D1765869

MW
TP09 016246
ACAKLAW

THE ROAD TO INDEPENDENCE FOR KOSOVO

This book tells the story of Kosovo's independence, ranging from the periodic bloodshed of the twentieth century to the diplomacy that led to a determination of Kosovo's final status as a state in 2008. Kosovo declared its independence from Serbia in February 2008 over the objections of Serbia and Russia. This culminated more than one hundred years of sometimes violent resistance to what the majority Albanian population considered to be "occupation" by foreign forces – first those of the Ottoman Empire, then those of Serbia, and finally by the United Nations. Kosovo's independence was the product of careful diplomacy, orchestrated by the United States and leading members of the European Union, under a framework brokered by former Finnish President Martti Ahtisaari, who subsequently won the Nobel Prize for Peace.

Henry H. Perritt, Jr., is a Professor of Law and former Dean of Chicago-Kent College of Law. He is a member of the Council on Foreign Relations and the board of directors of the Chicago Council on Global Affairs. He served on President Clinton's Transition Team and in the Ford administration, during which time he was on the White House staff and later was Deputy Under Secretary of Labor. He was a Democratic candidate for the U.S. Congress in 2002. Perritt is the author of more than ninety law review articles and fifteen books on international relations and law, technology and law, and employment law, most recently *Kosovo Liberation Army: The Inside Story of an Insurgency*. He also wrote *You Took Away My Flag – A Musical About Kosovo*, which opened in Chicago in 2009.

3030369

The Road to Independence for Kosovo

A CHRONICLE OF THE AHTISAARI PLAN

Henry H. Perritt, Jr.

Chicago-Kent College of Law

CAMBRIDGE
UNIVERSITY PRESS

CAMBRIDGE UNIVERSITY PRESS
Cambridge, New York, Melbourne, Madrid, Cape Town, Singapore,
São Paulo, Delhi, Dubai, Tokyo

Cambridge University Press
32 Avenue of the Americas, New York, NY 10013-2473, USA

www.cambridge.org
Information on this title: www.cambridge.org/9780521116244

© Henry H. Perritt, Jr., 2010

This publication is in copyright. Subject to statutory exception
and to the provisions of relevant collective licensing agreements,
no reproduction of any part may take place without the written
permission of Cambridge University Press.

First published 2010

Printed in the United States of America

A catalog record for this publication is available from the British Library.

Library of Congress Cataloging in Publication data

Perritt, Henry H.
The road to independence for Kosovo : a chronicle of the Ahtisaari
plan / Henry H. Perritt, Jr.
    p. cm.
Includes bibliographical references and index.
ISBN 978-0-521-11624-4 (hardback)
1. Kosovo (Republic) – History – Autonomy and independence movements.
2. Kosovo (Republic) – Politics and government – 21st century.   3. Kosovo
(Republic) – Ethnic relations.   4. United Nations Interim Mission in
Kosovo.   5. Ahtisaari, Martti.   6. Kosovo (Republic) – Ethnic relations.
7. Geopolitics – Balkan Peninsula.   I. Title.
DR2086.P465   2010
949.71 – dc22   2009014767

ISBN   978-0-521-11624-4 Hardback

Cambridge University Press has no responsibility for the persistence or
accuracy of URLs for external or third-party Internet Web sites referred to in
this publication and does not guarantee that any content on such Web sites is,
or will remain, accurate or appropriate.

UNIVERSITIES AT MEDWAY
0 9 SEP 2010
DRILL HALL LIBRARY

Contents

Acknowledgments

WRITING THIS BOOK PROVIDED A REMARKABLE OPPORTUNITY TO chronicle the final status process for Kosovo as it was unfolding. I am especially grateful to Frank Wisner and Martti Ahtisaari for getting me involved at an early stage. Both were generous with their time, candid in their communications, and wise in their assessments of the dynamics of the diplomacy and the prospects for success or failure.

Albert Rohan and Kai Sauer were equally generous, candid, and wise. They provided essential contextual information about President Ahtisaari and the Belgrade and Prishtina negotiating teams. Soren Jessen-Petersen filled in background on the Contact-Group-level discussions that led up to Ahtisaari's appointment and his terms of reference. He shared his unique insights about the dynamics of Kosovo's politics between the March 2004 riots and the first year after independence. He stands out as the best SRSG Kosovo had. Wolfgang Ischinger was probing in his analysis of intra-European politics during the Troika period of negotiations. The final status process would not have been successful without his unique skills.

Joachin Ruecker, as SRSG during the final status process, provided insights about the diplomatic forces operating on SRSGs and on intelligence about the potential for violence. Steven Schook, his deputy during the same period, manifested his charisma and was candid about the perils and potential of various final-status moves. Rosemary DiCarlo and Joshua Black at the U.S. State Department were open and forthcoming about U.S. attitudes toward the final status process as they evolved during 2007. Karen Pierce, Stephan Lehne, Hua Jiang, Jack Christofides, and Bardha Shpuza Azari shared their observations about the diplomatic process.

Rachel Bronson, Vice President of the Chicago Council on Global Affairs, helped get the whole project started. J. D. Bindenagel, former career ambassador in the U.S. Foreign Service provided valuable insight about the diplomatic process and about German and Russian interests. Evan Sult edited early drafts and persuaded me to develop this in a narrative format rather than in a more conventional academic one. Tim Sandusky, curious about everything, and smart, constantly challenged my assumptions.

I could not have accomplished a fraction of my Kosovo-related goals without the help and friendship of Alban Rafuna, who was always available to interpret, to arrange meetings, to provide background on the struggle, and to be a sounding board, wise beyond his years. Afrim Ademi always did what he said he was going to do and consistently helped arrange interviews and facilitate access.

Several of my other Kosovar Albanian friends illuminated popular attitudes toward the final status process. I first met Hashim Thaci, Prime Minister of Kosovo when independence was declared, shortly after the war. I have benefitted from regular conversations with him about politics in Kosovo and Kosovo's interaction with the international community. Ramush Haradinaj, former Prime Minister and now leader of the opposition, never fails to provide insights in the many conversations I have had with him. Fatmir Sejdui, President of Kosovo on Independence Day, similarly has been accessible and thoughtful about the final status process, even in the early days when it seemed it would never start. Rrustem Mustafa (Commender Remi), not only has always been available to educate me on the background of the conflict and the evolution of Kosovo's democracy; on several occasions, he has organized field trips allowing me to gain concrete perspective on the war and on economic development. Jakup Krasniqi, President of the Kosovo Assembly on Independence Day, was one of my first contacts among the leaders of the KLA and of Kosovo's new political leadership. He always has been generous with his time and his insights. Veton Surroi and Skender Hyseni were kind enough to offer insights during the frustrating months as the Security Council process was unraveling.

Bujar Bukoshi never failed, in multiple interviews, to offer trenchant insight into personalities and politics. Ahmet Shala and Besim Beqaj always went out of their way to deepen my understanding and open up doors. Albin Kurti, founder of Vetvendosje, offered critical analysis in several meetings of where the Ahtisaari concepts were likely to lead. Haki Abazi, one of the cleverest of his generation, presented novel perspectives on the geopolitical context. Chris Hall, President of the American University in Kosovo and former Democratic Leader of the Maine state senate, consistently was generous with his resources and his ideas about politics in Kosovo and the United States. Luan Dalipi, Ardian Jashari, and Driton Dalipi, organizers of the Kosovo consulting firm MDA, are examples of the accomplishments of Kosovo's new professional class. They always have enthusiastically supported my writing projects and provided good analysis of economic development potential and obstacles. Lisen Bashkurti, former Deputy Foreign Minister of Albania and now President of the Albanian Diplomatic Academy, offered insights into Albanian politics and arranged access to key actors in the 1998–1999 conflict. Fahri Rami, a former KLA soldier, provided moving stories about his own life experience and the motivations of the young men who put Kosovo's independence in motion through their bravery. Ardian Spahiu filled in gaps by relating his own experiences.

Andy Gridinsky once again proved to be a good critic and editor. Brekenda Rexhepi, Lundrim Aliu, and Veton Surroi, were generous with their time and insights.

Katriot Johaj, a promising and fearless young journalist, offered perspectives on the role of the press in Kosovo's civil society. Driton Kukalaj was an efficient interpreter and gave voice to some of the frustrations felt by young Kosovar Albanian professionals. Dastid Pallaska never minced words as he guided my understanding of Kosovo's evolution from the war forward. Valon Murati provided insights from his time as a KLA soldier through his development as a professional manager and policy analyst and leader of the Human Rights Centre at the University of Prishtina. Enver Hasani, Rector of the University of Prishtina and judge of Kosovo's new Constitutional Court, is a star of Kosovo's more senior legal professionals, inspiring young people to follow his example of intellectual courage. Everyone wants to hire Robert Muharremi, thoroughly modern lawyer and policy professional, who was generous on many occasions with his careful analysis of law and diplomacy. Lirim Greceivci, understated and quiet, not only regularly facilitated contacts with people active in politics but provided astute political insights. Fatmir Limaj, former KLA commander and now Minister of Transportation, spoke from the heart when he told me, "We did not fight this war so that anyone in Kosovo should be afraid to go out from their homes, including the Kosovo Serbs." Hajredin Kuqi, former director of international relations for the University of Prishtina and now Deputy Prime Minister, always was lively and insightful, whether we were talking about the antecedents of the KLA or the future of Kosovo's politics.

Sladjan Ilic, former major of Strpce, Tanja Petrovic, young organizer of interethnic projects in North Mitrovica, and Branislav Grbic, former Kosovo Minister of Returns and Communities, provided valuable perspectives on the experience and future expectations of Kosovo Serbs.

Several of my law-student research assistants were helpful in tracking down facts and writing up essays on crucial legal and political events: Dawson Brody, Jocelyn Floyd, Chris Bailey-Woon, and Kiki Mosley.

Irina Faskianos, Vice President of the Council on Foreign Relations, was kind enough to arrange a seminar to discuss draft chapters, in which good ideas were offered by J. D. Bindenagel, Richard Joseph, Edward A. Kolodziej, Gary E. MacDougal, Michael Sosin, Joseph Panza, and Christopher Bailey-Woon.

Two leaders of the Albanian community in Chicago, Freddie Mustafer and Arxhient Bajraktari, organized meetings with other Albanians and on many occasions were willing to vet my emerging thoughts and hypotheses. I also appreciate insights and support from Harry Bajraktari, Florin Krasniqi, and Dino Asajni in New York.

I appreciate the Rockefeller Brothers Fund's support for the project.

Patricia O'Neal provided her usual cheerful, resourceful, and energetic support. I also appreciate the support of my partner of twenty-five years, Mitchell Bergmann.

Introduction

THIS BOOK EXPLAINS HOW KOSOVO BECAME AN INDEPENDENT state in 2008, following more than a century of struggle to break free from political domination by others. Kosovo, formerly an autonomous province of Serbia within Yugoslavia, declared its independence on February 17, 2008, and was recognized as an independent state by fifty-four countries within a year. The recognizing states included the United States and most of the member states of the European Union (EU). The independence declaration was carefully crafted in concert among the elected officials of the provisional government of Kosovo, the United States, and the leadership of the EU. This process culminated three years of "final status" negotiations over Kosovo's future, launched by the United Nations (UN) Security Council in 2005. The key negotiations were guided by Martti Ahtisaari, former president of Finland, who subsequently won the Nobel Prize for Peace for his work on Kosovo and elsewhere. These negotiations and international diplomacy that preceded and followed them are the subject of this book.

Kosovo's independence and the diplomatic process that led up to it have significant implications for the effective conduct of multilateral decision making in the transatlantic alliance, even as they illustrate the reemergence of Russia as a thorn in the sides of those who seek broader multilateral cooperation to solve regional problems. It illustrates the limited role that international law plays in channeling the interests of major powers into established international institutions and represents yet another example of the impotence of the UN Security Council to resolve disagreements among its permanent members. It shows how the threat of violence is often an essential lever to force difficult decisions to be made, while representing the first time that a major decision with respect to conflict in the Balkans was made without an actual outbreak of sustained violence. Much uncertainty remains, however. The jury is still out on how successful Kosovo will be as an independent state. Its economy is weak and its democracy fragile. Enormous mistrust remains between its two largest ethnic communities, the dominant Kosovar Albanians and the minority Kosovo Serbs. Serbia continues to have difficulty coming to terms with its ultranationalist past, which led to the breakup of Yugoslavia and put the Kosovo crisis into motion. Serbia continues to challenge the legitimacy of Kosovo's independence in diplomatic channels and in a case brought before the International Court of Justice (ICJ). Despite this confrontation with European policy, the EU appears on a rush to admit Serbia to the Union. The result may be further paralysis and timidity in European security policy.

Kosovo is a landlocked territory in the Western Balkans roughly the size of Connecticut, with a population of about two million people, mostly Albanians, with a substantial minority of Serbs. For more than a century, the Albanians have chafed under the rule of the Ottoman Empire and then Serbia, seeking union with the separate state of Albania, autonomy within Yugoslavia and, more recently, independence. Serbia insisted that Kosovo remain part of Serbia, viewing the territory as the historic birthplace of Serbia and of its church. Violence over Albanian separatist aspirations broke out sporadically throughout the twentieth century and intensified after Serbian President Slobodan Milošević revoked Kosovo's political autonomy in 1989.

An insurgency, led by the Kosovo Liberation Army (KLA) after 1993, resulted in a scorched-earth policy of ethnic cleansing by Serbian secret police, interior ministry police, and army that resulted in the expulsion of some eight hundred thousand Albanians from their homes in 1999. The insurgency developed slowly and initially was opposed by the Kosovar Albanian political elites. It grew in strength after the Dayton Accords settled the armed conflict in Bosnia without addressing Kosovo's status, undercutting Kosovar Albanian hopes that the West would protect it from Serbian excesses. Then Serbian counterinsurgency forces escalated the use of armed force against Kosovar Albanian civilians, and the collapse of governmental authority in Albania opened up a route for supplying arms to the insurgents. The international community's sympathies shifted toward the side of the Kosovar Albanians as Milošević's human rights' violations increased and became more public. International concerns intensified as a significant portion of the Kosovar Albanian population were driven from their homes by Serb forces who executed civilians near the village of Racak in early 1999, condemned as a "massacre" by Ambassador William Walker, who was then heading the international monitoring force in Kosovo. This resulted in a high-level diplomatic conference in Rambouillet, France, where the KLA and other Kosovar Albanians agreed to a U.S./European-crafted peace deal, but Milošević refused.

The international community responded with a bombing campaign led by the North Atlantic Treaty Organization (NATO), aimed at forcing Serbia to withdraw its security forces from Kosovo. This led to a period of UN civil administration backed up by NATO forces while Kosovo's future was sorted out, after Milošević agreed to withdraw his forces and allow NATO and the UN to enter in June 1999. Thereafter, a United Nations Interim Administration Mission (UNMIK) exercised executive, legislative, and judicial authority in Kosovo. Security Council Resolution 1244, authorizing the UN and NATO presence, acknowledged continued formal sovereignty by Serbia during an interim period while the UN actually exercised the attributes of sovereignty. The Resolution envisioned some kind of process for resolving Kosovo's final status. Kosovar Albanians expected the process to lead to independence; the government of Serbia expected Kosovo to be returned to Serbian control. As Kosovar Albanians were elected to office in the provisional local government institutions (PISG) authorized by UNMIK, tensions grew between UNMIK and the PISG over the slow pace in devolving power to the PISG and the reluctance of the international community to grapple with Kosovo's future. Kosovar Albanian frustrations spilled over into widespread riots in March 2004, which galvanized the international community to kick-start a final status process led by Martii Ahtisaari, former president of Finland and widely respected international mediator.

Ahtisaari presided over two years of intensive negotiations involving the protagonists – the government of Serbia and the Kosovar Albanian leadership of the PISG – and the "Contact Group" – an informal committee of senior diplomats from the United States, Britain, Germany, France, Italy, and Russia. Unable to bridge the gap between Kosovar Albanian insistence on independence and Serbian insistence that Kosovo remain part of Serbia, Ahtisaari submitted a comprehensive plan for Kosovo's supervised independence to the UN Security Council in March 2007. The plan contained detailed institutional structures for protecting the human rights and self-government by Kosovo Serbs under the ultimate authority of EU and U.S. overseers. Russia blocked Security Council approval of the plan and another four months of diplomacy followed under a "Troika" of the EU, the United States, and Russia. Unable to procure agreement between Russia and Serbia on one side, and the EU, the United States, and the Kosovo political leadership on the other, the EU and the United States worked with the Kosovo political leadership to craft the declaration of independence and implementation of the Ahtisaari Plan outside the framework of a UN Security Council resolution.

This book details the steps toward Kosovo's independence finally put in motion by the 2004 riots, after a century or more of Albanian restlessness under "foreign occupation," as the Kosovar Albanians saw it. It begins with the riots themselves, and then puts the riots in the context of the political dynamics of the Albanian–Serbian struggle over Kosovo. Drawing on my work for an earlier book *Kosovo Liberation Army: The Inside Story of an Insurgency*, I explain how the KLA shaped international public opinion to expel Serbian forces from Kosovo in 1999 and to substitute the UN for Serbian exercise of the attributes of sovereignty. This book explores how UNMIK's moral authority to govern weakened between 1999 and 2004 as indigenous political leadership in Kosovo matured, sometimes split between the leaders of the now-disbanded KLA and longer-established Kosovar Albanian political elites centered in Kosovo's cities. Then it details the design and implementation of the final status process, paying close attention to the jockeying among members of the EU, the United States, Russia, the Serbian political leadership in Belgrade, and among the Kosovo Serbs and the Kosovar Albanian leadership. It reviews in some detail the issues considered during the Ahtisaari process and the institutional approaches to protecting minority rights in an independent Kosovo reflected in the Ahtisaari Plan. It explains why the Security Council was unable to agree on the Ahtisaari Plan, and takes readers inside the Troika process that followed the impasse.

It concludes with an on-the-scene portrayal of Independence Day in Kosovo, an analysis of Kosovo's future as an independent state, and an assessment of what Kosovo's independence portends for the international order.

I have been deeply involved in Kosovo since the run-up to the 1999 NATO bombing campaign, visiting Kosovo several times a year since December 1998, getting to know its political leaders well, and deploying groups of law and engineering students on several small projects supporting Kosovo's political, economic, and legal development. For this book and for the KLA book, beginning in the spring of 2004, I interviewed more than one hundred ordinary Kosovar Albanians, Kosovo Serbs, academics, diplomats, and guerrilla and secret service personnel from the region; and European and U.S. diplomatic and military leaders. President Ahtisaari, his deputy Ambassador Albert Rohan, and U.S. Ambassador Frank Wisner provided close cooperation and encouragement.

Because much of the data on which the book is based were obtained from personal observation and engagement with the Kosovar Albanian political and civil-society leadership, portions of the narrative are expressed in first person.

I conclude that Kosovo's independence was inevitable after the UN took over in 1999. The international community had great difficulty grappling with this reality, but Ahtisaari and the Troika deftly navigated the shoals of the conflict in 2006–2008 to avoid further violence in the region, and to avoid a split between the United States and the EU, a split that Russia would have welcomed. I explain why Russia's growing economic power, its assertive leadership under Vladimir Putin, and its geopolitical interests made it unlikely that the West and Russia could agree on Kosovo's future, unlike 1999 when Ahtisaari helped forge a shaky accommodation permitting the displacement of Serbian forces and the introduction of the UN and NATO. I also conclude that Kosovo's elected leadership under Prime Minister and former KLA leader Hashim Thaçi and President Fatmir Sejdiu did a good job in shepherding independence itself, but face considerable challenges in crafting a bright economic and political future for the country. For its other participants, the final status process illuminates opportunities for effective transatlantic cooperation while further exposing the limitations of the UN Security Council as the central institution for dealing with threats to international peace and security. In the long run, integration of Serbia and Kosovo into the EU holds the promise of mitigating tensions over independence. Whether Russia's perceptions of its geopolitical interests and its desire to restore Russian pride will lead to further East–West conflict or effective pursuit of mutual interests remains to be seen.

1   Riots in Kosovo

HE SIXTEENTH OF MARCH IN 2004 DAWNED CRISP AND CLEAR IN
Pristina, the capital of Kosovo.[1] The chill and rain of the previous
weeks had blown away, and the muddy gaps in the sidewalks were
finally drying up. A few clouds skirted the blue sky as the day warmed over
Kosovo, a diamond-shaped patch of land in the southwestern Balkans slightly
smaller than Connecticut.

By 10 A.M., stories were already spreading about a tragedy that occurred the
previous evening in Mitrovica, the tense city in Kosovo's north where Kosovo
Serbs and Kosovar Albanians lived in fear of each other on opposite sides
of the Ibar River. According to newspapers, radio, and gossip, four Albanian
youngsters had been playing on the northern, Serb side of the river when several older Serbian youths gave chase and set a dog on them. The Albanian
youngsters, terrified, tried to flee into or across the river, and three of the four
drowned. Alienated from international authorities, most Kosovar Albanians
throughout the rest of Kosovo did not expect the United Nations (UN) police
to do anything about the tragedy, let alone arrest and punish the perpetrators.
The Kosovar Albanian media fed the frenzy. They eagerly passed on information that later turned out to be wildly inaccurate, with little concern about the
impact on the public mood.

Expectations were high that something significant was going to happen
that day. Friction between the UN's political oversight and Kosovo's majority Albanian population had been building heat for years, and this spring
looked finally to catch fire. Kosovar Albanians in the national trade union,
angered by a recent halt in privatization, had organized busloads of trade
unionists to come to Pristina and engage in a peaceful march on the gates
of the Kosovo Trust Agency, the UN-established organization charged with
privatizing socialist enterprises. Also, the War Veterans Association, in which
some of the more militant elements of the former Albanian Kosovo Liberation
Army (KLA) were embedded, had been talking about organizing demonstrations against the government. Meanwhile, angry at the increasingly strident

---

[1] The account of the events described in this chapter is drawn primarily from my personal
observations. I was there during the riots, not only in Pristina but also in parts of western
Kosovo.

Albanian voices calling for the separation of Kosovo from Serbia, Serbs from Çaglaviça – the enclave that lay just beyond the hill south of Pristina – had barricaded the main highway from Pristina to Skopje, Macedonia, shutting off Kosovo's main transportation lifeline.

Relationships between Kosovo's majority Albanian population and its significant Serb minority had been tense for decades. Power between them had ebbed and flowed. Establishment of the Kingdom of Serbs, Croats, and Slovenes – Yugoslavia's predecessor[2] – after World War I frustrated Albanian ambitions to be part of the separate state of Albania. Then, Albanians enjoyed a period of political autonomy during Tito's leadership of Yugoslavia after World War II. That was followed by Slobodan Milošević's revocation of autonomy in 1989, by the emergence of the KLA insurgency in the late 1990s, and finally by the displacement of Yugoslav control by a NATO bombing campaign in 1999.

Caught in the middle of the struggle between Kosovo Serbs and Kosovar Albanians after 1999 was the United Nations civil administration (known as UNMIK) and KFOR (Kosovo Force), the NATO peacekeeping force. NATO had bombed Serbian forces in Kosovo and in Serbia proper to end human rights abuses against the majority Albanian population of Kosovo. UNMIK had been established by UN Security Council Resolution 1244 to govern Kosovo on an interim basis while its future was sorted out. It seemed that the last piece of what remained of Yugoslavia might become independent, ending the Kosovar Albanians' century-long quest for their own state.[3] The international community, however, was not prepared to embrace independence. Neither UNMIK nor KFOR was designed as a long-term political or security entity: the Security Council resolution had been negotiated among Russia, NATO, and Yugoslavia to establish interim security and civil-administration agencies while the question of Kosovo's international status was settled. As KFOR moved in, Serbian military and police withdrew. Originally a so-called autonomous Yugoslav province with a 90 percent or more Albanian majority, Kosovo had avoided the bloody conflicts suffered in Croatia and Bosnia

---

[2] The Kingdom of Serbs, Croats, and Slovenes was established in 1918. It was reestablished as the Democratic Federal Yugoslavia in 1943 and renamed the Federal People's Republic of Yugoslavia in 1946. In 1963, it was renamed again as the Socialist Federal Republic of Yugoslavia (SFRY). The Federal Republic of Yugoslavia (FRY) was established on March 27, 1992, comprising Serbia and Montenegro, after Slovenia, Croatia, Bosnia, and Macedonia seceded from Yugoslavia. This "rump Yugoslavia" was renamed the State Union of Serbia and Montenegro in 2006. After Montenegro seceded in 2006, only Serbia remained. For ease in exposition, the text refers to "Yugoslavia" for the period from the end of World War I until the breakup of Yugoslavia in 1991 and to "Serbia" thereafter.

[3] From the beginning of the twentieth century until Tito's Yugoslavia, most Kosovar Albanians wanted to be included into Albania. Then, the goal of the Kosovar Albanian political elites was for Kosovo to have the status of a Yugoslav republic. Only in 1991, when the Yugoslav Federation broke apart, did independence become the goal.

as Yugoslavia broke up. By 1999, however, the breakup of Yugoslavia had pitched the former province into a legal limbo – still formally a province of Serbia, Kosovo was in fact governed by UN-supervised elected local officials. While both Albanian and Serb populations seemed to recognize the need for international peacekeepers, both sides inevitably resented the foreign presence. Kosovar Albanians welcomed KFOR as liberators, but they chafed at the exercise of political authority by UNMIK.[4] The Kosovar Albanian political culture had been forged for generations almost entirely in terms of opposing foreign occupiers, and now it seemed to many Kosovar Albanians that UNMIK had simply replaced the Serbs, and the Ottomans before them, as colonial authorities determined to emasculate Kosovar Albanian dreams for genuine self-determination and self-government. Meanwhile, Kosovo Serbs resented the UN's displacement of their political dominance over a region they still considered a sovereign part of the existing state of Serbia.

By mid-afternoon, the Pristina air was sparking with rebellion, and the excitement spilled into the streets. Leaving a meeting at the Faculty of Law, I watched as what seemed like nearly all of the ten thousand students at the University of Pristina had finished – or abandoned – their classes to swarm down the incline from the university to Mother Theresa Street, Pristina's main boulevard. Laughing and talking among themselves, they followed the swelling crowd of Albanians headed toward the barricade Serbs had established on the main highway from Pristina to Skopje. The general plan seemed to be that the students and other protesters would meet up at the barricade and simply remove it.

At the traffic circle on the southern end of Mother Theresa Street, the mass gathered momentum. Here, Albanian-driven vehicles had completely blocked the way. Some feigned breakdowns; others simply parked in the middle of the street with their doors open. As trapped Kosovo Police Service vehicles uselessly flashed their lights and blared their sirens, the stream of young Albanians mingled among the cars, walking leisurely arm in arm through the chaos. Laughing and joking, they headed up the hill and wondered aloud about where they were going and what they would do when they got there.

The fine weather lessened the usual depressing effect of their walk down Pristina's main street, framed by monotonous blocks of communist apartment buildings made of splotched and graying concrete. Satellite television antennas pointed more or less south from balconies from which wires drooped. Neither UNMIK nor the elected local government had mastered the art of trash collection, so the already narrow pedestrian pathways along the street – they

---

[4] According to opinion surveys reported in 2002, only 27.2 percent of the population was satisfied with UNMIK's performance, while 60.2 percent were satisfied by the PISG performance, and 69.8 percent were satisfied with KFOR's performance. UNDP Early Warning Report No. 1 (May–August 2002).

could hardly be called sidewalks – were further narrowed by piles of trash and garbage. Each of the hundreds of small shops and cafes that had been built by Albanian entrepreneurs after the Serbian forces left had its own portable generator outside the door so that business could continue when the municipal electricity supply was interrupted, as it was several times a day.

By twilight, hundreds of Albanian and Serb teenagers and twenty-somethings were throwing rocks at each other and at KFOR across the boundary of Çaglaviça. As darkness stole over the hill, hundreds of Kosovar Albanians were still trying to reach the crest, dodging clouds of tear gas and trying to get around at least one KFOR tank blocking the road. A few gunshots were heard. The protesters slipped off the pavement and into the shrubs and bushes near the top of the hill, seeking to flank the tank on either side.

As the evening wore on, packs of high-school-aged youths ran energetically through the streets of Pristina, carrying large Albanian flags and blowing whistles, chanting slogans against UNMIK. In the center of the city, UNMIK's staff was barricaded in their headquarters adjacent to the Grand Hotel. Another hulking monument to communist architecture, the hotel was anything but grand to the foreign officials and peacekeepers who were caught there. UN and other foreign officials were afraid to leave the building but also fearful of what might happen if they stayed inside and were largely without direction. Mother Theresa Street was now mostly deserted of vehicular traffic, aside from a few white UNMIK Toyota SUVs burning fiercely with no police or fire trucks in sight. Passersby ducked as tires exploded from the heat. The excited students were looking for targets for their rebellion. One ran up to a young man who looked foreign and excitedly asked, "Do you work for UNMIK?" Discovering that the foreigner was an American, the kid responded, "Ahh, an American!" He grinned. "We like you. Come with us! We want to show you what we are about to do."

By midnight, rocks and Molotov cocktails were flying. They appeared to be aimed at the symbols of UN authority as much as at the Serbs. Almost every vehicle marked with the large black initials UN against an otherwise white paint job was destroyed by rocks, overturned by hand, or set on fire. Adjacent vehicles bearing the OSCE (Organization for Security and Cooperation in Europe) logo went unmolested. Kosovo Serbs were under attack in their home enclaves as well as in their Serbian Orthodox churches. Recently built religious and educational facilities dedicated to Kosovo Serbs were particular targets. Terrified, some Serbs tried to fight back, some sought police or KFOR protection, and some simply fled. Within and without Pristina, in villages and cities, UNMIK police were on the run as Albanian crowds increased their numbers and attacks. The UNMIK police, for the most part, abandoned their vehicles and ran away when confronted by rioters. NATO's KFOR, by contrast, took no particular notice of the rioting. Despite increasingly frantic calls from UN officials to NATO commanders, the riots were dismissed as simple spring exuberance. NATO officials calmly insisted that the night's events were not NATO concerns and could be handled easily by UNMIK and the Kosovo Police Service. The KFOR contingent responsible for Pristina dispatched a few tanks to block the route to Çaglaviça; elsewhere, other KFOR contingents responded according to their national proclivities.

Many of Kosovo's own political leaders, aware that riots could easily spill over into deadlier violence, called on the students and protesters to desist. Hashim Thaçi, former political director of the KLA and then leader of the number-two Kosovar Albanian political party, was in the United States making a speech at the United States Institute of Peace (USIP). He interrupted his trip and returned home after broadcasting an urgent call for calm in Albanian on Voice of America's Albanian service and in English on its Serbian service. Prime Minister Bajram Rexhepi, Thaçi's designee as prime minister in the coalition government, personally visited the scene of the greatest concentration of rioters near Çaglaviça and pleaded for people to go home. Ramush Haradinaj, a powerful former KLA commander and the then leader of Kosovo's third major political party, made a few statements urging calm. Meanwhile, Kosovar Albanian President Ibrahim Rugova, long an opponent of violence, remained silent.

The riots raged on, essentially unrestricted throughout the long night, backlit by the flames of Serbian Orthodox churches and Serbian homes burning as their residents fled into the dark. Albanian rage was directed as much at ordinary Kosovo Serbs as at the symbols of international authority.

The next morning found most of Kosovo implicated in the riots. As excited news spread from Pristina, more Kosovar Albanians took up the cause. On the streets of all Kosovo's major cities and villages were scores of colorfully dressed men and women parading through muddy streets, holding banners aloft celebrating Albanian nationalism. It was a young people's rebellion: chanting patriotic and anti-UNMIK slogans, waving enormous flags, student-aged Albanians were out in force. After the first night's violence, the following days' demonstrations were mostly peaceful and entirely unrestrained by the presence of police. Still, in the city of Prizren, smoke drifted from the ruins of Serbian Orthodox monasteries and homes on the steep slope defining the southern part of the city. The few Serbs who had not fled from their villages were holed up and scrambling to protect themselves from an expected renewal of assaults from Albanian mobs.

"How did you know about it? How did you know where to go and what to do?" one young Kosovar was asked afterward. Alban Rafuna was a polite, mild-mannered, and hard-working waiter in the Hotel Victory, one of the new hotels built after the war that catered to foreigners. "That was no problem," Rafuna answered, after a slightly embarrassed smile. "We simply called each other on our cell phones or sent text messages to each other. It wasn't too hard to agree that Çaglaviça was where the action should be." It was not formally organized, he explained. "We just decided what to do among ourselves," he said of himself and his friends. "We were fed up and we wanted to do something. Most of us were too young to have been part of the KLA, but we are not too young now to show that we have some pride, and that there are limits on what the Serbs and UNMIK can do to us."[5]

Despite its professed indifference, KFOR, comprising forces from a dozen or more member states, was in a state of confusion. Each national military contingent was seeking instruction from its national capital. The German contingent, responsible for the Prizren area, took the field to protect Serb civilians fleeing the violence but stood by as most of the buildings on the hill marking Prizren's southern boundary, including a Serbian Orthodox church, were firebombed. Protection of property was not part of their mandate, the Germans said. Swedish, Finnish, Norwegian, and Irish contingents, responsible for the Pristina area, had scrambled through the night to block reinforcements of the crowd at the top of the hill, moving a dozen tanks and armored personnel carriers on the road and on both sides of it. By the next morning, even KFOR recognized the violence as a crisis. Britain announced that it was sending some fifteen hundred troop reinforcements, but the first detachment would not arrive until the next day. International observers in Kosovo and around the world feared what might happen in the meantime. Rumors spread that a major march on UNMIK Headquarters was planned for that evening. The UN riot police hurriedly reorganized to present a more stalwart face to the rioters. UNMIK scrambled the policemen – mostly American and British Commonwealth nationals – who were already in-country – into teams bristling with automatic weapons, shotguns, and bulletproof vests, and hustled them into the Pristina streets. With the sudden increase in police presence came an increase in hostility, as unreliable rumors spread that UNMIK police or KFOR troops had shot and killed several unarmed Albanian demonstrators, and that other protesters had been shot by Serb civilians firing from balconies in residential areas near Pristina. Still, the huge new police presence succeeded in its objective: the anticipated assault on UNMIK Headquarters did not materialize, and when British reinforcements arrived the next day, the riots were over as quickly as they had started. For the moment, the international forces that kept Kosovo together had held – if barely so.

According to nongovernmental organization sources, fifty-one thousand people rioted, with the majority of the violence directed at Serb, Ashkali, and Roma minorities.[6] The United Nations reported thirty-one people died in the violence (both Crisis International and Human Rights Watch put total

---

[5] Conversation with Alban Rafuna, Pristina, March 17, 2004.

[6] *United Nations Peace Operations Year in Review 2004: UNMIK – Holding Kosovo to High Standards* (December 2004) located at http://www.un.org/Depts/dpko/dpko/pub/year_review04/yir2004.pdf (corroborates that large-scale violence during the March 2004 riots targeted the Serb, Ashkali, and Roma minorities).

fatalities at nineteen).[7] More than 950 injuries were reported among civilians and 184 injuries to police and military officers.[8] Approximately 935 buildings (mostly Serb owned) were damaged or destroyed as well as 36 Orthodox churches, monasteries, and other religious sites.[9] Approximately four thousand Serbs, Romas, and Ashkalis were displaced due to the riots: 42 percent from Pristina and 40 percent from Mitrovica, with the remaining percentage covering people from other regions of Kosovo.[10] Of the displaced peoples, 82 percent were Serb and 18 percent were Roma and Ashkali.

It was clear that the clock on this awkward political arrangement was running down. The advent of UN and NATO forces in Kosovo had so far kept Kosovar Albanians and Kosovo Serbs from open warfare, but the sustained international presence had become counterproductive over time. Without changing its mission, UNMIK had declined from being a stabilizing force to a destabilizing one, and the riots illustrated how close to the brink of war Kosovo had come. I was there, and I felt the fear as law and order broke down for twenty-four hours. The rhetorical question of Kosovo's status – state or province? – was fast becoming an existential one.

If Kosovo was to survive, its status had to be settled. Could it earn international recognition as a sovereign country? And what would happen if it did not?

---

[7] Id.; "Kosovo: Failure of NATO, U.N. to Protect Minorities: Reform of Security Structures Needed as New Administrator Takes Office" (July 26, 2004), located at http://www.hrw.org/english/docs/2004/07/27/serbia9136.htm; International Crisis Group, *Collapse in Kosovo* (April 22, 2004), located at http://www.crisisgroup.org/library/documents/europe/balkans/155_collapse_in_kosovo_revised.pdf.

[8] Collapse in Kosovo at 1.

[9] Id.

[10] Id. (stating that more than four thousand Serbs, Romas, and Ashkalis were displaced); Bock and Pham, *supra* note 1 (describing displaced persons by region).

2 Albanian Resentment Comes to a Boil

I WAS IN KOSOVO DURING THE MARCH 2004 RIOTS. I SAW THE SUVs burning, was confronted by the riot police, and took pictures of the tear gas and tanks at the top of the hill. I talked to young people who were involved. However, that was only the latest experience in what is now more than a decade-long involvement with Kosovo.

Shortly after I became Dean of Chicago-Kent College of Law in June 1997, I invited U.S. Ambassador Richard Holbrooke to speak at the law school. Holbrooke had mediated an end to the war in Bosnia, the bloodiest and most protracted conflict over the breakup of Yugoslavia. In his address at Chicago-Kent, Holbrooke emphasized the need for credible threats of NATO military action to facilitate diplomacy, criticizing the flaccid approach taken by the UN in Bosnia. I had gotten to know Holbrooke during the previous year via Project Bosnia, an initiative launched at my former institution Villanova University School of Law by my former student Stuart P. Ingis. Through Project Bosnia, scores of law students worked to establish capacity in new legal and press institutions in Bosnia.

We became part – albeit a small part – of engagement by the international community in nation-building activities in the Balkans. The phrase *international community* signifies an ill-defined class of foreign governments and other official organs. It generally encompasses such international organizations as the United Nations (UN), the Organization for Security and Cooperation in Europe (OSCE), and the North Atlantic Treaty Organization (NATO), all three of which had legal responsibilities to govern Kosovo. It also includes nongovernmental organizations (NGOs) such as Human Rights Watch, Amnesty International, Doctors Without Borders, the International Crisis Group (ICG), the United States Institute for Peace (USIP), the American Bar Association's Central and East European Law Initiative (ABA/CEELI), and Chicago-Kent's activities such as Project Bosnia and Operation Kosovo. The short form *internationals* refers to the foreigners in the country, usually but not always those working in the international organizations – hundreds of volunteers and paid staff working for human rights protection, nation building, establishment of a rule of law, and economic reform. Most of the larger institutional members of the international community had their headquarters elsewhere but maintained offices or missions in Kosovo.

Usually the local offices had considerable autonomy to frame their own positions regarding Kosovo. Separately, profit-seeking firms had their own interests in Kosovo, particularly regarding privatization, investment incentives, security, and business law. Although private firms had a stake in Kosovo's future, their self-interest distinguishes them from the loose grouping referred to as the international community.

A few months after that initial engagement, Holbrooke was in Chicago again. Assistant Dean Charles Rudnick and I gave him a ride to the airport. Bosnia had faded from the headlines by then, but trouble was brewing in Kosovo. Seeking to crush a nationalist Albanian guerrilla movement known as the Kosovo Liberation Army (KLA), Serbian President Slobodan Milošević's military and police forces had driven several hundred thousand Kosovar Albanians from their homes and across the borders into refugee camps in the neighboring Republic of Albania. "You know what Chicago-Kent has done in Bosnia," I said to Holbrooke. "Is there something we can do that would be helpful in connection with the Kosovo crisis?"

"Yes!" Holbrooke responded. "You can help the people in the refugee camps." Within a week, I made plans for Assistant Dean Rudnick and two law students to go to the refugee camp near Bajram Curri, located in the isolated north of Albania, through which the KLA was smuggling arms for its insurgency. During their weeklong trip in mid-July 1998, our Chicago-Kent representatives visited the refugee camps and met with a number of nongovernmental and international organizations, representatives of the Albanian and the U.S. governments, and telecommunications and technology experts.

After their return, they told stories of gunfire in the night and piles of shell casings on the ferry ride to Bajram Curri. They also told stories of bewildered grandmothers and grandsons, distraught at seeing their houses burned and their livestock killed. The refugees were proud of their self-sufficiency, but they now depended on help from others to survive. Excitement spread in our law school community for deepening our involvement in the crisis. We circulated plans for initiatives to support job creation in Albania for refugees, and did everything we could think of to raise public consciousness about the looming crisis and the need for greater international involvement. Being lawyers and law students, we also did what came naturally: intensive research. We dove into every source we could identify to learn about the history of the conflict. One early insight was that the new violence had roots in centuries of tension and conflict in the territory now defined as Kosovo, during which the Albanian population resisted what they called foreign occupiers. Although some observers of the Balkans argued that "ancient ethnic hatreds" made peace impossible,[1] the more sophisticated question was why there was peace at some

---

[1] Compare Robert D. Kaplan, *Balkan Ghosts* (1993) (painting picture of Balkan peoples imprisoned by historical myths emphasizing inhumane cruelty by other ethnic groups) with Richard Holbrooke, *To End a War* 22–3 (1998) (criticizing "ancient-ethnic-hatred" view); see

points in history and not at others. The bane of anyone who works on Kosovo issues is the insistence by both Albanian and Serb interlocutors that any meeting begin with a lengthy recitation of hundreds or thousands of years of history, and the celebration of their national heroes, the Serbian Prince Lazar and the Albanian Gjergj Kastrioti Skenderbeg, both of whom died before 1500. Although these figures may at first seem tangential to outsiders, historical context is crucial to understanding the modern-day crisis of Kosovo.

Kosovo collects the full range of geographic features from the rest of the world and stuffs them into its compact 4,200 square miles. More than half of its 2.2 million people are concentrated in the major cities of Pristina, roughly in the center; Peja in the west; Prizren in the southwest; Gjakova between Peja and Prizren; Mitrovica and Pudojevo in the north; Gjilane in the southeast, and Ferizaj in the south. Pristina was the administrative capital first of the Yugoslav communist authorities, and then later of UNMIK. Prizren was the historical center of Albanian resistance to the Ottoman Empire in the nineteenth and early twentieth centuries. Mitrovica was the industrial center with the largest Serb population. Ferizaj, another business center, abuts the Sharr Mountains that define Kosovo's border with Macedonia. The Cursed Mountains, sometimes known as the Dinaric Alps, separate the largely Albanian cities of Prizren, Gjakova, and Peja from Albania and Macedonia. The Dukagjini Plain (Metohija to Serbs) to the west, the Drenica Valley in the center, and the Kosovo Plain to the east comprise hilly areas dotted with farmland. Belgrade, the capital of Serbia, lies some 150 miles to the north of Pristina.

For several hundred years, Albanians were the dominant ethnic population in a geographic area that included the modern Republic of Albania, the present territory of Kosovo, the Preshevo Valley of southern Serbia, northwestern Macedonia, and a sliver of eastern Montenegro.

Considerable controversy surrounds the racial ancestry of Albanians and the linguistic roots of the Albanian language. No dispute exists, however, that the Albanian and Serbian languages are linguistically different and that Albanians and Serbs are ethnically distinct, in culture if not in racial and genetic characteristics. An outsider would have difficulty distinguishing a Kosovo Serb from a Kosovar Albanian by appearance, but the two languages sound completely different and are in totally different language groups. Throughout the nineteenth and the first part of the twentieth centuries, Albanians were isolated from other influences and relied on extended family connections and subsistence farming for their survival, whereas Serbs achieved greater integration with other Europeans.

Clark at 22 criticizing Rebecca West's *Black Lamb and Grey Falcon*, and Robert Kaplan's *Balkan Ghosts* as "bad history," with a pernicious effect on President Clinton and other senior decision makers in the United States and Europe, reinforcing the erroneous view that interethnic conflict was inevitable.

During that time, three national identities struggled for dominance on the territory of Kosovo: Ottoman, Albanian, and Serbian. As the Ottoman Empire withered, various nationalities in the Balkans struggled to achieve greater autonomy or to break free altogether. From about 1500 to World War I, Albanian tribes had periodically resisted Ottoman domination while enjoying a good deal of autonomy under the Ottoman Empire. A number of Albanian nationals were sent to serve in high imperial positions in the government of the Ottoman Empire.

Serbia was recognized as an independent state at the Congress of Berlin in 1878.[2] Serbia's population is predominantly Slavic. Central to Slavic nationalism in Serbia is the tale of Prince Lazar choosing God over victory on the "Field of Blackbirds" – a battlefield located in modern-day Kosovo – against the Ottoman Sultan's forces in 1389. In that battle, ironically, Albanians fought side by side with Serbs against the Ottoman Army. To nationalist Serbs, Kosovo is the cradle of the Serbian nation: a place where Serbian blood was shed for national identity, and a place where some of the oldest artifacts of the Serbian Orthodox Church were erected and remain.

In reaction to the recognition of Serbian boundaries that included Kosovo, representatives of Albanian tribes and territories formed the League of Prizren, major factions of which sought a unified state comprising all Albanian-populated territory.[3] Other factions within the League sought greater autonomy for Albanian *vilayets*[4] within the Ottoman Empire – not statehood. At that moment in history, many Albanian nationalists realized that it might be better to remain autonomous within the Ottoman Empire as the national awakening spread in Serbia. The Ottomans could defend the Albanians against Serbia. The League of Prizren organized a military resistance against the Ottomans, but the resistance was crushed in 1881. The League reflected Albanian optimism about obtaining self-government as the Ottoman Empire atrophied in the last half of the nineteenth century. Serbia was equally determined that Kosovo would be part of Serbia.

The ensuing forty years were punctuated by three major wars in the region: the First Balkan War, the Second Balkan War, and World War I. The conflicts were brutal, as one ethnicity lived in fear of its neighbors, and armed forces murdered, raped, burned, and plundered.[5] By 1920, the boundaries of new

---

[2] See Vickers at 32–40.

[3] Vickers at 33–5 (describing Albanian political mobilization during and after Congress of Berlin).

[4] A *vilayet* was a basic administrative unit within the Ottoman Empire, more or less equivalent to a province, with governors appointed by the Porte – the central Ottoman government – and increasingly, by the end of the nineteenth century, with locally elected assemblies.

[5] See Vickers at 69 (quoting Leon Trotsky reporting on villages being "turned into pillars of fire"); Carnegie Endowment for Peace, *The Other Balkan Wars: A 1913 Carnegie Endowment Inquiry* 74–5 (reprint 1993) (detailing atrocities against civilian population by all sides of the conflict); Robert D. Kaplan, *Balkan Ghosts* xvii (1993) (quoting young Kosovar Albanian: "Do you know what it is to throw a child in the air and catch it on a knife in front of its mother? To be tied to a burning log?").

states in the Balkans had been drawn and redrawn, the Turks had withdrawn to modern-day Turkey, the Republic of Albania had been founded,[6] and the province of Kosovo had been established within Serbia. In the military and diplomatic struggles over self-determination and boundaries, Albanians unsuccessfully pressed for creation of a larger Albanian state, encompassing most of the Albanian population in the area, while Serbs were successful in keeping Kosovo. The Serbs were unsuccessful, however, in their quest for a seaport on the Adriatic, at the expense of the new Republic of Albania. Although Kosovo was occupied by invading Serbian forces in 1912, as one of the last major developments of the Second Balkan War, the boundaries of modern-day Albania remained as they were before the war, because the Austro-Hungarian Empire pressed for a large Albanian state as a buffer between the Russian Empire and the Adriatic Sea. Russia preferred no Albanian state at all, with a seaport on the Adriatic for client state Serbia. Leon Trotsky chronicled the viciousness of Serbian ethnic cleansing directed at Albanian residents of Kosovo during the conflicts.[7]

Away from the cities, Kosovar Albanians and Kosovo Serbs lived similarly but separately in tiny villages. Albanian villages comprised a dozen or more small houses, often clustered inside walled *kulas* from which extended families cultivated livestock on communal pastures and private cropland, irrigated by water diverted from mountain streams and channeled through rock-framed ditches maintained by the village. Farming methods were those of the early eighteenth and nineteenth centuries, passed down from generation to generation in large families. Although many villages had a few shops maintained on the ground floor of traditional three-story Albanian brick houses, money was irrelevant, and governmental authorities in the cities were of even less relevance. The villages were self-sufficient and fiercely independent. The closely interspersed Serb and Albanian villages struggled with each other, often with violence, as they jockeyed for dominance. Unlike in Bosnia and Croatia, mixed marriages between Kosovar Albanians and Kosovo Serbs were virtually unknown.

The Kingdom of Yugoslavia, also known as the Kingdom of Serbs, Croats, and Slovenes, was founded in 1918 at the end of World War I and dominated by Serbia. After World War II, the communist-led opposition to Axis forces abolished the monarchy and established a new state known as Democratic

---

[6] Supported by Austria, Albania had declared independence on November 28, 1912, at the Congress of Vlore. Vickers at 68. After Serbia occupied northern and central Albania during the second Balkan War, in the 1913 Treaty of London, the Porte agreed to relinquish control over Albanian territories, including present-day Albania and Kosovo, but left it to further negotiations to decide the international status of both and the boundaries of Albania. Vickers at 74–5. Diplomatic and military conflict continued until an Albanian principality was agreed to in November 1913, with Prince William of Wied on its throne. Vickers at 82–3. Post–World War I diplomacy finally recognized Albania as an independent state, but without Kosovo.

[7] See Vickers at 69 (quoting Leon Trotsky reporting on villages being "turned into pillars of fire").

Federal Yugoslavia, renamed the Federal People's Republic of Yugoslavia in 1946, then renamed again in 1963 as the Socialist Federal Republic of Yugoslavia. Its boundaries remained more or less the same from 1918 to 1991, always including Kosovo.

Yugoslavia's communist boss Josip Broz – universally known as Tito – was a Machiavellian, charismatic figure who sought to accommodate separate national identities within Yugoslavia with an overarching Yugoslav identity.[8] He alternately placated Albanian demands for self-government and cracked down on Kosovar Albanian nationalists.[9]

Sharp controversy surrounds the facts relating to the demographic balance in Kosovo. Kosovar Albanians claim that the present territory and more, extending northward into Serbia proper, historically was populated primarily by Albanians. They also claim that the government of Serbia consciously pressed Serbs to migrate into Kosovo, and Albanians to migrate out, to achieve a more favorable mix of population groups. Serbs claim that the territory historically was dominated by Serbs, and that Albanians moved there over several centuries, sometimes as a matter of conscious policy and sometimes as a matter of natural migrations in search of better agricultural conditions.

Everyone agrees, however, that Albanians constituted a majority of the population in Kosovo throughout the twentieth century. The Serbs saw the Albanians as a threat to their culture and sovereignty, and the Albanians saw the Serbs as oppressors and foreign occupiers. Most of the interwar period was punctuated by periods of armed Albanian resistance to Serbian authorities, and a Serbian government policy that did little to draw Albanians into modern life from relatively primitive, self-sufficient farms anchored in a clan-based traditional society. Serbs thought it particularly undesirable for Albanians to receive education in the Albanian language, fearing that linguistic ties would fuel Albanian nationalism.

Tension between Kosovar Albanians and Kosovo Serbs was intensified by differences in religion. Serbs are overwhelmingly Orthodox Christians, and the Serbian Orthodox Church has long played a major role as a voice for Serb nationalism. Kosovar Albanians are predominantly Muslim, with significant minorities of Roman Catholics and a few Orthodox Christians. Islam, however, has played only a peripheral role historically in the culture of Kosovar Albanians. Islamic religious authorities within Kosovo have relatively little

---

[8] See generally Richard West, *Tito and the Rise and Fall of Yugoslavia* 331–337 (1994) (describing and evaluating critical treatment of Tito; id. at 244–7 (describing how Tito relaxed state controls on industry, the press, and culture); id. at 210–12 (describing Tito's efforts to moderate post–World War II efforts to take revenge on ethnic political opponents); id. 342 (describing Tito's channeling of investment into Kosovo, the poorest region of Yugoslavia).

[9] Susan L. Woodward, *Balkan Tragedy: Chaos and Dissolution After the Cold War* 45 (1995) (Yugoslavia was not held together by Tito's charisma, political dictatorship, or repression of national sentiments but by a complex balancing act at the international level and an extensive systems of rights of overlapping sovereignties.)

influence. While Kosovar Albanians go through the motions of celebrating Ramadan and other Muslim holidays, the majority consider themselves nationalist Albanians first, and only incidentally Muslims.

In the twentieth century, Serbian policy toward the "Albanian problem" was to cleanse Kosovo of as many Albanians as possible. In 1937, Vaso Cubrilovic, sentenced as a conspirator in the 1918 assassination of Austro-Hungarian Archduke Ferdinand in Sarajevo, and later a professor and cabinet officer in Serbia, authored a report proposing the expulsion of Albanians from Kosovo.[10] He proposed to reclassify Albanians as "Turks," and to make their lives in Kosovo so miserable that they would be eager to emigrate. Arrangements ultimately were made between Serbia and Turkey to encourage relocation of tens of thousands of Kosovar Albanians to Turkey – a policy that continued into the 1950s and 1960s under Tito.[11]

World War II intensified the division between Serbs and Albanians. Serbs were solidly on the side of the Allies, while Albanians enjoyed a period of unification and relative autonomy under Italian administration. After imposing military control over the southwestern Balkans, Italy organized all of the Albanian territories into one district of military administration. A "Greater Albania" existed, albeit under Axis control.

As the military tide began to run against the Axis forces, Yugoslavia and Albania became bloody battlefields on which five contending irregular forces fought each other with little restraint. Nationalists Serb Chetniks opposed the Nazi-allied and nationalist Croat Ustasha, while Tito's communist partisans and loosely allied communist forces under the political control of Enver Hoxha in Albania fought with everyone else. Some Kosovar Albanians fought on the side of the Italians and Germans, while others organized guerrilla groups to support Tito and to oppose the Chetniks.

After Germany surrendered, the battle over Yugoslavia continued, with Tito and Hoxha gradually gaining ground. Tito sought to sway more Albanians to join his side by promising Kosovo either political autonomy or absorption into the Republic of Albania through a referendum to be held after the fighting stopped. When it came time to deliver on this promise, however, Tito was confronted by political reality: Serbs were fiercely opposed to losing Kosovo. Tito needed Serb support for his emerging communist government in

---

[10] Dr. V. Cubrilovic, *The Expulsion of the Albanians* (1937), located at http://www.aacl.com/ expulsion2.html; see Julie A. Mertus, *Kosovo: How Myths and Truths Started a War* (1999) (describing Cubrilovic memorandum). Web sources, although sometime disfavored as authority, often are the best way to obtain access to historical documents.

[11] See Noel Malcolm, *Kosovo: A Short History* 322–3 (1998) (reporting that, under pressure from Yugoslav authorities from 1945 to 1966 for Muslims to identify themselves as "Turks," some one hundred thousand Kosovar Albanians migrated to Turkey); Paulin Kola, *The Search for Greater Albania* 100–6 (2003) (analyzing Cubrilovic memorandum and its impact on Serbian intellectuals and policy makers; detailing Yugoslav initiative to encourage Kosovar Albanians to migrate to Turkey).

Yugoslavia more than he needed continued Albanian military support, and so he backed away from his commitment to a plebicite. Kosovo remained a part of the Republic of Serbia within the reconstituted federal State of Yugoslavia after the war.[12]

Hoxha was not much interested in Kosovo. He was preoccupied with solidifying his control in Albania inside its existing borders, and his political support was weakest in the northern part of Albanian-populated territory – the part abutting Kosovo. He reneged on a provision in the Mukja Agreement, negotiated between Tito's Communist Party of Yugoslavia and Albanian nationalists, which provided for a plebiscite or referendum on Kosovo's future.[13]

Enraged by this betrayal of their aspirations for self-determination, many Albanians, especially in the Drenica region of Kosovo, continued to offer armed resistance through loosely organized *kaçaks*, an Albanian resistance movement dating back to 1918. Tito's worries about British and American attempts to subvert his political control were exacerbated by his break with Stalin in 1951, adding to his anxiety about the possibility that Soviet forces also would act to topple his regime. Significant to this geopolitical development was the fact that Enver Hoxha and the Republic of Albania remained solidly in Stalin's camp,[14] thus making the Republic of Albania a potential staging ground for a Soviet incursion into Yugoslavia.[15] The dominant Albanian population in Kosovo could become a fifth column for Hoxha. Albanian nationalist resistance combined with the Stalinist threat to cause Tito and the Serbian government to keep tight control over the Albanian population in Kosovo, implemented by Aleksandar Ranković, Tito's close political crony and Minister of the Interior in Serbia. Yugoslav – and this usually meant Serb – police and intelligence forces routinely raided Albanian homes searching for weapons, Albanian community leaders frequently were questioned and jailed on suspicion of subversion, and Albanian-language education and observances of Albanian culture were banned.

---

[12] Vickers at 161–2.

[13] See Bernd J. Fischer, "Enver Hoxha and the Stalinist Dictatorship in Albania," in Bernd J. Fischer, *Balkan Strongmen* 239, 246 (2007) (Yugoslavs forced Hoxha to renounce Mukja Agreement).

[14] Hoxha was confronted with sharp factionalism in the Communist Party of Albania, including a significant faction that he suspected of planning to depose him and draw Albania entirely within Yugoslavia's orbit. See http://www.marxistsfr.org/reference/archive/hoxha/works/stalin/meet2.htm. Only Stalin could protect him. Enver Hoxha's memoirs show a shift from telling Stalin in 1947 that relations between Albania and Yugoslavia were good (http://www.marxistsfr.org/reference/archive/hoxha/works/stalin/meet1.htm) to 1951, when he emphasized Stalin's warning to him that Albania must have the military capability to defend itself against Yugoslavia (http://www.marxistsfr.org/reference/archive/hoxha/works/stalin/meet5.htm).

[15] See Kola at 100 (summarizing the breakup between Tito, who sought to court the West, and Hoxha, who sought to consolidate his power by isolating Albania).

The resulting effect was to drive Albanians, even those with no particular appetite for armed resistance, underground and more solidly into their traditional folk- and clan-based networks. Thus, as Yugoslavia modernized under the tight control of a communist government in Belgrade, funded by generous Western supporters eager to see Yugoslavia flourish as a relatively neutral communist regime not dominated by the Soviets, opportunities for Albanians in public life were limited. They either sought – with Yugoslav government encouragement – to migrate abroad to start new lives in the West or in Turkey, or remained as part of an increasingly robust informal economy and political system, largely separate from official Yugoslav political institutions.

The Tito regime poured money into Kosovo, which was surely the most underdeveloped part of Yugoslavia.[16] Roads, railroads, telephone, and electricity grids were built to support the new factories splashed over the Kosovo landscape. Large hard-rock mining facilities were built in Trepca, near Mitrovica, and lignite mines were built near Pristina. Although many Albanians obtained good jobs in these projects, most of the managerial positions and many of the lower-level positions were occupied by Serbs. The Serbian government actively encouraged Serbs to migrate from elsewhere in Yugoslavia to Kosovo as part of its long-running effort to stabilize the population balance there. The high birth rate among Albanians, still locked into traditional family-oriented cultures, made this an uphill battle.

Meanwhile, Enver Hoxha had almost completely sealed off the Republic of Albania from outside influences, fearing subversion of his police state as much from Kosovar Albanians as from Yugoslav influences. This left Kosovar Albanians with an unrealistic fantasy about the conditions in the Enverist Albania,[17] while lacking much actual contact with Albanians in Albania.

A diffuse resentment by Albanians of Serb domination and Serbian Interior Minister Aleksandar Ranković's heavy-handed police-state methods boiled over into riots throughout Kosovo in 1969. Tito, always a deft accommodator and architect of power-sharing arrangements that would leave his dominance unchallenged, had already fired Ranković, who had been plotting against Tito anyway. Tito knew when to show his magnanimous side: he established the University of Pristina, the first Albanian-language university outside the Republic of Albania, and he opened up more opportunities for Albanians to enter political and economic life as teachers, judges, members of the police and intelligence forces, factory managers, and political actors.

Yugoslavia was a federal state, comprising the republics of Bosnia, Croatia, Macedonia, Montenegro, Slovenia, and Serbia. Tito was not willing to accede

---

[16] Howard Clark, *Civil Resistance in Kosovo* 37 (2000) (noting that investment in Kosovo before 1957 emphasized mineral extraction and production of electricity for use elsewhere in Yugoslavia); March 2003 discussions with Ahmet Shala and Besim Beqaj regarding geographic and ethnic patterns of Yugoslav investment.

[17] March 2005 discussions with Lisen Bashkurti, former Vice Minister of Albanian Foreign Service, and Besim Beqaj, now head of the Kosovo Chamber of Commerce.

to the Kosovar Albanian desire for Kosovo to become a republic, but he did revise the Yugoslav Constitution in 1974 to make Kosovo an "autonomous province" within the Republic of Serbia. Kosovo now had its own assembly, its own branch of the Communist Party, and other badges of self-government. It also sent voting representatives to central institutions in Belgrade. Its status as an autonomous province, however, like that of Vojvodina, the other autonomous province within the Republic of Serbia, withheld one of the hallmarks of a republic: the formal power to secede from Yugoslavia – a power enjoyed by the republics but denied to Kosovo. An elected Kosovo Assembly had wide governmental powers and Kosovo representatives also sat on the collective presidency of Yugoslavia, a committee on which the chairmanship rotated among representatives of the republics and autonomous provinces.

As frequently happens with relaxation of autocracy, the accommodations to the Kosovar Albanians calmed things down in the short run but opened up channels through which Albanian nationalism strengthened. Albanian consciousness was centered in the University of Pristina and in the Communist League of Kosovo, which dominated the Assembly. Newly minted Kosovar Albanian politicians and factory managers celebrated their power by expanding opportunities for ethnic Albanian friends and cousins, often at the expense of the Kosovo Serbs who now had lost their historic dominance in both political and economic realms. Nationalist sentiment within the young Albanian population particularly manifested itself in periodic strikes and demonstrations against the authorities – which were most often staffed by Albanians but controlled by Serbs. Kosovo Serbs thought that Kosovar Albanians had too much power and abused it, and felt particularly threatened by periodic outbreaks of Albanian violence.

The two communities had very different perspectives on the demonstrations and the unrest. The Kosovar Albanians saw them as a natural reaction to continued illegitimate governance of Kosovo by Serbia. The Kosovo Serbs saw them as a threatening street challenge to the legitimate governments of Yugoslavia and Serbia and their institutions.

Tito died in 1980, and the political elites in Belgrade felt insecure over the inevitable battles over succession. A year later, at this moment of high insecurity, Albanians rioted all across Kosovo, sparked by a controversy over food served to students in the University of Pristina cafeteria. The Serbian government overreacted, sending tanks into the streets of Pristina and thirty thousand troops to Kosovo, and arresting and incarcerating thousands of Albanian political activists. Although the Serbian government claimed that only eleven people were killed, Kosovar Albanians put the figure at about one thousand.[18]

A report issued in 1986 by the Serbian Academy of Sciences referred to "the physical, political, legal, and cultural genocide perpetrated against the Serbian population of Kosovo and Metohija..." as "the greatest defeat

_____

[18] Vickers at 205.

suffered by Serbia in the wars of liberation she waged between Orasac in 1804 and the uprising of 1941."[19]

The regime's heavy-handed overreaction alienated significant parts of the Kosovar Albanian political elite, causing them to question whether Yugoslavia would ever provide a climate within which Albanians could realize their aspirations. Ironically, the crackdown also facilitated networking among Kosovar Albanian militants who were now in jail together, able to communicate and plot more freely under the inattentive eyes of prison guards than they could outside, under the highly attentive eyes and ears of the Yugoslav secret police. Many activists escaped arrest by fleeing to small Albanian communities in Germany, Switzerland, and, to a lesser extent, the United States, where they began to stir up Albanian nationalism. Three of the most vocal – Jusef Gervalla, Kadri Zeka, and Bardosh Gervalla – were killed in Stuttgart, Germany, in 1982 as they were leaving an Albanian nationalist celebration. Most people think they were assassinated by the Yugoslav intelligence service. Their assassination provided symbolism for intensified Albanian nationalism and hostility to Yugoslav control of Kosovo more than it served to intimidate the remaining militants.

For many Kosovar Albanians, the Republic of Albania seemed to be a hallmark of what all Albanians should enjoy: their own state. Many dreamed of a day when Kosovo would separate from Serbia and become part of Albania. Enver Hoxha, the repressive head of the Republic of Albania, survived Tito by five years. Hoxha was ambivalent in his attitude toward the Albanian separatists. On the one hand, they provided an interesting tool for keeping the Yugoslav government distracted from any plans that might threaten Hoxha's regime in the Republic of Albania, and they could eventually tilt the political transformation of Kosovo in directions that would suit Albanian state interests. On the other hand, Hoxha wanted to continue the detente that he had forged with Tito by the early 1970s. Both sought a collective bulwark against Soviet adventures in Yugoslavia similar to the Soviet invasion of Hungary in 1956 and of Czechoslovakia in 1968. Moreover, Hoxha knew that Albanian militants now focused on resistance in Kosovo might easily provide leadership for anti-Enverist resistance in Albania. He reconciled these ostensibly incompatible concerns by providing modest financial support through his intelligence service, the Sigurimi, to fledgling Kosovar Albanian nationalist organizations in Switzerland and Germany. The most important of the beneficiaries was the Popular League for the Republic of Kosovo or LPRK. The level of financial support did not permit the LPRK and others to do much operationally, but it ensured that the Sigurimi maintained good intelligence about what the resisters were doing.

---

[19] Memorandum from the Serbian Academy of Arts and Sciences (1986), available at http://www.haverford.edu/relg/sells/reports/memorandumSANU.htm.

The disorder in Kosovo in 1981 frightened Kosovo Serbs. The vacuum left in Yugoslavia by Tito's death opened up opportunities for the politically ambitious to experiment with new forms of appeal. Traditional Marxist ideological rhetoric and Titoist advocacy of a multiethnic Yugoslavia in which a Yugoslav national identity would coexist with Serb, Croat, Slovene, Bosniak,[20] or Albanian identities were beginning to lose their resonance with the public. Instead, examples of nationalist resistance to Soviet control elsewhere in Central and Eastern Europe by Poles, Czechs, Hungarians, and others encouraged appeals to nationalist sentiment in Croat, Serb, Slovene, and Albanian communities in Yugoslavia.

Slobodan Milošević rose to power in Yugoslavia in the late 1980s by inciting Serb fears of Kosovar Albanians, only to be the architect of Yugoslavia's destruction through three bloody wars in Croatia, Bosnia, and Kosovo. Milošević was initially an ambitious but relatively obscure midlevel official in the Serbian Communist Party. He was not known for charisma or stirring rhetoric. In 1987, however, he gave a speech in the House of Culture in Fushë Kosova. The response was huge, and revealed the power of a political campaign to tap into growing Serb nationalism.[21] Milošević decided to play the Serb nationalist card in a way that would capitalize Kosovo Serb resentment about their diminishing dominance of political and economic affairs in Kosovo. If he could whip up the Kosovo Serbs and make their plight visible to other Serbs, he could build a tide of anger throughout Serbia that would lift him to control of the Communist Party of Serbia.

Emboldened by the success of this speech, Milošević defined his program as one of restoring Serbian pride and dignity against Kosovar Albanian political influence in Kosovo. With remarkable speed, he ascended to the head of the Serbian and then the Yugoslav Communist Party, betraying, and allegedly engineering the murders of his former patrons and opponents along the way. One of his victims was Ivan Stambolić, who had mentored Milošević and facilitated his rise in the Communist Party. Milošević orchestrated a campaign against Stambolić, resulting in his resignation from the Yugoslav presidency, by accusing him and his other protégés of being too soft on the Kosovar Albanians.[22] Subsequently, Milošević was indicted for ordering Stambolić's assassination.[23] By 1989, he was president of Serbia and intended to deliver on his promise to reinstate Kosovo Serbs in the seats of power in Kosovo.

---

[20] The term "Bosniak" has come into popular usage only in the last few years, replacing "Bosnian Muslim," which was more common during the 1990s. The term had been used in the nineteenth century and was officially embraced by the Second Bosniak Congress, held in September 1993.

[21] Sell at 1; Malcolm at 341–2; Clark at 18; Kola at 174.

[22] Sell at 48–9.

[23] See "Stambolic Murder Trial Opens in Belgrade," *Southeast European Times*, February 23, 2004 (describing indictment of Slobodan Milošević and others for ordering murder of Stambolic in 2000); Zelijko Cvijanovic, "Mira Faces Stambolic Murder Allegations, Inst.

His timing was propitious, as Yugoslavia followed the example of East Germany, Hungary, Czechoslovakia, Romania, and Bulgaria in throwing off communism and one-party control by the Communist Party. Democratization in Yugoslavia, however, soon was forestalled by successful Slovenian, Croatian, Bosnian, and Macedonian efforts to secede. Milošević, now in control of the political and state security apparatus in Serbia, could add national security arguments aimed at defending the political integrity of the Yugoslav state to his essentially racist arguments in support of Serb dominance of Yugoslavia. Although he lacked the capacity militarily to implement his policies in other parts of Yugoslavia outside Serbia, Kosovar Albanians were too poorly organized to resist his policies in Kosovo.

Milošević had solidified his power enough by 1989 that he stripped the province of Kosovo of its political autonomy and legislated most Kosovar Albanians out of all but the most menial jobs in industry, public institutions, and education. Albanian-language instruction at the University of Pristina was terminated. De facto Albanian control of socially owned enterprises was subverted by a so-called privatization process transferring these enterprises – which comprised most industry in Kosovo – into the hands of private investors who were of Serbian ethnicity or otherwise friendly to Milošević.

On March 23, 1989, as the seasons changed in Kosovo, so did the reins of control. In the wake of a month of chaos following a miners' strike, countless political arrests, and the steady threat of further violence, the voice of the people succumbed to the voice of intimidation. In the same month, Milošević had removed Azem Vllasi from his post as head of the Kosovo branch of the Yugoslav Communist Party and had him arrested for organizing unrest in Kosovo.[24] Vllasi had dominated the Party in Kosovo and had sought on the one hand to suppress Kosovar Albanian nationalism and on the other hand to protect Kosovo's political autonomy from growing Serbian nationalism.

When the members of the Assembly of Kosovo convened in Pristina to vote on constitutional amendments already passed by the Serbian assembly in Belgrade, Serbian tanks and armored cars "guarded" the entrance, and were stationed throughout the rest of the city. Police garbed in helmets and automatic weapons screened those entering the building. With the inclusion of various "guests" on the floor – members of the security police and Communist Party functionaries from Serbia – the parliamentary debate took less than four hours and, according to some reports, included active participation from the "guests" when it came time to vote. With a final vote of 168 to 10 (and two abstentions), the Assembly bowed before the might of Milošević, accepted the new Serbian constitution, and eradicated its own power – and, in essence, its own existence.

---

for War and Peace Reporting," January 4, 2003, located at http://www.iwpr.net/index.php?apc_state=hen&s=o&o=p=bcr&l=EN&s=f&o=157551 (reporting on suspicions that Milošević's wife masterminded the killing).

[24] Sell at 81–6.

Violence erupted on the streets of Kosovo's cities in reaction. In Ferizaj, one thrown stone multiplied into thousands of protestors flinging the primitive projectiles while the police retaliated with tear gas and batons. In Pristina itself, students swarmed from the halls of the university into the streets, only to be beaten back by police batons and automatic weapons. Heavy police presence, the continued presence of tanks in and around many towns, and a strict curfew in Pristina did little to stem the angry resistance. In less than a week, the official toll was 24 dead and 222 injured – but the unofficial toll was far higher, with estimates as high as 140 dead.[25] No one was spared the consequences of the riots; children as young as nine years of age were brought to hospitals with gunshot wounds.

On June 28, 1989, on the six hundredth anniversary of Prince Lazar's legendary victory, Milošević returned to the Field of Blackbirds. He spoke to a cheering crowd of one million Serbs from all over Serbia, crowing about his victory over the Albanians. Within a period of months, most Kosovar Albanians had been excluded from managerial, public policy making, teaching, judicial, and law-enforcement jobs in Kosovo.[26]

The initial response by the Kosovar Albanians – aside from the rioting – was measured. The Albanian leadership of the Kosovo Communist Party formed a new party, the Democratic League of Kosovo (LDK), and elected French-educated literature major Ibrahim Rugova as its president. Under LDK orchestration, an informal session of the Kosovo Assembly declared Kosovo to be an "independent unit" of Yugoslavia in July 1990.[27] Then, after Slovenia and Croatia declared independence from Yugoslavia in June 1991, the LDK organized a referendum – informal by necessity – on independence for Kosovo, which passed overwhelmingly on October 19, 1991. No state except Albania, however, recognized Kosovo's proclamation of independence.

Rugova established a parallel system of schools and social services, operated by volunteers, and appointed a Government in Exile, headed by urologist Bujar Bukoshi, who operated initially from Croatia, then from Switzerland, and finally from Germany. Rugova himself was eccentric.[28] He always wore a polka-dotted scarf and was usually taciturn and unresponsive in international gatherings. He was a whiz, however, at party politics. He knew every name, insisted on absolute loyalty, and established the LDK as the dominant institution in Kosovar Albanian public life, becoming an icon himself in the process.[29]

---

[25] Sell at 87–8.

[26] Sell at 95.

[27] Vickers at 226.

[28] See Sell at 91–2 (describing Rugova in sympathetic terms).

[29] August 2005 interview with Chad Rogers, then head of NDI office in Pristina. But see Troebst at 9–11 (describing growing criticism of Rugova, among other things for manipulating LDK rules and procedures to procure his reelection in February and March of 1998 to shore up his position as party leader despite growing opposition).

Although he was tireless in keeping up the drumbeat to expose Serbian abuses of Kosovar Albanian human rights, Rugova was consistently risk averse to any forceful means of protest, let alone violent resistance. Still, his steady resistance to Serbian authority built him strong and deep support within the Kosovar Albanian political elite and among many ordinary Kosovar Albanians.

Meanwhile, ordinary Kosovar Albanian kids were forming their own political views. They were not drawn to Rugova's passivity in the face of growing repression. Slowly, they formed a guerrilla insurgency that came to be known as the Kosovo Liberation Army (KLA, or UÇK in Albanian). Fahri Rama was a waiter in the Hotel Victory in Pristina when I first met him – strikingly handsome, but shy and reticent in his "waiter's English." He was twenty when he joined the KLA in a village near Pudejevo. When Fahri was in high school in the mid-1990s, he was walking home from school one day with his schoolbooks. A Serb policeman stopped him and demanded to know why he was carrying the books. He explained that he was just coming from school and was going home. The Serb policeman took him to the police station and told him that he had to eat the books because they were written in Albanian instead of Serbian, and then forced him to eat several pages.[30]

Throughout Kosovo, Kosovar Albanian fathers and mothers had been expelled from their jobs in state enterprises or in the government and had to fall back on traditional Albanian farms and family ties. Even in their insular family compounds, they were not secure. A pounding on the door in the middle of the night would announce a visit by the Serbian Interior Ministry (MUP) police, who would ransack the house, ostensibly looking for weapons. One or more brothers or cousins would be taken to the police station and beaten; sometimes they would not return. To sing an Albanian song or to criticize the revocation of Kosovo's autonomy was risky; it could earn a beating and a prison sentence.[31]

The Kosovar Albanians had tasted a measure of freedom to be themselves and to run their own affairs in the last years of the Tito regime, and now it had been jerked away. Throughout Eastern Europe – and in much of the rest of Yugoslavia – others were fighting for self-determination. Meanwhile, Rugova counseled only patience, even as economic conditions worsened and the baton of Serb control struck more frequently. If you were Albanian, there was no remedy if a particularly brutal MUP officer or secret-police official trashed your house or humiliated your mother and father. Young boys would go into the streets to sell cigarettes to try to fill the holes in family incomes, but Serb police would often take the cigarettes. If you were belligerent in response, they could kill you, as they had killed others, and there was nothing you could do

---

[30] January 2004 interview with Fahri Rama.
[31] February 2005 interview with Myzafer Mehmeti, Chicago.

about it.[32] The courts dismissed claims by Kosovar Albanians, and to make a complaint marked you as a troublemaker and separatist. The courts would register property transfers from Albanians to Serbs but not from Serbs to Albanians. Most Kosovar Albanians suffered sullenly – but they talked to their kids about a better life and held up Albanian culture as a source of strength.[33]

Milošević's abandonment of the Titoist model of a multiethnic Yugoslav society made it easier for advocates of Kosovar autonomy or independence to gain traction with the Albanian population both in Kosovo and in the growing exile communities abroad. Resistance by Kosovar Albanians to so-called foreign occupiers did not begin with Milošević or end with the March 2004 riots. The revocation of Kosovo's political autonomy in 1989, however, strengthened the numbers of Albanians who were willing to fight against their Serb masters and gradually broadened the base of popular support for armed resistance. The Popular League for the Republic of Kosovo (LPRK) changed its name to Popular League for Kosovo (LPK), signifying that its goal had expanded from the mere creation of a Republic of Kosovo within Yugoslavia to a fully independent Kosovo, perhaps aligned with the Republic of Albania.

Finally, Fahri and hundreds of other young adults like him decided that they could take it no more and would fight. At first they thought only of defending their families and homes and friends from Serbian police raids. Yet it was not long before they decided to take resistance to Serbian bases of operation – particularly to MUP police stations. They would fight back, they told each other, even if they were killed in the process. Rumors were growing of a deeply clandestine guerrilla movement – the KLA. Fahri decided to join it. First, though, he had to find it. "I knew I might get killed," said Fahri, "but I vowed to fight for our dignity."[34]

Through one of his uncles, Fahri made contact with the KLA and participated in training, where the young men learned to take orders and were schooled in basic guerrilla tactics. Later, I asked Fahri whether he and his buddies really thought the KLA could win against the overwhelming forces they faced. "I always knew we would win because we were fighting for our land, for our country, and for our families and the Serbs were not," he said.

Lirim Greiçevci, another young man, described it this way:

> In 1996, I was still in secondary school in the Drenica Valley and there began to be rumors of people seeing armed men in the woods. In 1997, actual armed attacks began in Drenica. These armed attacks got across the message: the KLA might be real after all and that armed resistance was possible. Even so, most people thought that the Serbs were doing it to themselves, as part of a plot to justify the repression. I wasn't so sure. I could see the Serbs panicking. They

---

[32] January 2004 interview with Alban Rafuna, Pristina.
[33] January 2005 interview with Arianit Zeka, Pristina.
[34] March 2004 interview with Fahri Rama.

clearly were concerned, and I couldn't believe they would be so concerned if it really was a Serb conspiracy. I was glad that something was being done, but I really didn't think about strategy or the possibility of victory.[35]

Milošević's Serbian forces were confident about their ability to suppress the Albanian nationalists. Milošević responded to KLA attacks with a ruthless decapitation strategy: removing the leaders of the separatist movements.[36] Throughout the 1990s, the Serbian intelligence service, the SDB, and the Ministry of Interior police tightened the vice, arresting young Albanians by the thousands.

The Serb Intelligence Service was efficient and had penetrated deeply into Albanian society. Milošević thus had been able in 1991 to penetrate and then disrupt an Albanian operation to train a guerrilla force in the northern mountains of Albania and infiltrate them into Kosovo.[37] In conjunction with that operation, he rounded up young leaders of the emerging resistance movement. Then, in 1996, he assassinated Zahir Pajaziti, the most effective leader of resistance in Kosovo's north, centered on the Llap Valley, and arrested another one hundred leaders of what was steadily becoming a more coherent KLA.[38]

---

[35] March 2005 interview with Greicevci.

[36] See James Pettifer, *Kosova Express: A Journey in Wartime* 33 (2005) (describing his interview with a Serbian police official in Pristina who told him that "some liquidations" of Albanian militants had taken place).

[37] July 2005 interview with Xhavit Haliti, Pristina; July 2005 interview with Bujar Bukoshi.

[38] For more detail on the growth of the KLA and its expanding popular support, see Henry H. Perritt, Jr., *Kosovo Liberation Army: The Inside Story of an Insurgency*, ch. 3 (2008).

3 Armed Conflict Grows

ALTHOUGH IT MAY HAVE SEEMED OTHERWISE TO MANY AMERICANS, the crisis in Kosovo had not developed overnight. The wars in Croatia and Bosnia were over and had dropped off the evening news, and now Milošević seemed to be up to his old ethnic-cleansing tricks in this place called Kosovo. A war in Kosovo had been incubating for a long time; its sudden emergence onto the front pages paralleled a last-ditch effort by the international community to bring under control a conflict that even senior policy makers did not understand much better than my students and I did, although close observers of the region had foreseen an escalating conflict there for some time.

The violence in Kosovo developed gradually; it was not a matter of a large guerrilla army taking to the field on the Albanian side, or of the VJ (the Yugoslav army) springing into a massive campaign of ethnic cleansing. What happened instead is that the Serbian police were aggressive in enforcing Milošević's apartheid regime in Kosovo even as other parts of Eastern Europe were breaking free of totalitarian Communist rule, and other parts of Yugoslavia were fighting to set up their own states. The voices in the Kosovar Albanian community favoring separation from Serbia grew louder. As they did so, the police tried to arrest them. Often the Serbian authorities did not know who the separatists were, or if they did know the identities, they did not know their locations, so the police began to target friends and neighbors instead. The more militant of the separatists fought back and the police became still more aggressive, treating Albanian troublemakers as terrorists. They were prepared to shoot first and ask questions afterwards. The regime began to expel populations from larger and larger areas believed to support the terrorists. To do so, they fired heavy weapons at houses and fortified family compounds, burned crops, killed livestock, and poisoned wells. Now, for the Kosovar Albanians, it was not merely a matter of pugnacious sons being arrested or killed; it was a matter of defending families and homesteads.

What began as defensive defiance by a handful of Kosovar Albanians morphed into an organized insurgency, willing to take the fight to the Serbian authorities on their own turf.

Later, when I was writing a book on the KLA,[1] I realized that the transformation involved two relatively distinct groups of Kosovar Albanian militants. One, which can be called the Defenders at Home, concentrated on defending against raids by Serbian authorities. The second, which can be called the Planners in Exile, emerged from clandestine Albanian political organizations then operating outside Kosovo, mostly associated with the LPK. As the wars in Croatia and Bosnia intensified in the early 1990s, the LPK had formed a group to plan an armed insurgency in Kosovo, seeking to tie together scattered but largely ineffective pockets of armed resistance to Yugoslav authority in various regions of Kosovo.[2] Adopting the name "Kosovo Liberation Army" (KLA or UÇK in Albanian) in 1993, the LPK group organized increasingly frequent and bold attacks against Serb police stations, intelligence agents, and Albanian collaborators with the Serb authorities.

A very prominent Kosovar Albanian political leader, insisting on anonymity, told this story of his early involvement with the KLA:

> A Serbian police convoy came out of a police station, traveled through the edge of town, traversed a traffic circle, and proceeded down a main road to a railroad crossing. We in the KLA had good intelligence, so our fighters were ready in their places. Careful preplanning allowed everyone to play roles flawlessly, opening fire just as the leading edge of the convoy reached the railroad track. We killed five policemen and wounded three others.
>
> Later, outside a restaurant, the KLA killed three policemen known by everyone to have abused Kosovar Albanians and their families. Our mission accomplished, we immediately melted into the crowd and appeared again in public in civilian clothes as soon as we could.[3]

This militant youth was not the only one. When he was eighteen, Valon Murati and a handful of others organized the National Movement for the Liberation of Kosova (NMLA, or LKÇK in Albanian). The NMLA comprised young urban sons of professionals who had reached the conclusion that there was little difference between Rugova's LDK and Milošević's regime.[4] Rugova was on television regularly, never failing to reaffirm his commitment to independence but discouraging any form of real resistance. Valon and friends began to publish a newsletter, staying one step ahead of the Serbian security services. In 1997, several of Valon's friends were arrested and killed. When he too became a target, he took refuge in a secure apartment maintained by the NMLA in the Prizren region. He subsequently escaped to Albania, where he spent a year in Tirana; by the time he returned, the KLA and NMLA were

---

[1] Henry H. Perritt, Jr., *Kosovo Liberation Army: The Inside Story of an Insurgency* (2008).
[2] July 2005 interview with Xhavit Haliti, Pristina; July 2005 interview with Azem Syla, Pristina; July 2005 interview with Jakup Krasniqi.
[3] Confidential interview, Pristina, March 2005.
[4] Interview with Valon Murati, Pristina, March 2005.

virtually merged. Murati got a gun and joined the KLA. KLA attacks on Serbian targets remained sporadic and isolated, but the Serbian forces responded ferociously, rounding up or harassing entire families suspected by the intelligence service of having nationalist sympathies. Young men were arrested and beaten. Serbian police were trigger-happy. Sons who saw their fathers gunned down in front of them were eager to find a way to respond.

At this point, no one could have predicted with any confidence the likely outcome of these relatively low-level struggles between Kosovar Albanian separatists and the Milošević regime. Even as the shooting war in Croatia was sputtering to a close, the international community seemed impotent to stop the bloody fighting in Bosnia. Most of the diplomatic pronouncements about the Bosnian War insisted that a comprehensive solution for Yugoslavia was the only way to put an end to the violence.[5] Meanwhile, the most prominent Kosovar Albanian political leader, President Rugova, successfully urged his compatriots to avoid the bloodshed then destroying Croatia and Bosnia, and to confine themselves to peaceful advocacy of their self-determination aspirations. For the moment, he was able to convince most angry Kosovar Albanians to wait for a comprehensive Yugoslav settlement that would assure them of at least autonomy and perhaps even independence.[6]

The reality, however, was that the conflict in Bosnia was too complicated and too intense to settle through any sort of comprehensive Yugoslav political arrangement. Indeed, U.S. Ambassador Holbrooke and others were barely able to craft a viable settlement in 1995. The settlement, which came to be known as the Dayton Accords, succeeded only by keeping the agenda as narrow as possible. Rugova went to the Dayton negotiations, but was unable to participate constructively – and when the Accords were signed, they said nothing about Kosovo.[7]

---

[5] See David Owen, *Balkan Odyssey* (1995) (describing diplomacy related to breakup of Yugoslavia); Michael Libal, *Limits of Persuasion: Germany and the Yugoslav Crisis, 1991– 1992* at 109–12 (1997) (arguing that German policy did not favor self-determination for national groups at the expense of existing borders; that's why Kosovo was not entitled to independence).

[6] Sell at 91–3.

[7] In his book about his successful mediation of the negotiations that resulted in the Dayton Accords, Richard Holbrooke barely mentions Kosovo, except to note that once when he and Milošević were out for a walk, they passed about a hundred Albanian American demonstrators outside the fence with megaphones pleading the case for Kosovo, Richard Holbrooke, *To End a War* 234 (1998), and to report that, at Dayton, he repeatedly emphasized to Milošević the need to restore the rights of Kosovo's Albanian Muslims. Id. at 357. Throughout the book, Holbrooke emphasizes how difficult it was to reach an agreement on Bosnia. See, e.g., id. at 261 ("our chances of getting an agreement were poor"). Wolfgang Ischinger, later the European representative to the Troika, represented Germany at the Dayton negotiations. "My instructions from Klaus Kinkle [German Foreign Minister] were to try to include Kosovo in the Dayton Accords. It was a good idea, but it was not possible to implement. I would have been thrown out of the room if I had raised Kosovo." October 2008 interview with Ischinger.

This disappointment shifted public sentiment among Kosovar Albanians, and within Albanian communities abroad, against the pacifist Rugova approach; most significantly, it created a more sympathetic climate for the KLA's argument that armed resistance and complete independence were necessary.[8] Still, as violence by Serbs against Albanians increased, Rugova continued to publicize it, and his efforts were crucial to alerting the West that Serbia was violating human rights on a large scale inside Kosovo.[9] Internally, Rugova was doing nothing about the repression, merely counseling patience until the West could come to the rescue. The KLA was doing something about it. Beginning in 1996, popular opinion among Kosovar Albanians shifted dramatically away from Rugova's party to the KLA as the only plausible way to end Serb oppression. Some prominent local LDK party leaders began to work to help the KLA get better organized.[10]

KLA attacks began to increase in frequency and spread over most parts of Kosovo – but Milošević no longer had his hands full with large-scale wars in Croatia and Bosnia. Before, with the Bosnian War still active, his Interior Ministry Police had occasionally cracked down on suspected leaders of the KLA, while Interior Ministry Police presence actually decreased in the regions where the KLA exerted real control. Now, fresh from other conflicts, Milošević responded with savage counterinsurgency tactics directed more and more at the general population of Kosovo, which did increasingly offer aid and comfort to the KLA.

Two problems remained for the KLA: first, it was by necessity a deeply clandestine organization, in order to evade intensified Serb efforts to decapitate it; and second, it faced enormous difficulties in getting sufficient arms to mount a real insurgency. Then, two major events (one in the spring of 1997 and other in the spring of 1998) removed these two obstacles to a full-blown guerrilla insurgency in Kosovo.

The KLA was so clandestine that it was nearly invisible,[11] and Milošević was able to convince most Kosovar Albanians that the KLA either did not exist at all or was simply a fantasy in the minds of a handful of bandits and archaic Marxist ideologues.[12] Separately, Rugova also sought to minimize the

---

[8] See Stefan Troebst, *Conflict in Kosovo: Failure of Prevention?* 9–11 (ECM Working Paper #1, May 1998) [hereinafter "Troebst"] (describing Dayton Accords as a shock that led to unraveling of uneasy peace preferred by Rugova).

[9] Pettifer, *Kosova Express* at 47, 57.

[10] See Howard Clark, *Civil Resistance in Kosovo* 116–19 (2000) (describing loyalty to Rugova even though parallel system functioned badly for ordinary people; detailing Rugova's increasingly undemocratic consolidation of power in LDK, emasculating most of opposition voices by 1994 LDK Assembly meeting); Kola at 306 (describing split between Rugova and Bukoshi and Rugova's 1994 modification of LDK structures to overcome opposition by Bukoshi forces, which apparently constituted a majority within LDK).

[11] See Perritt, KLA at ch. 3–4 (describing KLA's emergence from obscurity).

[12] See generally James Pettifer, "Killing Fields of Kosovo," *The Times*, August 6, 1998, at p. 18 (denouncing those who equate KLA "terrorists" with Milošević; "the Serbs are fighting a colonial war in Kosovo; few live there anymore").

KLA because it was political movement with the potential to derail the LDK's dominance over Kosovo political life. The LDK's funding came mainly from what came to be known as the "Three Percent Fund," so named from the expectation that Albanians abroad would contribute 3 percent of their income to it.[13] Many of the Three Percent Fund donors were Kosovar Albanian businesspeople who had amassed considerable wealth from a variety of business activities, most at least formally illegal under Serbian law, some involving various kinds of trafficking in weapons, narcotics, and human beings, and many involving efforts to evade economic sanctions imposed on Serbia. This money was beginning to flow more heavily into support for the KLA. So Rugova made a political decision to reinforce Milošević's propaganda minimizing the significance of the KLA, often arguing that what appeared to KLA activities actually were provocation by the Serb secret police aimed at justifying intensified Serb repression.

Unavailability of weapons remained a major problem for the KLA.[14] Kosovo is landlocked and surrounded by regimes that, with the exception of the Republic of Albania, were hardly inclined to be sympathetic to the cause of an Albanian guerrilla movement aimed at creating an independent Albanian state in Kosovo. The state of Albania, of course, was instinctively sympathetic at some level, but early expressions of sympathy with Kosovar Albanian separatists had earned Albania a diplomatic slap in the face and a threat to withdraw increasing Western economic support for its modernization and alignment with the West. So Albania was cautious about allowing the KLA to recruit, train, and organize weapon supply lines through Albanian territory, and certainly was not going to provide such support openly.

In early 1997, the Albanian economy collapsed suddenly as huge pyramid funds – holding most of the savings of ordinary Albanian citizens – no longer had enough new contributions to finance withdrawals. With astounding speed, most political and security institutions collapsed as well. Albania spent more than a year mired in near-complete anarchy, and its government was unable to prevent the KLA from doing whatever it wanted.[15] By this time, the KLA was sufficiently organized to take full advantage of the opportunity,[16] and seized thousands of weapons from unprotected Albanian army arsenals. Of greater

---

[13] March 2005 interview with Bujar Bukoshi, Pristina.

[14] See Perritt, KLA at ch. 8 (describing weapons quantities and supply chain for KLA).

[15] See Tom Walker, "Serbia Sends in Tanks," *The Times*, June 18, 1998 (reporting that when a reporter checked into hotel in Bajram Curri, he was presented with an automatic pistol along with a room key).

[16] See James Pettifer, "Kosovo Gunmen Force Serb Police to Beat," *The Times*, January 8, 1998, at p. 15 (reporting that KLA has forced Serb police to withdraw from large parts of Kosovo's territory; Rugova looks increasingly irrelevant); "Clashes in Kosovo leave at least 22 dead," CNN Interactive (March 5, 1998) (reporting on shelling of villages by Serbian security forces, leaving at least twenty-two dead); James Pettifer, "Albanian Exile Groups Recruit Volunteers," *The Times*, March 6, 1999, at p. 17 (describing KLA recruitment drive for volunteers in Europe).

significance, because the Albanian army weapons were of poor quality, it organized more robust weapons supply lines from the Albanian Port of Durres into the northern Albanian mountains near Bajram Curri, Tropoja, and Kukes, which quickly became major staging areas for KLA training.[17]

In March 1998, Milošević decided to strike a hard blow to eliminate the KLA threat once and for all, and in doing so gave the KLA needed publicity and credibility. Serb artillery, tanks, and aircraft organized an assault on the family compound of Adem Jashari in Prekaz.[18] Jashari and his family were the undisputed leaders of the separatist movement in the Drenica region: the region of Kosovo with the strongest culture of resistance. Indeed, a portrait of Jashari wearing a black beard and holding an automatic weapon adorns the walls of many Kosovar Albanian homes,[19] and many of them regard Jashari as the father of the KLA. Serb forces at about the same time also organized assaults on the compounds of other families in Drenica and Dukagjini that were most prominent in the resistance to Serb authority, including those of future KLA commander Ramush Haradinaj. Until then, Serb forces had largely stayed away from these compounds, but now Milošević had decided that Serbia needed to show some muscle. Serb forces stormed family compounds, reducing them to rubble and killing everyone inside.

Fifty-seven family members, including children as young as three and elderly people as old as eighty-five, were killed in the Jashari "massacre," as Kosovar Albanians called it. Milošević's scorched-earth tactics had the opposite of the intended effect, however: the casualties galvanized Albanian communities around the world and led to an explosion of KLA recruits. Almost overnight, the KLA became a visible and viable political and military entity. Before, it was easy to believe that any violence, whether Albanian or Serb inspired, would be limited to people – mostly young men – directly involved in resisting law enforcement personnel; now it seemed every Albanian family was in jeopardy if one resisted Serb control.[20] Beyond the relatively abstract political goal of independence, the KLA now could recruit on the grounds that Albanians had to fight to protect their families as well. Albanian youth from Germany, Switzerland, Scandinavia, and the United States flocked to Albania on their way to Kosovo to join the fight. Milošević's brutal response was to expel hundreds of thousands of Kosovar Albanian civilians from their homes

---

[17] July 2005 interview with Xhavit Haliti, Pristina; August 2005 interview with Ramush Haradinaj, Pristina; August 2005 interview with Rrustem Mustafa ("Commander Remi").

[18] See "Serbs Say Kosovo Guerrilla Leader Killed in Crackdown," CNN Interactive, March 6, 1998 (reporting Serbian police claim that the killing of Adem Jashari "destroyed the core" of the KLA); "Milošević Defiant over Kosovo Crackdown," CNN Interactive, March 8, 1998 (describing how journalists saw half of the village's fifty houses destroyed after assault on Jashari compound).

[19] A picture of Jashari hangs in almost every one of the dozens of Kosovar Albanian homes I have visited.

[20] Interview with Ardian Spajiu, July 2005.

and across the borders to Albania and Macedonia. The Milošević regime intended for them never to return. By fall 1998, more than 250,000 Kosovar Albanians were massed in refugee camps outside Kosovo.[21]

Hashim Thaçi and other Kosovar Albanian rebels sneaked across the Albanian border into Kosovo to provide crucial military experience and organization to the KLA.[22] Thaçi himself had not served in the Yugoslav Army, but many other Kosovar Albanians had, and the KLA set out to recruit them. The KLA set up logistics operations in Tirana, the capital of the Republic of Albania. By late summer 1998, with the Yugoslav Army actively engaged in shelling and expelling entire villages in order to eradicate guerrillas, the KLA's insurgency was in full swing.

Throughout Kosovo, young Albanians decided that they had to do something. Many joined the KLA; some helped in other ways. Lirim Greiçevci, the university student who had early doubts about whether the KLA really existed, said in an interview:

> The Jashari massacre occurred in March, and I left the University of Pristina to go home to see what I could do. We got caught up in the summer offensive. The Serbs had a number of tanks who were shelling a hill near my village where they thought a KLA unit was located. We could see that they had tanks and troops on three sides of the village. The KLA saw it also and therefore was absent from the village. The Serbs rolled into the village with tanks and infantry, but everyone was gone, fled into a valley nearby. The KLA had retreated by that time, and melted back into the civilian population. They had to do this in order to save themselves from annihilation. The Serbs searched every house, and burned about ten. I guess they were looking for guns or KLA.
>
> Meanwhile about 3,000 of us were in a kind of camp towards the southwest. The Serbs must have known where we were, but for some reason they never attacked us. I wanted to do something to protect my family, friends, and neighbors, but there really wasn't anything I could do. I couldn't join the KLA as a fighter because the KLA had disappeared.
>
> Then I realized: I could use my English and my cell phone. I was able to make contact with international journalists, and two of them came to our encampment. Over time, I established regular contact with about seven journalists and some NGOs. Journalists passed my cell phone number around to others. They were, of course, enthusiastic to have some way of finding out what actually was happening on the ground. Journalists would come in and out, and NGOs occasionally would bring aid. I was the coordinator.
>
> Occasionally some of the people, especially when they gathered around the only water source in the encampment, started to panic. "The Serbs will shoot

---

[21] Human Rights Watch, *Under Orders: War Crimes in Kosovo* 47 (2001) By the end of the NATO bombing campaign, more than 850,000 Kosovar Albanians had been forcibly expelled from Kosovo. *Under Orders* at 4. See Ivo H. Daalder and Michael E. O'Hanlon, *Winning Ugly* 23 (2000).

[22] July, August, October 2005 interviews with Hashim Thaci; July 2005 interview with Ramush Haradinaj.

us! The Serbs will shoot us!" I tried to calm them down. I couldn't protect them but I could try to give them hope. When journalists came, they felt safer. We listened to the Voice of America and to BBC and anything else we could find to keep abreast of what was going on.

At one point, I managed to contact someone at USIS [the United States Information Service, the only official U.S. government presence in Pristina at the time]. I told him people were suffering and that we really needed help. Within a few days, a truck with some supplies showed up. Later, I met him and he told me, "You're the first actual person who ever called me from the woods. I thought about you for several nights. I couldn't sleep."

The Serbs withdrew in October, when the Holbrooke/Milošević agreement[23] was signed, dismantling some checkpoints. We all went home. The Serbs had looted everything and burned ten houses. We didn't know why they burned those particular ten. Maybe they found some leaflets or something in those houses.

Later, I became part of the team that produced *Koha Ditore Times*, the only source of news from the Albanian resistance published in English. We also had a Web site – Arta – available in English. We would email the stories to a server located outside Kosovo. The newspaper and the Web site broke the news blackout maintained by Rugova and the LDK. Otherwise, journalists would have viewed the war through an LDK lens. The LDK could hardly deny the existence of the KLA by this time, but they still were trying to minimize its significance and to reinforce the idea that the KLA was just a handful of extremists.

We had pictures and stories right away because Veton Surroi [the publisher of *Koha Ditore*] was a genius. He sent his reporters right along with the international reporters.[24] It was a good deal for both sides: The international reporters had people with them who knew the territory. The *Koha Ditore* reporters had company that tended to protect them from arrest and harassment by the Serbs.

I didn't ever take up a gun, but I think I made an important contribution shaping public opinion the international community which eventually led to the NATO intervention.[25]

The international press, free from reporting on the Bosnian War, and cynical about Milošević and the Serbs because of their brutality there, were eager for new stories about the breakup of Yugoslavia. Reporters made sure that the KLA's fight – and Milošević's scorched-earth retaliations – were on Western TV screens and front pages. The KLA ran a sophisticated public relations campaign, making use of new Internet and cell phone tools, and organizing effective lobbies in Germany, Britain, and the United States.[26]

---

[23] See *Winning Ugly* at 48–62 (describing Holbrooke/Milošević Agreement and its limitations).

[24] See Helen Rumbelow, "My Safety Means Nothing," *The Times*, June 12, 1998 (describing 24-year-old Kosovar Albanian journalist working for *Koha Ditore* discussing risks and his commitment to get the Kosovar Albanian story out).

[25] March 2005 interview with Lirim Greiçevici.

[26] September 2005 interview with Florin Krasniqi, New York; June 2005 interview with Jakup Krasniqi, Pristina; August 2005 interview with Jock Martini, Detroit; October 2005 interview

By the end of the summer, Western diplomats were alarmed, and pressed by their home constituencies to do something to prevent a wider war. Ambassadors scrambled to find a diplomatic solution that would be acceptable to both the Albanians and to Milošević. Only slowly did the West realize that the KLA was now a real political force in Kosovo, and a deal between Rugova and Milošević would be of no use if the KLA did not support it.

By late spring, after a series of UN Security Council resolutions, the international community persuaded Milošević to allow a "Kosovo Diplomatic Observer Mission" (KDOM) into Kosovo to monitor the activities of the contending Serb and KLA forces. In late August, Ambassador Holbrooke met with a group of KLA fighters in the Dukagjini region,[27] signaling that the international community was prepared to deal with the KLA. In October 1998, as the fighting continued to intensify, Holbrooke, backed by a NATO activation order threatening to bomb Serb anti-insurgency forces in Kosovo, managed to craft a cease-fire with Milošević.[28]

Under the agreement, the KLA was to cease attacks on Serbian police stations and other symbols of authority, and Serbia was to remove its heavy forces from Kosovo and to pull Serbian police forces back to their bases. Milošević agreed to allow a team of unarmed international monitors to be deployed by the Organization for Security and Cooperation in Europe (OSCE) inside Kosovo. This Kosovo Verification Mission (KVM) would monitor compliance with the terms of the cease-fire. Milošević also agreed to negotiate a settlement with the Kosovar Albanians, although the terms of an acceptable settlement and the process of negotiation were ill defined. All Kosovar refugees and internally displaced persons were entitled to return to their homes and villages. The Yugoslav government agreed not to impede refugees in exercising this right, and the KVM would ensure compliance.

Back in Chicago, my students and faculty were keeping close watch on the negotiation process and results. Now the people and place names in the news were not unfamiliar. We had been there – and planned to go back. Following the agreement, Mr. Rudnick and several Chicago-Kent students traveled to Pristina to explore the possibilities for extending our reach into Kosovo itself, as well as in Albania, to help implement the agreement. As our Chicago-Kent team worked face to face with refugees and with international refugee-relief efforts, and as we learned more details about the crisis, we felt our commitment increase. We decided that we could help on multiple fronts. This would be a major project for us, and we dubbed it "Operation Kosovo," obtaining a small grant from George Soros's Open Society Institute to support our efforts.

---

with former Congressman Richard Bonior, Detroit; July 2005 interview with Harry Bajraktari, New York; July 2005 interview with Dino Asanaj, Pristina.

[27] August 2005 interview with Ramush Haradinaj.

[28] General Wesley K. Clark, *Waging Modern War* 137–54 (2001) (describing negotiation of Milošević/Holbrooke agreement and its limitations, under treat of NATO bombing).

Utilizing Internet technology, our project sought to connect Kosovar relief organizations to a centralized database containing essential information about the status of refugees, their homes, and their villages. This database would bring together reports from Kosovo about security, housing, and transportation; information about governmental and nongovernmental capabilities for assisting refugees; and data from Kosovo and Albania about the location, identity, and desired destination of refugees. It would also provide the opportunity for those seeking asylum or refugee status in other countries to obtain information regarding that process and their rights under appropriate laws.

Implementation of our plan, however, was not going to be so simple. Even as we began work to create these crucial streams of information, our project was derailed by intensified fighting. The fragile cease-fire between Serbia and the KLA was over.

4 Cease-Fire Breaks Down

I N DECEMBER 1998, STILL HOPEFUL THAT OUR PLAN FOR A REFUGEE-return database could be realized, I led a small group of Chicago-Kent staff and students to Pristina. We had to sneak in. There was no point in Americans applying at the Chicago Consulate General of Yugoslavia for visas to go to Kosovo; the applications would be denied. Therefore, our team flew to Zagreb, Croatia, and applied for visas there – to visit a friend in Belgrade, we said. Fortunately, the consular officer at the Yugoslav Embassy had spent some time in Chicago and was far more interested in talking to us about our home city than in scrutinizing our visa applications. Visas stamped in our passports, we flew into Skopje, Macedonia, and rented a car for the seventy-five-mile drive to Pristina.

"You're not going to take this car into Yugoslavia, are you?" the car rental attendant asked. "Going to Yugoslavia is not permitted."

"Into Yugoslavia!" we responded. "No, of course not. Why would we want to go to Yugoslavia?"

We filled up the gas tank, and headed toward Kosovo, then still in Yugoslavia. We were greeted with great suspicion at the border. Fortunately, our visas said nothing about the imaginary friend in Belgrade, and our passage was eased by the presence of a white SUV with UNHCR emblazoned on the side. This truck was to be our escort. We were taking a few computers to the Pristina office of the United Nations High Commissioner for Refugees, which had arranged the escort. UNHCR was struggling heroically to coordinate relief for tens of thousands of Kosovar Albanians who had been displaced from their homes, and who faced a brutal winter without shelter or reliable supplies of food, water, and medical attention. The head of the UNHCR office in Pristina, Joe Hegennauer, had been enthusiastic in e-mail contacts about our plan to equip UNHCR with a database and Internet connections to facilitate its operations. Hegennauer was clear and articulate about UNHCR's immediate and long-term goals: the first was to get people sheltered for the winter. That task seemed fairly well under control. Next was to determine why refugees and internally displaced persons were not returning to those Kosovo villages that had sustained relatively little damage. Refugees' return to their homes was a crucial aspect of reducing refugee populations. With this information, Hegennauer hoped to stabilize the humanitarian situation so efforts could be shifted away from immediate, life-threatening calamities and toward building civilian institutions for political stability. He displayed an interesting combination of no-nonsense goal orientation and low-key patience and supportiveness.

We spent several days connecting the computers, demonstrating the database to UNHCR personnel, and making contact with some of the hundreds of NGOs then present in Pristina to enlist their support for our Internet-based network to facilitate UNHCR coordination of their activities. Pristina was filthy. It appeared that no window had been washed in a decade, and trash remained on the streets and sidewalks where it had been thrown by passersby. Every time we went out in our rental car, we were stopped by blue-uniformed Serb policemen with automatic weapons, who repeatedly asked us to open our luggage for inspection while pointing their weapons at us. The hotel staff and other, predominantly Serbian, customer-service personnel at banks and stores were surly.

The internationals we talked to – UN, U.S., and NGO personnel – were worried that the cease-fire between Serb forces and the KLA was breaking down and that fighting would resume in earnest in the spring – if not during the winter. Only the physical presence of the international community had prevented an immediate outbreak of fighting. However, the OSCE did not have its Kosovo Verification Mission act together. Threats to security were becoming diffuse as the KLA recovered from a disorganized summer, and armed Serb paramilitary forces began to attack Kosovar Albanian populations, reinforcing formal Serbian government forces. In a village near the road from Pristina to Skopje earlier that week, a group of armed Serb paramilitaries had held a German aid group hostage for five hours.

A negotiated solution was made more difficult by the KLA's belief that it could obtain a military victory over the Serbs on its own, and a belief by the larger Albanian community that if they continued to fight over a long enough period of time, Kosovo eventually would obtain independence from Milošević's Serbia, either because the international community would rescue them or because the Serbs eventually would give up. The KLA had such fragmented leadership that it was difficult to know whom to bring to any negotiating table – if the time ever came to negotiate with the KLA, and many were opposed to the very idea.[1] There was no command-and-control system as any real army would have.

The West's demands seemed to decrease the longer the Serbs refused to negotiate, but the KLA was placing a "floor" on how much the West could ratchet down the price of settlement. There was no one to deal with on the Albanian side, however, to determine what the floor was.

---

[1] See "Holbrook proposes bringing Kosovo rebels to peace table," CNN Interactive, June 18, 1998 (quoting Holbrooke as saying that KLA deserved a seat at peace negotiations if they could show that they were in control of their fighters).

I pestered the UNHCR personnel to take us to a place where the KLA was active. They eventually acquiesced with great reluctance, and we drove in a bulletproof SUV to KLA stronghold Malisheva, passing burned-out police stations and houses destroyed by tank fire, and doing our best to circumnavigate Serbian and KLA checkpoints. We saw occasional civilians, most over seventy or under twelve years old, driving cows along the road or carrying water in buckets. Everyone else seemed to be holed up somewhere. Our driver and guide were tense and did not relax until we agreed, after a few very quiet hours, to return to Pristina.

Kosovar Albanians, in general, were annoyed by the international community's preoccupation with refugees. They worried that all the international community wanted was to get the refugees and displaced Kosovars back in their homes so that the world could forget about Kosovo. They did not understand the West's reluctance to send an occupation army into a sovereign country. The leadership of the KLA, however, did understand that focusing on human rights issues could bring much stronger support from the international community for the Albanian position.[2] The most effective strategy for Albanian separatists might be to provoke overreaction by Serbian authorities in order to enlist international community involvement.

At that moment in late 1998, two scenarios seemed possible.[3] The pessimistic scenario involved a resumption of armed conflict and its continuation until the balance of military and political power changed. The optimistic scenario envisioned preservation of the October 1998 cease-fire, stabilized initially by the physical presence and high visibility of international KVM personnel, and reinforced over time by reform of police, judicial, and educational institutions.

International NGOs were involved during the late 1990s in trying to promote dialogue between the Serbian government and the Kosovar Albanians. For example, the Community of St. Egidio, a Catholic peace organization,[4] worked with Rugova and Milošević to implement an agreement on education signed by Rugova and Milošević on September 1, 1996, characterized as the "first official agreement of any kind reached between the Serb government and the Albanian community in this century." Under the agreement, Albanians began to reenter the public schools and universities in March 1998, just as the conflict was escalating.[5] Kosovo Serbs bitterly opposed the agreement.[6]

---

[2] January 2005 interview with Jakup Krasniqi, Pristina.

[3] December 1998 interviews with USIS and ICRC personnel, Pristina.

[4] See generally the Community of Sant'Egidio, located at http://www.santegidio.org/en/contatto/cosa_e.html (describing origins and mission).

[5] Community of St. Egidio in Kosovo (report May 30, 1998), located at http://www.santegidio.org/news/rassegna/0000, 0/19980530_peaceworks1_EN.htm.

[6] See "Thousands Protest Kosovo Education Accord," CNN Interactive, March 23, 1998 (reporting that fifteen thousand Kosovo Serbs demonstrated to protest education agreement).

It was, by then, too late for such peacemaking efforts to succeed. Milošević's counterinsurgency tactics were driving Kosovar Albanians into the camp of the KLA and Rugova's credibility was on the decline.

The pessimistic scenario was made more likely by forces at work in the Albanian, Serbian, and international communities. The KLA's inexperience led to exaggerated expectations about the likely results of further armed conflict. That, in turn, led to inflexibility on the Albanian side. To a significant degree, KLA activists believed they could prevail militarily, despite the fact that they were considerably outgunned, and almost certain to remain so.[7] They could smuggle in light weapons through Albania, but they could not smuggle in tanks and artillery, which the Serbs had in abundance.

Fragmentation of KLA leadership made it difficult to identify relevant leaders with whom the international community could negotiate; it was also difficult to assemble a manageable negotiating team even when relevant leaders were known, and difficult to make a deal stick in a polycentric power situation. Fragmentation also led to competition within the Albanian community, which further complicated both agreement formation and implementation. President Rugova continued to enjoy iconic status within the Kosovar Albanian political elite. His party, the Democratic League of Kosovo (LDK), had a presence throughout Kosovo and coordinated the educational and health-care activities of the parallel system of institutions. For most educated, urban Kosovar Albanians, Rugova was the symbol of Albanian resistance to Milošević, and he opposed any official international contact with the KLA. KLA voices sniped at him for betraying Albanian aspirations for independence by being open to restoration of Kosovo's autonomy within Serbia as the core of a political settlement. LDK representatives in Europe and the U.S. actively opposed efforts to raise money for the KLA.

The Serbs were similarly inflexible and increasingly fragmented themselves. Three factors determined the Serbian position: sovereignty, political insecurity of the Belgrade regime, and militancy among Kosovo Serbs. Serbia was a sovereign state, and involvement by the international community in the conflict in Kosovo affronted Serbian sovereignty. Allowing international verifiers and humanitarian assistance in Serbian territory was an admission that Milošević's government had lost the capacity to govern that territory. Slobodan Milošević, although politically canny and remarkably successful in maintaining power through extreme turbulence in Yugoslavian affairs, was not unopposed by other Serbians. The most effective opposition came from forces within the Serbian political setting that were more nationalist and apparently less pragmatic than Milošević. He risked strengthening this opposition and weakening his own political position by seeming to be less than completely vigilant in promoting the interests of the Serb minority in Kosovo, especially

---

[7] March 2004 interview with Rrustem Mustafa ("Commander Remi"), Dubrava; July 2005 interview with Ramush Haradinaj, Pristina.

given Kosovo's central role in Serbian history. Allowing more autonomy to Kosovar Albanians would jeopardize his leadership, because autonomy might be the first step on a slippery slope toward Albanian independence. He did not want to be accused of having "lost" Kosovo. Milošević was a pragmatic populist above all; he was responsive to these popular currents in Serbian politics.

Regardless of the position taken by the government in Belgrade, the Serb minority in Kosovo also had crucial interests at stake. There was ample empirical evidence that greater autonomy for Kosovar Albanians would come at Serb expense. Thus, especially after partial withdrawal of Serbian police and security forces under the Holbrooke-Milošević agreement, Serb paramilitaries in Kosovo were arming themselves and engaging in hostile acts against Albanians and international organizations.[8] This led to an equally debilitating fragmentation of political and military authority on the Serb side, making it far more difficult to organize a viable negotiating process. A simple military conflict between a KLA with tight command and control and the Yugoslav Army would have made diplomacy much easier. The real situation, however, was more complex: armed Serb paramilitaries battled village defense forces loosely associated with the KLA; Serbian Interior Police (MUP) coordinated badly with the Yugoslav Army (VJ); and a bitter intra-Albanian conflict poisoned relations between Rugova and the KLA.[9]

The international community had learned from the Bosnian experience that early and forceful intervention in the post-Yugoslavia Balkans was desirable – but intervention was nevertheless inhibited by multiple considerations. Multilateral decision making always is difficult when military force is under consideration. International law regarding intervention into sovereign nations' affairs is far from clear, and many of the interested nations were dealing with ethnically based insurgencies of their own – in Chechnya, Ireland, the Kurd areas of Turkey, and the Basque areas of Spain. Moreover, there was no clear path to resolving the Kosovo conflict, making it hard to mobilize effective arguments to bolster political will for more forceful intervention. If the situation was hopeless anyway, many foreign political leaders reasoned, why pay the cost of intervention?

Any viable international strategy had to mitigate the forces that animated the pessimistic scenario. It had to reduce Albanian fragmentation. It had to protect Milošević's position vis-à-vis more nationalistic elements within Serbian politics, while saving face for Yugoslav sovereignty. It had to arrest the trend toward Kosovo Serb vigilantism. Moreover, it could not impose costs on the international community greater than those nations were willing to pay.

---

[8] March 2005 interview with Adem Demaci, Pristina (Serbian government turned things over to "mafia thugs").

[9] March 2005, July 2005 interviews with Hashim Thaçi, Pristina; March 2005 interview with Bujar Bukoshi.

After our contingent returned to Chicago, we kept anxious eyes on the news reports describing escalating conflict. Harry "IV" Ashton, who had become deeply involved in Operation Kosovo as a law student and now as my executive assistant, made telephone contact with UNHCR head Hegennauer and learned that the UNHCR was being evacuated, taking our computers and Internet routers with them. By the end of December 1998, the cease-fire had broken down on both sides, and Milošević was mobilizing regular Yugoslav Army troops for a massive assault on KLA forces and population centers.[10] Increasingly, his goal was not limited to annihilating the KLA, but extended to driving most of the Albanian population out of Kosovo.

The international community scrambled for one last diplomatic initiative to end the fighting. It took place in the French resort of Rambouillet under the mediation of U.S. Secretary of State Madeleine Albright and European co-chairs Robin Cook and Hubert Vedrine. Along with Holbrooke, Albright was the most assertive voice in the administration of U.S. President Bill Clinton, and she urged forceful international action, including military force if necessary, to stop Milošević's human rights abuses in Kosovo. By the time the Rambouillet conference convened, international public opinion had shifted further against Milošević, in large part because of a mass killing of civilians by Serb forces that occurred at Račak in January 1999.[11] U.S. Ambassador William Walker, head of KVM, denounced the killings as an obvious massacre by Serb forces. Louise Arbour was the chief prosecutor of the International Criminal Tribunal for the former Yugoslavia (ICTY), which had been established in 1993. She unsuccessfully attempted to visit Račak, and her confrontation with Serb border guards who refused to let her enter Kosovo was widely publicized.[12] This added to the opprobrium directed at Milošević, who by then was widely rumored to be subject to imminent indictment by the Tribunal for war crimes.

Milošević did not attend the Rambouillet negotiations but Hashim Thaçi, political director of the KLA, headed the Kosovo delegation. Albright and the other conveners came prepared with a draft agreement that would have introduced NATO forces and an international civil administration to run Kosovo as heavier Serb forces were withdrawn. Milošević's representatives rejected the proposal out of hand; Kosovo's representatives agreed only after a recess permitted Thaçi to build consensus within the group of relatively autonomous

[10] *Under Orders* at 59 (citing reports that six months before Rambouillet, Milošević had crystallized plans for "Operation Horseshoe" to drive Albanians out of Kosovo).

[11] See *Under Orders* at 57 (describing the massacre of forty-five Albanian civilians at Račak and characterizing it as a "turning point" in international public opinion).

[12] See, e.g., Jane Perlez, "NATO Fails in Belgrade Talks to Halt Kosovo Attacks," *New York Times*, January 20, 1999; Jane Perlez, "Defiant Yugoslav Orders Expulsion of U.S. Diplomat," *New York Times*, January 19, 1999 (reporting refusal to admit Louise Arbour to investigate events at Račak); Jane Perlez, "U.S. Weighs Its Reaction to Massacre in Kosovo," *New York Times*, January 17, 1999 (reporting announcement by Arbour of plans to go to Kosovo).

KLA field commanders. The Rambouillet conference brought Hashim Thaçi to international prominence and heightened tensions between the established Kosovar Albanian political elite and the young KLA militants. At Rambouillet, Madeline Albright was reported to have described Thaçi as "the only Albanian politician who knows what he wants."[13]

Rambouillet paved the way for armed NATO intervention against Serb forces, which began on March 24 and continued until June 11, 1999. Initially limited to attacks on Serb forces in Kosovo, the NATO bombing campaign then expanded to include strategic targets such as electric power grids in Serbia proper.[14] The NATO campaign had less effect inside Kosovo than many expected, and the unity of NATO members was fragile, raising questions about whether the West could sustain its pressure on Milošević.[15] The campaign, however, gave Milošević political cover for intensifying his campaign of ethnic cleansing. Transcripts of the later war crimes trials of Milošević and his senior security and military officials take hundreds of pages to detail the horrific acts committed in 1999 by Serbian forces in Kosovo.[16]

Following are excerpts from prosecution lawyer Thomas Hannis's opening statement in the trial of six of Milošević's top advisers Milan Milutinovic, Nikola Sainovic, Dragolub Ojdanic, Nebojsa Pavkovic, Vladimir Lazarevic, and Sreten Lukic:

> All across Kosovo, in a concerted and coordinated manner, the forces of the FRY [Federal Republic of Yugoslavia] and Serbia began their widespread and systematic attack on the Kosovo Albanian civilian population, going from one tiny village to the next and from one town to another, murdering, beating, robbing, looting, destroying businesses and mosques, and forcing out the Kosovar Albanians in front of them. They burned and destroyed villages or towns as they went in order to leave nothing behind for those expelled to return to.
>
> [A] typical pattern occurred in which the Serb forces would nearly encircle a town or village, leaving one avenue of escape. The VJ would commence shelling with artillery and heavy weapons. Then the MUP [Interior Ministry] units, including special units and volunteers, incorporated or otherwise attached to the MUP or VJ, would enter the town, force the people out,

---

[13] March 2005 interview with Hashim Thaçi, Pristina. See Madeleine Albright, *Madam Secretary* 398–406 (2003) (describing difficulties in persuading Thaçi to accept Rambouillet Accord, and his subsequent efforts to sell it to KLA commanders); Testimony by Wolfgang Petritsch, Milošević trial transcript at 7300–5 (July 2, 2002), http://www.un.org/icty/transe54/020702ED.htm.

[14] See David Halberstam, *War in a Time of Peace* 450–73 (2001) (describing internal debate within the United States and NATO about bombing targets and over the use of ground troops).

[15] See Clark at 89–93 (offering one example of disputes within NATO and within U.S. government about sustaining NATO military pressure on Serbia); id. at 274–7 (describing limited effectiveness of bombing targets within Kosovo).

[16] The transcripts are available on the ICTY's Web site, www.un.org/icty.

sometimes killing or raping as they did so, and often looting and then burning the abandoned houses.

This kind of activity understandably created an atmosphere of terror, and the inhabitants of neighboring villages seeing this happen and hearing the stories of the primary victims would join in fleeing to avoid a similar fate as that suffered by their neighbors. And so the massive convoys seen in the international media quickly came into existence from the end of March 1999, as thousands and thousands of Kosovo Albanians literally fled for their very lives.

[E]n route out of the country and at the borders, forces of the FRY and Serbia regularly forced the refugees to hand over their identity documents, and they took the vehicle license plates off their tractors and their cars and the wagons before they'd left Kosovo and went into Albania or Macedonia.

[The] objective [was] to modify the ethnic balance of Kosovo in order to maintain Serb control. Once outside the country and with no official identity documents, how were those refugees going to be able to return to Kosovo under Serb authorities who could simply say, "Sorry, it looks like you're simply an illegal immigrant from Albania, you can't come in now,"? [The] intention [was] that those Kosovar Albanians, once removed, would not be allowed to return, thus effecting the desired modification of the ethnic balance necessary to solve the Kosovo problem.

Forces of the FRY and Serbia attacked the village of Bela Crkva in Orahovac. Many of the villagers fled along a small river and hid under a railroad bridge. Serbian police opened fire on one group of villagers hiding under the bridge, killing twelve people, ten of them women and children. The remaining villagers were ordered out of the streambed and out from under the bridge. The men and the older boys were separated, ordered to strip, and then they were robbed of their valuables and their identity documents. The women were then ordered to leave, to go to another nearby village. The village doctor tried to intercede with the police commander, but he and his nephew were shot and killed on the spot. The remaining boys and men then were ordered back into the streambed. The Serb forces opened fire, killing most of them. A few survivors lived to tell the tale.

In the municipality of Srbica, as many as 4,500 people fleeing from Serbian forces had gathered in a field. Serbian forces surrounded them, demanded money, and ordered the women and children to leave and go to Albania.

Two disabled elderly women were seated in a trailer, unable to walk, Serb forces set fire to the trailer and burned those women alive. The men were separated from the women and children and then the men were divided into two groups. One group was taken towards the woods and a stream, where they were then told to kneel down. And then the Serb forces began shooting them. The second group was marched off in another direction, made to line up, before they, too, were shot.[17]

The details changed, but the scene repeated itself all over Kosovo as Milošević's forces killed and deported the Kosovar Albanians in an attempt

---

[17] *Prosecutor v. Milutonivic*, IT-05–87 trial transcript 060710IT at 452–67 (opening statement by Office of the Prosecutor).

to balance the ethnic population. From the east, the Kosovars were driven south to Macedonia; from the west, directly over the border into Albania. For months, rape, beatings, looting, destruction, and dead bodies littered the path behind them. No corner, no politics, no social caste was spared.[18]

The KLA used models of guerrilla and conventional warfare to resist annihilation by the Serbs[19] while building domestic and international support by proving that it would continue to fight. The KLA employed "fourth-generation warfare," a term coined by retired U.S. Marine Colonel Thomas Hammes to describe the shaping of guerrilla military strategy and tactics to achieve political objectives.[20] The KLA targeted collaborators with the Serbian regime, but avoided broader forms of terrorism.

The KLA had enough light arms, acquired from excess stockpiles in Croatia, Bosnia, and Eastern Europe,[21] but few heavy weapons necessary to oppose regular Serb army forces' weapons. Guerrilla fighters need little training, but by the end of 1998, most zone commanders had organized multiweek training programs using NATO curricula. Some, like Rrustem Mustafa, universally known as "Commander Remi," organized training – and his own military tactics – by watching American war movies.[22]

Perseverance was part of the KLA strategy. Milošević almost annihilated the KLA on several occasions, but each time the KLA reconstituted itself around a core of committed individuals, and Milošević was never able to put the fire out. Equally important, the KLA was tough enough to resist international pressure to stop fighting. The KLA demonstrated that it would not stay in the locker room while Milošević reentered the field. It resisted Milošević with arms, regardless of protests from the international community. This defiant stance by the KLA sent a clear signal to the international community: the conflict in Kosovo would not be resolved until Milošević's repressive forces were removed from Kosovo and a viable path to independence was established.

---

[18] See also Tom Walker, "Serbs Ignore Surrender Call," *The Times*, June 29, 1998, at p. 12 (reporting conversation with Serbian police commander who planned "cleansing of villages" and who denounced Holbrooke meeting with KLA in Junik); Anthony Loyd, "Serbs Force Albanian Refugees Back," *The Times*, September 14, 1998, at p. 13 (reporting that four hundred thousand Kosovar Albanians had been displaced from their homes by Serbian forces).

[19] See Tom Walker, "Kosovo Rebels Dig in to Face Serbs," *The Times*, June 1, 1998, p. 12 (describing conflicts between KLA and Serbian forces reaching within twenty miles of Pristina by reporter accompanying KLA unit).

[20] Thomas X. Hammes, *The Sling and The Stone: On War in the 21st Century* 2 (2004) (explaining concept of fourth-generation war); Perritt, KLA at 143–5 (explaining how KLA used fourth-generation warfare).

[21] March 2005 interviews with Lisen Bashkurti, former deputy foreign minister of Albania, General Kulishi Lama, head of Albanian army logistics branch, Fatos Klosi, former head of Albanian intelligence service; August 2005 interviews with Rrustem Mustafa (Commander Remi), Ramush Haradinaj.

[22] March 2004 interview with Commander Remi.

There is no evidence of any KLA operation motivated primarily by the goal of provoking Serb reaction, but KLA leaders knew that one of the results of continued fighting would be intensified Serb repression of the innocent – so the insurgents grew more sophisticated in their ability to make sure the outside world knew of Serb forces' growing repression.[23]

The KLA knew not to undercut growing international support. It avoided terrorist attacks on civilian targets. It steered clear of militant Islamic influences. It kept the fight inside Kosovo. It raised money openly in other countries. As a result, it blunted attempts by critics to portray the KLA as a terrorist organization and a vanguard of militant Islam.

Moreover, despite the ethnic nationalism central to its existence, the KLA disavowed the objective of creating a "Greater Albania." KLA leaders understood international fears of uncontrollable instability, with the breakup of Serbia and Macedonia, and expansion of Albania. In any case, the bankrupt Republic of Albania of the mid-1990s was far from a model of either democracy or viable market economy.

The growing violence in Kosovo limited further on-the-ground activities by our Chicago-Kent team after December 1998. We used the time to deepen our knowledge of Kosovar Albanian political conflicts. I took advantage of law-school business in Europe to meet with some leaders of the Kosovar Albanian diaspora in Germany and Albanian political party leaders in Macedonia.

Diaspora leaders lamented the fact that the KLA lacked any real political capacity.[24] Bujar Bukoshi, the prime minister of the government in exile while in Germany, was still loyal to Rugova's LDK. Bukoshi warned in a German newspaper that Thaçi and his men could change the Kosovo of tomorrow into "Cuba within Europe." He was under pressure to shift support to KLA, however, as support for the KLA grew within the diaspora.[25]

As violence increased, diaspora leaders predicted, the KLA would win; it would be very different from the summer of 1998. They would not need armor to overcome the Serb forces when more skillful guerrilla tactics would suffice. Kosovo was not fundamentally a humanitarian problem; from their perspective, it was a political problem. Difficulties would only grow if Kosovo did not gain its independence.

---

[23] August 2005 interview with Jakup Krasniqi, Pristina; July 2005 interview with Ramush Haradinaj, Pristina.

[24] Confidential interview with member of Kosovar Albanian diaspora, April 1999, Berlin.

[25] January 2005 interview with Bujar Bukoshi, Pristina.

5 Establishing the United Nations' First Colony

IN JUNE 1999, MILOŠEVIĆ DECIDED THAT HE HAD HAD ENOUGH. After prolonged negotiations, he agreed in the Kumanovo Accord to withdraw almost all of his forces from Kosovo, and to allow a NATO stabilization force (KFOR) and a UN-run civil administration to govern the province.[1] The peace agreement was procured only after intense diplomatic activity, involving mediation by Finnish President Martti Ahtisaari between Russian representative (and former Prime Minister) Chernomyrdin and U.S./NATO representative Strobe Talbott, which eventually induced Russia to withdraw its support for continued Serb military activities.[2]

The Kumanovo Accord was codified in UN Security Council Resolution 1244, which provided the constitutional basis for NATO's security presence and the UN civil administration. For its part, the KLA agreed to disarm and disband, with many of its members entitled to join a newly established Kosovo Police Service and civilian emergency force, the Kosovo Protection Corps.

The facts support different inferences about why Milošević capitulated to NATO in June 1999. One possibility is that he thought he had won. He had cleansed Kosovo of most of its Albanian population and doubted that they would return. Temporary exercise of sovereignty over Kosovo by the UN was a small price to pay for the possibility of eventual Serb reoccupation of the territory without the Albanians. With Russia's veto on the Security Council, he could hamstring the UN's exercise of authority. Another inference, not necessarily inconsistent with the first, is that NATO's strategic bombing of electric power and transportation infrastructure in Serbia proper had begun to alienate the centers of political power on which Milošević depended.[3]

---

[1] Military Technical Agreement (June 9, 1999), http://www.nato.int/kosovo/docu/a990609a.htm.

[2] John Norris, *Collision Course: NATO, Russia, and Kosovo* 207–26 (2005) (describing difficult negotiations over Kumanovo agreement).

[3] See Stephen T. Hosmer, *Why Milosevic Decided to Settle When He Did* (Rand, 2001) (emphasizing effect of strategic bombing in Serbia and its effect on political elites on which Milosevic depended; fear of ground invasion also played a role); Halberstam at 473 (evaluating Milosevic's motives for giving in the West and ending NATO bombing).

The UN, never having run a country before,[4] was slow to organize its "UN Interim Administration Mission in Kosovo" (UNMIK), and it also took a while – although significantly less time – for the NATO forces to establish the KFOR security presence.

The young fighters of the KLA were the heroes of all of Albanian Kosovo, willingly sharing the acclaim with NATO. They naturally moved into the vacuum left by withdrawing Serbs, occupying not only territory, but also factories, schools, and town halls. Returning Albanian refugees and expatriates, many of whom had run these same institutions before 1989, expected to resume their places and provide political and economic leadership for the new Kosovo. However, they were ten years older than the returning heroes, most had not fought, and the day belonged to the young men of the KLA, many of whom lacked any more than basic schooling and experience in anything except fighting. Resentment against the KLA simmered among those who thought they themselves deserved the places and leadership positions now occupied by the former fighters.[5] The prewar and intrawar tensions between the urban elites and the mostly rural militants increased.

Greg Campbell, a Boulder, Colorado, newspaper reporter, was in Kosovo in July 1999 with several students from Chicago-Kent College of Law. He reported that the KLA took advantage of the relatively slow deployment of NATO forces and UN agencies and quickly assumed many of the duties that officially belonged to UNMIK under Security Council Resolution 1244. Campbell quoted Sandra Mitchell, the outgoing human rights director of the OSCE, as saying that "KLA civil control is filling in the gaps" left by UN and KFOR. Because the population of most of the villages where the KLA was strong was predominantly Albanian, KLA initiatives were enthusiastically received, and they enjoyed the support and loyalty of the locals from the beginning. In Peja, the KLA "liberated" the electricity substation and the Pecko brewery from their Serb bosses and replaced the staff with ethnic Albanian workers, some of whom had once held similar positions in the brewery before 1989. Thanks to the KLA, Peja had power before many other areas of the province, and Kosovo had a new national beer.[6]

---

[4] But see Christian Eric Ford and Ben A. Oppenheim, "Neotrusteeship or Mistrusteeship? The 'Authority Creep' Dilemma in United Nationals Transitional Administration," 41 *Vand. J. Transnat'l L.* 55(58, n. 6), (2008) (referring to Namibia from 1989 to 1990, Cambodia from 1992 to 1993, Eastern Slavonia from 1996–1998, East Timor from 1999 to 2002, and Kosovo, as instances in which the UN exercised broad attributes of sovereignty).

[5] November 1999 interviews with Ahmet Shala, Jakup Krasniqi, Agron Dida, and Agim Gjinali, Pristina.

[6] See generally Greg Campbell, *The Road to Kosovo: A Balkan Diary* 239–49 (2000) (detailing observations of anti-Serb violence by people claiming to be KLA after NATO intervention ended and political control of Kosovo by former KLA forces); id. at 235 (referring to deployment as part of Operation Kosovo). Campbell wrote a report to me in late summer 1999. The quotations in the text are from that report.

Throughout Kosovo, the KLA won popular support by providing basic services such as utilities, mine clearing, and law-enforcement duties. When a top KFOR officer arrived in Mitrovica, he announced that "there will be no police force acting independently of me, I assure you" – but less than ten blocks away, according to Campbell, the main market in Mitrovica was being patrolled by armed KLA military police and a KLA commander who only gave the name Tyson. He said that the KLA was actively training a police force in Srbica (Skenderaj, in Albanian), weeks ahead of when the UN-sanctioned police force was scheduled to begin training. Campbell reported, "Across Kosovo, it's clear ... that the KLA is granted an astronomically greater degree of respect by the common population than KFOR or the UN."

Nevertheless, not everything done in the KLA's name was so well received. Groups of Albanians, some wearing KLA regalia, roamed the capital city of Pristina evicting, and in some cases murdering, anyone who was not Albanian. Robberies and beatings occurred with alarming frequency, sometimes within sight of KFOR soldiers. For many Kosovar Albanians, it was an opportunity to exact revenge on the Kosovo Serb community for the suffering of Kosovar Albanians during the conflict. Kosovo Serb and other non-Albanian properties were targets, but so also were those of prominent Kosovar Albanians who had not supported the KLA.[7]

Both sides had victims. Albanians who lived in the de facto Serb sector in north Mitrovica were regularly beaten and evicted from their homes. Serbs trying to cross the Ibar River to their homes in the city's southern half were harassed and threatened by Albanian loiterers, who gathered at the bridge daily. Albanians and some Americans who crossed the bridge into the northern half were threatened by Serb bridge-watchers on the northern side of the bridge. Although the bridge had a nominal French KFOR presence patrolling it around the clock, there were a number of clashes and confrontations on the bridge that included gunfire, rioting, and rock throwing. Both sides accused KFOR of not doing enough to protect those who lived on the side of the "enemy."

Two of my Chicago-Kent students were in Kosovo during this time, and crossed the bridge to the north. They were immediately surrounded by a gang of angry Serbs. Frightened, they asked for protection from a group of French KFOR troops on a nearby street corner. The troops merely shrugged, leaving it to my students to extricate themselves and retreat back across the bridge.

"Without an immediate and forceful response to the situation in Mitrovica – which serves as a main gateway to northern Kosovo and the valuable Trepça and Stari Trn mines," reported Campbell,[8] "Kosovo will effectively be

---

[7] See *Report of the Secretary-General on the United Nations Interim Administration Mission in Kosovo*, S/1999/779 (July 12, 1999) (reporting on postwar violence as UNMIK was struggling to get established).

[8] Campbell report to author (1999) (on file with author).

partitioned in the same manner that Bosnia was de facto partitioned along ethnic lines with the creation of two semi-autonomous halves, and ethnic cleansing will again be validated by the world community."[9]

The KLA set up its own government for Kosovo, constituting the core of
Hashim Thaçi's new political party, the Democratic Party of Kosovo (PDK).
Strikingly handsome, and a young thirty, Thaçi had consolidated his power
within the KLA, put together an "interim government" headed by "ministers,"
and designated himself as Prime Minister of the Interim Government. Rugova
initially agreed to participate, but then withdrew. Thaçi pressured UNMIK to
allow Kosovars to begin operating factories they had seized from the Serbs –
or occupied, anyway, after Serb withdrawal at the end of the NATO bombing
campaign. The interim government developed inventories of facility damage,
and worked up estimates of the investment capital required to restart the economy. It mobilized foreign expertise, some from the Albanian diaspora, some
from Switzerland, some from Britain, some from America, to advise it on procurement policy and selection of a contractor to start Kosovo-based cellular
telephone service, to crystallize alternatives to deal with property disputes,
and to explore the potential of e-commerce.

However, UNMIK would not deal forthrightly with the Thaçi interim
government because it, UNMIK said, lacked political legitimacy. UNMIK's
head, Bernard Kouchner, the Special Representative of the Secretary General
(SRSG), preferred consultation through his Transitions Council, which was a
kind of super-advisory committee comprising heads of all the major political
factions.

UNMIK itself was established by the Secretary General of the UN under
the authority of Security Council Resolution 1244.[10] All legislative and executive powers, including the administration of the judiciary were vested in
UNMIK.[11] UNMIK was organized into four "pillars." Pillar I, the responsibility of the UN itself, was interim civil administration. Pillar II, the responsibility of UNHCR, was humanitarian affairs. Pillar III, the responsibility of
OSCE, was institution building. Pillar IV, the responsibility of the EU, was
reconstruction.[12]

---

[9] Considering the difficulties integrating Mitrovica into independent Kosovo in 2008, detailed
in Chapter 13, Campbell's warnings were prophetic.

[10] UNSCR 1244 sec. 10 (authorizing Secretary General to establish "international civil presence" in Kosovo); *Report of the Secretary-General Pursuant to Paragraph 10 of Security Council Resolution 1244*, S/1999/672 (June 12, 1999) [hereinafter "1999 SG Report"] (reporting
intention to establish UNMIK, headed by a Special Representative of the Secretary General
("SRSG"). UNMIK was organized into four "pillars." Pillar I, the responsibility of the UN
itself, was interim civil administration. Pillar II, the responsibility of UNHCR, was humanitarian affairs. Pillar III, the responsibility of OSCE, was institution building. Pillar IV, the
responsibility of the EU, was reconstruction. Report of the Secretary General, para. 5.

[11] *Report of the Secretary-General on the United Nations Interim Administration Mission in
Kosovo*, S/1999/779 (July 12, 1999).

[12] 1999 SG Report ¶ 5.

In September 1999, I met with Jakup Krasniqi and Ahmet Shala in Washington. Krasniqi had been a member of the General Staff of the KLA and, for a time, its public spokesperson. He now was Minister of Reconstruction and Development in Thaçi's interim government. Shala was an economist by training, later to be the top Kosovar Albanian official in the privatization entity known as the Kosovo Trust Agency, and then, after independence, Minister of Economy and Finance. As a result of the meeting, we initiated an intensive research effort on institutional approaches to privatization, preparing a report that I later delivered to Krasniqi and Shala. To blunt skepticism that UNMIK possessed legal authority to reform economic institutions in Kosovo and to move enterprises into the private sector through privatization, my students and I[13] wrote a paper on a "trustee occupant" concept, a doctrine in international law that would give the UN greater powers than a "belligerent occupant" historically possessed under international law. We presented the report at several conferences in the United States and distributed it as widely as we could among internationals and Kosovar Albanians in Kosovo.[14]

Chicago-Kent loaned Assistant Dean Charles Rudnick to the American Bar Association to set up an office in Pristina for the ABA's Center for East European Law Initiative (ABA/CEELI). Rudnick, who had led the Center's office in Sarajevo, Bosnia, before I recruited him to come to Chicago-Kent, spent the months of August and September 1999 in Pristina, helping to coordinate early efforts to reestablish a judiciary, to publish reformed laws for Kosovo, and to reestablish a system of legal education.

In late November 1999, law student Scott Waguespack (later a Chicago alderman) and I visited Agim Gjinali, a Kosovar Albanian expatriate and head of a successful engineering firm in Lugano, Switzerland, who had been a generous financial contributor to the KLA. The three of us then proceeded to Kosovo. I took with me a five-page white paper explaining how Internet connectivity and e-commerce could facilitate economic development.

Because the Pristina airport was closed to commercial traffic, we flew from Lugano into Skopje, Macedonia, and crossed the border at Tetovo, Macedonia, to avoid the backup of truck traffic at the usual border crossing north of Skopje. The crossing itself was uneventful – even the Macedonian border guards were uncharacteristically efficient and friendly – but we immediately ran into a gridlock resulting from heavy truck traffic between Kosovo and Macedonia. On the two-lane road, some trucks had passed the southbound line by pulling into the northbound lane, only to become stuck; others had tried to pass on the northbound shoulder. Some had jack-knifed into the ditch, and still others were blocked by oncoming northbound traffic. Gjinali miraculously figured out how to unscramble the mess and gave appropriate orders

---

[13] Former student John Scheib, then a lawyer at Covington and Burling, was especially active in crafting the report.

[14] See Chapter 6 n.6 infra (describing report and its subsequent citation by others).

to the truck drivers who, surprisingly, complied. After about two hours, we were able to crawl on a rutted dirt road over the mountains, and then joined the main road from Macedonia and drove through thick fog into Pristina. We checked into the Grand Hotel, which was much improved in efficiency and physical condition from the previous December. Minister Krasniqi, who was to meet us in the hotel, apparently had given up due to our late arrival.

We then went to a mostly darkened headquarters of the Post and Telecom of Kosovo, where Mr. Gjinali, Mr. Waguespack, and I met for several hours, including dinner, with General Manager Agron Dida. Charles Rudnick and I had met and befriended Mr. Dida in December 1998, when he was attached to the UNHCR mission in Pristina and helped us set up the computerized database to track refugee relief. Mr. Dida's English was flawless and his manner friendly.

Dida and his associates were worked up about UNMIK having jerked the rug out from under their bidding process to select a cell phone operator for Kosovo. The formal bid process had selected a company called Siemens; UNMIK peremptorily announced that the winner instead would be Alcatel. UNMIK had seen neither of the proposals, and there had been almost no communication about why UNMIK preferred Alcatel. The UNMIK decision violated the letter and spirit of UNMIK's own procurement policy, as well as derogating the delegation of authority to the Post and Telecom. UNMIK's commitment to a "rule of law" was off to a bad start.

The next day, on December 1, 1999, we met with Minister Krasniqi and his Vice Minister Dr. Muje Gjonbalaj. We talked about the potential to advance economic development by a special emphasis on e-commerce through Mr. Dida's plans to establish an Internet backbone, and urged a joint effort to promote diaspora investment in Kosovo. Mr. Krasniqi expressed enthusiasm for the electronic commerce idea, and reiterated his appreciation for our technical assistance and support.

In the afternoon we met Hashim Thaçi in an unpretentious three-room office suite three flights up from a back entrance guarded by polite young men who presumably were former members of the KLA. Thaçi was physically quite striking, immaculately tailored, tall, and good-looking. He welcomed us through an interpreter and thanked us for our work for Mr. Krasniqi and Mr. Dida. We discussed our conclusions about the cell phone imbroglio. I invited him to come to Chicago and he laughed and said he would. We concluded with a short photo session.

I myself had a very favorable impression of Thaçi and his demeanor during the meeting; he acted like any senior political leader would in deflecting substantive comments and questions to his subordinates. I noticed only the occasional awkwardness, as though he was asking himself, "What should I do next?" and that was only because I was sitting right beside him at the head of a long table and could easily observe his movements and facial expressions in detail.

Our Albanian friends, however, were concerned about what they thought was Thaçi's disengagement and lack of interest in substance. They acknowledged that Thaçi had shown an instinct for political success, and had a track record and the core charisma that supports power in any ultimately successful major political figure. Their criticism reflected the attitudes of a slightly older generation who had enjoyed great self-respect, had endured much, and who expected to be installed in major positions of power once the Serb "occupation" was displaced. Instead, they found themselves displaced by a younger generation that had little to recommend it, in their view, besides its fighting credentials.

Afterward we met again with Minister Krasniqi, a meeting that continued through dinner until after midnight. Krasniqi observed that UNMIK's biggest mistake so far had been to adopt Yugoslav law as of March 1999 as the law under which it would govern Kosovo. Yugoslav law on that date was inherently discriminatory, perpetuating major uncertainty about property rights under UNMIK rule. The legal regime as of 1999 codified Milošević's displacement of Kosovar Albanians from private and social ownership of assets; now French, Italians, and UNMIK itself were honoring those illegitimate property interests. Krasniqi suggested a rollback of property interests to their state in 1989, but admitted this was an imperfect solution. He also gave examples of some fifty-five facilities that, due to KFOR physical occupation, were unavailable for resumed operation and economic productivity. I encouraged him to go ahead and resume operations where he could and seek permission later. He noted also that the French KFOR prevented Kosovar Albanians from working in or asserting property rights in assets located north of the Ibar River, while KFOR and UNMIK were enforcing Serb property rights and employment everywhere else in Kosovo.

In none of our discussions did we hear a hint of the need for revenge or retribution against Serbs. There were complaints about UNMIK, but almost all of the attention was focused on what the Kosovar Albanians wanted to do on their own, to develop their human capital and economic capacity with or without Serbs and with or without UNMIK.

During the same visit to Kosovo, we met with the acting dean of the Pristina Law Faculty, Rexhep Murati, and several of his colleagues. The permanent dean had disappeared during the war, and most Kosovar Albanians believed that he was dead. Murati had refused to accept the title "dean," however, because he and his colleagues hoped for the permanent dean's safe return.

They explained how the Law Faculty, displaced from their professorial positions by the Serbs in 1989, kept legal education going nevertheless, motivated by a commitment not to let an entire generation of Kosovar Albanians lose the chance to become lawyers. They taught their classes in private facilities, went without salary, were denied access to their law library – but nevertheless taught hundreds of students about the rule of law, and had so far managed to publish four volumes of articles.[15] They gave me a set with pride.

As our meeting concluded, Murati was eager to take us through their criminology museum in the basement, which the faculty had set up after cleaning up the debris and havoc wrought by the Serbs during the war. On the way to the museum, he showed me a composite of student photographs for the classes taught during the occupation. Several young faces were marked with red; those students had been killed. Others had pictures of bars superimposed on them; those were still in Serbian prisons.

The criminology museum was a small room with exhibits of weapons used in crimes over the last hundred years or so. It also contained photographs of the naked bodies of young men and women who had been scarred and burned over major parts of their bodies, and one who had been disemboweled – all the results of systematic torture by Serb occupiers.

During the war, museum areas apparently had been used for sexual assaults on young women and children. The paraphernalia of these activities – semen-soiled undergarments, drug syringes, handcuffs – were in the display case, along with photographs of some of the victims.

On our way out of the building, Murati opened the side door of one of the lecture halls, inviting us to look inside. A lecture in constitutional law was underway for about four hundred and fifty students packing the hall. It was very cold; everyone was wearing heavy jackets and overcoats. The lecturer stopped and beckoned us inside. Murati explained who we were. The students started clapping. The lecturer motioned for us to come down to the front of the hall.

The lecturer signaled that I should move to the front of the platform, as Murati introduced me and explained that we had come to meet with the Law Faculty. I was, I realized only at that moment, the first American to have done so.

The students started to cheer.

I asked Gjinali to translate, and said: "We have been watching your struggle from America. I have heard what your faculty did to keep opportunities open to you, despite unbelievable hardship. I want you to know how much your faculty's – and your – courage, perseverance, commitment, and energy have inspired my students and so many others in America."

Without waiting for the translation, about half of the students – those who understood English – jumped to their feet, cheering and pounding their desks. The other half followed as the translation unfolded. As I had been speaking (for no more than five minutes), another hundred or so students had crowded into the hall from the corridors of the building and the lobby. We waved goodbye and slowly left the hall as the cheering and clapping continued unabated.

---

[15] Fakukulteti Juridik I Universitetit te Prishtines, E drejta – Law (nr. 1–2) (2003).

Murati, Gjinali, Waguespack, and I were wiping away tears. It was several minutes before we could speak.

We also met with Veton Surroi, publisher of *Koha Ditore*, the major newspaper in Pristina. Surroi was a hero of the civil society movement in Kosovo and elsewhere. He had used his newspaper to get stories and images out of Kosovo during some of the darkest hours of Serbian attacks on civilians in 1997, 1998, and 1999. He was instrumental in holding the Kosovar Albanian delegation to the Rambouillet talks together, helping Madeleine Albright work effectively with Thaçi. During and immediately after the war he functioned as a de facto foreign minister for Kosovo, interpreting the dynamics of Kosovar politics for the internationals.

Tension between Surroi and Thaçi and between each of them and Rugova had roots in the Rambouillet conference and before. Surroi was highly regarded by the international community for his sophisticated understanding of international diplomacy and his flawless English. Thaçi, at Rambouillet, was an upstart, challenging not only Rugova's long-standing primacy as the non-violent spokesperson of the Kosovar Albanians, but also Surroi's comfortable position as the main interlocutor between the internationals and the Kosovar Albanians. Surroi helped fill in gaps left by Thaçi's inexperience and need not to get too far out in front of what the relatively independent KLA commanders would accept.[16] The split between Thaçi and Rugova was more fundamental. Rugova represented the traditional Kosovar Albanian political elites, mostly urban, who had held power in Kosovo before Milošević's revocation of autonomy in 1989. Thaçi represented a new generation of more muscular resisters, drawn mainly from villages and the countryside, outside the establishment. Surroi and Rugova both represented the traditional political elites, but they were rivals for international attention.

In our meeting, Surroi was self-absorbed and cynical, but his political analysis was insightful. I asked him for his assessment of the relative strength of Thaçi, Rugova, and the minor parties and the relationship between UNMIK and the interim government. He rejected the proposition that there was any effective interim government, scoffing at Krasniqi's pretensions to have organized reconstruction and development. He said that some of the facilities may have been reopened, but that was only because of "inertia" at the local level, with people just resuming their former jobs. No interim government could have legitimacy because there had been no elections. Thaçi, said Surroi, needed to "go to school."

Rugova and the others were passive, he said, because no one could accomplish anything yet and Thaçi, the leader of the interim government, would get blamed for everything that went wrong.

---

[16] Madame Secretary at 401–5 (describing roles of Thaçi and Surroi at Rambouillet, sometimes conflicting, sometimes complementary).

Thaçi had emerged as the de facto leader of the former KLA, Surroi said, only because the United States had picked him in Rambouillet, and that earlier favorable Western press perceptions of Thaçi were changing. I asked, "What do you mean – perceptions of corruption and the propensity for violence?" "Yes," he answered. I asked if there was anything to those perceptions, and he said, "It doesn't matter. It's perceptions that matter."

Surroi contended that elections could not be held immediately, because parties and other political institutions had not crystallized. There really were no parties; only personal followings. He also observed that the LDK had never favored or exhibited democracy with respect to internal matters. Surroi thought elections should be held in September 2000 and that it was important for national and local elections to be held at the same time. If local elections were held first, they would tend to establish municipal fiefdoms. This was discouraging. How can people know what the issues are and express themselves if everyone lays back and no political aspirants mobilize public opinion? That, Surroi said, was the job of the press. In order for decent elections to be held, the parties had to mature, and television had to be operational in order for people to see the candidates.

Surroi was an apostle of – or at least an apologist for – inaction. Other political and opinion leaders that he disdained would suffer the consequences of action. His air of superiority bespoke the contempt that the Kosovar Albanian political elite felt for the country bumpkins who had led the KLA. Surroi, like other members of the elite, resented Thaçi's ascendance in the public eye. His criticism of every other center of political power, including Rugova, suggested that he hoped political lightning would strike Surroi himself instead.

Ibrahim Rugova, very different from Surroi in personality, was an icon for most Kosovar Albanians. He had been the symbol of Kosovar Albanian resistance to the Milošević regime since 1991, keeping Serbian human rights violations in the forefront of diplomatic and journalist minds, and meeting tirelessly to reiterate the Albanian position. He had built a party, the Democratic League of Kosovo (LDK), which had tentacles into every village in Kosovo. He never forgot a name.

Yet Rugova had lost support as an effective instrument for realizing Kosovar aspirations when the KLA took to the field, and then substantially undermined his own credibility further by appearing on television with Milošević during the war,[17] at a meeting that Javier Solana publicly said at the time might have been the result of duress, as Serbian forces had extended their ethnic cleansing campaign in Kosovo. He added insult to injury by moving with his entire family to Italy until the bombing stopped. Some educated and well-informed Kosovars predicted at the end of 1999 that Rugova was finished,

---

[17] July 2005 interview with Bujar Bukoshi, Pristina; Kola at 358–9 (describing Rugova–Milosevic meeting in Belgrade and KLA denunciation of it).

supported only by a handful of the elite who were paid through the Three Per-cent Fund before the KLA came to the fore. There was much resentment of Rugova and Bukoshi for hoarding the fund paid by the Albanian diaspora over a ten-year period, refusing to make it available for "humanitarian purposes" (a code word for support of the KLA) during the war and during the period of ethnic cleansing. The only remaining supporters for Rugova were said to be quasi-intellectuals ages fifty or older who lived well on the diaspora money, and Kosovar Albanians who were against revolution altogether.

Yet others, Surroi most obviously, disagreed, and said that Rugova contin-ued to enjoy considerable support. They pointed to polls showing that Rugova would win the presidency four to one. "If Kosovo is to have a democratic government," Surroi maintained, "LDK may be the best approach, although under different leadership from Rugova." No one was entirely comfortable with Thaçi and his interim government. They feared his inexperience, and wor-ried that the KLA background would lead to a seizure of power much as the communists seized power in Yugoslavia at the end of World War II – by phys-ical occupation of factories, schools, and town halls, daring anyone to tangle with them. The mechanisms for financing the KLA represented a beachhead for corruption, but at least Thaçi and Krasniqi and the PDK were doing some-thing, rather than urging inaction to gain political advantage. Legitimacy could come from action, as well as elections, and action was what Kosovo needed. Support for Kosovo's action-oriented political centers could be accompanied by tutelage in democracy and rule of law, filling the void of inexperience. The risk of corruption and racketeering, Thaçi defenders said, came not from Thaçi or KLA elements, but from Albanians from Albania who were infiltrating Kosovo, trying to extend their proven talents for protection rackets, prostitu-tion, and drug running. Too often, the international community ignored them and supported the Rugova laissez-faire approach.

In any event, Kosovo had to have some kind of indigenous political insti-tutions; UNMIK and KFOR and the hundreds of NGOs simply could not do the job by ignoring and excluding the locals. Only Kosovar Albanians had the expertise on what needed to be done and how to do it.[18] Unwilling to delegate power to the Thaçi interim government, UNMIK could have called elections sooner rather than later so some locally selected political entities could be legitimated to exercise power. However, the international community, which controlled UNMIK through the UN Security Council, was afraid that the KLA veterans would win early elections. Internationals wanted to shore up alterna-tives such as Rugova, or to split the KLA vote, before the elections were held.

Regardless of what UNMIK was accomplishing, it was doing a terrible job of grassroots politics. No one had come to the University of Pristina's law

---

[18] See *Report of the Secretary-General on the United Nations Interim Administration Mission in Kosovo*, S/1999/779 (July 12, 1999) (acknowledging that UNMIK needed to enlist Kosovar Albanians to govern postwar Kosovo).

faculty to congratulate the faculty or the students on their achievements and perseverance with little pay. No one responded to invitations to attend the opening of new telephone operations in major cities outside Pristina. UNMIK and Kouchner made no response to inquiries. Senior UNMIK representatives simply did not show up for scheduled meetings about the cell phone procurement.[19] Whatever the tensions might be between UNMIK and the Thaçi government, many Kosovar Albanians – some from the KLA, some not – trying to rebuild were thoroughly decent and thoroughly competent professionals who were the soul of courtesy and accommodation. In order for UNMIK to govern Kosovo effectively, it had to succeed in winning the hearts and minds of the people. It not only was not doing so, it ostentatiously was making no effort even to try.

Gjinali and Daka drove me to the border. On the way out of Pristina, we passed Rugova's house, where there was a great bustle of activity, with limousines in front, bodyguards and important-looking businessmen or governmental officials hurrying in and out. It was an interesting contrast to the quiet waiting area and handful of bodyguards outside Thaçi's modest office at a nondescript entrance off a side street.

Kosovar Albanians thought they were ready to govern themselves. UNMIK disagreed.

---

[19] November 1999 interview with Agron Dida, Pristina.

6 Living Under a Colonial Regime

BY THE START OF 2000, UNMIK HAD ESTABLISHED ITSELF MORE firmly and begun issuing legislative acts in the form of "UNMIK Regulations." An interim administrative council that included Thaçi, Rugova, and other political party leaders provided an indigenous locus for shared governmental authority with UNMIK. UNMIK promulgated a "constitutional framework" that provided for power sharing with newly minted, local Provisional Institutions of Self-Government (PISG). UNMIK retained ultimate decision-making authority, however.[1]

Resolution 1244 directed the Secretary General to devolve power to locally elected institutions and to oversee a process for determining the final status of Kosovo.[2] The constitutional framework was a natural step under these authorities. It did not create Kosovar Albanian political institutions from the dust; it delegated some of the executive and legislative power given to the Secretary General by the Security Council and delegated by him to the Special Representative of the Secretary General (SRSG). Nevertheless, the constitutional framework was quite controversial because it created popularly accountable political institutions in Kosovo that were independent of the political authorities in Belgrade – a clear step toward eventual independence for Kosovo.[3]

Two quite different interpretations of Resolution 1244 bedeviled UNMIK from the beginning. The first interpretation, embraced by the Kosovar Albanians and the Americans, envisioned UNMIK as a political trusteeship intended to nurture the peoples of Kosovo and their democratically elected leaders in developing their own distinct political entity. This entity would, in a few years, attain some "final status," which might be a form of autonomy within what remained of Yugoslavia (Serbia and Montenegro still used the name Yugoslavia, although only those two republics remained within the federation)

---

[1] Constitutional Framework, UNMIK Reg. 2001/9 art. 9.1.45 (reserving power in SRSG to promulgate acts adopted by Kosovo Assembly).

[2] UNSCR Resolution 1244 art. 11(e) ("Facilitating a political process designed to determine Kosovo's future status, taking into account the Rambouillet accords").

[3] Carlotta Gall, "Putin Urges Global Pressure to Disarm Rebels in Kosovo," *New York Times*, June 18, 2001 (reporting on Putin's criticism of constitutional framework as being too like a constitution and not emphasizing strongly enough that Kosovo remained a sovereign and territorial part of Yugoslavia).

or might be independence. (The word *independence* was a politically incorrect usage at the time.) Under this view, UNMIK had the legislative power to make whatever laws seemed most helpful in a broad nation-building and democratization effort and to delegate that power as it saw fit to legitimate local institutions. The adherents of this view emphasized the "side letter" issued by the U.S. Secretary of State to the Kosovar Albanian delegation at the Rambouillet conference containing the phrase, "Three years after the entry into force of this Agreement, an international meeting shall be convened to determine a mechanism for a final settlement for Kosovo, on the basis of the will of the people...."[4] That letter promised Kosovo a referendum in three years. Little doubt existed that such a referendum would produce a mandate for independence.[5]

The second interpretation was that UNMIK was analogous to a belligerent occupant in international law – a modest transitional effort, aimed at keeping the peace after the withdrawal of Serbian security forces. According to this view, UNMIK was obligated to disturb existing institutions as little as possible, so that Kosovo could be handed back to a reformed Serbia. After this transfer, it would have a status similar to that enjoyed by Kosovo before Milošević stripped away its autonomy beginning in 1989.[6]

If UNMIK had the status of belligerent occupant under international law, it was obligated to leave Serbian law and political authority undisturbed except where changes could be justified on the grounds of protecting its own security and the security of the population. This would severely hamstring its exercise of final executive and legislative power. Under this view, certainly embraced by Serbia and Russia, but also by other advisers in Western governments and in the UN, the establishment of an elected assembly and a president, prime minister, and cabinet for Kosovo was questionable. The effort, beginning to

---

[4] Article I(1) of the "Amendment, Comprehensive Assessment, and Final Clauses," of the Rambouillet Agreement, made applicable to UNMIK's administration by art. 11(e), SCR 1244 ("Facilitating a political process designed to determine Kosovo's future status, taking into account the Rambouillet accords").

[5] Madeleine Albright, *Madam Secretary* 402 (2003) ("We made clear the agreement would not prevent them from holding a referendum, although that wouldn't be the sole criterion in determining Kosovo's future status").

[6] The legal concept was derived from the doctrine of "belligerent occupancy" in international law, under which an occupying military force may make only those institutional and legal changes necessary to protect its own security and the security of the occupied people, anticipating a return of the occupied territory to its previous government. See "Article 43 of the Annex of the Fourth Hague Convention, 36 Stat. 2306, requires that the commander of a force occupying enemy territory, as was petitioner, 'shall take all the measures in his power to restore, and ensure, as far as possible, public order and safety, while respecting, unless absolutely prevented, the laws in force in the country.'" *Application of Yamishita*, 327 U.S. 1, 16 (1946) (denying petition for habeas corpus by Japanese officer tried by U.S. military commission in Philippines); *Cobb v. United States*, 191 F.2d 604, 610 (9th Cir. 1951) (United States, as military governor of Okinawa had duty, under Hague Convention Art. 43, to maintain preexisting tort law in occupied territory).

be crafted in late 2001 and 2002, to privatize Kosovo's socialist enterprises was impermissible. Adherents to this view emphasized the phrase, "*Reaffirming* the commitment of all Member States to the sovereignty and territorial integrity of the Federal Republic of Yugoslavia," in the preamble to Resolution 1244.[7]

The political trustee concept was an alternative to belligerent occupancy. As a political trustee, UNMIK temporarily exercised sovereignty on behalf of the peoples of Kosovo, with a reversionary interest[8] that would be transferred eventually according to the final status determination. The political trustee concept allowed UNMIK to exercise full sovereign authority, limited only by what served the interests of the peoples of Kosovo and by what would be consistent with its mandate to move toward final status.

Working with Kosovar Albanian political leadership and my former student John Scheib – by then a lawyer with the law firm of Covington and Burling in Washington – I crafted a legal analysis, subsequently subsumed into several law review articles,[9] explaining that UNMIK had broad powers, as a "political trustee" of Kosovo. Its mandate was to administer Kosovo in the interests of its peoples until Kosovo's final status could be determined. This final status would be decided according to the will of the peoples of Kosovo, through referendum or otherwise. The paper apparently was used by elements within

---

[7] SCR 1244, preamble.

[8] A reversionary interest in the law of trusts, and its rough analogy – truehand – in German law is the legal interest in property held by a trustee that eventually passes to someone else, either the person or entity who owned the property before the trust was established, or the beneficiaries of the trust.

[9] Henry H. Perritt, Jr., "Structures and Standards for Political Trusteeship," 8 *U.C.L.A. J. Int'l and Foreign Aff.* 385 (2003); Henry H. Perritt, Jr., *Economic Sustainability and Final Status for Kosovo*, 25 *U. Pa. J. Int'l Econ. L.* 259 (2004); Henry H. Perritt, Jr., "Providing Judicial Review for Decisions by Political Trustees," 15 *Duke J. Comp. and Int'l L.* 1 (2004). The author and the concept of political trusteeship has been cited by other commentators: Christian Eric Ford and Ben A. Oppenheim, "Neotrusteeship or Mistrusteeship? The 'Authority Creep' Dilemma in United Nationals Transitional Administration," 41 *Vand. J. Transnat'l L.* 55, 103 (2008); Jared Schott, "Chapter VII as an Exception: Security Council Action and the Regulatory Ideal of Emergency," 6 *Northwestern U. J. Int'l Hum. Rts* 24, 142 n. 282 (2007); Carlos L. Yordan, "Why Did the U.N. Security Council Support the Anglo-American Project to Transform Postwar Iraq? The Evolution of International Law in the Shadow of the American Hegemon," *Journal of Int'l L. and Int'l Relations* 61, 78 (2007) (citing Henry H. Perritt, "Note on the 'Political Trustee' Concept," Symposium – Final Status for Kosovo (Chicago, IL: Chicago-Kent College of Law, April 16, 2004), online: http://operationkosovo.kentlaw.edu/symposium/note-on-political-trusteeship.htm); Grant T. Harris, "The Era of Multilateral Occupation," 24 *Berkeley J. Int'l L.* 1, 20 n. 71 (2006); Rosa Ehrenreich Brooks, "Failed States, or the State as Failure?" 72 *U. Chi. L. Rev.* 1159, 1160 n.1 (2005); Bernhard Knoll, "From Benchmarking to Final Status? Kosovo and the Problem of an International Administration's Open-Ended Mandate," 16 *Eur. J. Int'l L.* 637, 653 n. 74 (2005); Asli U. Bali, "Justice Under Occupation: Rule of Law and the Ethics of Nation-Building in Iraq," 30 *Yale J. Int'l L.* 431, 469 n. 119 (2005).

UNMIK to persuade the legal advisers in New York to allow privatization to proceed.[10]

Despite UNMIK's flexible powers, the internationals who swarmed into Kosovo with UNMIK were remarkably incurious about the Kosovar Albanian population, its culture, and its experiences during the Milošević era. The pattern for civil administration and for reform of the legal, economic, and political system was to act as if the territory was unpopulated before the international presence was established. Western legal advisers tended to put forward their own country's corporation law or criminal code, with relatively minor modifications to adapt them to Kosovo's legal history. Economic orthodoxy, whether of the free-market or socialist persuasion, drove economic policy for Kosovo. UNMIK favored local institutional arrangements that made it relatively easy for senior international officials to deal with a limited number of Kosovar Albanians who could be presumed to speak for the entire population.

These predispositions resulted in a less effective UNMIK administration than could have occurred if most internationals had worked harder to understand the coping mechanisms developed by the Albanian population in the parallel system and the patterns of economic activity associated with the Three Percent Fund and the separate system for financing the KLA. Too often, however, the past was viewed as corrupt or violent or primitive. It was vaguely unseemly to be interested in it.[11] This was a mistake.

Because the internationals did not understand the informal folkways, it was easy for the international organizations to churn out policies among themselves that had relatively little impact on the way that Kosovo actually worked.

Meanwhile, things were changing in Serbia. The Serbian government had been licking its wounds since its expulsion from Kosovo in June 1999. Milošević claimed that Serbia had been the victim of U.S.-led NATO aggression. Rather than adapting to a new reality for Kosovo and crafting a strategy for the future, the government of Serbia sought prosecution of NATO commanders in the ICTY for war crimes and sued NATO members in the International Court of Justice.[12] Neither maneuver was successful, but both showed that Serbia was unbowed.

---

[10] March 18, 2004, conversation with Ernst U. Tschoepke, deputy legal adviser to the SRSG, Pristina.

[11] For example, the head of the ABA/CEELI office in Kosovo in 2003 prohibited three of my law students, in Kosovo for a CEELI project, from attending a prearranged meeting with Hashim Thaçi and Ramush Haradinaj on the grounds that it was too "political." Although she had been working for two years on a USAID-funded project to reform the Law Faculty at the University of Pristina, she had not met any member of the law faculty until I introduced her in late 2003, preferring to limit her contact to an independent OSCE-funded NGO.

[12] Aaron Schwabach, "Yugoslavia v. NATO, Security Council Resolution and the Law of Humanitarian Intervention," 27 *Syracuse J. Int'l L & Com.* 77, 83 (2000) (describing Yugoslavia's lawsuit filed April 29, 1999, against NATO members involved in aerial attacks within the Federal Republic of Yugoslavia).

The establishment of the UN- and NATO-run political trusteeship over Kosovo in June 1999 significantly weakened Milošević's hold on power in Serbia. His indictment for war crimes by the ICTY, although it increased his popularity among radical Serb elements, was an additional distraction. The habitually fragmented opposition came together at last, with eighteen parties forming the Democratic Opposition of Serbia. Having changed the format of the election to a direct vote, Milošević announced that democratic elections would be held on September 24, 2000, thinking that this move would secure him another term of office. He banned all international observers who wanted to view the elections, and refused to allow opposition candidates to appear on state-controlled television or radio stations.

In the days before the election, Milošević trailed his main opponent Vojislav Koštunica. Citizens of Serbia worried that Milošević was preparing to steal the election. After the election was conducted, early returns indicated that Koštunica had received 49 percent of the vote, with Milošević receiving only 39 percent. The Constitutional Court of Serbia heard complaints of electoral fraud. The court acknowledged ballot irregularities and ordered a new vote. The opposition declared that it would not participate in the runoff election because its candidate won a majority in the first round.

Milošević refused to yield. After the court's decision, he made a television appearance accusing the opposition movement of simply being a "puppet of the Western powers.... For a whole decade, efforts have been underway to place the entire Balkans under the control of certain Western powers," he declared. "Most of that work has been done by installing puppet governments in certain countries, by turning these countries into countries of limited sovereignty or depriving them of any sovereignty."[13]

Citizens took to the streets all over Serbia, outraged by the failure to implement the first election's results. Hundreds of thousands of people protested and launched a general strike on October 4, 2000. "Slobo, save Serbia: kill yourself" was heard from the opposition supporters as they demanded that Milošević give up his seat as president. The protestors, numbering more than five hundred thousand, demanded that Milošević resign immediately. As crowds of Serbs protested outside the Federal Parliament building, they were attacked with tear gas, but the protestors burst through police lines with a bulldozer, smashing up furniture and setting the parliament building on fire. Demonstrators torched police cars and took control of the state-run television station. Although some police tried to stop the violence, others instead joined the protesters. Koštunica stood in front of Belgrade's city hall and declared that "today is making history," while the crowd called for Milošević's arrest and chanted "Kill him! Kill him!" Finally, the state news station declared Vojislav Koštunica, now in control of the parliament and the media, the new

---

[13] "Milošević Speech: Beware External Threats," BBC News, October 1, 2000, located at http://news.bbc.co.uk/2/hi/world/monitoring/media_eports/953697.stm.

"president elect." The international community eagerly recognized the new government.[14]

The protests and strikes were organized by Zoran Djindjić, the coordinator of the Democratic Opposition of Serbia bloc. Democratic Opposition of Serbia supporters were reinforced by an "irreverent, nonviolent, student-led movement" known as Optor, or "Resistance." Optor was led by Čedomir Jovanović, a charismatic young theater student, who subsequently emerged as one of the few voices for a more moderate Serbian policy on Kosovo. The group's only goal was to remove Milošević, who had "spoiled their youth," from power. Even before the elections and the protests, Optor organized a get-out-the-vote campaign centered on the message: "He's finished! It's time for him to go!" Six months after the presidential elections, and after an armed standoff, former President Milošević was arrested outside of his mansion and turned over to ICTY authorities to be tried on his indictment for war crimes.[15]

After Milošević's removal, senior foreign visitors went to see Koštunica, including Albert Rohan, Secretary General of the Austrian Foreign Service. Rohan remembers Koštunica standing in the president's office almost by himself.[16] There were no secretaries, few lights, no telephones ringing: nothing. Koštunica met with Rohan as the official representative of the OSCE, and together they worked through their agenda, focusing on the political situation in Serbia and on Kosovo. Finally, Rohan asked Koštunica when the inauguration would be, to which he replied, "I hoped you could tell me. I don't know." Despite his victory, Koštunica did not smile much, although he was courteous. He professed limited power over Serbian political developments. Foreshadowing a later resort to legalisms, he said, "I am only the president; the prime minister controls the government." Rohan told Koštunica that he had enormous practical power as the symbol of the success of the anti-Milošević forces. After their meeting, Rohan encountered an Austrian TV crew on his way out. He suddenly remembered that he had promised to ask if they could have the first interview with the new leader of Serbia. Rohan went back and asked Koštunica: the TV crew got their wish.

The inauguration ceremony was delayed for two hours as Parliament wrangled over some relatively minor matters. Once the details were in order, and Parliament was finally organized enough to swear in Koštunica, the entire Serbian political class was there, with the notable exception of any senior military representatives. Then, before the actual swearing in, the huge doors at the end of the hall banged open and four generals marched in together. They clicked their way straight through the crowd and up to Koštunica. They saluted

[14] See Steven Erlanger, "Milošević Concedes Defeat; Yugoslavs Celebrate New Era," *New York Times*, October 7, 2000.

[15] *Prosecutor v. Milošević*, Case No. IT-99–37 (indictment, May 24, 1999), located at http://www.un.org/icty/indictment/english/mil-ii990524e.htm.

[16] August 2007 interview of Albert Rohan, Vienna.

and greeted him as "Mr. President." "That was the real inauguration," Rohan observed later. "The military supported him."[17]

The international community was jubilant about Milošević's removal from power through mostly peaceful elections and demonstrations. Those concerned with writing the final chapter on the dissolution of Yugoslavia were hopeful that Serbia had entered a new era, one that would allow Kosovo to seek its own course and embrace European integration for what remained of Serbia. Koštunica and Djindjić were hailed as the leaders of this new era; Djindjić in particular, the more polished and European-oriented of the two, was the darling of Western capitals. Djindjić was respected for his pro-European orientation and for his ability to craft viable deals in the maelstrom of Serbian politics.

It appeared to many international decision makers that the ultimate decisions about Kosovo's future might be made in Belgrade. In Serb-dominated north Kosovo, including the city of Mitrovica, Kosovo Serbs still looked to the capital. Most Kosovo Serbs in the northern areas received salaries or pensions from Belgrade, and the citizens generally did not respect decisions made in Pristina by either UNMIK or the PISG. UNMIK thought this problem would recede under a moderate Serbian government. It would not.

By late 2000, UNMIK decided it was safe to hold local elections in Kosovo. Besides Thaçi, who had been the political director of the KLA, a highly respected KLA commander, Ramush Haradinaj, had started his own political party (known as the Alliance for the Future of Kosova – "AAK"). Haradinaj entered politics for his own reasons – a desire to build on his proven leadership in the KLA and a belief that he could forge a broader political coalition than Thaçi.[18] He was encouraged by the international community. UNMIK hoped he would split the KLA vote with Thaçi's party. When the elections actually occurred, Rugova's LDK received a convincing majority of votes – partially induced by tradition and partially a reaction to the near anarchy of the last few months of 1999, which most people blamed on the KLA. The 2000 elections for local assemblies in the municipalities were followed in 2001 and 2002 by elections for the national assembly. In the municipal election, Rugova's LDK received 58 percent of the vote, and Thaçi's PDK received 27 percent. In the 2001 elections, the LDK vote had dropped to 45.6 percent, with PDK at 25.7 percent, and Haradinaj's AAK at 7.8 percent. That rough share of the vote did not change appreciably until the 2007 elections.

UNMIK's constitutional framework envisioned a power-sharing arrangement, with an elected assembly appointing a president and constituting a government headed by a prime minister. Twenty seats in the 120-member assembly were reserved for minorities – mainly Kosovo Serbs – regardless of the election results. Together, these institutions comprised the PISG, which would

---

[17] May 2007 interview with Albert Rohan.
[18] August 2005 interview with Ramush Haradinaj, Pristina.

make day-to-day policy decisions and execute them, while UNMIK retained overall control through the power to veto PISG decisions, including the power to nullify legislation passed by the assembly. After the elections, the power sharing materialized: Rugova became the president, and Thaçi was in charge of selecting the prime minister. Haradinaj's party was part of the grand coalition.

Despite its desire to split the KLA vote, UNMIK was fearful of political division among Kosovar Albanians, recognizing that an elected parliamentary opposition might target UNMIK for criticism. From its first days on the ground in Kosovo, the SRSG had sought to prevent the seizure of political power by the KLA, which, he feared, would undercut the ability of UNMIK to fulfill its mandate. If elections were held before UNMIK could consolidate control, the highly popular KLA could achieve a popular mandate, perhaps reinforced by intimidation, which would make it impossible for UNMIK to exercise paramount executive and legislative authority.[19] Such political competition was unwelcome.

Therefore, it encouraged the formation of the grand coalition, allowing all three of the largest parties to share in the political spoils. The U.S. government applied considerable pressure on all three Albanian leaders to participate in the coalition. The assembly proceeded to ratify Rugova's presidency and accept Thaçi's designee as prime minister: Bajram Rexhepi, the former KLA physician. Ramush Haradinaj's AAK had placed a distant third in the voting, and he was included in the coalition government. For the first time, Kosovo had its own government – even if it was provisional for the moment, and subject to UNMIK oversight and veto.

The coalition began to operate while taking little initiative in the policy arena. Most legislative and executive authority continued to be exercised by UNMIK, and the most active parts of the judiciary were superintended by international judges.

During 2002, as the Democratic nominee for the U.S. House of Representatives from the Tenth Congressional District of Illinois, I played up the importance of U.S. and international nation-building efforts in Kosovo – and elsewhere. My potential constituents were not much interested in this theme, but my experience as a political candidate deepened my convictions about potential effectiveness of grassroots politics in Kosovo.

By early 2003, when I visited Kosovo again, substantial development of local political institutions had occurred. As on previous trips, I met with Thaçi, Haradinaj, and General Secretary Fatmir Sejdiu of the LDK. Thaçi and Haradinaj were very focused on action: recruiting and training a younger generation of Kosovars for effective political leadership. Their success in

---

[19] 1999 UNSG report to Security Council ¶¶ 5–7 (reporting challenges to UNMIK authority by KLA and other local elements, and suggesting need to involve political leaders of all communities in consultation with UNMIK).

recruiting some of the best and brightest in the generation in its late twenties and early thirties was evident in the economic, legal, and political spheres.[20] The LDK was more passive, but enjoyed support and participation from significant parts of the intellectual and professional elite in the more senior generation. The parliament, the governments, and the court were functioning. A visit to a session of the Kosovo Assembly was like visiting any one of hundreds of legislative bodies around the world.

There was, however, huge and growing frustration within the PISG and in the Kosovar Albanian citizenry over the slow pace at which power was being devolved from UNMIK to local institutions.

UNMIK's resistance to shifting authority onto local institutions seemed to come not only from national governments but from UN bureaucrats, especially UN lawyers. Stronger support from the members of the Security Council for such devolution of power would have been both feasible and effective; behind the scenes, however, some national capitals in Europe and Russia opposed even modest empowerment of elected institutions in Kosovo, fearing that this would pave the path toward eventual independence.

On the one hand, popular pressure increased for real self-government by Kosovar Albanians, because there were now popular political institutions. On the other hand, there was not much direct democracy. Although members of the Kosovo Assembly credibly claimed to represent the people of Kosovo, they really represented the parties of Kosovo – the Kosovar Albanian parties. Under UNMIK's constitutional framework, the 120 members of the Assembly were elected on a proportional basis to represent a single multimember electoral district for all of Kosovo. In this "closed list" system, each political party developed its own slate of candidates – and only the names of the parties, not the names of the individual candidates, appeared on the ballot for the Assembly of Kosovo and for municipal assemblies.

Accordingly, the real power lay with the political parties. The UNMIK head, the SRSG, understood this. German diplomat Michael Steiner, the third SRSG, consulted with local institutions more than his two predecessors but he limited his consultations to Rugova, Thaçi, and Haradinaj, the heads of the three major political parties, while ignoring the ministers of government and leaders or individual members of the assembly. Steiner was more colorful than his predecessor Hans Haekkerup, but he had the reputation of mistreating his subordinates and being overbearing with the locals. Limiting consultations to the party leaders added to the frustration of senior officials of the government and the assembly. Given the realities of the allocation of political power among local actors and institutions, however, it was hard to fault this practice.

---

[20] They included Besim Beqaj, a rising young economist in the Kosovo Chamber of Commerce; Ahmet Shala, another economist who became the senior Albanian official in the privatization agency and later Minister of Finance and Economy, both recruited by Thaçi; and Valon Murati, an economist who later became head of the Human Rights Center at the University of Pristina.

In 2003, I toured several factories in Kosovo, meeting reinstalled Kosovar Albanian management teams. Each presented a business plan and expressed eagerness to attract foreign investment and restart operations. My conversations with Ahmet Shala, by then the top Kosovar official in the Kosovo Trust Agency, however, were troubling. Shala said that the postwar euphoria, in which managers and workers at socially owned enterprises donated their time to clean up facilities and restart machinery, was fading, being replaced by a growing frustration and antipathy for UNMIK as an imperial authority more intrusive in some ways than the Serbs. Much of the frustration was unnecessary, and could be reduced by more transparency, greater promptness in making decisions and greater willingness to consult.

He also argued for the need for some kind of statement on Kosovo's final status. Albright's side letter had promised that final status talks would begin in 2002 – three years after the Albanians signed the Rambouillet Accords. Not only was the absence of any kind of commitment – a year after the promised date – frustrating for the Kosovar population, it represented a degree of political uncertainty that discouraged investors. While the international community remained silent about final status, Kosovar Albanians aggressively stated their commitment to it, and foreign investors feared a renewal of violence during the terms of their investment. Shala said that a commitment not only to a process but also to eventual independence was necessary. He was unable to describe a final status that would be acceptable to everyone, however. He said that the international community could not accept complete independence, and that Kosovar Albanians could not accept partition. Thus, even he found himself a prisoner of the same impasse.

Almost every other Kosovar Albanian I talked to agreed that final status for Kosovo must be resolved sooner rather than later. They perceived UN staff as the greatest barriers to both final status resolution and devolution of power to local institutions, because UN staff liked their jobs and liked the power associated with being part of a colonial regency.[21] Kosovar Albanians perceived the United States as consistently pushing for faster devolution, and Europeans generally objecting to it.

---

[21] Kosovo was not literally a colonial regime, as the term was understood in the eighteenth and nineteenth centuries. However, the allocation of political and legal authority between UNMIK and the local population resembled in many respects the allocation of authority between colonial powers such as Britain, for example, and the peoples of India, before Indian independence in 1947. Final legislative and executive authority lay with the SRSG, as it did with the British viceroy in India. Some of that authority had been delegated to local leaders, as had been done in India. There was a vague promise that, eventually, all political power would pass to locally accountable officials and institutions. See generally Lawrence James, *Raj: the Making and Unmaking of British India* (1997); *European Stability Initiative, Travails of the European Raj* (2003) (report available on ESI Web site, located at http://www.esiweb.org/ index.php?lang=en&id=156&document_ID=59) (comparing international authority in Bosnia to British authority in India). The scope of legal authority exercised by UNMIK was greater than that exercised by the High Representative in Bosnia.

A major problem with the Kosovar Albanian preoccupation with final status and independence was that independence would have little meaning unless it was accompanied by realization of two other goals: economic viability and security. Neither of these goals could be satisfied if Kosovo were completely isolated. Kosovo was too small to be self-sustaining economically, and it was too small to be militarily secure on its own, even if it put half its male population under arms. So final status necessarily implied a geographic, political, and economic context within which Kosovo would have relationships with other states to sustain its economy and assure its security. The absence of a resolution of final status was an impediment to political and economic development – but it was not a complete block. Some people were willing to invest despite uncertainty about final status.

The best guarantee of eventual independence was a track record of concrete success in political and economic development. If Kosovo developed a modern, viable economy, if it developed political institutions that made a difference in the lives of ordinary people and were democratic and transparent, no one would be able to take that away. If, on the other hand, municipal governments failed to use their existing power to pick up the garbage and remove the snow; if the parliament and other local institutions spent all their energy complaining that they did not have more competence and that UNMIK was too slow in transferring authority to them, and did not do anything with their existing authority, people would lose hope and eventually the international community would simply walk away.

Despite significant progress, things were beginning to stagnate. Uncertainty about final status was the cause – or the excuse for – growing paralysis. UNMIK was reluctant to hand over more governing power to the locals, who were frustrated with the deteriorating social and economic development of Kosovo and the apparent unwillingness of the international community to begin the process of determining Kosovo's final status. There was no organized or widespread violence during this period, although sporadic assassinations and detonation of explosives continued to make people nervous about the security situation. It was generally perceived that NATO was in full control of security on the ground. Even if the KLA had not turned in all its weapons – and it almost surely had not – the likelihood of war returning was perceived as slight. Still, the Kosovar Albanians felt increasingly betrayed by UNMIK's failure to move toward any kind of process for determining Kosovo's final status as provided for in UN Security Council Resolution 1244. While the Kosovars viewed KFOR as a liberating force, it viewed UNMIK, almost from the outset of its administration, as a neocolonial Raj, reluctant to let go.

Kosovo Serbs felt humiliated, disempowered, and threatened by the dominance of Albanians and the PISG, despite Serbs having been guaranteed almost 20 percent of the Assembly seats and one or two ministries. Kosovo Serbs had boycotted the Kosovo Assembly after Nexhat Daci, the speaker of the Assembly, commissioned the painting of a mural of Albanian nationalist scenes for a wall of the assembly building, art that the Kosovo Serbs considered a slap in the face and a repudiation of the goal of multiethnic tolerance. It took months for UNMIK to have the murals covered over. Few Serbs who had fled Kosovo during the conflict returned, and it was undeniable that many of the Serbs remaining in Kosovo were subjected to regular harassment and not protected by either the international or the local police. Despite international emphasis on interethnic reconciliation, the Serbian government in Belgrade did everything it could to prevent Kosovo Serb participation in the PISG's government. The Kosovar Albanians did little to welcome them.[22]

Significant progress had been made, to be sure. The housing stock, badly damaged during 1998 and 1999, was largely restored during this period and substantial investments had been made in improving the physical infrastructure, especially the Pristina airport and major roads. However, little progress was made on building a viable market economy. Underground businesses continued to flourish much as they had during the ten years that Milošević's regime excluded Albanians from most officially recognized governmental organizations and enterprises, and the privatization of socialist enterprises stalled after its German administrator halted all privatization activities for more than a year in response to Serb protests of the transfer of property interests from Serb owners to new investors. Although the telephone and Internet communications infrastructure was good, the electric power supply was intermittent and nothing had been done to exploit lignite reserves or to build new electric-generating capacity necessary for the domestic supply. Unemployment was high; official figures put it at about 60 percent, although this figure overstated the problem because many Kosovars were employed in enterprises operating off the books.

Kosovo lacked its own telephone country code and was unrepresented (except through UNMIK) in the international bodies that regulate civil aviation and telecommunications. The organizations of many multinational corporations such as McDonald's viewed Kosovo as part of a corporate region managed in Belgrade.[23] Potential investors were inclined to defer major investments until Kosovo's status was sorted out.

It was generally believed that corruption was pervasive throughout the society, penetrating to the very top of the political establishment. Few anticorruption investigations had been pursued against influential figures, and no convictions had been obtained. The corruption problem was complicated by the tendency of Kosovars to perceive ordinary profit-seeking business ventures as examples of corruption. In addition, there was a lack of any widely shared social consensus about whether behavior such as nepotism constituted

---

[22] July 2007 interview with Sladjan Ilic, Pristina.

[23] At the request of Dino Asanaj, I had several telephone conversations with senior executives of McDonald's, headquartered near Chicago. They did not seem to know where Kosovo was and had little interest in exploring business opportunities there. One suggested that any franchises in Kosovo would have to be approved in Belgrade.

corruption or was a desirable part of the distribution of political spoils. Education at the University of Pristina was infected with petty corruption and faculty incompetence. Often, professors simply failed to show up to teach their scheduled classes.

SRSG Steiner needed to respond to the growing pressure from Kosovar Albanians to address final status, although Russia and major European powers discouraged him from doing so. His solution was to announce that certain standards of human rights protection, democracy, and rule of law had to be met as preconditions for final-status determination. This "standards before status" policy was widely criticized by the Kosovar Albanians because of its aspirational character and the vagueness of some of its benchmarks. Some close observers joked that if Kosovo met Steiner's standards, it should be immediately granted the chairmanship of the Council in Europe, because its human rights record would surpass that of any Western European country. Many Kosovar Albanians saw the policy as a subterfuge for deferring status negotiations forever.

At a March 2003 open forum at the University of Pristina Law Faculty, Steiner gave an articulate, crisp, and animated explanation of his eight standards and explained why they had to be satisfied before final status determination. "Standards before Status," he said, simply meant that no nation can be considered functionally civilized until it meets all eight standards, and that logically must come first. He pointedly did not use the word *independence*. He was received politely and with applause after his prepared remarks but otherwise not warmly, and a buzz of conversation was frequently quite audible during his overly long answers to questions. Questions were submitted only in writing, but were respectful in tone and thoughtful in content. Steiner spoke forcefully, without notes, like the persuasive German politician that he was.

Several conversations with well-informed Kosovars and internationals reinforced two hypotheses: First, the international community had given far too little thought to the impact the experience of the 1990s had on Kosovar behavior. During that period, Milošević's repressive regime constituted the "rule of law," and Kosovar Albanians could exist only outside it because they had been intentionally excluded from it. They learned to cope through a variety of informal institutions and arrangements. The lessons learned during that period constituted both a strength and a weakness as Kosovo moved toward democracy, rule of law in the international sense, and a market economy. These improvised arrangements provided strengths to the extent that Kosovars had become adept at "cutting through red tape," in the quaint American expression, or adhering to the maxim "just do it and ask for permission later," as I had advised Krasniqi right after the war. These were tendencies that, if encouraged, could have accelerated the pace of political, economic, and legal development. However, too many internationals saw such behavior as undermining a rule of law or constituting corruption.

To be blind to these learned traits was to invite a subtle replacement of the Serbian government with UNMIK as colonial occupiers in Kosovar Albanian consciousness: the Kosovar tendency was indifference to official institutions – a posture that served them so well during the repressive 1990s. The danger was that this attitude created only the illusion of progress, based on cosmetic changes like the number of UN regulations or NGO reports, while ordinary Kosovars experienced no real improvement in day-to-day life. Such a result obviously was inimical to everyone's goals.

An alternative, and ultimately preferable, approach would have been for UNMIK and other international organizations to seek out Kosovar Albanian businesspeople, especially those who had been most successful in the grey economy. It would have been possible to forge an economically oriented alliance between the internationals and the business community that would have enlisted the most effective local actors in economic development. Instead, too many internationals ignored local businesspeople, often characterizing them as corrupt for their activities during the Milošević regime.

UNMIK, however, with significant flaws of its own, also was a scapegoat for the broader international community's unwillingness to confront the question of final status. UNMIK could do no more than its masters on the Security Council would allow. In addition, neither Washington, DC, nor any of the major Europe capitals were willing to grasp the nettle of independence for Kosovo, which surely would be at the center of any explicit discussion of final status. The prevailing view was that even discussion of final status should be deferred.[24] The deputy chief of the U.S. Office-Pristina was officially uncomfortable in late 2003 when I briefed him on plans for a symposium on final status at Chicago-Kent. Even UNMIK's modest steps to empower the PISG and to launch privatization of enterprises were criticized in diplomatic circles as inconsistent with maintenance of Serbian sovereignty.

Progress on Kosovo's future was stymied by a crucial contradiction. The Kosovar Albanians thought they had won independence from Serbia in 1999 and that UNMIK's administration was just a barricade on the road to their own state. Kosovo Serbs and the Serbian government in Belgrade viewed the expulsion of Serbian authorities from Kosovo as aggression in violation of international law. A critical mass of the UN staff, both in Pristina and New York, believed that UNMIK represented something quite limited: a shepherd for the construction of a multiethnic society of Albanians and Serbs who one day might be restored to the government by a reformed Serbia.[25] Top political

---

[24] See *Independent International Commission on Kosovo: Kosovo Report* 261 (2000) [hereinafter "IICK Report"] (deferring discussions about final status can create a "constructive ambiguity" that encourages people to work together; noting unwillingness of major powers to confront the issue).

[25] See Iain King and Whit Mason, *Peace at Any Price: How the World Failed Kosovo* 70–1 (2006) (criticizing UNMIK and other international organizations for not trying harder to facilitate interethnic contacts).

leaders in the United States, Europe, and Russia were not yet prepared to choose among these differing visions.

Kosovo was slowly embracing democracy, but a central reality of Kosovo political development during this period was that the LDK, representing the old communist elite, and the PDK, representing the new wartime elite, were blocking access to the levers of power by others. Young Kosovar Albanian professionals yearned for a new political reality that could address the existing parties' neglect of important public policy issues. Yet with final status unresolved, Kosovar criticism was focused on UNMIK and its perceived hurdles to full democratic development.

As progress occurred in Kosovo, however slowly, politics in Serbia circa 2003 seemed to be moving in a positive direction as well. Djindjić and Koštunica were distancing themselves from the Milošević era, and hope was growing in the international community that the time would come before long when Serbia would be prepared to accept Kosovo's independence.

Then, on March 12, 2003, a warm spring day in Belgrade, Serbian Prime Minister Zoran Djindjić exited his bulletproof BMW to chair a session of the newly created Anti-Corruption Council. He was wobbly on his feet due to a football injury that had left him on crutches, and he was escorted up the stairs of the main government building by his personal security unit. Suddenly he dropped, struck by two sniper shots from a nearby building. The first bullet struck Djindjić in his stomach; the second went through his chest. Another wounded his bodyguard in the stomach. He was rushed unconscious from the chaos on the stairs to his car and thence to the hospital, where he was pronounced dead.

It soon became clear that the assassination was carefully planned and executed by the notorious Zemun Gang, led by Milorad Lukovic, former commander of Milošević's special police. Only a few weeks earlier, there had been another attempt on Djindjić's life, when a truck driven by a member of the Zemun Gang had tried to force Djindjić's car off the highway. Even after that experience, Djindjić had declined to wear a bulletproof vest – a decision that cost both Djindjić and all of Serbia dearly.

The death of Djindjić removed the only political figure in Serbia who had both a sufficiently broad political base and the courage to chart a course for Serbia that could permit it to let go of Kosovo and direct Serbia's attention to eventual integration into the European Union.

Before this, some of the more astute international figures such as U.S. Public Affairs Officer Mike McClellan had been optimistic about the future. "Nobody in Serbia cares about Kosovo," McClellan had asserted. "They know it's already independent. They want to worry about other things and they want their leaders to worry about other things. The Serbian connection is only about how much they get for agreeing to Kosovo's independence."[26] However, the

---

[26] January 2003 conversation with Michael McClellan, Pristina.

turmoil in Serbian politics after the Djindjić assassination raised doubts about McClellan's rosy characterization.

I returned to Kosovo in July 2003, this time with four law students from Chicago-Kent. The Djindjić assassination seemed to have little impact in Kosovo itself; indeed, some Kosovar Albanians thought it might prove to be a blessing in disguise. Djindjić's popularity in the West had created a situation in which the West might have been reluctant to destabilize Serbian politics by insisting on final status resolution for Kosovo. If, without Djindjić, Serbian politics shifted in a more nationalist direction, rebuffing opportunities for integration with Europe, Kosovar independence might actually be easier to attain, because the international community would be less reliant on Serbia as a partner in resolving the question of Kosovo's future.

There were in fact encouraging signs that the provisional self-government was becoming more effective. Pristina was, physically, a much cleaner city: city workers and contractors were patrolling the streets for garbage, the trash had all been picked up, and dumpsters and trashcans were prominent. All this was having an affect on Kosovar behavior – even the head of the student union picked up trash from the floor of the Law Faculty as we walked around.

Nevertheless, no one outside Kosovo seemed to have the stomach for beginning real final status negotiations – until the March 2004 riots.

7 Responding to the Wake-Up Call

PRIOR TO THE MARCH 2004 RIOTS, THERE HAD BEEN LITTLE INCEN-tive for international decision makers to rock the boat. Kosovo was calm, progress was obviously being made in developing local political capacity, and lots of money was being spent on physical reconstruction, studies, and education. The status quo could continue for another ten years or more, many hoped.

The March 2004 riots changed all that. Although sharp disagreement exists about the nature of the riots, it is indisputable that they were spontaneous, at least to a considerable extent, and reflected the impatience and rage of Kosovar Albanians.[1] Claims persist that the violence was orchestrated behind the scenes by clandestine Kosovar Albanian organizations centered on the war veterans.[2] Whether or not that is true, no evidence exists that the senior Kosovar Albanian government officials led them. To the contrary, Rexhepi and Thaçi went out of their way – under considerable international pressure – to call for calm, and they seemed genuinely worried that they might not be able to regain control.

It is undeniable that the paroxysm of Kosovar Albanian rage directed against UNMIK and Kosovo Serbs on those two days reflected a deep-seated Albanian frustration with political affairs and with the pace of transition from UN administration of Kosovo to final status. Nearly every Kosovar Albanian interpreted final status to mean independence.

The riots also showed the unhappy synergy between a nationalist and professionally immature press and media and thousands of restless Kosovar Albanian youths who were ready to throw rocks and set fires – and worse. They also struck a body blow against anyone in the Kosovo Serb community prepared to entrust Serb security to an indigenous Kosovo government that

---

[1] See *Human Rights Watch, Failure to Protect: Anti-Minority Violence in Kosovo*, March 2004 at 28 (July 2004) (vol. 16, No. 6(D)) ("while the majority of the ethnic Albanian rioters probably came to join the protests spontaneously, there is little doubt that some ethnic Albanian extremist elements worked to organize and accelerate the violence"; summarizing opposing views about degree of organization).

[2] August 2007 interview with Soren Jessen-Petersen. Former SRSG Jessen-Petersen does not assert that the riots were organized, but notes that many UN and NATO personnel believed they were.

would inevitably be dominated by Kosovar Albanians. The greatest long-term damage resulting from the riots was that they reinforced mistrust between the Kosovar Albanian and Kosovo Serb communities. The Albanians would always fear a return of Serb control to Kosovo; the Serbs would never feel safe in a Kosovo run by the Albanians.[3]

The riots galvanized the international community into critical evaluation; it was time to determine the future of the international presence in Kosovo and finally to act to address final status. It was crucial to begin a new process that was acceptable to both the greater UN and specifically to the Contact Group – and hopefully to the Serbs and Albanians as well.

The Contact Group is an informal group comprising the United States, Great Britain, France, Germany, Italy, and Russia.[4] It was established in 1994 to provide a continuing forum in which the most interested powers could seek common ground on the conflict in Bosnia. Lacking a staff or other indicia of most intergovernmental institutions, it continued to function after the end of the Bosnian War and became the central diplomatic forum for dealing with the Kosovo crisis in 1998 and thereafter. Because its membership included four of the five permanent members of the Security Council (excluding China, which generally deferred to the others on Kosovo matters)[5] and also the leading members of the EU and NATO, its decisions generally translated into decisions by the EU, NATO, and the UN Security Council. The United States was the dominant member because it was the only one with the capacity to project massive military force into the Balkans. Some European countries had the troops but lacked the transport and the command, control, and communications capability to use them effectively. Because of well-known differences between Russia and the other members, a functional subset within the Contact Group was established, known as the *Quint*, comprising the Contact Group without Russia. Usually the major challenge for the Contact Group was to forge a common position between Russia and the Quint. Other states, of course, claimed an interest in Kosovo's future, and often they resented being presented with a Contact Group decision – or a Quint position – as a fait accompli respecting Kosovo.[6]

Two conclusions emerged after the riots: First, UNMIK needed more forceful leadership – someone able to stand up to the UN staff in New York, which had micromanaged SRSG Harri Holkeri. When the Kosovar Albanian leadership approached Holkeri in August 2003 pressing for greater political independence and less UNMIK control, Holkeri was forbidden by UN Headquarters from acceding. New York pounded on Holkeri to focus on

---

[3] July 2008 interview with Soren Jessen-Petersen, Washington.

[4] IICK Report at 40–1 (describing formation of Contact Group and its eventual focus on Kosovo).

[5] Confidential interviews with European diplomats posted to UN, June 2007.

[6] October 2008 interview with Wolfgang Ischinger, Minneapolis.

implementation of the Steiner standards.[7] Second, some kind of process for determining Kosovo's final status had to be launched without delay. A vision for Kosovo's future had to be articulated, and key governments had to support the vision. When Holkeri resigned for health reasons in June 2004, new leadership for UNMIK came in the form of Soren Jessen-Petersen, an experienced, charismatic Danish diplomat. A lawyer and journalist by training, Jessen-Petersen had served in several senior positions with the United Nations High Commissioner for Refugees (UNHCR) in the Balkans and at its headquarters, and had been the European Union's Special Representative to the government of Macedonia.

When Jessen-Petersen was asked by the UN Secretary General if he would become the SRSG, Jessen-Petersen said, "The only terms on which I will agree to do it is if I can be forthright about the need to move quickly to final status negotiations, and if I can be decisive in devolving further power to the elected governmental institutions of Kosovo."[8] He said the same thing to the Contact Group. There was some twitching in the room when – unlike almost everybody else involved – he used the term "independence," but all the members agreed.

Serious talk about final status would not have been possible without the March 2004 riots. Jessen-Petersen believes that he himself could not have persuaded the Contact Group or UN Headquarters to put final status at the top of the agenda in, say, 2001, or even as late as January 2004.[9] Indeed, when Jessen-Petersen met with then-SRSG Steiner in 2002, Steiner was quite annoyed "Have you seen the op-ed piece that Carl Bildt wrote in the *International Herald Tribune*?" Steiner asked Jessen-Petersen. Bildt was a former prime minister and future foreign minister of Sweden and prided himself on his Balkan expertise. Bildt had written, "The issue of Kosovo's final status, and thus the structure of the region, cannot be avoided for long. The international community missed a window of opportunity after the fall of Slobodan Milošević to deal with the issue.... Three years after the end of the Kosovo war, it is thus high time that we dare to address the issue of the Kosovo peace. We can't have another peace failure."[10] Steiner disagreed with Bildt's assessment, arguing forcefully that final status negotiations, and the attendant issue of independence, could not possibly be undertaken yet and should not even be discussed by prominent diplomats. Steiner wrote his own op-ed opposing Bildt's suggestion on July 24, 2002: "Kosovo's final status cannot be considered

[7] Confidential interview with European diplomat who worked for UNMIK during Holkeri administration, July 2008.

[8] July 2007 interview with Jessen-Peterson.

[9] See *Independent International Commission on Kosovo: Kosovo Report* 261 (2000) [hereinafter "IICK Report"] (deferring discussions about final status can create a "constructive ambiguity" that encourages people to work together; noting unwillingness of major powers to confront the issue).

[10] Carl Bildt, *The Balkans: An Unreal Peace Process, International Herald Tribune*, July 10, 2002, available at http://www.iht.com/articles/2002/07/10/edbildt_ed3_.php.

in a meaningful way until its institutions, economy, and political culture have evolved so that it can administer itself without extensive outside support or interference."[11] Jessen-Petersen, in contrast, thought Bildt had done rather a good job in his op-ed piece, by raising an issue that needed to be addressed.

On taking the role of SRSG, Jessen-Petersen's first order of business was to visit the Kosovar political leadership. His staff began to make plans under the assumption that those leaders would come to the SRSG's office. He brought them up short. "No," he declared flatly. "I will go to see them." There was intense bureaucratic handwringing over his going to both PDK and AAK party headquarters to meet with Thaçi and Haradinaj. Not only was the established protocol that local political leaders defer to the SRSG by coming to his office, Thaçi and Haradinaj were party leaders, not government officials. Moreover, UNMIK advisers continued to be wary of the continued KLA legacy in Kosovar politics. Nevertheless, Jessen-Petersen went; the reality was that Thaçi and Haradinaj were the most influential voices in Kosovar Albanian politics.

Jessen-Petersen visited Ramush Haradinaj at the AAK Headquarters in Pristina. The Headquarters' building occupies half a block on Mother Theresa Street adjacent to the University of Pristina and not far from the post and telecom building. Haradinaj's second-floor office includes two principal meeting rooms; the first – a large, elongated hall dominated by a massive conference table – is where Haradinaj habitually met with visitors beneath a pair of Albanian and American flags.

There also is a smaller room across the hall, which has the coziness of a small study. Here, Haradinaj usually sits in a chair with his back to the window, his visitors facing him on couches and chairs around a small coffee table. This was the room in which he received Jessen-Petersen. Jessen-Petersen had heard about Haradinaj's charm, and now he felt it. He began the meeting with a brief introduction and a request to hear Haradinaj's views on the political situation in Kosovo. Haradinaj proceeded to be quite critical of UNMIK and of his fellow Kosovar Albanians, focusing some of his strongest attention on the March 2004 riots and on the failure to respond quickly, not only by UNMIK and NATO, but also by the Kosovar political leadership.

Jessen-Petersen was hugely impressed by Haradinaj's proficient English, his quickness, his candor, and his overall charisma. Haradinaj had a mixed reputation with others, however. Some internationals and Kosovar Albanians worried about his brutality during the war, and rumors ran rampant that he controlled a criminal network responsible for smuggling, human trafficking, and worse. The Serbian government reviled him, and Kosovo Serbs feared him. It was widely believed that he would be indicted by the ICTY for war

---

[11] Michael Steiner, "First Things First: Step by Step in Kosovo," *International Herald Tribune*, July 24, 2002, available at http://www.iht.com/articles/2002/07/24/edsteiner_ed3_.php.

crimes.[12] His younger brother Daut and a number of other close associates had been convicted by an internationally staffed Kosovo court of brutalizing Kosovar Albanian political opponents after the war.[13] Their sentencing was followed by murders of most of the key witnesses against them and the assassination of at least one police officer involved in the investigation.

On the other hand, Haradinaj had made effective use of his reputation as a tough KLA commander, not to polarize Kosovo politics, but to start a political party that emphasized reconciliation and rule of law. Unlike Thaçi's PDK right after the war, Haradinaj's AAK welcomed a broad spectrum of political views. Haradinaj had learned English, was completing his studies in law at the University of Pristina, and greeted Western visitors with an arm around the shoulder and apparently heartfelt expressions of the need to build a future state in Kosovo that would respect the rights of all Kosovo's peoples. To all appearances, postwar Haradinaj was a statesman, an unusual Balkans politician whose word was his bond.

At the conclusion of the meeting, as was his custom, Haradinaj presented a copy of his book about the war to Jessen-Petersen, but he did not have a pen. Jessen-Petersen lent him his own pen – rather a favorite – and Haradinaj signed the book and gave it to Jessen-Petersen. Later, in Skopje, as Jessen-Petersen was preparing to leave the region, he discovered that he did not have the pen. He called Haradinaj and said, "You kept my pen." A car from the AAK showed up at the airport as Jessen-Petersen prepared to board. The driver presented the missing pen and departed. It was a small symbol of Haradinaj's commitment to follow through.

Haradinaj, already a major political force as a member of the grand coalition government, sprang to the very top of the Kosovar political order after the October 2004 elections. He and the LDK leadership in Kosovo shocked their political rivals and the international community by forming a proposed coalition that made Haradinaj prime minister but excluded Thaçi's PDK from the coalition. Thaçi was dismayed: in the previous grand coalition, Thaçi had reserved the right to select the prime minister himself. Jessen-Petersen was besieged with phone calls and visits, demanding that he veto the proposed arrangement and prevent Haradinaj from becoming prime minister. The demands came broadly from European capitals (the United States seemed to be more relaxed about the proposal), from Thaçi, and from other Kosovars. Jessen-Petersen was unwilling to overrule the results of a free and fair election and subsequent democratic discussions about coalition formation. He argued that progress in Kosovo meant respecting democracy there.[14]

---

[12] Haradinaj was indicted and tried, but acquitted.

[13] United Nations Interim Administration Mission in Kosovo, Peja District Court, *People v. Daut Haradinaj*, C.C. No. 190/02 (December 17, 2002) (verdict finding Daut Haradinaj and co-defendants guilty of beating, torturing, and killing), aff'd in material part, *People v. Daut Haradinaj*, AP. 95/2003 (Supreme Court of Kosovo, December 1, 2003).

[14] July 2007 interview with Soren Jessen-Petersen, Geneva.

Much of the protest against Haradinaj was fueled by the widespread rumors that he was about to be indicted by the ICTY. "Well, that may happen in the future," Jessen-Petersen responded, "but it hasn't happened yet. Rumors of a possible indictment provide no legitimate basis for me to act."

He did, however, visit Haradinaj privately. He told him about the international and local pressure and said, "I'm inclined to let you go forward with your proposal. I respect democracy. But I want your promise that if you are indicted, you will resign immediately and voluntarily go to The Hague." Haradinaj agreed and took office as prime minister. Thaçi's PDK was out, and the newly formed coalition had survived its first challenge.

The indictment was handed down in March 2005. It charged Haradinaj and two co-defendants, Idriz Balaj and Lahi Brahimaj, with "attacking and persecuting certain sections of the civilian population [by] the unlawful removal of Serb civilians from [the Dukagjini] area, and the forcible, violent suppression of any real or perceived form of collaboration with the Serbs by Albanian or Roma civilians there. The criminal purpose included the intimidation, abduction, imprisonment, beating, torture, and murder of targeted civilians."[15]

NATO wanted to mobilize considerable force to make a formal arrest, surrounding the AAK offices, Haradinaj's home, and possibly the government building with troops. Jessen-Petersen demurred and told NATO, "I want to do it my way." Jessen-Petersen and Haradinaj met again. Jessen-Petersen told him about the indictment and said, "I expect you to keep your promise." Haradinaj quickly responded, "You have no need to worry. I will keep it. But I haven't seen the indictment yet. Can you let me see it?" Before the meeting concluded, Jessen-Petersen asked for Haradinaj's advice on how the arrests of his two co-defendants should be handled. "Don't worry about them," Haradinaj said, "I'll handle that. They will voluntarily go to The Hague as well."

Haradinaj resigned as prime minister and voluntarily surrendered to pretrial detention by the ICTY in The Hague, taking Balaj and Brahimaj with him.

Haradinaj's graceful handling of his indictment was widely praised by the international community; a potentially disastrous moment had been transformed into a tangible artifact of Kosovo's political maturity and commitment to a rule of law. Despite some pressure, especially from Thaçi, to dissolve the LDK/AAK coalition, Jessen-Petersen allowed the coalition to continue under Bajram Kosumi, Haradinaj's designee. Kosumi had served as minister of the environment under Haradinaj.

Later, Jessen-Petersen reflected about Haradinaj, "I learned that I always could trust him to keep his word," he said. "There never was the slightest doubt. I could not say that about many others."[16]

---

[15] International Criminal Tribunal for the Former Yugoslavia, *Prosecutor v. Ramush Haradinaj*, Case. No. IT-04–84I ¶ 24 (original indictment, March 4, 2005).

[16] July 2007 interview with Soren Jessen-Petersen, Geneva.

Jessen-Petersen's outreach was not limited to political leaders in the Kosovar Albanian community; he also sought to improve relations with the Serbian political leadership, although once he embraced commencement of final status talks more publicly, the government of Serbia increasingly demonized him.

In February 2005, Serbian President Boris Tadić, part of the opposition team who had succeeded Milošević, traveled to Kosovo, paying the first visit by a head of state of Serbia since 1999. Tadić was the leader of DS, the Serbian political party perceived by the West as more moderate than Prime Minister Koštunica's DSS. He told reporters that his trip was designed to remind the world of the plight of Serbs in Kosovo. "Kosovo is part of Serbia and Montenegro, not only according to our law but also international law. This is my stance in Belgrade, in Kosovo, in Pristina, in Silovo, wherever I go," Tadić told the Kosovo Serb villagers as he presented them with a Serbian flag. In discussions preceding the visit, SRSG Jessen-Petersen chided Tadić for an itinerary that had him visiting only Serb areas. Jessen-Petersen said, "Mr. President, this is an opportunity for you. You should show that you also care about the Albanian people of Kosovo by visiting some Albanian areas." Tadić agreed and there was a certain amount of scurrying around to amend the plans to include visits to some mixed areas, a mere twenty-four hours before the visit actually took place.

Everything went well except for the fact that Tadić had presented the Serbian flag to the Kosovo Serb villagers. The display of the flag drove the headlines in the Kosovo press. After he returned to Belgrade, Tadić called Jessen-Petersen, thanking him for the well-organized visit and the good security. Then he asked, "Has there been much reaction to my showing the flag? I probably should not have done that." Jessen-Petersen told him that it was dominating the press reports. Tadić lamented that fact and urged Jessen-Petersen to talk to the Albanian political leadership and ask them not to criticize Tadić too militantly for the flag incident. Jessen-Petersen did so, and the criticism died down.

Tadić and the Serbian Prime Minister Vojislav Koštunica had very different personalities and approaches to diplomacy. Tadić craved approval; routinely, after a meeting or some other significant event, he would call colleagues and ask them, "How did I do? What was the reaction?" Koštunica, on the other hand, was antagonistic and rigid. He was dashing hopes that the political leadership of Serbia would recognize the inevitability of Kosovo's independence and help turn Serbian popular attention away from Kosovo and toward Europe. Koštunica had shed the moderate cloak he seemed to wear after Milošević's removal and had emerged as a champion of radical Serb voices, rivaling Milošević in his demagoguery about the future of Kosovo. Not only was he determined to prevent Kosovo Serb participation in the internationally established political institutions of Kosovo (for example, by thwarting their participation in Kosovo elections), he also was determined to derail any final status process in whatever ways he could. Koštunica almost always framed his arguments with reference to his interpretations of international law. He resisted discussions of political reality, returning time and again to "the law, the law, the law." Both Tadić and Koštunica had visited Kosovo, but Koštunica's two visits, unlike Tadić's, were limited to Serb areas in the north and to the Serb monastery town of Gračanica.

Nevertheless, international diplomats worked hard to bring Koštunica around, courting him regularly. Their meetings with Koštunica always took place in a large meeting room where Koštunica had five to ten aides flanking him. He usually was courteous, but "he never smiled," observed Albert Rohan. "He was like a different man from the one I met the day after Milošević capitulated."

Koštunica rarely devoted any time to the agreed-upon agenda. Instead, he would begin each meeting with a diatribe, usually focused on some failure by the international community to use one of his suggestions – sometimes made months or years before – as the basis for further drafting and discussion. He typically refused to talk about a matter unless his contribution anchored further work. Then he would turn the meeting over to one of his subordinates and sit with a scowl on his face while subordinates excoriated his visitors, often in quite undiplomatic and insulting terms.

On one occasion his diatribe was focused on the failure of UNMIK to use his own plan for decentralization of governmental authority in Kosovo. Koštunica's position was that Kosovo was still part of Serbia and therefore that any plans for Kosovo's future had to originate with the Serbian government in Belgrade. SRSG Jessen-Petersen had had enough. He said, "Mr. Prime Minister, you apparently have forgotten that UN Security Council Resolution 1244 took away your authority over Kosovo. You do not have the authority to decide what the plans are for Kosovo. We will be happy to consider your suggestions, but we are not obligated to adopt them." For once, there was a flicker in Koštunica's eyes suggesting that Jessen-Petersen had scored a point.

Koštunica had emerged as an extreme nationalist – more so than Milošević, who was an opportunist. Koštunica also had been smart in manipulating Serbian politics regarding Kosovo: he put resisting Kosovar independence back at the top of Serbia's agenda, while Djindjić, had he survived, would have prioritized European integration.

Jessen-Petersen's outreach to Serbs was not limited to Belgrade. Remembering that the war in 1999 had been fought to protect human rights and ensure interethnic tolerance, he worked hard to promote the integration of the dwindling number of Kosovo Serbs into the maturing political life of Kosovo. One success story in that regard was the ethnically mixed municipality of Strpce, led by a popular young mayor, Sladjan Ilic, a former champion skier. Jessen-Petersen was determined to do whatever he could to increase the profile and credibility of moderate Kosovo Serbs like Ilic.

On October 21, 2004, SRSG Jessen-Petersen went to Strpce to meet Ilic and a group of Serb residents. One of their goals was to urge Kosovo Serbs to participate in the forthcoming national elections. Strpce is in the south of Kosovo bordering Macedonia. It had a Serb majority in its assembly and Ilic, a Serb, as its mayor. UNMIK often looked to Strpce as a potential model of interethnic government, but efforts by Ilic to encourage Kosovo Serb participation in elections and other institutional processes of UNMIK-run Kosovo had led to attempts from Mitrovica and Belgrade to intimidate him and his allies. On this occasion, when Jessen-Petersen arrived, Ilic was friendly and welcoming. Then an aide came in and whispered in his ear and the mayor's face blanched. "What's the matter?" asked Jessen-Petersen.

"Word has come down that no one is to attend the meeting," said Ilic. "I don't know what to do."

"I would ask you to do this," responded Jessen-Petersen. "Open the meeting with us. Introduce us to however many people are there. Then you can excuse yourself and go outside and talk to the people who are leaving." That is what happened, and Jessen-Petersen was able to accomplish his mission while Ilic saved face. Still, the young Serbian mayor faced high risks working with Jessen-Petersen's agenda: later, on a visit to Belgrade, Ilic was beaten up, and fled Kosovo for a time. Here, he tells the story of what happened:

> I had enough supporters in my community that I had problems not so much in Strpce. But I had a hard time with hardliners, paid hardliners, "patriots" who were paid to make trouble.
>
> At first I was against participation in the elections of 2004 – when I was mayor. I said, "We lost three years in the previous assembly. We had twenty-two Serbs there, and what did they achieve? Nothing. Why should we be there?" But then I was thinking, thinking, and thinking. I came to the conclusion that our votes would allow us communicate through the only institution which is respectable to the Western countries. That was enough to persuade me to participate in the election.
>
> I had a meeting in Belgrade, in Tadić's office. They asked me what I thought about the elections. I said, "A couple of days ago I was against participating, but I changed my mind because I was thinking that maybe we can accomplish something." We were expecting negotiation over final status, you know, and all the time we had a bad reputation in the international community because of the fact that we always accused them of everything. And so we talked, and two days after this meeting Tadić said, "We will support the election. Some conditions are necessary, but we will participate."
>
> At that time there was the big, big pressure from the church and accusations from the press that we were betrayers, that we were American spies, that we got money . . . that we . . . everything. In the Strpce municipality itself, I had good relations with my community, but I had problems with those hardliners from outside.
>
> It was after the election, on November 8, 2004, I think. We had a meeting with Tadić's office in the morning. In the evening, I got a phone call. They said, "We are journalists from *Berliner Zeitung*," something like that. "Could you come to a bar on the river?" I went there but nobody was waiting. All they

wanted to do was to locate me. They followed me. I was alone. They – three of them – they had a pistol. They pulled out the pistol and said, "Stop! Stop! We are going to kill you." I said, "You can shoot, but I will not stop." I was a very, very fast runner and strong – a former professional skier.

They punched me once, but I didn't fall down. I hit one of them and ran out to the light. They started running behind me with the pistol, but I was faster and took a taxi to police. When I come back they had demolished my car. I lost my mobile phone and my keys, but I survived.

The police promised me protection, but I didn't trust them. I had a pistol but not with me at the time. So I took my pistol and called some friends. I said, "I need an escort to the border." I left Serbia.[17]

Like Ilic, some Kosovo Serbs wanted to participate in forging institutions to promote ethnic tolerance, but factions in Belgrade and Serb extremists in Kosovo were prepared to use violence to prevent cooperation. For them, at the beginning of 2005, cooperation with UNMIK meant a beating, or worse, because Belgrade portrayed UNMIK as favoring the Kosovar Albanians. The Kosovar Albanians, for their part, were clearly restless because UNMIK was not doing enough. From the end of the bombing campaign to early 2004, tensions grew between the PISG, Kosovar journalists, and other Kosovar Albanian political actors on the one hand, and UNMIK on the other.

No one knew when a paroxysm of violence might reoccur. Still, with Jessen-Petersen as SRSG and Haradinaj in the prime minister's seat, Kosovo had the strongest leadership ever. Both were committed to reach out to the Kosovo Serbs and try to define a future that they and Belgrade could accept.

The Kosovar Albanians were reluctant, however, to engage in direct talks with Belgrade, even if Belgrade had been willing to talk to them, which it was not. The Belgrade government refused to sit down with "terrorists," as they consistently characterized the Kosovar Albanian political leadership. The Kosovar Albanians were worried that direct talks would undermine their image with the Kosovar Albanian population and that they might be overmatched by greater Serbian diplomatic experience. Ironically, says one senior UNMIK staffer, Rugova and Daci were more willing to talk to Belgrade than Thaçi and the PDK.

By early 2005, the Contact Group and the Secretary General had decided on a two-step process. First, a high-level UN emissary would determine whether Kosovo was ready for final status negotiations to begin. Then, if that determination was affirmative, another envoy would be appointed to guide the final status process.

Kai Eide, Norway's ambassador to NATO, was designated in June 2005 to perform the first mission. He visited Kosovo many times, held intensive discussions with local Kosovar Albanian and Kosovo Serb political leaders, engaged in discussions with the government of Serbia, and met many times with the

---

[17] July 2007 interview with Sladjan Ilic.

Contact Group and other state representatives. On October 7, 2005, he presented his report to the UN Security Council. Eide's report reviewed many areas in which progress had been made and also acknowledged that progress was still insufficient in many other areas:

> Following a period of political stagnation and widespread frustration, Kosovo has entered a new period of dynamic development. A political process is underway and is gaining momentum. It is based on a comprehensive political strategy, which includes the prospects for a future status process.
>
> With regard to the economy, significant progress has been made. Economic structures have been established and modern legislation exists in many essential areas. Nevertheless, the current economic situation remains bleak. If a future status process is launched, this will certainly have a positive effect on the economy of Kosovo. However, the Kosovo authorities must understand that they cannot depend on the international community to solve their problems. They must take steps to ensure that shortcomings are addressed. Investment and integration will depend not only on status, but also on a predictable and stable Kosovo, where the rule of law is respected.
>
> The Kosovo Serbs have chosen to stay outside the central political institutions and maintain parallel structures for health and educational services. The Kosovo Serbs fear that they will become a decoration to any central-level political institution, with little ability to yield tangible results. The Kosovo Albanians have done little to dispel this fear. The interests of the Kosovo Serbs would be better served if their representatives returned to the Assembly. The Kosovo Albanian parties should stimulate such a process. The time has also come for Belgrade to abandon its negative position towards Kosovo Serb participation.
>
> Organized crime and corruption have been characterized as the biggest threats to the stability of Kosovo and to the sustainability of its institutions....Over the past six years, international police, prosecutors, and intelligence officials have tried to address corruption, but have failed to go much beyond the surface of the problem. Clan solidarity, codes of silence, language problems, and inexperienced local law enforcement institutions have all contributed to this failure.
>
> There will...not be any good moment for addressing the future status of Kosovo. Determining Kosovo's future status remains – and will continue to be – a highly sensitive political issue with serious regional and wider international implications. Nevertheless, an overall assessment leads to the conclusion that the time has come to commence this process.[18]

Thus, ultimately, Eide concluded that the time was right to begin a process for determining final status. Skeptics claimed that the center of gravity of his report was critical of progress in Kosovo and that his conclusion was coerced by the United States.[19]

---

[18] Kai Eide, *A Comprehensive Review of the Situation in Kosovo*, U.N. Doc. S/2005/635 (October 7, 2005).

[19] Confidential interview with European diplomat, August 2007, describing European critics of U.S. arm-twisting.

8 The Politics of Purgatory

KOSOVO'S FATE LAY IN THE HANDS OF THE "INTERNATIONAL COM-
munity." At the highest level of abstraction, the international
community had common goals: forestalling violence and trans-
forming Kosovo into a modern society with interethnic tolerance. Significant
differences existed, however, on how this should be done. State interests and
ideas for Kosovo's future spanned a wide spectrum.

Some governments, like that of the United States, and some NGOs, like
the International Crisis Group (ICG),[1] urged prompt action on Kosovo's final
status and were inclined to believe that the only viable final status was independence from Serbia. Other governments, like that of Russia, and many individuals working for NGOs, hoped that Kosovo eventually could be folded back
into Serbia. Serbia insisted that the question of final status should be kept
open for an indefinite period until Kosovo had made greater progress, especially with respect to reintegrating Kosovo Serbs into Kosovo's political and
economic life.[2] Even in the United States divisions existed. Some members
of Congress and some voices within the administration questioned whether
the United States had sufficient interest in Kosovo to spend political capital
or military resources on it.[3] At the beginning of the George W. Bush administration, several of the president's advisers questioned whether the administration should adhere to the Clinton administration's commitment to the
Balkans.[4] The growing weight of opinion, however, was that the United States
needed to finish what it had started. The UN and other intergovernmental

---

[1] See International Crisis Group, *A Kosovo Roadmap (I): Addressing Final Status*, Europe
Report No. 124 (March 1, 2002) ("The refusal to address Kosovo's final status perpetuates an
inherently unstable situation."); ICG, *Kosovo: Toward Final Status*, Europe Report No. 161
(January 24, 2005).

[2] See United Nations, Transcript of Security Council Meeting, October 24, 2005, S/PV.5389 at 8
(statement of Serbian Prime Minister Koštunica, emphasizing negative aspects of Eide report
and raising doubts about commencement of final status talks).

[3] See Remarks of Senator Inhofe, 145 Cong. Rec. S4515, S4538 (May 3, 1999) (criticizing commitment to Kosovo because the United States does not have strategic interests there).

[4] Steven A. Holmes, "The 2000 Campaign: Foreign Policy; Gore Assails Bush on Plan to Recall
U.S. Balkan Force," *New York Times*, October 22, 2000 (describing Bush campaign's call to
withdraw U.S. troops from Bosnia and Kosovo, as expressed in interview with Condoleezza
Rice).

organizations had no official position independent of the conflicted positions of their members, although individual staff members' opinions ranged over the full spectrum of national and NGO opinion.

Eide's report and his recommendation that final status negotiations begin did not reduce these disagreements; indeed, critics of his recommendation used major parts of his report to argue that Kosovo was far from ready to have the UNMIK yoke lightened,[5] let alone to be independent. Many argued that the thrust of Eide's report supported deferring final status determination and that his recommendation had been grafted onto the report at the end, only to accede to demands by the United States that Kosovo move toward independence as soon as possible. The United States had crystallized its argument that resolution of Kosovo's status was necessary to tie up the last major loose end in the Balkans and to permit a drawdown of NATO forces there.

Until Djindjić's assassination in 2003, many influential internationals plausibly argued that Serbia was at the threshold of a new, post-Milošević, democratic era. They argued that the international community should keep its emphasis on strengthening democratic forces in Serbia and on integrating Serbia into Europe.[6] Kosovo's status could best be resolved later, they said, after a reoriented Serbia came around to the view that it was better off with Kosovo as an independent, sovereign neighbor rather than with Kosovo as an unwilling part of Serbia prepared to use armed resistance against any reinstitution of Serbian sovereignty.

Djindjić's assassination, the continued political success of radical elements in Serbian politics, and the March 2004 riots in Kosovo cast dark shadows over these optimistic and apparently risk-free scenarios. However, it was difficult to frame alternative scenarios that could be pursued with acceptable levels of risk.

Some held out hope that Belgrade and Pristina could agree on "autonomy" for a Kosovo political entity within Serbia.[7] Serbia preferred autonomy to independence, because autonomy would maintain the fiction of formal sovereignty of Serbia over Kosovo. However, autonomy was a fighting word for the Kosovar Albanians. That was Kosovo's status prior to 1989, and Milošević had revoked it. Kosovar Albanians did not trust a renewed Serbian commitment to autonomy; moreover, Belgrade now was unwilling to agree to

---

[5] See UN Security Council, Statement of Serbian Prime Minister Koštunica, S/PV.5289 at 8 (October 24, 2005) (quoting Eide report that prospect of multiethnic society is "grim," that harassment occurs frequently, and that the return process has halted; concluding that future status talks cannot succeed because crucial human rights standards have not been met).

[6] See Commission of the European Communities, Commission Staff Working Paper Federal Republic of Yugoslavia Stabilisation and Association Report, SEC (2002) 343 sec. 2.1 (referring to "progress and a strong commitment to reform" during 2001).

[7] See U.S. Institute for Peace, *Special Report No. 100: Kosovo Decision Time: How and When?* (February 2003) (noting that many Europeans preferred that Kosovo remain part of a larger multiethnic entity).

as much autonomy as Kosovo had enjoyed before, when it had representation in the Serbian parliament and membership in the Serbian cabinet.[8]

Others hoped Belgrade and Pristina might agree to partition Kosovo,[9] with the area south of the Ibar River and the city of Mitrovica being governed by the Albanian majority, and the area north of the river being governed by the Serb majority there, or by Belgrade directly.[10] It would be hard, partition proponents argued, for any international body to resist agreement between Belgrade and Pristina on partition. The Serbs might well agree to it, they said, because it would be a way of getting Kosovo off the Serbian agenda and preserving Serb control over the north of Kosovo, and perhaps integrating the north into Serbia proper. Partition could be enough to satisfy Serb radicals in the domestic politics of Serbia. Even though Albanian Kosovars hated the idea and it was hard to see them agreeing to it, anything was possible if the West told them they should agree. In any case, Kosovo already was effectively partitioned: neither UNMIK nor the PISG exercised any real governmental authority north of the Ibar River, and the international community was not prepared to change this fact on the ground. Public officials in that part of Kosovo received salaries and retirees received pensions from Belgrade, not from Pristina.

However, partition would be a Pandora's box. It would abandon at least 50 percent of Kosovo's Serbs who lived south of the Ibar River – and in fact, southern Kosovo Serbs had always been fearful of partition for just that reason. Partition would probably lead to an exodus of Serbs from the enclaves from the south of Kosovo. Furthermore, it was unlikely that Koštunica would agree to partition – not because he was concerned about the Kosovo Serbs, but because agreement would dilute the image of his willingness to fall on his sword to keep all of Kosovo. Even if they were not left completely adrift, resulting in a population exchange, heavy international supervision would be required to make sure their lives remained tolerable.

Partition posed other threats as well. Albanians in the Preshevo Valley of southern Serbia, and perhaps those in Macedonia and Montenegro as well, could seek partition of their own states and integration of their communities into Albanian areas of rump Kosovo, making a complete mess that nobody could clean up. Elsewhere, Republika Srpska might use partition of Kosovo

---

[8] IICK Report at 277 (Resolution 1244 is unsustainable in the long run because it would maintain the fiction of continued Serbian sovereignty over an unwilling Kosovar Albanian population).

[9] See "Russia Admits Kosovo Split Possible," *France 24 International News* (August 31, 2007) (quoting Russian Foreign Minister Lavrov regarding possible agreement to partition Kosovo). Located at http://www.france24.com/france24Public/en/archives/news/europe/20070831-Kosovo-Russia-Serbia-Albanians-Belgrade.php.

[10] But see IICK Report at 266–8 (evaluating partition option for Kosovo's future and concluding that it would be inconsistent with long-standing international opposition to partition elsewhere and would be unacceptable to the majority Albanian population in Kosovo).

as an excuse to partition Bosnia. Kosovar leaders probably could not agree to it without a more general redrawing of borders. Unification of Kosovo with Albania was unlikely, however, because Albania's top priority was joining NATO, followed by accession to the EU. Absorption of Kosovo during this process would completely derail those top-priority efforts. At the same time, Kosovo's present and emerging political leaders wanted an opportunity to run their own state and not to play secondary roles in a larger Albanian state.

In any event, the Serbian government was unwilling to consider partition. Two years later, on the Troika's first trip to Belgrade, its members met with Tadić and Koštunica and they reviewed the options for Kosovo's status together. The Serbian leaders said, "Forget partition," according to Wisner.[11] Partition of Kosovo would imply a partition of Serbia, and that is exactly what Belgrade was determined to avoid. "Partition was a non-starter," says Wisner, "and we never came back to it."

Absent the likelihood of agreement on autonomy, partition, or independence, the default was ongoing limbo or *drift* – commitment to the status quo, which in this case meant keeping the UN in charge of a nonsovereign territory. It also meant prolonged, indefinite international management of militant elements within the Kosovar Albanian and Kosovo Serb communities, and continued efforts to improve the capacity of elected local institutions to assure a rule of law, human rights protection, and economic progress. UNMIK's effectiveness was declining, however, because of both increasing Kosovar Albanian opposition and the growing difficulty in recruiting and retaining high-quality staff. The problem with staff quality and morale existed, not at the top level, but further down in the organization.[12]

Drift, although it would avoid the need to make difficult and risk-laden political decisions about the future, also brought to center stage an eventual return to war: this time a multipolar conflict, with Serbia and the Kosovo Serbs on one side, Kosovar Albanian militants on another, UNMIK and NATO in the middle, and governments of interested states choosing sides as they wished. This scenario was unattractive to almost everyone and could very well constitute a bloody mess worse than what drew international intervention in 1999. Yet many believed this was Kosovo's most likely fate if the international community sought to preserve the status quo.

Continued Serbian opposition to anything other than a reinstitution of Serbian sovereignty over Kosovo could be preempted by a unilateral declaration of independence (known as UDI) by the elected government in Kosovo. This could be followed by recognition of Kosovar sovereignty by several major states, presumably including the United States but certainly excluding Serbia, and likely Russia (an option labeled UDIR).[13] The ramifications of UDIR on UN-member states' own internal conflicts could be profound, and profoundly

---

[11] May 2008 interview with Frank Wisner, New York.
[12] October 2008 interview with Wolfgang Ischinger, Minneapolis.
[13] The acronym stands for "Unilateral Declaration of Independence with Recognition."

destabilizing. The UDIR scenario might be associated with partition, with all its attendant problems.

Everyone inside and outside Kosovo recognized that the international community would have to chart Kosovo's future course because both the Serbian government and the elected Kosovar Albanian institutions were too weak, economically and militarily, to impose their wills on one another. They also lacked the political capital to transform popular opinion in their respective territories opposed to compromise.

Crafting a viable future status for Kosovo would require success on multiple fronts: Serbia had to be brought along as far as possible, and anyone managing diplomatic negotiations over final status would have to bend over backwards to accommodate Serbia's concerns. Moreover, as the March 2004 riots made clear, the Kosovo Albanians had to accept any status solution. Whether any common ground existed between Belgrade and Pristina remained to be seen. Moreover, when Eide recommended that the final status process start, all players assumed that any new status for Kosovo would be implemented through a UN Security Council resolution replacing Resolution 1244. Therefore, Russia had to agree to any plan; otherwise it would cast a veto in the Security Council. Europe also would have to be unified behind any plan, and U.S. support was crucial. If Europe and the United States were united, everyone (outside Belgrade) hoped, the Russians would not stand in the way.

Serbia was not in a position directly to block a status determination it did not favor. Nevertheless, it was hardly without influence. Serbia expected Russia to take its side and further expected to be able to write the script for Russian involvement. Belgrade also was hopeful that the large Serbian diaspora in the United States could be mobilized to dilute U.S. enthusiasm for independence for Kosovo. However, few well-informed Serbs believed that Serbia could ever again govern Kosovo as it had before 1999 – de facto independence from Serbian control was too firmly implanted in realities on the ground in Kosovo.

The architects of the final status process wanted to craft a plan that would protect Kosovo Serbs and protect Serbian religious sites in Kosovo, thereby moderating Serbian opposition to a redefined status for Kosovo – or at least muting its persuasiveness. At the beginning of the negotiations, a few international diplomats held out hope for a status not including independence, which represented such a red line in Serbian politics. However, says Wisner, "No senior policy person believed there was any way to solve the problem except to cut Kosovo loose from formal Serbian sovereignty. From the very beginning, the problem was not whether to do it, but how to do it, and how to forge trans-Atlantic unity behind such an approach."[14]

---

[14] May 2008 interview with Frank Wisner. Accord, IICK Report at 277 (Resolution 1244 is unsustainable in the long run because it would maintain the fiction of continued Serbian sovereignty over an unwilling Kosovar Albanian population).

From the perspective of most Western states, Serbia's long-term interests would best be served by gracefully acceding to the independence of Kosovo, while Serbia directed its attention to successful membership in the EU. Many Western observers believed that if Djindjić had survived, he would have had the political capital and the statesmanship to bring Serbian public opinion around. He could have put the Milošević era to rest and directed Serbian energies to a European future. Djindjić's assassination in 2003 had removed that possibility. Djindjić was not a miracle worker; he could not have magically eliminated all the factionalism that pervaded the Democratic Opposition of Serbia, especially because Koštunica was already making trouble before Djindjić was killed. Nevertheless, Djindjić could have moved more aggressively to apprehend Serbian war-crimes fugitives, an issue of great interest to Europe, and that would have permitted Serbia to be moving toward EU accession at the same pace as Croatia. With membership in the European Union on the agenda, the West would have had much more leverage to get Serbia to let go of Kosovo. A consummate deal maker, Djindjić might have been able to partition Kosovo and let 90 percent of it become independent. This line of reasoning assumes that the Kosovar Albanians would have agreed to partition as the price for independence in 2003, and it is far from clear that would have occurred. Djindjić, however, surely would have managed Serbia's part of the final status negotiations constructively.

Serbia's remaining political leaders, however, lacked both the political capital and the skills that Djindjić possessed. They were badly divided and, as former U.S. Ambassador to Belgrade William Montgomery pointed out in a series of columns in Serbia's Radio B92, it was an illusion to suppose that a "democratic bloc" existed in Serbian politics that was moderate on the question of Kosovo.[15] Instead, the shaky coalition governments after Djindjić were coalitions of pragmatic convenience and did not embody any consensus on Kosovo.

Politics in Serbia were framed by the Democratic Party (DS) of President Tadić, the Democratic Party of Serbia (DSS) of Prime Minister Koštunica, the Serbian Radical Party (SRS) of accused war-criminal Vojislav Seselj, the Socialist Party of Serbia (SPS) of Milošević, and G17+. G17+ was a pro-Western party named after the seventeen social scientists who formed an NGO in 1997 and subsequently became part of the Democratic Opposition of Serbia (DOS), headed by Miroljub Labus. It had been part of various Serbian coalition governments since Milošević's downfall. The DOS was a coalition of eighteen Serbian political parties that successfully opposed Milošević's SPS in the December 2000 elections, in which the DOS won 177 out of 250 seats in

---

[15] See William Montgomery, "Ten Inconvenient Truths about Serbia," *Radio B92*, August 19, 2007, located at http://www.b92.net/eng/insight/opinions.php?nav_id=43127 (arguing that Europe and the United States exaggerate the transformative potential of Serbian politics).

the Serbian assembly. In those elections the radical parties suffered a humil-iating defeat: the SRS polled only 8.6 percent and the SPS only 12.2 percent. After the DSS withdrew in 2001, the DOS re-formed into the DS and smaller parties clustered in G17+.

In subsequent elections, the radical parties rebounded strongly. In the December 2003 elections, the SRS won 32.8 percent of the vote and became the largest party in the assembly. The SPS won 8 percent. The most European-oriented parties continued to suffer from factionalism, and their electoral sup-port waned. Miroljub Labus resigned as president of G17+ over Serbia's fail-ure to cooperate with the ICTY in turning over war-crimes fugitives.

The middle – to the extent there was one – was occupied by two major figures: Boris Tadić, leader of the DS party, and Vojislav Koštunica, leader of the DSS party. Tadić firmly believed that Serbia's future lay with Europe and appeared willing to acquiesce in putting the Kosovo conundrum to rest. He lacked the political capital to say so forthrightly, however, and did not com-mand enough electoral support to drive Serbian foreign policy in the direction he thought best. The problem with Tadić, said one diplomat who dealt with him, is that "he is very nice and dignified, but he's completely ineffective. He does not deliver on anything he says he will." Another wag said, "He couldn't deliver a pizza."[16] Koštunica, on the other end of the spectrum, wanted to make a place for himself in Serbian history books as the man who had stood alone on the barricades and prevented the United States from ripping Kosovo out of Serbia. For him, no compromise on the future of Kosovo was possible, and his personal political interests would be almost as well served by going down fighting as by winning – after all, that is what happened to Prince Lazar at the Battle of Blackbirds in 1389. Koštunica's demeanor was dour. He deflected efforts to make small talk with rudeness. He could be charming and could make others want to help him – at least in the early days after his accession to power. There was always a slight distance, however. As a political player, he regularly outmaneuvered Tadić.

Čedomir Jovanović was a lonely voice favoring moderation on Kosovo. He had helped lead student forces that deposed Milošević and had been elected to the Serbian Assembly afterward. He was expelled from Tadić's party, how-ever, amid controversy over his associates, and seemed to gain little political traction except among the very young who admired his looks and his celebrity as a theatre professional.

In fact, it was highly unlikely that any of the major Serbian parties would be willing to give Kosovo independence. Their differences related not so much to Kosovo as to philosophies of economic policy and development; their rel-ative receptiveness to pressure imposed by the EU on Kosovo; and other issues related to the pace with which Serbia could be integrated into the

---

[16] Confidential interview, August 2007.

EU. Demagoguery over Kosovo continued to be a powerful tool of ambitious candidates in Serbia, and would continue to be so for the foreseeable
future.

Serb actors inside Serbia, Kosovo, and elsewhere continued their arguments that an independent Kosovo would become a safe haven for organized
crime and Islamic extremism in Europe, and that the UN Security Council
lacked the authority to divest a member state of sovereignty over part of its
territory. More extreme voices in the Serbian Orthodox Church emphasized
the Islamic threat.

Belgrade, through its experienced and effective diplomatic machinery, consistently sought the moral high ground in any discussion about the future of
Kosovo. Its theme was that Serbia had consistently been a victim of U.S. impe-
rialism. The United States had led what Serbia characterized as an unlawful
attack on its soil in 1999 by NATO. Serbia's people were victims of post-KLA
violence and organized crime rings, and the Serbian state was the only bulwark against Islamic fundamentalism in Europe, Serbian officials said. Now
the United States was prodding the Europeans to divest Serbia of sovereignty
over part of its territory.

International audiences were split. Some sympathized with apparent vic-
timization of the Serbs by NATO and the Kosovar Albanians. Others considered Serbian intransigence on Kosovo as proof that Serbia was still mired in
the racist and militarist adventures of the Milošević era rather than engaging
in pragmatic participation in international decision-making councils. Serbia's
moral position was considerably diluted when an order came from Belgrade
forbidding Kosovo Serbs to participate in the 2004 Kosovo elections.

If Serbia was confronted with imposed independence for Kosovo, it
certainly would press to achieve as much autonomy as possible for Serb-
dominated areas in Kosovo, up to and including full independence through
partition. This was Belgrade's position even though partition had been
strongly resisted by the West, and well might stir up pressures for secession in
the Preshevo Valley, one of the Albanian-dominated areas of Serbia proper.
Serbia would resist such secession fiercely because the main north–south transportation route from Serbia to Greece and the Adriatic and Aegean Seas runs
through the Preshevo Valley.

However, independence also was a red line in Kosovo, and the Kosovar
Albanians were on the other side of it. Kosovar Albanians were transfixed by
the prospect of imminent independence, but their capacity to act in a unified
way was questionable. Kosovar politics remained in a state of considerable
uncertainty. The capacity of local institutions to make any significant decisions
was essentially null because of these political problems and because of the
growing preoccupation with final status and independence.

The October 2004 national elections in Kosovo had poisoned relations
between the leading ex-KLA political figures: Hashim Thaçi and Ramush
Haradinaj. Before those elections, Thaçi's PDK and Haradinaj's AAK had

worked together in the grand coalition government with Rugova's LDK. The PDK and AAK frequently supported each other in election campaigns. That spirit of cooperation was fractured when Haradinaj and Rugova froze Thaçi's PDK out of the new government.

The AAK–LDK coalition, however, provided an opportunity for Kosovo to become accustomed to a real political opposition. Lacking experience in heading a democratic opposition party, Thaçi was at first inclined simply to throw rhetorical stones at Haradinaj's government. Over time, the PDK – joined in opposition by newspaper publisher Veton Surroi's much smaller ORA – framed a more coherent message concentrating on the alleged corruption and manifest ineffectiveness of the LDK–AAK coalition. The ability of Kosovo to accommodate one of its major parties in opposition on programmatic and efficient grounds was a significant sign of growing political maturity.

As prime minister, Haradinaj got along famously with SRSG Jessen-Petersen. As Jessen-Petersen said, "Ramush Haradinaj constantly worked to improve his old skills. He mastered English. He got a law degree. If he wanted to become a great tennis player, he would take lessons and be able to play good tennis in a week."

Haradinaj's indictment and arrest in March 2005 threatened to destabilize Kosovo politics again, until Jessen-Petersen and Haradinaj managed it so well that the event became a symbol of Kosovo's growing respectability instead of a disaster. As a result, the ICTY acquiesced to Jessen-Petersen's official request that Haradinaj be released from detention to return to Kosovo until his trial started,[17] and Haradinaj was restored as an active participant in Kosovo politics – although much of his influence was exerted, by necessity, behind the scenes.

The decks thus were cleared on the Kosovo political ship for cooperation with the international community and serious engagement in the final status process – at least in the short run. The major political figures were cooperative with the international community. They also were subject to considerable leverage if they were tempted to become uncooperative – Thaçi understood that his return to power depended on keeping the internationals relatively pleased with his performance. Haradinaj in particular knew that he could not make public statements without approval by the SRSG, and that he was vulnerable to being returned to jail if he proved politically disruptive.

Kosovo Serbs mainly remained outside these machinations. Despite strong international encouragement to participate in the October 2004 elections, Kosovo Serbs boycotted the elections on instructions from the authorities in Belgrade. This withdrawal from the Kosovar political process not only deprived Serbs of the most efficient channels to express their views, it also

---

[17] ICTY, *Prosecutor v. Haradinaj*, Case No. IT-04–84-PT, (decision granting provisional release, June 6, 2005) ¶¶ 10 and 13 referring to formal submissions by UNMIK guaranteeing compliance by Haradinaj with terms of provisional release).

poisoned international public opinion against them and against Belgrade's spirit toward good faith negotiations over final status.

The Kosovar Albanians were disadvantaged in the early diplomatic stages of the final status process by two realities. First, they were entirely inexperienced in high-level diplomacy. They lacked sophistication, were unsure how to behave, and had no confidence in their mastery of technical substance. In Kosovo, critics said, there were no political leaders who remotely qualified as statesmen. Thaçi's performance got mixed reviews. "He looked like he was scared in every meeting, fearful he would be overmatched by the Serbs," reported one international participant. "He never quite knew what to do, and would rarely venture beyond reading a prepared statement."[18] Others disagree and say that Thaçi always handled himself well. Haradinaj had a more forceful presence, but the terms of his provisional release prevented him from playing a formal public role. Veton Surroi, the former publisher of *Koha Ditore*, looked and acted like a seasoned diplomat, but other Kosovar Albanian political figures felt threatened by him. They failed to take advantage of his experience with respect to their own participation, and he undercut his own influence through his arrogant and disdainful manner. The Serbs, in contrast, were among the most seasoned diplomats in Europe. Historically, diplomats from other states liked and respected most of them. Now, however, the Serbian Foreign Service was in some disarray, faced with bribery and politicization scandals.

The Kosovar Albanians' second disadvantage was isolation: UN Headquarters and the UNMIK legal office had for the most part succeeded in preventing the Kosovar leadership from having direct contact with the outside world. They consistently took the position that no Kosovar political leader could participate in any official international forum independently, but rather could do so only through an UNMIK representative – if the Kosovars could be present at all.

Even after many arguments with the UN bureaucracy, Jessen-Petersen was unable to persuade UN officials that the Kosovars should be allowed to make unchaperoned diplomatic trips. Jessen-Petersen worked around this obstacle by making sure he sent only junior UNMIK representatives, with instructions that the senior Kosovar was to take the lead in any meetings. Only by such direct participation, Jessen-Petersen believed, could the Kosovars get their story out, demonstrate their reasonableness and credibility to the international community, and – probably most important – gain some eleventh-hour seasoning in the diplomatic process.

By the later stages of the final status process, however, the Kosovar Albanian participants had become comfortable and effective as negotiators. "I attended every meeting of the Troika," says Wisner. "I never saw Thaçi scared. I don't believe he lacked sophistication. He and the other Kosovar Albanians

---

[18] Confidential interview, July 2007.

were shrewd and knew their position. They had great self-confidence that represented political sophistication honed for years in the KLA and in Kosovar politics. These guys were good."[19] Thaçi also reportedly had a back channel to Tadić.

Although political developments in Kosovo were shaping up to facilitate stability during final status negotiations, economic life for ordinary Kosovar Albanians and Kosovo Serbs was getting worse. The riots of March 2004 had badly frightened the Serbs remaining in Kosovo. They hunkered down in their communities north of the Ibar River and in enclaves scattered about the rest of Kosovo, any remaining will to participate in Kosovo's political institutions diminished. They continued to look to Belgrade for pensions and salary supplements.

On a trip to Pristina in January 2005, I saw large groups of young men wiling away the time in the coffee shops that dotted every block, and clusters of old men sitting uselessly in the guard rooms that adjoined the entrance to every public building. Almost every new Kosovar Albanian house constructed since the war had a convenience store on the ground level, but few customers. The streets of Pristina were crowded with kiosks selling cigarettes, cigarette lighters, CDs, and DVDs. Friends of the proprietors chatted throughout the day. A customer was a welcome but infrequent break. Most Kosovar Albanian families depended on remittances sent from sons, brothers, and cousins working abroad, but the welcome extended by foreign host countries for them was growing cooler, and many had been forced to return home.[20] As UNMIK reduced its presence, well-paying jobs for the better educated were harder to come by. Half-finished warehouses and shopping malls dotted the suburbs. Despite the sense that the politics of final status were beginning to lurch forward, hope for economic prosperity was diminishing.

Serbia and Kosovo were not the only political entities in the region, of course. Albania, Macedonia, and Montenegro share borders with Kosovo. Kosovo's immediate neighbors, aside from Serbia, recognized that the ultimate decisions about Kosovo's future would be determined by the Kosovar Albanian majority in Kosovo, the government of Serbia, and the international community acting through the Contact Group and the UN Security Council. The Republic of Albania, governed from 1997 by the Socialist Party (the successor to Enver Hoxha's Communist Party), was inherently sympathetic to Kosovo's quest for independence, but was preoccupied with recovering from the anarchy of 1997, and convincing the EU and the United States that it was ready to move toward EU succession. There was little doubt that Albania would support independence as the final status for Kosovo.

---

[19] June 2008 interview with Frank Wisner.

[20] See European Security Initiative, "Towards a Kosovo Development Plan. The State of the Kosovo Economy and Possible Ways Forward." (August 24, 2004), located at http://www.esiweb.org/index.php?lang=en&id=156&document_ID=58 (emphasizing need for Kosovo to reduce dependence on remittances).

Montenegro had been part of a political union with the Kingdom of Serbs, Croats, and Slovenes after 1918 and then a constituent republic of Yugoslavia. After Yugoslavia broke up, Montenegro remained in a federation with Serbia, first denominated "Yugoslavia," and then after separatist forces in Montenegro began to grow, in a Union of Serbia and Montenegro. The Union agreement gave Montenegro the power to hold a referendum on independence from Serbia in 2006, three years after the Union agreement was crafted under pressure from EU officials, especially de facto EU Foreign Minister Javier Solana. Indeed, some sarcastically called the Union of Serbia and Montenegro "Solania." According to the 2003 census, Montenegro's population comprised 43 percent ethnic Montenegrins, 32 percent Serbs, and 5 percent Albanians. The Albanian population was concentrated along the border with western Kosovo and Albania, primarily in Ulcinj municipality and there was ongoing fear that this population would seek independence from Montenegro and possible inclusion in a Greater Albania. NATO had bombed sites in Montenegro during the 1999 conflict, causing public hostility to the international community's intervention on behalf of the Kosovar Albanians. Growing sentiment in favor of Montenegro's independence from Serbia, however, blunted Montenegrin tendencies to support the Serbian position with respect to Kosovo. The Montenegrin government was preoccupied with its own questions of statehood, which eclipsed Montenegrin attention to the growing unrest in Kosovo.

Macedonia's attitude toward Kosovo was complicated. It had a significant Albanian minority – 25 percent according to the official Macedonia census, and more than 30 percent according to the Albanian community there.[21] Albanian political parties had been part of the coalition governments following Macedonia's secession from Yugoslavia in 1991, but conflict broke out in 2000–2001 between the Macedonia government and Albanian guerrillas. The Albanian forces were suppressed by prompt NATO action, and the Ohrid Agreement was crafted through international mediation, which devolved greater political power to municipal levels of government and thus gave greater cultural autonomy to Albanian-dominated areas.[22] Tensions remained high between the Macedonian majority, which tended to identify with Serbia, and the Albanian minority. The Macedonian government signaled that it favored action to resolve Kosovo's status and that it would acquiesce to whatever solution, including independence, was adopted by the international community. The international community feared, however, that mismanagement of Kosovo's movement toward final status could destabilize Macedonia.

In the international community, the transatlantic partnership of NATO powers, represented by the five members of the Contact Group known as the

---

[21] June 2003 discussions with Macedonian–Albanian students as South East European University, Tetovo, Macedonia.
[22] See International Crisis Group, *Macedonia: War on Hold*, Europe Briefing No. 21 (August 15, 2001) (analyzing conflict and Ohrid agreement, which established a cease-fire and political reform).

Quint, sought to use the Contact Group to bridge the anticipated gap with Russia. Within the six-member Contact Group, there was a tendency to think of Russia as a partner in matters relating to Kosovo – a reluctant partner, but one that could be brought along to consensus. It was, after all, an active participant in the Contact Group. It had acquiesced in the adoption by the UN Security Council of Resolution 1244. However, memories had dimmed about how hard it had been to bring Russia to that position, and how much had changed since then. In 1999, the challenge had been to close the gap between NATO and Russia on the terms for ending the NATO bombing of Kosovo and Serbia. The Russian government had been in chaos. President Boris Yeltsin was incapacitated much of the time, and he had designated Viktor Chernomyrdin to take the lead in negotiations with the West over the crisis in Kosovo. Chernomyrdin previously had been prime minister of Russia, and had a significant political base because of his relationship with Yeltsin. Chernomyrdin had good relations with U.S. Vice President Al Gore, Secretary of State Madeleine Albright, and Deputy Secretary of State Strobe Talbott, but his special role with respect to Kosovo was widely resented by other power centers within Russia, particularly by Foreign Minister Igor Ivanov and by the Russian military, who challenged the legitimacy of his mandate.[23] Chernomyrdin had also constantly faced competition from General Leonid Ivashov, who sought to scuttle the talks. Under enormous pressure brought to bear by NATO – mainly by Britain and the United States, who were preparing plans for a ground invasion of Kosovo, and possibly Serbia proper – Chernomyrdin had agreed to NATO's terms for ending the bombing campaign: ultimately codified in UN Resolution 1244. Strobe Talbott, representing the United States, and Martti Ahtisaari, representing Europe, had orchestrated the deal with Chernomyrdin. Russian critics of the deal viewed it as Russia's "days of humiliation."

Now Yeltsin was gone, and Vladimir Putin was president and in firm control of Russian policy. Russia was stronger economically and politically, not least in its role as a major energy supplier for Europe.

The Europeans and Americans tried to address Russian concerns by making Russia a player and ensuring that features of the ultimate outcome reflected Russian input – the more dramatic the better. On the other hand, if what Russia mainly wanted to do was to demonstrate its power by simply throwing a monkey wrench into something it thought the United States had arranged, it would be far more difficult to bring Russia on board. Acquiescence to any U.S.-sponsored outcome would show Russian weakness. "I believed it was worth a try," says Wisner, "but I thought Russian acquiescence was far from certain. In any event, the best we would hope for was that Russia would let it happen rather than actually agreeing to Kosovo's independence."

---

[23] See John Norris, *Collision Course: NATO, Russia, and Kosovo* (2005) (describing diplomacy over NATO bombing campaign in 1999, including frictions within Russian leadership).

After the March 2004 riots, the Contact Group was reinvigorated and began to press the UN for stronger leadership of UNMIK – realized with the appointment of Jessen-Petersen. Jointly, the UN and the Contact Group began to consider options for dealing with the aftermath of the riots. Individual diplomats who had served in Kosovo or otherwise followed it closely had, of course, been thinking on their own about what sort of governing entity should follow UNMIK, mindful that UNMIK's mandate was to be exercised "pending a final settlement," and that the Resolution required UNMIK to "facilit[ate]a political process designed to determine Kosovo's future status," and "in a final stage, [to oversee] the transfer of authority from Kosovo's provisional institutions to institutions established under a political settlement."[24]

The United States' approach to the Balkans in general, and to Kosovo in particular, was complex. Washington had initially sought to disassociate itself from the breakup of Yugoslavia, believing that international relations in Europe would be simplified if Yugoslavia remained intact. Part of the problem in framing a coherent U.S. position on the Balkans was that many in the U.S. foreign policy establishment did not believe that the United States had strategic interests in Bosnia or Kosovo, although Europe did. U.S. Secretary of State James Baker's famous statement on Yugoslavia – "We don't have a dog in that fight" – summed up the U.S. position in 1991. Nevertheless, before leaving office, the first President Bush signed a "Christmas warning," drafted by Acting Secretary of State Lawrence Eagleburger, which threatened U.S. military intervention if Milošević escalated his campaign against Albanian separatists in Kosovo.[25]

When the Clinton administration took office at the beginning of 1993, it ratified the Christmas warning with respect to Kosovo and initially sought a more active U.S. role to forge a solution to the Bosnian conflict. However, the Clinton administration was thwarted and probably too easily discouraged by the difficulties in crafting a common Western position. So the United States remained mainly on the sidelines with respect to the Bosnian conflict until 1994 and 1995, when Ambassador Holbrooke was able to craft the Dayton Accords.[26] It turned out that the American "dog in the fight" was Europe: as European decision making proved unequal to the challenge of managing the breakup of Yugoslavia without war, the United States had a clear interest in working with Europe to shore up the credibility of the transatlantic alliance and of European progress toward playing a meaningful role in resolving security threats in Europe.[27] Then, however, the Clinton administration faced

---

[24] S.C. Res. 1244, ¶11, U.N. Doc. S/RES/1244 (June 10, 1999).

[25] President Bush is reported to have said during this period, however, "Don't talk to me about foreign policy until after the election."

[26] Other factors were at play, as well, including French elections, which produced a government more willing to use force in Bosnia.

[27] J. D. Bindenagle, former ambassador and deputy chief of missions of the U.S. embassy in Berlin, provided this insight in an October 2008 discussion.

major opposition from the Republican foreign-policy establishment when it sought to introduce U.S. troops as part of a multinational force to secure the peace envisioned by the Dayton Accords.

As the conflict in Kosovo heated up in 1997 and 1998, the Clinton administration was more prepared to get involved and exercise stronger leadership, in part because of a sense of guilt about having waited too long in Bosnia. Additionally, Milošević was by this time discredited as someone who could be worked with through ordinary diplomacy – especially after he began his scorched-earth techniques in Kosovo. Moreover, the U.S. public had been sensitized by the bloodshed in Bosnia, and was more open to an assertive U.S. policy to prevent Milošević from bringing further violence to Kosovo. The U.S. press, outraged by what it had witnessed in Bosnia, was prepared – even eager – to fan the flames of public opinion in favor of intervention against Milošević. Finally, the second Clinton administration had an extraordinary array of individual talent, tempered by earlier conflicts in the region. Richard Holbrooke, Wesley Clark, and especially Madeleine Albright were forceful advocates of an interventionist U.S. policy with respect to Kosovo, and they had the president's ear.

Although the Clinton administration organized the NATO bombing campaign and the de facto independence of Kosovo in 1999, the Republican majority in Congress continued to raise questions about U.S. interests in Kosovo,[28] although some Republicans like former senator and presidential candidate Robert Dole strongly supported Kosovar Albanian aspirations for independence. The second Bush administration reflected that skepticism. Before becoming National Security Adviser and then Secretary of State in the second Bush administration, Condoleezza Rice served as Candidate Bush's top foreign policy adviser. Shortly before the 2000 election, she published an article criticizing the Clinton administration's intervention in Kosovo.[29] While the new Bush administration did not withdraw U.S. troops, it generally viewed the Kosovo intervention as a "Clinton project" unworthy of significant investment of political capital or other resources by the new administration. Moreover, the foreign policy of the Bush administration before September 11, 2001, was, if not isolationist, at most focused on strategic concerns with respect to the

---

[28] See 145 Cong. Rec. S11189 (September 22, 1999) (statement of Senator Domenici arguing that Kosovo intervention threatened U.S. interests and resulted from inadequate definition of those interests).

[29] Condoleezza Rice, "Promoting the National Interest," 79 *Foreign Affairs* No. 1 at 45, 46 (January/February 2000) (arguing that Clinton administration foreign policy failed to separate the "important from the trivial"; acknowledging that strategic interests relating to NATO were involved in Kosovo conflict, but concluding that Clinton administration conducted Kosovo war "incompetently"). See also Michael Mandelbaum, "Foreign Policy as Social Work," *Foreign Aff.* (January/February 1996) (describing Clinton foreign policy as concerned more with social, economic, and political development with small countries on the periphery of U.S. interests than in strategic interests of the United States).

great powers – relations with the Soviet Union and China and with national defense projects such as a missile defense shield.

The September 11, 2001, attack changed all that: refocusing American attention on the terrorist threat, the attack legitimated the United States acting in its own interest in smaller states where festering resentments might spawn violent groups. This is exactly what happened in Kosovo in the late 1990s, of course, when the KLA emerged as a real political force and gradually supplanted the pacifist Rugova as the architect of the Albanian response to Serb repression. The new legitimacy for intervention in the affairs of more remote parts of the globe combined with a strategic desire to reduce troop commitments in Kosovo and elsewhere. Together, these two factors shifted U.S. policy in favor of attending to Kosovo in a way that would produce some kind of final status and permit a reduction in international commitments to administer Kosovo and to protect it, which in turn would permit a drawdown of U.S. troops there. The United States pushed the Contact Group and the Security Council hard to get final status determined promptly.

Nevertheless, it was implausible to argue that U.S. interest in the independence of Kosovo was stronger than U.S. interest in cooperation with Russia on problems such as Islamic fundamentalism, containing Iranian nuclear weapons ambitions, or disarming North Korean nuclear warfare capability. There was some tension within the U.S. government (most notably between National Security Council [NSC] staff and the State Department – NSC staff had lots of Russian experts) and they tended to be more interested in future relations with Russia and Serbia than in Kosovo.

During President Bush's first term, his administration had met its commitments in Kosovo but was not eager to make new commitments. In the second term, its attitude changed. Condoleezza Rice was now Secretary of State, and Nicholas Burns was her Under Secretary for Political Affairs. Burns had come out of NATO and emphasized that both the United States and Europe were out on a limb with respect to Kosovo. It was important to the long-term credibility of American foreign policy for one administration to follow through with the commitments of the previous one. Europe would not be able to coalesce without U.S. leadership. However, Burns also realized that the United States must avoid its tendency to "lead" through loud breast-beating. Instead, the United States should keep a relatively low profile but act energetically to allow Europe to reach its own footing. The United States should get things moving in the right direction in Europe without pounding the table, and then stand back. "U.S. economic and security interests required good relations with Europe, and there was an implicit recognition within U.S. policy councils," says Frank Wisner, "that the Atlantic Alliance was frayed over Iraq – though Iraq was never explicitly a part of the discussion over Kosovo. The Kosovo issue provided an opportunity for the U.S. and Europe to find common ground." Such an approach would provide perhaps the best chance the Bush administration had for a foreign policy success on a record that offered mostly foreign policy failures. By 2005, the U.S. government stuck to a common line on Kosovo: Kosovo's status must be resolved without further delay and independence was the only plausible status.

Historically, France was as pro-Serbian as Germany was anti-Serbian. France was credibly viewed during the conflicts in Croatia and Bosnia as favoring Serb interests. During the NATO bombing campaign over Kosovo, the French military was accused of leaking information about targets to the Serbian government. However, the pro-Serbian tilt in French policy was not evident during the final status negotiations.

In the summer of 2005, the intra-European part of the process was simplified when France made a dramatic U-turn in its attitude toward Serbia and the negotiations. Philipee Douste-Blazy had succeeded Michel Barnier as French Foreign Minister, and he brought new insights to French policy toward Kosovo. He had been a physician in Bosnia and saw with his own eyes the horrors of ethnic cleansing and interethnic violence. If one saw that, one understood what happened in Kosovo in 1998 and 1999 – it logically led to the conclusion that Serbia had lost the privilege of ever governing Kosovo again. Douste-Blazy reorganized the department within the Foreign Ministry that was responsible for policy on Serbia and Kosovo. Afterwards, considerable influence was wielded by Douste-Blazy's Balkan adviser Arnaud Danjean, who was a seasoned Balkan expert despite his relatively young age, and Jean-Francois Terral, former ambassador to Macedonia, whose crystal-clear interventions in EU and Contact Group meetings left no room for misinterpreting France's position.

Now, France embraced the proposition that the only conceivable status for Kosovo was independence. Unless Kosovo became independent, Serbia could never lay its past to rest and prepare for effective membership in the European Union.

Great Britain was, after the United States, the most muscular advocate of Kosovar independence. This represented a dramatic change from British policy in the 1990s when, as convincingly detailed in James Pettifer's *Kosova Express*, John Major's government tilted strongly against the Kosovar Albanian separatists.[30] Tony Blair's government transformed British policy: during the 1999 NATO intervention, Britain was out in front of the United States in advocating the introduction of ground troops if necessary to expel Serb forces from Kosovo. After the March 2004 riots, Britain took the lead in favor of independence for Kosovo.

---

[30] See James Pettifer, *Kosova Express: A Journey in Wartime* 18 (2005) (characterizing British Foreign Office as pro-Belgrade and anti-United States with respect to early stages of Kosovo conflict); id. at 34 (referring to collaboration between British and Yugoslav intelligence services in mid-1990s and "hidden wiring linking Whitehall and Belgrade); id. at 69 (reporting that senior British diplomat at Dayton negotiations ensured that Kosovo would not be considered); id. at 114 (describing British Foreign Office rejection of increasing evidence that violent resistance was developing in Kosovo).

Smaller European states had additional, more specific interests in the outcome of Kosovo's final status negotiations. Switzerland had a large Albanian
diaspora. It had close-up experience with accommodating large refugee flows
from conflicts in the region in the past and did not want to experience the
same pressure again. The Swiss government made public statements early on
that signaled sympathy with Kosovar independence as the best final status. As
a nonmember of the European Union, Switzerland had only limited influence
in the shaping of a uniform European position, but its historic role as the host
country for many international organizations and diplomatic missions gave it
an influence disproportionate to its size and population. In July 2005, Swiss
Foreign Minister Micheline Calmy-Rey vocally supported Kosovo's independence. In retaliation, Belgrade cancelled a scheduled visit to Serbia by Calmy-
Rey, and some Swiss diplomats were privately very critical of her getting too
far out in front of European diplomacy. The Swiss position attracted great
attention within the Kosovar Albanian community but had little influence on
European diplomacy.

Others were wary of independence for Kosovo. Spain worried about the
effect on its restive Basque minority, Greece about Cyprus, Slovakia and
Romania about the Hungarians.

The governments of Serbia and of Kosovo had almost no direct contact
with each other – the exceptions being occasional casual encounters between
a Serbian official and a Kosovar Albanian official at international conferences.
UNMIK was the only bridge between the two, and each viewed UNMIK with
mistrust. Whatever the process for determining final status turned out to be,
UNMIK would be in the middle. Until final status was implemented, Security
Council Resolution 1244 had given UNMIK responsibility for civil administration, while it gave KFOR responsibility for maintaining the peace. UNMIK
and KFOR ultimately bore the responsibility of governing Kosovo.

UNMIK was subjected to continuing oversight, both formal and informal,
by the UN Security Council. Its SRSGs were acutely mindful of this chain of
command.[31] Despite differences in their personalities and in their personal
judgments about what was best for Kosovo, no SRSG could get too far out in
front of the permanent members of the Security Council – the United States,
Russia, Great Britain, France, and China – without being replaced. Permanent
UN staff in New York in the Secretariat, especially in the Legal Adviser's
Office, attempted to keep a tight rein on the exercise of SRSG discretion.
Permanent staff in UNMIK itself, especially the Pristina Legal Adviser's
Office, also exercised tight control, usually backed up by formal and con-
servative interpretations of UNMIK's legal mandate under Resolution 1244.
The presence of Russian- and Serb-sympathetic staff made sure that national

---

[31] July 2007 interview with SRSG Joachim Rueker, Pristina; July 2007 interview with Deputy
SRSG Steven Schook, Pristina.

differences over Kosovo's future were reflected in a – frequently incoherent – UNMIK approach. Through these mechanisms, the senior UNMIK leadership was held hostage by the unwillingness of the Security Council and the EU leadership to make fundamental decisions about Kosovo's future.

The five SRSGs who held office since June 1999 each embraced different priorities. Sérgio Vieira de Mello served as acting SRSG in 1999, and struggled to get UNMIK established after Resolution 1244 was adopted. The first official SRSG, Bernard Kouchner (July 1999 through January 2001), focused on getting UNMIK organized, working with KFOR to stabilize the remaining hot spots of unrest, and issuing UNMIK regulations that provided a constitutional framework for local government and Western-oriented law. Hans Haekkerup (January 2001 to February 2002) continued UNMIK's momentum as a lawmaker. Michael Steiner (February 2002 to July 2003) deflected increasing local pressure for final status determination by creating a so-called standards before status policy, which required Kosovo to demonstrate progress toward rule of law, market reform, and interethnic integration before discussion over final status could occur. Harri Holkeri (July 2003 to June 2004) faced resistance from New York and from his own staff in moving toward final status discussions. He also faced resistance from local government institutions on implementation of Steiner's standards. The March 2004 riots occurred on his watch. Soren Jessen-Petersen (June 2004 to September 2006) insisted in being given a freer hand to begin the final status process. He embraced local Kosovar Albanian leaders more warmly than had his predecessors and also reached out, with limited success, to major figures in both the Serbian government and to Kosovo Serbs.

By some measures, UNMIK had succeeded in doing what had never been done before: imposing a UN government on a postconflict society. It had set up courts, imposed an interim constitution, written and adopted hundreds of new laws, supervised four rounds of free and fair elections for locally accountable political institutions, and navigated through the interstices of a policy set by a badly divided UN Security Council. UNMIK, however, was generally perceived as pro-Albanian by Belgrade and Kosovo Serbs, and as a foreign occupier by Kosovar Albanians.

UNMIK's position was untenable for the long term, and the events of March 2004 forced its sponsors to acknowledge that inconvenient fact. Now, even more than before, its capacity to carry out its mission depended on NATO's KFOR. Kosovo's emergence from Serbian domination was a product of NATO's military intervention, and NATO forces continued to keep the peace in Kosovo. Any political decision on Kosovo's final status would have to be implemented with NATO's support.

NATO comprised military forces contributed by member states, under the direction of a joint military staff, with policy decisions made by the North Atlantic Council – a group of ambassadors from each member state. By late

2005, the context for NATO's role in Kosovo had shifted considerably. The difficulty of maintaining NATO cohesion during the 1999 bombing campaign and lapses in the KFOR command and control during the March 2004 riots had shaken confidence that NATO could once again be a coherent and unbeatable military force in a new Kosovo crisis. Meanwhile, the UN Security Council had designated NATO to lead a military intervention in Afghanistan, which committed significant U.S., Canadian, and European forces to that theater. The national interests of NATO member states in Afghanistan were as great as or greater than their interests in Kosovo. Enlargement of NATO membership from nineteen members in 1999 to twenty-six members in 2005 complicated decision making.

Still, NATO's reputation was on the line in Kosovo, and KFOR regularly reiterated its determination to prevail over any forces inclined to deal with Kosovo's future through violence. NATO still provided a diplomatic forum preferable to the alternatives – but whether its members could mobilize the political will to take risks in Kosovo as great as the ones taken in 1999 was uncertain. As with the UN, NATO members might fear that they would jeopardize the future of the organization more by taking a firm stand than by backing away and delaying difficult decisions.

Sorting out all these conflicting interests and articulating and then building support for a coherent plan for Kosovo would require a strong hand.

9 Enter Martti Ahtisaari

EVEN AS KAI EIDE WAS DECIDING THAT KOSOVO WAS READY FOR final status talks, the process of deciding who should be the special envoy for final status was underway. Several distinguished international diplomats had experienced close contact with Kosovo or Bosnia, and therefore were credible candidates. Eide himself was a candidate, and most inside observers thought he wanted the additional role. His country, however, was not a member of the EU. Other contenders surfaced during the course of 2005, including Giulano Amato, former prime minister of Italy, and George Robertson, former NATO Secretary General. Robertson turned out not to be interested, and Amato was seen as too aggressive in promoting his own candidacy. From early 2005, the two leading candidates were Carl Bildt and former president of Finland Martti Ahtisaari. Bildt was ultimately rejected because of his reputation for being a bull in a china shop, and because the United States mistrusted him, as unpredictable and tied too closely to Belgrade.[1] The United States did not pick a fight with him, but the fact was Bildt was a marginal player in major decisions, and he never really tried to buck the tide.

Martti Ahtisaari was appointed Special Envoy of the Secretary General of the United Nations for the Future Status Process for Kosovo in October 2005. "There were many people who were qualified, in some sense, to guide the final status negotiations," said one experienced diplomat, "but Martti Ahtisaari was the best of them. Everyone knew him and respected him."[2]

Later, Ahtisaari won the 2008 Nobel Peace Prize for "his important efforts, on several continents and over more than three decades, to resolve

---

[1] Richard Holbrooke, however, reports favorably on Bildt's involvement in negotiation and implementation of the Dayton Accords. Holbrooke at 233, 242–4 (describing Carl Bildt's central role as European representative to the Dayton negotiations over the Bosnian War, but uncertainty about "whom he spoke for" in Europe); id. at 116 (describing Holbrooke's friendship with Bildt and favorably describing his capabilities); id. at 324 (describing criticism of Bildt's slow start as high representative in Bosnia, but pointing out that he was so starved of resources, he had to use his private cell phone to communicate).

[2] July 2007 interview with Søren Jessen-Petersen, Geneva.

international conflicts." According to a press release issued by the Nobel Committee:

> Throughout all his adult life, whether as a senior Finnish public servant and president or in an international capacity, often connected to the United Nations, Ahtisaari has worked for peace and reconciliation. For the past twenty years, he has figured prominently in endeavours to resolve several serious and long-lasting conflicts. In 1989–90 he played a significant part in the establishment of Namibia's independence; in 2005 he and his organization Crisis Management Initiative (CMI) were central to the solution of the complicated Aceh question in Indonesia. In 1999 and again in 2005–7, he sought under especially difficult circumstances to find a solution to the conflict in Kosovo. In 2008, through the CMI and in cooperation with other institutions, Ahtisaari has tried to help find a peaceful conclusion to the problems in Iraq. He has also made constructive contributions to the resolution of conflicts in Northern Ireland, in Central Asia, and on the Horn of Africa.
>
> Through his untiring efforts and good results, he has shown what role mediation of various kinds can play in the resolution of international conflicts. The Norwegian Nobel Committee wishes to express the hope that others may be inspired by his efforts and his achievements.[3]

Educated as a teacher and having worked in Pakistan supervising an NGO education mission, Ahtisaari's diplomatic career began in 1965. "I wasn't a career diplomat then," Ahtisaari explains. "I was recruited as part of an effort to bring people with a development background into the Foreign Service. I had been associated with the Swedish-Pakistani Institute of Technology, which reached out to students who had 'disappeared' after graduation. It was a great learning experience."[4] In 1973 when Ahtisaari was thirty-six years old, the president of Finland appointed him to be Finland's ambassador to Tanzania. In 1993, Ahtisaari was himself elected president of Finland as the candidate of the center-left Social Democratic Party. His integrity, forthright manner, successful international engagements, and practice of wading into crowds – and generally relishing contact with ordinary citizens – made him immensely popular. As president, he sparred with the Centre Party prime minister, who was unenthusiastic about Ahtisaari's emphasis on foreign affairs – or at least Ahtisaari's active personal participation in them. Ahtisaari actively campaigned for Finland to join the European Union, which occurred after a 1994 referendum vote of 56 percent in favor of membership. His activist foreign policy frequently was thwarted by parliament, and he decided not to seek reelection as president in 2000.

Ahtisaari had a distinguished record as an international mediator. As a young man, he had persisted more than ten years to shepherd the new state

---

[3] Nobel Committee, Press Release, Oslo (October 10, 2008), located at http://nobelprize.org/nobel_prizes/peace/laureates/2008/press.html.

[4] March 2008 interview with Martti Ahtisaari, New York.

of Namibia into independence, ending South African rule under a post–World War I League of Nations mandate. He had a particularly notable track record in mediating apparently intractable disputes arising from separatist violence. He also had played a major role in ending the 1999 NATO bombing campaign over Kosovo, by forging the agreement that led to UNMIK and KFOR's interim administration of Kosovo. He knew the Kosovo territory well, and he had the toughness and diplomatic skills to serve as an effective intermediary in the final status process. He was not a publicity hound.

In 2001 at the request of the Irish and British governments, he had verified the disarming of the Irish Republican Army (IRA), thus permitting the Good Friday Agreement of 1998 to come into full effect. "I should not receive too much credit for implementation of the Agreement," Ahtisaari says, "my role was symbolic; we simply verified that the arms dumps had not been tampered with." Still, his recruitment demonstrated his credibility and respect throughout Europe. Most relevant, while helping bring NATO, Russia, and Serbia to an agreement ending the 1999 bombing campaign over Kosovo, he maintained the trust of all sides while adroitly finding sources of leverage to produce an agreement. Indeed, some credited Ahtisaari with saving Schroeder's government in Germany by the way he handled European political fallout over the NATO bombing campaign.

In 2005, Ahtisaari mediated an agreement between the free Aceh movement and the government of Indonesia. The agreement resulted in the removal of Indonesian troops from domestic policing functions in Aceh and in the abandonment by Aceh separatists of their demands for full independence.

He had a reputation for adopting a pragmatic, no-nonsense approach. After the Aceh success, Ahtisaari admitted that there were several instances where he had had to be "very strict, even hard." When he first met with separatist negotiators, he told them he was unsure if "any government would support [a deal with] them," he said. He also told them that "if they did not immediately grasp this opportunity, they might never get back to their homes in Aceh, but would die here in the North."

In conversation, Ahtisaari repeatedly describes his actions in international diplomacy with the words: "I was very candid." Everyone gives him credit for delivering unwelcome messages but doing so in a way that minimized offense. "A young man came to me once," he reports, "and said, 'I want to spend a year with you, just to learn how to say difficult things nicely.'"

Ahtisaari's background, combined with his availability, made him the obvious choice. No one could match the key elements of his background. In addition to his public political and international mediation successes, he had worked as a UN Under Secretary General for management, and therefore knew the UN bureaucracy and political folkways well. He even maintained a good relationship with the Russians, although others viewed him as the architect of Russia's humiliation in the Kosovo crisis of 1999. The Russians dealt with him politely but warily. He enjoyed enormous respect throughout the international diplomatic community, with few instances of major criticism.

Søren Jessen-Petersen said flatly, "Martti Ahtisaari was the only guy to lead the final status process. The best news I had as SRSG was when Martti called me and told me he had been asked to clear his calendar because he was under consideration to be the special envoy. I have known Martti for twenty-five years. He has a broad range of experience, framed by notable successes in situations that proved intractable for everyone else. He takes a no-nonsense approach. He is very direct and extremely honest. He also is a good strategist and tactician: once he crystallizes a goal, he always knows how to get there."

UN Secretary General Kofi Annan had settled on Ahtisaari as the Secretary General's Special Envoy for the Future Status Process for Kosovo by September 2005, after having first asked him to consider it on August 14. Ahtisaari told Annan he must have Albert Rohan as his deputy. On October 31, the Secretary General informed the Security Council of his intention to appoint Ahtisaari, with Albert Rohan as Deputy to the Special Envoy. The Security Council supported their appointment in a letter dated November 10, 2005. Formal announcement of the appointment was delayed by private negotiations over the content of the Contact Group's "appendix" to the letter of appointment. Collectively, Ahtisaari, Rohan, and their staff were known as UNOSEK: United Nations Office of the Special Envoy for Kosovo.

Ahtisaari is a bear of a man who speaks directly, but with a smile and a twinkle in his eye. On first meeting, he is quick to jump into engaging stories that reveal the personalities involved in difficult diplomatic engagements of the past, as well as his own deftness in tweaking pomposity and twisting the knife just enough to expose the weaknesses of intransigent positions or of the inconsistency between positions and underlying interests.

He knows that negotiators must be clear on what they want. In November 2005, while Ahtisaari was being selected as the special envoy, he came to a Contact Group meeting straight from a meeting with The World Bank. He was full of stories about how Kosovo could not develop economically with international financial support unless its final status was resolved. He was direct with the Contact Group, saying, "It's very important that we know exactly what we're talking about, both in terms of the ultimate goal, and in terms of how we can get there."[5]

At one point in the final status negotiations, he responded to Russian Foreign Minister Lavrov's insistence that the EU and the United States must give more respect to Russia's prerogatives as a great power – a respect, Lavrov said, that had been lacking as the UN administration of Kosovo was put together in 1999. "So," Ahtisaari said to him, "Russia is a great power, entitled to help shape the Security Council's decision about Kosovo. I agree. So why is your foreign policy on this subject being made in Belgrade?"[6]

---

[5] July 2007 interview with Søren Jessen-Petersen, Geneva.
[6] March 2007 interview with Martti Ahtisaari, New York.

Despite his success as a peacemaker, Ahtisaari is tough. "He goes straight for the jugular," observed Albert Rohan. He knows that parties to a conflict often give ground only when their backs are to the wall, when a negotiated solution offers a better outcome than continuation of the conflict or waiting for some other diplomatic development. In South Africa, Ahtisaari endorsed military response to conduct by Namibian insurgents that threatened to derail the peace process there. He does not leap at diplomatic opportunities until he is sure there is some prospect for success. He insisted on deferring meetings with Milosevic over the NATO bombing in 1999 until he made sure he had broad European support and sufficient agreement to confront Milosevic with a united front.[7] He began his mediation of the Aceh conflict by warning that he did not intend to waste his time with them if they were not serious. He constantly prodded the Contact Group in the final status negotiations to be clear about the desired outcome and to communicate it clearly to Serbia. Once he knew that independence for Kosovo was the goal of the Quint (the non-Russian members of the Contact Group), he was forthright in telling the Serbs that fact – although this created the possibility for criticism that he had begun the negotiation process with his mind made up.

Despite this toughness, he does not fly solo when recruited for a difficult mission. After each of his notable successes, he regularly emphasized the essential contributions his handpicked team made to the outcome.

To his staff, Ahtisaari was avuncular. He enjoyed immense respect throughout Europe, and his younger staffers initially were in awe of him. Only a few days into her tenure as press spokesperson, Hua Jiang had been consistently calling him "Mr. Ahtisaari" or "President Ahtisaari." As Hua started to say it again, Ahtisaari extended his hand and said to her, "Let me introduce myself. My name is Martti Ahtisaari. You should call me 'Martti.'" Hua was stunned and completely disarmed.[8]

Ahtisaari was a master of knowing what and how much to say at meetings. Sometimes he would say virtually nothing and simply listen. Other times, he would say the bare minimum that protocol required, as in ceremonial meetings with institutions like the OSCE, which were eager to be involved in the final status negotiations but actually had little to contribute. Other times, when he thought it might make a difference in the dynamics of the meeting or the positions of the parties, he would speak at greater length, forcefully advocating a particular perspective on events. He would always ask his staff to prepare talking points in advance of meetings, but he rarely used them. He was a voracious reader, not only of all of the documents prepared in conjunction with the negotiations, but also of press reports, articles, and books. He almost always knew more about the subject under discussion than anyone else in the room – at least at the strategic level. This meant that he could react to the course of the discussion spontaneously, without fear that his words would come back

---

[7] February 2008 interview with Martti Ahtisaari, New York.
[8] June 2007 interview with Jiang Hua, New York.

to haunt him because of some nuance he had failed to appreciate at the time.

Once his appointment was finalized, Ahtisaari set up an office for UNOSEK in Vienna. Senior political adviser Kai Sauer described Ahtisaari's UNOSEK team as being like a family. For the most part Ahtisaari's staff members were detailed from other institutions, thereby removing the competition and rivalry that might have been natural if they had all been permanent employees of the UN. Deputy Special Envoy Albert Rohan had served as Secretary General of the Austrian Foreign Service and in a number of other diplomatic posts, including as ambassador to Argentina, director of the Executive Office of the UN Secretary General, and as Special Envoy of the Austrian Chairman in Office of OSCE. "Albert knew more about the Balkans than I did," says Ahtisaari. Kai Sauer became Ahtisaari's senior political adviser. Sauer was director of the Unit for Western Balkans in the Finnish Ministry for Foreign Affairs. He had served with UNMIK, as well as with the OSCE in Bosnia–Herzegovina, with the Finnish Embassy in Croatia, and with the Permanent Mission of Finland to the United Nations in New York.

Bernhard Schlagheck was a senior German diplomat with extensive expertise on decentralization, and former deputy head of UNMIK's Office for Political Affairs. Petr Ivantsov, a senior Russian diplomat, had been head of UNMIK's Office for Political Affairs since 1999, and became head of UNOSEK's Office of Political Affairs. Hua Jiang, who had served as the SRSG's public affairs officer, performed the same role for UNOSEK.

To ensure a coherent approach, UNOSEK established liaison arrangements with the U.S. State Department, the EU, and NATO. These institutions had representatives embedded in UNOSEK, and became integral members of the team. Russia had been offered a formal liaison representative, but had declined – so Ahtisaari was careful to recruit Ivantsov to the UNOSEK staff to tie Moscow into the process. These arrangements ensured a smooth flow of information and provided political backup for UNOSEK from these major players in other decision-making councils. The senior UNOSEK staff received regular intelligence briefings. The U.S. Central Intelligence Agency's (CIA) briefings were generally not helpful. British MI6's (the British intelligence service) were better, and the Slovenian intelligence service's often the best.

Several other governments tried to get their people into UNOSEK. Ahtisaari, through Sauer, resisted their efforts, wanting to keep his team small and efficient. Unknown personalities and political loyalties were not desirable.

Ahtisaari's relationship with Rohan was one of genuine partnership. The two had worked together in the 1970s, when Rohan was chef de cabinet for Secretary General Kurt Waldheim and Ahtisaari was the UN commissioner for Namibia. Rohan also had a good relationship with Secretary General Kofi Annan, who was the chief administrative officer when Rohan was director of the Executive Office of Secretary General Waldheim. The two knew each other well: both Ahtisaari and Rohan served on an advisory board for George

Soros's Open Society Institute. Ahtisaari chaired the Independent Commission on Turkey, and Rohan was the rapporteur for the commission. Once, when Ahtisaari was running for president of Finland, Rohan asked him, "I hear you are running for president. How is it going?" "It's going astonishingly well," responded Ahtisaari. "My advisers tell me that as long as I stay out of the country until the election, I will surely win."[9]

When the two agreed to work together in UNOSEK, they had no formal hierarchical arrangement; they were interchangeable. They sometimes played on status, however: Rohan would chair meetings that were "not at Ahtisaari's level," while Ahtisaari chaired meetings at the summit level. Based on their friendship and mutual esteem, however, they always operated on the same wavelength.

There were differences in style, to be sure: both men understood this and used the differences to further the negotiations. Ahtisaari was direct, sometimes brutally so; Rohan was more diplomatic. Ahtisaari was more standoffish with the press than Rohan, who had learned through his career that the press often were a valuable diplomatic tool. Rohan also had deeper knowledge of the details regarding Kosovo than Ahtisaari, whose earlier involvement had been limited to a higher international level.

As members of the UNOSEK team discussed plans for formal meetings with a host of other organizations, ranging from the Contact Group to the governments of smaller states to international press, the process was open and relaxed. Everyone on the staff consistently was invited not only to attend meetings but also to contribute freely. From the most junior staff member to the most senior, all felt free to offer a comment or a suggestion. Ahtisaari always listened carefully to what anyone had to say, and on occasion helped team members formulate their suggestions more crisply and express them more clearly. Ahtisaari seemed to consider it a personal achievement when a subordinate came up with a good idea.[10] His early training as a teacher showed admirably.

Some staff members characterized the relationship between Ahtisaari and others as "like father and son." On occasion there was disagreement between two staff members regarding the most appropriate course of action, as when Sauer and Jiang disagreed on Sauer's proposal that Ahtisaari hold a background briefing for the press. Ahtisaari was careful not to choose sides, which could have caused someone to lose face in the larger staff meeting context, but rather to follow up with a private meeting involving just Sauer and Jiang before rendering a judgment. Thus, all three of them could be made comfortable with the process and the decision.

It was not unusual for the staff to get excited or angry about some external development. On such occasions, Ahtisaari would say cheerfully, "Calm down,

---

[9] July 2007 interview with Albert Rohan, Vienna.
[10] June 2007 interview with Kai Sauer.

kids. This was to be expected, and we are strong enough and smart enough to work our way through this." The team never saw him flustered. When the Serbs unveiled a vicious ad-hominem attack on him in late 2006 and early 2007, demanding that he be replaced as special envoy, his reaction was a shrug and a comment: "I'm surprised it took them so long."

There was some awkward history between Bildt and Ahtisaari, growing out of the period when Ahtisaari, Chernomyrdin, and Milosevic worked to craft an agreement to end the NATO bombing campaign. Just as these mediation exercises were at their most critical point, UN Secretary General Kofi Annan inexplicably appointed Carl Bildt and Eduard Kukan, foreign minister of Slovakia, as UN special envoys to the process. There was nothing really for them to do, but the insertion of these entrepreneurial personalities threatened to interfere with the unity of Ahtisaari's mediation process. Ultimately the United States made sure they were sidelined. However, even on the occasion when staff members would rail at the inadequacies of individuals on the periphery – or at the center – of the final status process, Ahtisaari never joined in the private criticism. Instead, he would most often respond in the form, "Oh, you're being too harsh. He's not so bad; I've seen him at his best."

There were scores of meetings in which Ahtisaari was obligated to repeat almost exactly the same thing he had said in previous meetings. These repetitions became excruciatingly boring for the staff, in part because Ahtisaari is an enthusiastic storyteller, and would tell the same stories over and over again. Before long, the staff could know exactly which story was coming after the first two or three words. They would exchange glances and smiles, and whoever was taking notes would make an abbreviated entry signifying which story occurred at that point. They joked with each other about the recurring stories and even occasionally with Ahtisaari himself. "If you can come up with some better stories," Ahtisaari offered, "I'll tell them instead."[11]

Ahtisaari deeply believed in Europe's potential to be a leader of initiatives to enhance international peace and security but also understood that Europe has a center of gravity only with U.S. leadership.

---

[11] June 2007 interview with Kai Sauer and Hua Jiang, New York.

10 The Stage for Final Status

AS AHTISAARI'S APPOINTMENT WAS BEING FINALIZED IN NOVEM-
ber 2005, the members of the Contact Group (France, Germany,
Italy, Russian Federation, the UK, and the United States) issued
ten "Guiding Principles for a settlement of the Status of Kosovo" to support Ahtisaari's efforts.[1] These principles stated that any settlement should
strengthen regional security and stability, ensure Kosovo's multiethnicity, provide for protection of the cultural and religious heritage in Kosovo, and enable
Kosovo to cooperate effectively with international organizations and international financial institutions. They declared partition of Kosovo or its annexa-
tion to any other state unacceptable. The Contact Group position was popularly characterized as expressing "three no's": no partitioning of Kosovo, no
going back to the status before 1999, and no merging with other states.[2]

In recruiting Ahtisaari for the special envoy position, the Quint had not
yet officially committed itself to the goal of independence for Kosovo – and
Russia, as the sixth member of the Contact Group, certainly had not. On the
other hand, everyone including Ahtisaari agreed that there was no way that
Kosovo could be folded back under Serbian control, and they also agreed
that the status quo of international administration was not viable. Within the
Contact Group, Britain and the United States were pushing hardest for some
clear resolution of Kosovo's status and knew that independence would be the
outcome.

The challenge, all members of the Quint agreed, was to square the circle: to find some political and legal structure that would permit the people of
the region to coexist without violence. This almost certainly meant independence; the issue was how to get there. Any institutional arrangement needed
to be palatable to Russia, and to include sufficient constraint over democratic

---

[1] Guiding principles of the Contact Group for a settlement of the status of Kosovo located at http://www.unosek.org/docref/Contact%20Group%20-%20Ten%20Guiding%
20principles%20for%20Ahtisaari.pdf (October 7, 2005).

[2] Statement on the future of Kosovo after the Contact Group meeting held at ministerial
level in London – January 31, 2006, http://www.unosek.org/docref/fevrier/STATEMENT%
20BY%20THE%20CONTACT%20GROUP%20ON%20THE%20FUTURE%20OF%
20KOSOVO%20-%20Eng.pdf ("no return of Kosovo to the pre-1999 situation, no partition
of Kosovo, and no union of Kosovo with any or part of another country").

political power in Kosovo that the rights of Kosovo's Serbs would be protected. Just as importantly, the solution also had to be acceptable to Kosovo's Albanians. It probably would involve a staged approach, with international involvement gradually diminishing until the entire region was integrated into the EU. This approach came to be referred to as "supervised independence."[3] From the outset, however, the status process was perceived as a pathway to determining Kosovo's final status, and both Serbian and Kosovar participants regularly characterized it as focusing on independence.

"You have lost Kosovo," Ahtisaari said directly to Serb leaders in Belgrade in November 2005. "The challenge now is how to clean up Milosevic's mess. The best way to do it is with your leadership." Koštunica's response – "No one has told me that" – reinforced Ahtisaari's convictions that a consistent message needed to be communicated to Serbian leadership about the range of feasible outcomes from the status process.

The two parties most directly concerned – Serbia and Kosovo – had diametrically different views of Ahtisaari's role. Serbia had steadfastly opposed beginning the final status process in 2005, arguing that Kosovo had to make further progress toward meeting Steiner's "standards before status" benchmarks. Serbia hoped that the Ahtisaari process would highlight Kosovo's unreadiness to have its future status determined. In any event, Belgrade was completely opposed to any movement toward independence for Kosovo. The Albanian-dominated government of Kosovo, on the other hand, saw the Ahtisaari process as a direct pathway to independence and expected to achieve that goal no later than the end of 2006.

International decisions regarding Kosovo had never been determined by legal analysis, because all those decisions have always been political in the end. Law, however, empowers rhetoric and political argument, so it was relevant. Russia and Serbia presented a number of legal arguments against imposed independence, arguing that only negotiated changes to state boundaries are permissible. This argument proceeds from each state's obligation under Article 2(3) and (4) of the UN Charter to settle disputes peacefully; likewise, Article 33 obligates states to settle any dispute that endangers international peace and security by negotiation or other peaceful means. The Commission on Security and Cooperation in Europe stated in the 1975 Helsinki Final Act that frontiers could be changed only through peaceful means and settlement.[4]

---

[3] IICK Report at 272 (Kosovo can only aspire to conditional independence, supervised by international community).

[4] Conference on Security and Co-operation in Europe, Helsinki Final Act art. 3–4 (August 1 1975), located at http://www.hri.org/docs/Helsinki75.html#H4.3 (frontiers "inviolable;" territorial integrity to be respected); see Enver Hasani, *Self-Determination, Territorial Integrity, and International Stability: The Case of Yugoslavia* 119–22 (2003) (explaining politics of formulating the Helsinki Determination statement on inviolability of state boundaries; although not legally binding, the Determination had considerable impact on European attitudes toward self-determination).

Indeed, the Contact Group's guiding principles for a settlement of Kosovo's status emphasized a negotiated, rather than imposed, solution.

Russia and Serbia argued that the principle of self-determination did not allow portions of states to secede over the objection of the overarching state controlling their territory. Outside the colonial context, no state formed since 1945 had been admitted to the United Nations over the objection of the overarching state. International law, they said, did not permit self-determination to trump state sovereignty, because a contrary rule would be completely disruptive to the existing international, state-based, system of law. In addition, in the 1986 *Burkina Faso in Mali* case,[5] the International Court of Justice emphasized the sanctity of existing frontiers, even when new states were formed out of colonial regimes. The Badinter Commission similarly honored state boundaries as Yugoslavia broke up: it recommended allowing new states to be formed along the boundaries of existing republics in Yugoslavia,[6] recognizing that republics had the power to secede under the Yugoslav constitution. It declined, however, to consider the possibility that Kosovo could become an independent state, because Kosovo was not a republic under that constitution.[7]

Russia and Serbia argued that UN Security Council Resolution 1244 did not recognize the possibility of Kosovo's independence. Although Resolution 1244 envisioned a process for determining Kosovo's final status, it spoke of that status as "autonomy" and "self administration," which implied continued Serbian sovereignty as the context.

Proponents of independence presented opposing legal arguments: first and most fundamentally, they said, Serbia had forfeited its right to govern Kosovo by breaching its *responsibility to protect* – an emerging principle of international law that obligates a sovereign to shield its citizens from violence and human rights violations.[8] The Serbian government not only had failed to shield

---

[5] Frontier Dispute (Burkina Faso/Republic of Mali), 1986 I.C.J. 554 (December 22).

[6] Conference on Yugoslavia Arbitration Commission: *Opinions on Questions Arising from the Dissolution of Yugoslavia*, 31 I.L.M. 1488, 1499–1500 (1992) (stating that boundaries of newly independent states of the former SFRY must not be altered except by agreement freely arrived at and that former boundaries were to become frontiers protected by international law). See Hasani at 267–73 (explaining political and legal context of Badinter Commission decision making).

[7] See Richard Caplan, *Europe and the Recognition of New States in Yugoslavia* 70 (2005) (noting Badinter's rejection of Kosovo's and other sub-federal units claim to self-determination and characterizing it as based on a "novel" distinction); id. at 139 (reporting on basis for rejection of request for recognition of independence submitted to EU by Kosovo authorities in December 1991); Hasani at 236–8 (detailing early unsuccessful efforts by Albanian authorities in Kosovo to persuade international community to accept Kosovo's legal right to become independent as Yugoslavia broke up).

[8] See *The Responsibility to Protect:* Report of the International Commission on Intervention and State Sovereignty (December 2001); Christopher C. Joyner, "'The Responsibility to Protect': Humanitarian Concern and the Lawfulness of Armed Intervention," 47 *Va. J. Int'l L.* 693, 703–10 (2007) (describing emergency of doctrine of "responsibility to protect" as an attribute of sovereignty in international law); Vesselin Popovski, "Sovereignty as

the Kosovar Albanian population, it was the source of a program of violence organized to drive them out of their homeland. This breach entitled the international community to intervene and to take such action as might be necessary to preserve international peace and security.

The Responsibility to Protect document was summarized by an international commission established by the government of Canada:

(1) Basic Principles
A. State sovereignty implies responsibility, and the primary responsibility for the protection of its people lies with the state itself.
B. Where a population is suffering serious harm, as a result of internal war, insurgency, repression or state failure, and the state in question is unwilling or unable to halt or avert it, the principle of non-intervention yields to the international responsibility to protect.[9]

The commission report has had significant influence on discussion of the principles it articulated. Many have accepted it as an emerging principle of international law,[10] but some have questioned its legal status.[11]

Duty to Protect Human Rights," *UN Chronicle Online Edition*, December 1, 2004, located at http://www.un.org/Pubs/chronicle/2004/issue4/0404p16.html. See also Stephan A. Wangsgard, "Secession, Humanitarian Intervention, and Clear Objectives: When to Commit United States Military Forces," 3 *Tulsa J. Comp. and Int'l Law* 313 (1996) (arguing that self-determination evolved from a weak norm in the Aland Islands case into a limited power when regime violates human rights). In the Aland Islands case, the League of Nations International Committee of Jurists refused to find self-determination to be a positive rule of the Law of Nations. It rejected secession by the Aland Islands in an advisory opinion. The population of the Islands favored union with Sweden although the Islands were claimed by Finland. Salvatore Massa, "Secession by Mutual Assent: A Comparative Analysis of the Dissolution of Czechoslovakia and the Separatist Movement in Canada," 14 *Wis. Int'l L. J.* 183, 212–13 (1995) (analyzing Aland Islands case and concluding that self-determination is a relatively weak norm in international law).

[9] *The Responsibility to Protect*, Report of the International Commission on Intervention and State Sovereignty, xi (2001).

[10] See Christopher C. Joyner, "'The Responsibility to Protect': Humanitarian Concern and the Lawfulness of Armed Intervention," 47 *Va. J. Int'l Law* 693, 704–5 (2007) (responsibility to protect has evolved from mere aspirations to a norm in the process of becoming a legal principle); Gareth Evans, "From Humanitarian Intervention to the Responsibility to Protect," 24 *Wis. Int'l L. J.* 703, 704 (2006) (international community is close to consensus on the emergence of a new international norm, one that may ultimately become a new rule of customary international law) Evans was co-chair of the Commission. See also Rebecca J. Hamilton, "The Responsibility to Protect: From Document to Doctrine – But What of Implementation?" 19 *Harv. Hum. Rts J.* 289, 293 (2006) (surveying reaction to report; concluding that its contents infiltrate almost all discussions of humanitarian crises); Alicia L. Bannon, "The Responsbility to Protect: The UN World Summit and the Question of Unilateralism," 115 *Yale L. J.* 1157, 1158 (2006) (reporting on results of United Nations 2005 World Summit, concluding that Responsibility to Protect privileges limited forms of unilateral and regional action).

[11] See Carsten Stahn, "Responsibility to Protect: Political Rhetoric or Emerging Legal Norm?," 101 *Am. J. Int'l L.* 99, 102 (2007) ("concept currently encompasses a spectrum of different normative propositions that vary considerably in their status and degree of legal support").

Although the norm is focused on circumstances in which intervention into the affairs of a sovereign state is permissible, it implicitly recognizes the limits of sovereignty and thus logically supports loss of sovereignty over a territory systematically victimized by a breach of the duty to protect its population.

Second, said proponents, depriving Kosovo of independence threatened international peace and security by perpetuating a continuing source of conflict and violence. The UN Charter gives the Security Council great flexibility in determining what means are appropriate to protect international peace and security, and the Security Council regularly had addressed boundary questions in order to deal with threats.[12]

Third they argued, a close reading of Security Council Resolution 1244 showed that the words *autonomy*, *self-administration*, and *self-government* were used in the context of the interim arrangement for Kosovo pending a final settlement. The Resolution thus did not foreclose any option for the final status of Kosovo.

Beyond these arguments was the long-standing, generally accepted principle that one of the hallmarks of statehood is governmental control over the territory defining the state. Sovereignty and statehood depend in part on the ability of the government of the purported state to exercise effective control over the state itself, such that it can enter into enforceable agreements with other states.[13] During Kosovo's period of de facto independence under UNMIK, Serbia had not been exerting effective control over Kosovo, and could not do so in the future. To be sure, Security Council Resolution 1244 recites in its preamble that Serbian sovereignty extends to Kosovo for the duration of the UNMIK civil administration and KFOR security missions. Serbia and Russia interpreted it to extend Serbian sovereignty over Kosovo until Resolution 1244 is repealed or replaced by the Security Council. Regardless of the interpretation of the Serbian-sovereignty provision of the preamble, however, Serbia had not exercised control over the territory of Kosovo for nine years when independence was declared. Serbia withdrew all of its sovereign institutions from Kosovo as a condition for ending the NATO bombing campaign.[14] Nor did it have any reasonable prospect of exercising traditional governmental

---

[12] See General Assembly Resolution 181 (1947) (defining the boundary between the Jewish and Arab states within Palestine); other examples include the establishment of the Iraq–Kuwait Boundary Demarcation Commission in 1991 under Security Council Resolution 687 (1991); U.S. Security Council Resolution 1272 (1999) (establishing a transitional administration in East Timor that resulted in the independence of that territory).

[13] See Montevideo Convention on the Rights and Duties of States (December 26, 1933), located at http://www.cfr.org/publication/15897/montevideo_convention_on_the_rights_and_duties_of_states.html.

[14] NATO, Military Technical Agreement between the International Security Force ("KFOR") and the Governments of the Federal Republic of Yugoslavia and the Republic of Serbia ("Kumanovo Agreement") (June 9, 1999) art. II ¶§2 (providing for withdrawal of Serbian forces from Kosovo), located at http://www.nato.int/kosovo/docu/a990609a.htm.

control over the territory, even if UNMIK and KFOR pulled out before independence was declared.

Therefore, with respect to this hallmark of sovereignty considered by itself, Serbia was not sovereign in Kosovo on the day before Independence Day.

Many of the arguments focused on whether the Security Council had the power to impose independence over Serbian objections. The strongest relevant principle of international law defines statehood not in terms of a grant from the Security Council, but in terms of certain political realities. This principle states that, in order to become a state, a territory must be contiguous; it must comprise a population that has formally declared its desire to be independent; and it must have institutions capable of exercising governmental control over the territory.[15] Once these institutions declare independence – a unilateral act – then the territory becomes a state when, and only when, other states recognize it. International law provides no magic quantitative threshold for recognition; rather, a new state is born when the realities of international power – military, political, and economic – allow the new state to be viable.[16] International law ultimately tossed the ball back to political and diplomatic arenas.

Ahtisaari knew he was taking on a difficult assignment, and his experience had taught him that, in any negotiation, the positions of stakeholders are guided by their perceptions of their interests. Any agreement, whether explicit or imposed and acquiesced to, must fulfill the overlapping interests of all parties.

He also knew that any negotiation over a difficult issue takes place in the face of uncertainty about mutually undesirable outcomes. The science of negotiations teaches that any party's position in a negotiation is determined by its perceived "best alternative to negotiated agreement."[17] In the context of Ahtisaari's mission, "negotiated agreement" did not refer to a negotiated agreement between Belgrade and Pristina – everyone understood that agreement was most likely impossible. Instead, those terms referred to a course of action such as putting a plan for Kosovo's final status to a vote in the Security Council and thereby risking a Russian veto, or encouraging Kosovo to declare independence followed by some states' recognizing independence. Each of these scenarios would in some sense be a negotiated one because a consensus – or

[15] Montevideo Convention. See also Alain Pellet, "The Opinions of the Badinter Arbitration Committee: A Second Breath for the Self-Determination of Peoples," 3 *E. J. I. L.* 178 (1992), located at http://www.ejil.org/journal/Vol3/No1/art12–13.pdf (analyzing attributes and limitations of sovereignty).

[16] See Caplan at 57 (criticizing "declaratory" view of statehood, which says that recognition simply acknowledges that statehood exists; that view ignores inescapably political and normative dimensions of state creation; acknowledging, however that opposing "constitutive" view may leave too much to political discretion).

[17] Roger Fisher, Bruce M. Patton, and William L. Ury, *Getting to Yes* (2nd ed. 1992) (explaining BATNA concept).

at least multistate support – would be necessary to allow the vote, and might prove necessary before the United States and others would be willing to recognize a unilateral declaration of independence.

Uncertainty always exists with respect to the alternatives to a negotiated agreement, and human nature being what it is, negotiators often are unduly optimistic that the alternative will favor their side. Optimism often results from the belief that, with the passage of time, external developments will strengthen a party's position. Delaying a decision is almost always an alternative. Although failing to negotiate a solution may well worsen the terms of the final resolution, postponement can be rationalized in the hopes that the alternatives will improve – the downsides will be less bad. In Kosovo deliberations, the temptation of delay was a formidable barrier to success. Both Russia and Serbia knew that. So did Ahtisaari.

Ahtisaari's challenge was to create momentum toward implementing a plan for independence that commanded maximum support from members of the Security Council, which would be responsible for imposing it. However, politics and the dynamics of the negotiation process were not all that mattered; the content of the plan mattered as well. Ahtisaari was determined that any solution he mediated, and any recommendation he made to the Security Council for an imposed solution, be functional. He believed that the solution imposed in Bosnia looked fine on paper but was impracticable to execute on the ground. Under the 1995 Dayton Accords, Bosnia enjoyed sovereignty, but was split into two "entities," one – Republika Srpska – dominated by Bosnian Serbs, and the other controlled by an uneasy alliance of Bosnian Muslims and Croats. An international High Representative exercised a veto power over legislation and could remove political officials. In Ahtisaari's opinion, Republika Srpska was too separate, and the thin layer of international supervision allowed too much political autonomy for squabbling Bosnian factions to make any real progress. Ahtisaari was convinced that the Bosnian compromise would not be functional for Kosovo.

Ahtisaari, however, accepted the reality that governmental administration in Kosovo already was decentralized to a considerable extent. No plan that sought to roll back Kosovo Serb self-government in areas of Kosovo where Serbs predominated would be workable.[18] Already, UNMIK and the PISG had devoted considerable attention to decentralizing governmental power in Kosovo, to allow areas with heavy concentrations of Kosovo Serbs a measure of self-government and political power. Kosovo Serbs also wanted ties between their communities and the Serbian government in Belgrade. Such an approach probably would prove to be the best way to protect Kosovo Serbs from a Pristina government that inevitably would be dominated by Kosovar Albanians. Nevertheless, too much decentralization and autonomy would make Kosovo ungovernable by anyone.

---

[18] Interview with Martii Ahtisaari, August 2008, Geneva.

Ahtisaari recognized that negotiations over Kosovo's final status took place in a very different geopolitical environment than the one that framed 1999's NATO intervention that he had helped guide to a conclusion. In 1999, the United States was riding a wave of confidence about the efficacy of its military power and political leadership, reinforced by the stunning military success of the first Iraq war and by the American perception that the conflict in Bosnia had been brought to a conclusion only after the United States asserted its leadership in international relations. At that time almost everyone, whether discomfited by U.S. "exceptionalism" or not, still believed that a "new world order," to use President H. W. Bush's phrase, was under construction. The 1999 intervention in Kosovo was an important symbolic step in that direction.

By 2006 and 2007, 1999-era confidence in the ability of the great powers to nurture democratization and to control events by relying on U.S. military leadership had receded considerably. The United States was bogged down in a quagmire in Iraq, uncertain how to extricate itself. It obviously needed help from other major states in dealing with the possibility that North Korea and Iran were about to emerge as significant nuclear powers. In addition, major segments of the U.S. political leadership and public opinion were embarrassed by the arrogance displayed by the Bush administration in the run-up to the second Iraq war, and hoped that it was possible to prove that the United States could still be a reliable partner in international affairs. Nevertheless, a muscular assertiveness continued to shape the way the Bush administration thought U.S. power and influence should be used. The combination of the remaining assertiveness and the desire once again to act multilaterally could be a potent force. It meant, in the context of final status, that the U.S. administration was willing to field some of its most experienced diplomats regardless of political and ideological identification. It also meant that the United States was willing to shape its policy to accommodate major concerns by the EU and, ultimately, Russia. It also meant, however, that the United States might be willing – and certainly was perceived as willing – to act unilaterally to recognize Kosovo independence if the international mechanisms for the UN failed to produce a satisfactory result.

Russia, still part of the Contact Group, had withdrawn its troops from KFOR in July 2003, signaling possible moderation in its hard-line position that Kosovo's status as part of Serbia must be protected. Russia in 2006, however, was a very different entity than the Russia of 1999. In 1999, Russia was at the nadir of its power and felt powerless, lost in a leadership vacuum. Vladimir Putin's Russia was assertive and determined to return to the center of the world stage. The other members of the Contact Group were hopeful that in 2006 a plan for Kosovo could be crafted in the West and sold to Russia with persuasive diplomacy.

The need for decisive international action felt far less urgent in 2006 than in 1999, however. There is nothing like an active war to support the perception of crisis: in 1999, images of massive refugee flows filled Western television

screens, and leaders in the United States, Europe, and Russia were all franti-
cally trying to figure out some way to stop the shooting war that had gone on
far longer than anyone expected. By contrast, Kosovo in 2006 was outwardly
peaceful. Outside Serbia, Kosovo was off the front page.

Nevertheless, Ahtisaari and the Contact Group believed after March 2004
that the status quo could not long remain, and that independence probably
would prove to be the only path forward. Of paramount concern was stability
in the Balkans, with the ultimate goal of integrating the Balkans into Europe.
Ahtisaari believed that even Serbia and Russia could be brought around to
accepting the inevitability of independence, although he did not believe either
would embrace it. Nevertheless, he felt both nations would acquiesce if an
independent Kosovo respected the rights and aspirations of Kosovo's Serbs.

Ahtisaari faced several challenges, and he had to meet all of them: first,
he had to bring Russia along so that it would not veto his recommendation
to the Security Council. He had to blunt Serbian opposition so that it would
not be persuasive with Russia or with those European states perched on the
fence. He had to extract meaningful concrete concessions from the Kosovar
Albanians. He had to manage intra-European politics so that Europe would
go to the Security Council united behind his plan. And he had to keep the
United States on board by working for a final resolution of Kosovo's status.

The Serbian strategy from the beginning of the final status negotiations
was driven by rejection of the legitimacy of the process altogether. Jessen-
Petersen, who adhered to a priority of reaching out to the Serbs, discovered that once he had embraced the need to begin final status talks, the
Serbs treated him as their enemy. They would not engage him seriously, and
Belgrade put enormous pressure on Kosovo Serbs who were tempted to talk
to him.

The Serb strategy was framed by four D's: delay, destabilize, divide, and
discredit. One after another, Serbia seized on every possible reason for delaying the final status process as long as possible. Meanwhile, Belgrade did its best
to destabilize security in Kosovo, on the grounds that violence or other threats
to security in Kosovo would sour the international community on Kosovo's
fitness for independence. Maximum diplomatic efforts were made to divide
the Contact Group, and were reinforced by a public relations campaign. The
Serbian goal was to peel Russia away from the rest of the Contact Group, and
then to divide the European Union and to drive a wedge between the United
States and the EU. Simultaneously, Serbian diplomats did their best to discredit Martti Ahtisaari as an honest broker.[19]

Ahtisaari was sanguine about Serbian intransigence. He had confronted
it head on when he helped Russia and the West end the NATO bombing

---

[19] See Mikhail Yambaev, "Whom Does the Future of the Balkans Depend On?," Strategic Culture Foundation, located at http://en.fondsk.ru/article.php?id=842 (July 11, 2007) (reporting
Serbian charges that Ahtisaari had financial problems and received illicit money from Pacolli).

campaign by overcoming Milošević's resistance to withdrawal from Kosovo. No one believed that the Serbian government could be persuaded to make Kosovo independent itself. The best that could be done would be to give sufficient attention to Serbia's expressed concerns about Kosovo: protection of Kosovo Serbs, maintenance of links between Kosovo Serb communities and Belgrade, and protection of historic religious sites, so that some or all of Serbia's top political leadership would become unwilling to invest all their political capital in opposing independence. Also, Ahtisaari calculated that a good plan addressing Serbian interests in Kosovo would dilute some popular support in Serbia for extreme nationalist positions. At the same time, the Contact Group had to make it clear to Serbia that Kosovar independence was inevitable, and it was therefore in Serbia's interest to devote its energies to formulating the most favorable elements of the institutional framework for independence.

However inexperienced, the political leadership in Kosovo was enthusiastic about commencing the Ahtisaari process and they were prepared to be cooperative, because they believed that Ahtisaari was charting a course toward independence. The expectations in Kosovo were overblown, however. Most ordinary Kosovar Albanian citizens – and much of the more sophisticated political leadership – expected that independence would be handed to Kosovo. Unless independence was relatively immediate and relatively unconditional, the Kosovar political leadership would have difficulty in managing public opinion. Virtually all of them had promised that independence would occur by the end of 2006. The most salient question, therefore, was not whether the major Kosovar leaders would cooperate with Ahtisaari and the Contact Group, but rather whether they could deliver independence by the end of 2006 and, if not, whether they could maintain sufficient credibility with the Kosovar public to provide any relevant leadership at all.

The manner of Haradinaj's exit from the office of prime minister had been better than the alternative, but it still left a vacuum in the Kosovar Albanian political leadership. Rugova was unwilling to reform the government coalition to include Thaçi, while Haradinaj's AAK had no leadership talent to replace Haradinaj himself. Bajram Kosumi, Haradinaj's handpicked successor, never really gained political traction and committed a number of small but embarrassing gaffes, such as accepting favors from rich businesspeople. Worried about this leadership vacuum, SRSG Jessen-Petersen persuaded the ICTY[20] to take the unprecedented step of releasing Haradinaj from confinement in June 2005 so that he could support the political process in Kosovo, albeit under tight UNMIK control.

---

[20] ICTY, *Prosecutor v. Haradinaj*, Case No. IT-04–84-PT, (decision granting provisional release, June 6, 2005) ¶¶ 10 & 13 referring to formal submissions by UNMIK guaranteeing compliance by Haradinaj with terms of provisional release).

That left the problem of Thaçi. How could the international community keep the breach between Thaçi and Haradinaj from poisoning effective Kosovar Albanian participation in the final status process? The international community, led by SRSG Søren Jessen-Petersen and U.S. Chief of Mission Phillip Goldberg, decided to forge a Kosovar *Unity Team*, a kind of parallel governmental coalition that included Thaçi but was chaired nominally by Rugova – who was in fact critically ill with late-stage lung cancer. For the time being, the Unity Team forestalled further fragmentation of Kosovar Albanian political structures. It was particularly successful in bringing Thaçi inside the tent. Indeed, it was reasonable to regard Thaçi as the dominant member of the Unity Team, given the restraints on Haradinaj's open participation in governmental institutions and Rugova's illness and subsequent death. The Unity Team was a backdoor way of reestablishing a grand coalition that included Thaçi. Still, political immaturity in Kosovo's local institutions presented challenges, and the gap between popular expectations in Kosovo and the real need for compromise and concession had to be monitored closely.

Ultimately, the final status of Kosovo would not be determined by either Serbia or Kosovo; it would be determined by the great powers and international institutions. The most powerful of the great powers was, of course, the United States.

U.S. participation in final status negotiations was led by three experienced, knowledgeable, and widely respected diplomats. R. Nicholas Burns was the Under Secretary of State for Political Affairs, the Department of State's third ranking official, and the senior career Foreign Service official at the Department. Prior to his assignment in Kosovo, he was the United States' Permanent Representative to the North Atlantic Treaty Organization, U.S. Ambassador to Greece, on the National Security Council staff at the White House, and Director for Soviet (and then Russian) Affairs.

Rosemary DiCarlo was Deputy Assistant Secretary of State in the Bureau of European and Eurasian Affairs, a career member of the Senior Foreign Service. She previously served as Director for United Nations Affairs at the National Security Council and as the Washington Deputy to the U.S. Permanent Representative to the United Nations. She also served as U.S. Coordinator for Stability Pact Implementation (Southeast Europe) in two assignments at the U.S. Embassy in Moscow. Before joining the Foreign Service, Ms. DiCarlo was a member of the Secretariat of the the United Nations Educational, Scientific and Cultural Organization (UNESCO).

Frank G. Wisner was appointed as the U.S. Secretary of State's Special Envoy for Kosovo Final Status Talks on December 19, 2005. Wisner had been a Foreign Service Officer since December 1961; he served in Vietnam, and became Director of the Office of Southern African Affairs in July 1976, where he first worked with Ahtisaari. He was Under-Secretary of State for International Security Affairs and then Ambassador to India, and also served as Under Secretary of Defense for Policy. After he retired from the Foreign

Service in 1997 with the rank of Career Ambassador, he joined the American International Group as Vice Chairman, External Affairs. Wisner was diplomatic with everyone but never allowed doubt to develop about the U.S. position: support for Ahtisaari and his recommendations, explicitly including independence for Kosovo.

Anna Mansfield, of the State Department Legal Adviser's office, regularly participated in providing legal support to Wisner, alongside Joshua Black, Desk Officer for Kosovo, on the diplomatic side. Both of them also provided support to UNOSEK, spending many months in Vienna as members of the UNOSEK team. Wisner and senior European diplomats had great confidence in both.

The United States had been the most steadfast supporter of beginning final status negotiations and pushing them to an early conclusion. There was no ambivalence in public statements of the U.S. position or in its participation in the Contact Group. There was reason to doubt, however, how far the United States would push matters if it got into loggerheads with Russia or the EU. There was some disagreement between the State Department and the National Security Council staff on U.S. priorities: NSC experts on Russia and on Europe could conclude that independence for Kosovo was not worth a major breach with Russia or with the EU. In addition, it would be hard for the United States to implement a Kosovo policy opposed by the EU; Kosovo was in Europe, after all, not in Kansas.

Although there were occasional rumors of disagreement within the U.S. team, the White House unequivocally assigned the Kosovo issue to the State Department and, whenever it counted, relied on State. Wisner reports that the U.S. government was more unified on Kosovo's final status than on any issue he could remember, but not without constant debate, review, and reconfirmation of the U.S. position through the National Security Council with State, the CIA, the Joint Chiefs of Staff, and the president participating. Congressional leadership was regularly involved. "This administration has been quite good in its handling of Kosovo," Ahtisaari said, in mid-2008.

The only sniping was from the NSC staff, motivated by a healthy skepticism about whether Kosovo's independence was worth the long-term alienation of Serbia. Yet these questions were never a threat to the three policy principles that the United States would support Ahtisaari, that it would support the Troika, and that independence was the only conceivable status for Kosovo. There was no significant criticism of these principles from Capitol Hill; on the contrary, Joe Biden, Chairman of the Senate Foreign Relations Committee (and later Vice President of the United States), forthrightly supported independence for Kosovo and U.S. leadership of the effort to achieve independence. "We made sure that Democrats who had been actively involved in the Kosovo crisis of 1999 were kept informed of our efforts," says Wisner. "This was a genuinely bi-partisan U.S. position." In the process, the Serbian lobby was nearly invisible. Senator Vojinovic, for example, never drew a hard line or expended real political capital on the issue, although he raised questions in public hearings.

Russia's interests regarding final status negotiations initially were opaque. Most knowledgeable observers believed that Russia's approach to final status negotiations was driven primarily by a desire to demonstrate its revived influence in the region, thus rebounding from what it saw as a low point in its influence when the initial intervention in Kosovo occurred in 1999. Moreover, individual Russian policy makers still smarted from the slights of 1999. Foreign Minister Lavrov, for example, was Russia's ambassador to the UN in 1999 and is thought to have felt handled roughly when the NATO bombing campaign was arranged and executed. There was also a Russian sense that it was "payback time" for the United States' aiding accession of Baltic and Eastern European nations to NATO, as well as U.S. involvement in Russia's own sphere of influence: the Caucasus Region, Ukraine, and Georgia.

Still, Russia seemed to be on board with Ahtisaari at first. In September 2004, Lavrov had told SRSG Jessen-Petersen, "We know that Kosovo is lost, but we need to talk about Abkhazia, Ossetia, Transnistria, Karabakh, and a few other places." In November 2005, Lavrov told Jessen-Petersen that he had warned the Serbs in Belgrade, "Do not isolate yourselves," and he also had told them, "Do not expect Russia to join you in isolation." At every step of the way toward development of the Ahtisaari plan, beginning with the decision to undertake a comprehensive review in mid-2005, Russia complained and objected, but eventually agreed on what the other members of the Contact Group wanted to do, in exchange for some usually innocuous concession to Russian sensibilities, which always was written into the policy decision under consideration.

The rest of the Contact Group repeatedly insisted on a clear declaration that Kosovo could never become part of Serbia again, and the Russians agreed to the formulation, "Kosovo cannot go back to its pre-1999 status."[21] With that compromise in wording, there were no quibbles about Ahtisaari's mission. By the January 2006 London ministerial meeting, Western members of the Contact Group were pushing hard for a public statement that any solution must be "acceptable to the people of Kosovo." The Quint was encouraged that Russia had joined the Contact Group in including the phrase in the criteria for the outcome of final status negotiations: all players understood that "people of Kosovo" meant the majority Kosovar Albanians, and that independence was

---

[21] Statement on the future of Kosovo after the Contact Group meeting held at ministerial level in London – January 31, 2006, located at http://www.unosek.org/docref/fevrier/STATEMENT%20BY%20THE%20CONTACT%20GROUP%20ON%20THE%20FUTURE%20OF%20KOSOVO%20-%20Eng.pdf ("no return of Kosovo to the pre-1999 situation").

the only outcome "acceptable" to them. Russia agreed privately but was skittish about saying so publicly; it eventually agreed on a formal Contact Group statement to that effect.[22]

Ahtisaari was no novice when it came to the whirlpools of Russian politics on issues relating to Kosovo. His experience in the 1999 negotiations to end the NATO bombing campaign taught him that Russia often started with a hard, unyielding position but would give ground at the last minute when confronted with an inevitable outcome. The 1999 experience also highlighted for him the internal tensions that often define Russian positions. His strategy for bringing Russia along was to include it in every possible way in the process so that Russia would have ownership of Ahtisaari's final recommendations, rather than feeling that it had been kept on the sidelines and presented with something on a take-it-or-leave-it basis. He also hoped that Russia would evaluate institutional arrangements for protecting the Kosovo Serbs on their own merits. If Russia thought everything possible had been done to address legitimate Serbian interests in Kosovo – other than maintenance of its sovereignty – then Ahtisaari hoped Russia would be less inclined to support Serbian intransigence with a Security Council veto. He extended an olive branch to Russia by including a Russian representative in UNOSEK, while helping the Contact Group maintain its resolve to be explicit with Russia that the only viable outcome of final status negotiations was independence. He never failed to point out, however, that Serbia could not be expected to agree to this outcome. The effort to include Russia fully had already begun in Contact Group discussions.

Russia's diplomatic effort was led by a cluster of experienced diplomats. Sergey Lavrov was the Russian Minister of Foreign Affairs. He was a career diplomat, having served as Russia's Permanent Representative to the UN before his present position and was at the UN during the 1999 NATO bombing campaign. Vladimir Titov was Deputy Foreign Minister, overseeing relations with European countries. He had served in the Ministry since 1980 as Russia's ambassador to Bulgaria among other things. Vitaly Churkin was Russia's Permanent Representative to the UN. He was a career diplomat, having served as Deputy Foreign Minister and as First Secretary in Russia's Embassy in Washington. Igor N. Shcherbak was Churkin's deputy. He also was a career diplomat, having served in a variety of senior positions in the Russian mission to the UN in Geneva, as deputy head of OSCE missions to Croatia and Yugoslavia, and as deputy director of the Department of International Organizations in the Ministry. Shcherbak was an important back channel between UNOSEK and the Russian government, although as time went on, his

---

[22] See Statement of the Contact Group after first Pristina-Belgrade High-level meeting held in Vienna – July 24, 2006, located at http://www.unosek.org/docref/Statement_of_the_ Contact_Group_after_first_Pristina-Belgrade_High-level_meeting_held_in_Vienna.pdf ("all possible efforts should be made to achieve a negotiated settlement in the course of 2006 that is, inter alia, acceptable to the people of Kosovo").

relatively soft messages clashed with Russia's public positions and actual behavior. Ambassador Aleksanar Botshan-Khartshenko was Special Envoy to the Western Balkans.

Kosovo often was characterized as a problem mainly for the European Union: German Political Director Michael Schäfer declared Kosovo "a vital security interest of Europe." Although the members of the European Union cared deeply about demonstrating the capacity of the EU to act effectively and in concerted fashion, they had to overcome divergent individual approaches to the Balkans. Although diplomats involved with Kosovo tend to talk about "the European position," and "Europe's concerns," there was no common European position or set of concerns. Britain supported independence, as did France explicitly after Sarkozy's election. Germany was ambivalent but assured a leadership position. Many smaller European states had major doubts. The EU was in a period of uncertainty and anxiety following 2005's failed ratification of the draft EU Constitution in both France and the Netherlands, and the admission of new members from Central and Eastern Europe. The angst was magnified by skepticism in Poland and Hungary about their own newly acquired EU membership.

The goal of European unity should not be underestimated. Not only the biggest European states – Germany and France – but also the smaller and newer EU member states perceived an effective European Union as a central pillar in their long-term economic and political security strategies. They all knew that Europe had yet to prove its capacity to pursue a robust foreign policy – and that Kosovo offered the best opportunity to do that. Determination of final status through the UN-brokered process provided an opportunity for the EU to demonstrate its capacity to act effectively in foreign policy and to put together and carry out operational missions in support of the UN. This was also an opportunity for the EU to work productively with the United States and Russia in a multilateral context. Everyone in the diplomatic community had been shaken by the Bush administration's disdain for multilateralism in the run-up to the war in Iraq; at the same time, transatlantic interests were undeniably intertwined, and those shared interests provided a push on both sides of the Atlantic to demonstrate that Europe and America could work together again.

In almost no case were the doubters concerned about the actual merits of a solution for Kosovo, according to one senior European diplomat intimately involved in the negotiations. To be sure, there was an undercurrent of opinion that moving too quickly to grant Kosovo independence would create a failed state in the middle of the Balkans; Carl Bildt was an active proponent of this view. Cyprus, however, was preoccupied about the future of northern Cyprus. Hungary was concerned that independence for Kosovo would produce a flood of Serb refugees into Vojvodina (the other autonomous province in Serbia). Earlier, Serb refugees from Croatia and Bosnia had radicalized interethnic politics there to the detriment of the large Hungarian population. Many

European states approached the question of Kosovo's future relative to their own intractable ethnic problems. Romania was concerned only about Transylvania, Spain about the Basques, and Greece about its client Cyprus. Each nation single-mindedly pursued its own interests "while babbling about European unity," in the words of one senior negotiator.

Managing these divergent concerns fell mostly to Britain, France, and Germany, and to senior diplomats representing EU institutions. Germany and France were the founders of the European Union, and the leaders of both states had long been committed to nurturing the EU's development. The attitudes of these two key states toward Serbia, however, had been disparate.

A month after Ahtisaari was appointed, in November 2005, a new government took office in Germany under Chancellor Angela Merkel. Merkel faced conflicting domestic pressures over Kosovo. Major figures within the German Intelligence Service and Foreign Ministry supported independence for Kosovo. Historically, Germany had opposed Serbia. Germany had pushed Europe to recognize Croatia and Slovenia as independent states, short-circuiting an elaborate diplomatic – and probably doomed – effort to forestall war over Yugoslavia's breakup, after Serbian forces began military action against Croatia.[23] The German intelligence services were long rumored to be involved in encouraging separatist Albanian forces in Kosovo.[24] After the Dayton Accords, Germany had favored intervention in Kosovo. As the final status process began, Germany was regarded as the most reliable advocate, after the United States and Britain, for independence. Germany's leadership often was muted, however, by sharp fissures in its domestic politics. As a general rule, the Left in German politics opposed international involvements and was particularly hostile to initiatives embraced by the United States. The position of the Social Democrats, historically the dominant center-Left party, had sought a German position equidistant from that of the United States and Russia. Of late, the Social Democrats were feeling threatened by inroads from newer and feistier leftist parties, which attracted considerable support from young people. The Greens in particular insisted that a Security Council resolution was necessary to resolve Kosovo's final status. Accordingly, Germany, while recognizing the inevitability of Kosovo's separation from Serbia, never was too enthusiastic about it.

---

[23] See Caplan at 41–2 (analyzing evolution of German position after Slovenia and Croatia seceded from Yugoslavia and war broke out).

[24] Sources within the KLA and the Albanian foreign ministry claim that the German intelligence service offered support and encouragement to predecessors of the KLA in the early 1990s. Wolfgang Ischinger doubts the accuracy of these reports because "Germany did not have a clear policy on Yugoslavia at that time." October 2008 interview with Wolfgang Ischinger. See also Michael Libal, *Limits of Persuasion: Germany and the Yugoslav Crisis 1991–1992* at 133 (1997) (criticizing Dutch proposal for redrawing borders because it would have supported demands of Albanians in Kosovo who would have asked for independence from Serbia). Libal was head of the Southeast European Department of the German Foreign Ministry from 1991 to 1995.

At first, Chancellor Merkel showed strong leadership – but senior German diplomats quickly pulled her back into the Kohl mold. From 1982 to 1998, the German government had pursued a cautious approach under Chancellor Helmut Kohl, who served as Chancellor of Germany longer than Bismark, and presided over the unification of East and West Germany in 1990. He "always wanted to have a Europeanized Germany rather than a Germanized Europe. It was an absolute necessity [for him] that the unification of Germany [be] carried out within a very firm framework of European and Atlantic integration," said Rohan. "He did not want to revive the fears of the past." Under the Kohl approach, Germany was cautious never to overassert itself. Instead, Kohl interpreted Germany's role more as a chairman of Europe rather than an advocate, and often sided with smaller European states in order to seek European unity above all.

Below the ministerial level, Germany was served by experienced diplomats. Emily Haber was Balkan Director in the Ministry preceded by Johannes Haindl. Michael Schäfer was the Political Director in the German Foreign Ministry. He joined the German Foreign Service in 1978 and since that time served in a variety of capacities in Germany and abroad. He had been a member of the German delegation to the UN, Head of the Western Balkans Task Force and Berlin Special Envoy for South Eastern Europe, and Director-General for Legal Affairs at the German Foreign Ministry. Schäfer was so close to Serbian President Tadić that he could simply pick up the phone and call him directly. Often, Schäfer would return from a meeting brimming with enthusiastic sympathy for the Serb position, and the political actors, both senior and junior, would try to force him back into line. France's leadership turnaround regarding independence for Kosovo already has been described in Chapter 8. Other major European states were even more ambivalent about Kosovo's independence. Greece historically had maintained close ties with Serbia and therefore was opposed instinctively to any solution that would override Serbia's concerns and interests. Greek Foreign Minister Dora Bakoyannis was the eldest child of Constantine Mitsotakis, the former prime minister of Greece who had conspired with Milošević to divide Macedonia, and even traveled personally to Tirana to ask Albanian Prime Minister Berisha if he would acquiesce in the division.[25]

The Italian government and people historically had close ties with Albania, and considered Albania a kind of informal protectorate through much of the twentieth century. Italy also had taken the brunt of refugee flows across the Adriatic Sea after the collapse of the Albanian state in 1997, and the later conflict in Kosovo. Italy thus was expected to be as strong a proponent of independence as Switzerland, but Italy had difficulty formulating a coherent foreign policy and sticking to it.

---

[25] Confidential interview, August 2007.

Spain was twitchy about the idea of imposed independence because of its long struggle with centrifugal pressures in Spain, most notably the Basque insurgency. Spain was worried that an imposition of independence for Kosovo by the UN Security Council might inflame Basque aspirations to achieve the same result, by setting a bad precedent under international law.

The Nordic countries had supplied a large number of skilled mediators for conflicts in the Balkans, and the political elites in those countries thus had a more sophisticated view of the Kosovo conflict than some other European states. This was sometimes a boon for the final status process and sometimes a bane. It was a boon in the sense that these political elites appreciated the improbability of Serbian/Albanian conciliation. It was a bane in that many of these same mediators were unduly confident in their own ability to craft unique solutions to the Kosovar question; their tendency to overestimate their knowledge of statecraft resulted in the launching of personal diplomatic missions, which were well intentioned but nevertheless disruptive to an orderly final status process.

Managing the disparate interests and personalities within Europe fell to a small group of experienced diplomats representing EU institutions. Javier Solana was the de facto foreign minister of the EU – although absent ratification of a constitution for the EU, his official title was High Representative for the Common Foreign and Security Policy. He was also, for a considerable period of time, the Archduke of Delay. He had been a proponent of a reinvented Yugoslavia comprising a confederation of Serbia, Montenegro, and Kosovo, and had thus opposed both Montenegro's Declaration of Independence and beginning final status talks for Kosovo. Also, as a Spanish national he was anxious about the effect Kosovo's independence would have on Basque claims for autonomy. By July 2007, however, he had become quite worried about the implications of further delay, and he argued that Europe needed to make hard decisions now or be confronted with a much more difficult situation later. His advocacy of short delays after Ahtisaari's recommendation was presented to the UN and the Troika process started was motivated by a desire to have plenty of time to forge European unity. He pressed Wisner and Ischinger to try to find a compromise. Wisner said, "Yes, we will try, but in the end we must make sure that the U.S. and Europe are solidly together on Kosovo." Solana agreed.

Stefan Lehne was the Special Envoy of High Representative Javier Solana to the final status talks – Solana's representative to UNOSEK. He was a career diplomat in the Austrian Foreign Service, serving in Austria's UN Mission and as Director for Balkans, Eastern Europe, and Central Asia for the EU Council Secretariat.

Olli Rehn was the Member of the European Commission responsible for enlargement of the EU. He formerly served as Head of Cabinet for the European Commission, as a member of the European Parliament, as an adviser to the prime minister of Finland and as a member of the Parliament of Finland.

Pieter Feith had been designated by the EU as the International Representative to head an EU mission in Kosovo, expected under the Ahtisaari plan. A veteran of the Dutch Diplomatic service, he held a number of high-level assignments for the EU, serving as the Head of Mission for the Aceh Monitoring Mission, Deputy Director General of the EU for Politico-Military Affairs, Political Adviser to the Commander of IFOR in Bosnia, and Head of NATO's Balkans Task Force. He was deeply involved in mediating the 2001 conflicts in southern Serbia and Macedonia.

Britain's involvement was led first by John Sawyers, Political Director of the British Foreign Service until March 2007, then UN Permanent Representative, former Balkan Director Karen Pierce, and Michael Tatham, Balkan Director. All were sophisticated about Balkans politics. Pierce followed final status negotiations particularly closely, and was brutally realistic about what was possible and what was not. She was impatient with ill-informed calls for further delay.

China, despite its veto power as a permanent member of the UN Security Council, was inclined to take the sidelines. Many international observers worried in the early stages about China. China consistently opposed international intervention into the sovereign affairs of other countries, and held a broadly traditional view of the scope of sovereign prerogatives. Chinese leaders also had been, for hundreds of years, paranoiac about centrifugal forces that might threaten to break China apart – in Tibet and Taiwan, to name two notable examples. Therefore, it was feared that China could be as militant as Russia, maybe even more so, in opposing any imposed independence. However, early contacts with senior Chinese officials by Ahtisaari yielded the conclusion that China saw Kosovo as a "European problem." China's attitude was that resolution of the Kosovo issue would be easy if the EU solidly backed a plan and brought it to the Security Council. Some EU representatives to the UN, however, had told their Chinese colleagues not to support the emerging EU "solidarity" in support of Ahtisaari's process.[26] The lack of European unity was manifest halfway around the world.

It is too easy for American observers of international relations to underestimate the importance that other states, particularly in Europe, attach to the continued effectiveness of United Nations machinery. The United Nations, as much as the European Union, represents a regime that permits European states, especially smaller European states, to activate diplomatic forces in a way that keeps them more secure economically and strategically than they could do on their own through bilateral negotiations – and certainly more than they could do on their own through unilateral measures. Moreover, the continued effectiveness of the United Nations represents an important potential bulwark against the unilateral exercise of American power that might be inimical to European interests.

---

[26] Confidential interview, July 2007.

As James Traub points out in his book *The Best Intentions: Kofi Annan and the UN in the Era of American World Power*, many people who work on the staff of the UN and other international organizations, including the EU, worship process. That should not be surprising, because in many cases their jobs and careers exist only because of formal institutional processes. Within this culture, what matters is not any particular decision or results; rather, primary importance is attached to the formality itself. For such people, a resolution that might get vetoed should not be put to a vote in the Security Council. A decision that might breach Security Council unity should not be sought.

The UN does not lack bold creative decision makers; but such people were frequently sucked into the quicksand represented by the much larger number of process worshippers. Nor do the process worshippers necessarily dominate the midlevel bureaucracy against which senior policy makers struggle; rather senior policy makers, at least at the ministerial level, and sometimes at the head-of-government level, often are themselves process worshippers. They can escape the political risks of making hard decisions by explaining to their constituencies that they must not risk breaching European or UN unity.

The only way that diplomacy could work effectively in such an environment was if someone – some state or some political leader who mattered – was prepared to do something that imposed higher costs for inaction than the expected cost of acting. In addition, in this context, patience is not always a virtue. Ahtisaari, Rohan, and Sauer knew the UN well. They inoculated themselves from bureaucratic interference and process-worship through their close relationship with Secretary General Annan.

Navigating UN processes was complicated by the broad perception that UNMIK must be succeeded in Kosovo by a predominately European "international civilian presence." At first, many European diplomats argued that it was infeasible to organize and deploy such a European mission in the absence of a new Security Council resolution. Resolution 1244 authorized the UNMIK mission and until 1244 was replaced by another resolution, they said, there would be no legal authority for an EU mission to replace UNMIK. That was not true, as a legal matter. Resolution 1244 authorized the Secretary General to organize a civil administration mission in Kosovo;[27] it did not say anything about the actual structure that UNMIK had assumed. So with Resolution 1244 still in place, the UN Secretary General could dismantle UNMIK and delegate his authority under the resolution to a new EU-led mission, essentially along the same lines as the Ahtisaari plan. Nevertheless, the Secretary General would be far more likely to take such a step if it was supported by the members of the Security Council, which left deployment of an EU mission still at the mercy of Security Council decision making, as a matter of political reality.

---

[27] UNSCR 1244, art. 10 (authorizing Secretary General to establish civilian presence); id. art. 6 (requesting Secretary General to appoint Special Representative to coordinate civilian presence).

Ahtisaari also faced some idiosyncratic personalities. In his book *Collision Course* about the diplomacy over the 1999 NATO bombing campaign, John Norris evocatively identified a major reality of high-profile diplomatic negotiations as "envoy envy." The phrase refers to the jockeying for public attention that almost always occurs when a single individual has been designated to lead negotiations. Despite Martti Ahtisaari's strength, and the profound esteem he enjoyed among members of the European, Russian, and U.S. diplomatic communities, there were others who envied his role and periodically sought to displace him from the limelight.

One was Carl Bildt, who served as prime minister of Sweden from 1991 to 1994, and was, after late 2006, the Minister of Foreign Affairs for Sweden. After his term as prime minister, he served as the EU's Special Envoy to Former Yugoslavia, co-chair of the Dayton Peace Conference, High Representative for Bosnia, and, from 1999 to 2001, as the UN Secretary General's Special Envoy for the Balkans. His energetic and continued involvement in diplomacy focused on the Balkans was exemplified by a blog he published on the Web, http://bildt.blogspot.com, which had hundreds of postings bearing Bildt's by-line on European politics, the conflict in Iraq, Russia's political evolution, and the Balkans. In a post in April 2005, he declared, "The aim ought to be that Kosovo gets its full independence as it enters the framework of interdependence of the European Union." Then his position seemed to shift. In an entry posted on July 27, 2005, he praised Kai Eide's qualifications and observed that European and U.S. figures were throwing "cold water" on Kosovar Albanian political leadership for its failure to promote multiethnicity, and said that moving too quickly toward independence for Kosovo would set up a failed state in Europe. He observed that final status negotiations following Eide's report would prove more difficult and protracted than most people expected. When Eide's report was accepted by the Security Council and Ahtisaari appointed as Special Envoy, Bildt said in his blog that the Security Council statement was "naïve." While acknowledging that Eide's central conclusion accorded with views he had publicly expressed, he somewhat artificially sought to distance himself from the Eide report: "I certainly share the Eide assessment that the status issues must be on the table. Indeed, I have advocated this for years. But I certainly don't share the belief that this will be easy or that everything will be better."

He was gloomy about the future: "I see a substantial risk that standards will deteriorate rather than improve as we accelerate the status issue. And if we neglect the risk of us setting up a failed state in a fragile region, and don't take firm action to try to prevent this, we are almost certain of doing precisely that. There will be convulsions ahead." Then, he implied that Ahtisaari might not be the right man: "Let's hope that President Ahtisaari has the stamina and patience to maneuver the process through the time it will take."

Bildt, however, was more of a problem for Ahtisaari in 1999 than during final status negotiations. In 1999, Ahtisaari's mandate came from the EU;

in 2005 it came from the Secretary General of the UN. "I accept the reality that political leaders who have knowledge and experience with an issue like Kosovo want to offer their views," Ahtisaari says.

Other bouts with envoy envy occurred after Ahtisaari's plan and recommendation had been submitted to the Security Council.

11 "Practical" Negotiations

AS THE UN SECRETARY GENERAL'S SPECIAL ENVOY, AHTISAARI'S main role was to create a Proposal for Kosovo Status Settlement, which he would then submit to the UN Security Council through the Secretary General. In preparation for this proposal, Ahtisaari and his team conducted a series of direct talks between representatives of Belgrade and Pristina, as well as meetings in which experts on the various issues visited Belgrade and Pristina to speak separately with each side on those issues. Under Ahtisaari's guiding principles from the Contact Group:

> A negotiated solution should be an international priority. Once the process has started, it cannot be blocked and must be brought to a conclusion. The Contact Group calls on the parties to engage in good faith and constructively, to refrain from unilateral steps and to reject any form of violence. Those advocating violence will have no role. The Special Envoy can take appropriate action within his United Nations mandate to suspend or exclude any individual or group, if he judges that their actions are not conducive to progress.
>
> The Contact Group calls on all parties to establish unified negotiating teams and agree on common positions.
>
> The process should provide for the effective participation of the Kosovo Serbs and other Kosovo citizens and communities. Regional neighbours and other interested parties should also be consulted as necessary.[1]

Serbia's delegation comprised Leon Kojen, Slobodan Samardzic, Goran Bogdanovic, Marko Jaksic, Aleksandar Simic, Boris Begovic, Bosko Mijatovic, and Thomas Fleiner, with President Boris Tadić and Prime Minister Vojislav Koštunica as co-chairs and Minister of Foreign Affairs Vuk Drašković as chief negotiator. There was criticism from some internationals and some Kosovar Albanians, especially Veton Surroi, that Kosovo Serbs were underrepresented in the delegation relative to the Serbian presence from Belgrade. Randjel Nojkic, head of the Kosovo Serb parliamentary group in the Kosovo Assembly, was excluded from the delegation because he refused to hew

---

[1] Guiding principles of the Contact Group for a settlement of the status of Kosovo (October 7, 2005), located at http://www.unosek.org/docref/Contact%20Group%20-%20Ten%20Guiding%20principles%20for%20Ahtisaari.pdf.

to Belgrade's line, among other things, by participating in the elections in Kosovo.[2]

The original Pristina delegation comprised Kosovo President Ibrahim Rugova as chairman, Parliamentary Speaker Nexhat Daci, Prime Minister Bajram Kosumi, PDK president Hashim Thaçi, newspaper editor Blerim Shala, and ORA party president Veton Surroi. Ahtisaari visited Rugova in Pristina, but Rugova never actively participated in the talks. Shala served as Coordinator of the Team of Unity and was present at every round of negotiation.

Membership in the negotiating teams varied in the specific negotiation sessions depending on the subject matter – and on the internal politics of the delegations.[3] Both delegations for the first round of discussions comprised eight members. The Belgrade delegation was co-chaired by Slobodan Samardzic, adviser to Prime Minister Koštunica and Leon Kojen, advisor to President Tadić. The Pristina delegation was led by Minister of Local Government Lutfi Haziri. The only constant elements on the Serbian side were the trio Tadić, Koštunica, and Drašković on the political level, present at the second "elephant rounds" and Kojen/Samardzic for the fifteen rounds on practical matters. On the Kosovar side: the entire Unity Team participated in the elephant rounds,[4] with Haziri many times, but not always, leading on practical matters.

The Austrian government had taken responsibility for providing physical facilities for the meetings. Offices for the negotiating teams and for UNOSEK were provided in rented facilities in Vienna. The meetings themselves were held in various places arranged for the particular negotiation session, sometimes at the Palais Auersperg or the Palais Kinsky, and in several instances at the Vienna International Center. The consistent configuration for negotiation meetings was a horseshoe table with eight seats per delegation. At one point, UNOSEK found this to be too constraining and added a "secretariat" table simply for the purpose of providing two additional seats for UNOSEK staff.

UNOSEK handled the negotiations on practical matters in the following way: Ahtisaari received both delegations in the morning in the UNOSEK office, one after the other and told them bluntly what behavior he expected from them during the talks. The Kosovars unfailingly promised full cooperation, the Serbs often presented wishes or criticism regarding the conduct of the talks.

Then the delegations moved to the facilities – first Palais Kinsky. Rohan usually chaired the meetings; Bernhard Schlageck did so in his absence. After

---

[2] Radio B92, "Nojkic booted from SNC" (March 7, 2006), located at http://www.b92.net/eng/news/comments.php?nav_id=33992.

[3] Factual information in this chapter comes from several interviews with Albert Rohan, Martii Ahtisaari, and Kai Sauer, and several e-mail exchanges with Bernard Schlageck.

[4] The "elephant rounds" were negotiations when the most senior representatives of Belgrade and Pristina met face to face.

the meeting UNOSEK had press conferences, the first by Rohan, followed separately by the two delegations. The departure times of the respective flights out of Vienna determined who would go first. Ahtisaari chaired the last round (lasting a week) himself, sharing the chair with Rohan and Stefan Lehne, depending on the subject under consideration. The "elephant rounds" were more formal occasions, in the Redoutensaal of the Hofburg (the Imperial Castle), chaired by Ahtisaari.

During practical negotiations, the UNOSEK delegation always included experts from Council of Europe, the Council's Venice Commission, the United Nations Educational, Scientific and Cultural Organization (UNESCO), the World Bank, the European Commission, and sometimes the International Monetary Fund (IMF). UNMIK was represented in each meeting.

After the first UNOSEK visit with the political leadership in Serbia and Kosovo, it was obvious that the two parties would not agree voluntarily on a status program. The first negotiation session reinforced this conclusion. Party representatives mainly wanted to talk about status, although they also discussed decentralization and community rights. The Serb delegation made it clear that Serbia would never agree to anything except continued sovereignty over Kosovo. They also made it clear that the term *minority rights* must not be used to refer to Kosovo Serbs; Belgrade insisted on the term *community rights* instead. The Kosovar delegation likewise made it clear that it would never agree to anything less than independence from Serbia.

Ahtisaari concluded that the only way to address the very real problems Kosovar Serbs faced was to start with technical talks over practical issues such as decentralization, protection of human rights, security for religious shrines, and economic issues and to work backwards toward the nature of final status. Beginning with the heart of the question – the status issue itself – would only harden irreconcilable positions and block progress on practical matters.

Decentralization was seen by UNOSEK as the only way to allow Kosovo Serbs (and smaller minorities) to run their own affairs, albeit within the legal and institutional framework of Kosovo. Community rights should enable minorities to preserve their identity and to participate effectively in Kosovo's political decision-making process. The measures for religious and cultural sites had the purpose of protecting these sites physically and allowing churches and monasteries, in particular those in purely Kosovar Albanian surroundings, to continue their ecclesiastic/monastic activities. The economic-issues subject mainly dealt with the division between Serbia and Kosovo of public assets and debt.

Approaching negotiations from a practical point established a degree of commonality on matters of municipal-level competency such as health care, education, culture, social welfare, police, and justice. As Ahtisaari said afterwards, the issues discussed at this point were "not earth-shattering matters in the political sense," but they did serve both to address the needs of the actual population of Kosovo and to begin the process with positive results to create a stronger foundation for negotiation over larger issues.

The styles of the Belgrade and Pristina negotiating teams differed considerably. The Serbian delegation was far more experienced in diplomacy, but had a mandate to undermine the negotiations as much as possible. For their part, the Albanians lacked experience, but were enthusiastic about where the process would lead.

The Serb delegation made it clear at the outset that they did not intend to take the negotiations seriously, although they did not say so explicitly. Shortly after he was appointed, Ahtisaari went to meet with them privately. "I know you may not be happy with where we end up," he said, "but I hope you will participate actively to make sure we understand and take account of your interests as we work out the details." The response was a brick wall, with Serbs essentially saying, "We do not agree on the outcome the Contact Group wants, we do not agree to this process, and we are not going to play your game." There were some agreements along the way on decentralization and protective zones for churches, but the Serbs took almost everything back in the last week, apparently because Belgrade was concerned that too much agreement might prejudice matters in favor of independence.

During the whole process, Belgrade moved only slightly from its original positions and offered only very limited concessions, usually in a rather improvised way, starting every meeting as if from scratch, trying to sway the negotiation agenda by refusing to discuss minority rights arrangements until very late in the process and using every opportunity to delay and complicate procedures and individual sessions without, however, walking out. While the Belgrade diplomats were more experienced, they were only interested and engaged in the macro-level – when it came to the detailed questions of decentralization and other subjects they were at times rather badly informed and prepared.[5]

Jaksic, on the Serb side, was extremely aggressive, calling the Kosovar Albanian participants "terrorists" and "separatists." Participants found him frequently insulting and destructive. For his part, Simic seemed to be slow. Participants did respect Kojen and Samardzic professionally, even though their role was often to be intentionally difficult.

The Kosovar Albanian delegation members eventually gained more self-assurance with increased experience and more exposure to the UNOSEK team and to the Serb delegation. Hashim Thaçi was very eager to lead the delegation, and came to an early decentralization meeting only to face a ferocious personal attack: Serbian representatives had lodged a formal protest against his presence, claiming that his role in the KLA made him a terrorist. Thaçi, according to one participant, read his prepared statement and then sat silent. Lutfi Haziri, Kosovo's deputy prime minister and a regular participant on the Kosovar side, was well informed, especially in decentralization matters.

The Kosovar Albanians matured through the process, says one UNOSEK participant. At first, the Pristina delegation had no authority to negotiate – all

---

[5] May 2008 e-mail exchange with Bernard Schlageck.

they would do was read a prepared statement and then refuse to talk about anything else. This was apparently a strategy arrived at by their political constituencies in Kosovo. In response to any issue that arose, they could only say "That's off the table! We won't even discuss that!" Finally, in frustration, Rohan traveled to Pristina to talk to the top members of the Unity Team. "We can't conduct business this way," he said flatly. "Whoever you send – or you could go yourselves – must have the authority to participate meaningfully in discussions and negotiations."[6] Thereafter, it got better.

The process itself was less paper intensive than anticipated. The UNOSEK team often prepared resource papers, and brought outside experts to negotiating sessions, and regularly asked each side to prepare position papers. The Serb delegation almost never prepared papers, even when it came time to discuss issues of greatest importance to them such as community protection. This only reinforced the view held by many participants – and by Kosovo Serbs – that the Belgrade negotiating team cared about Belgrade's geopolitical interests, but not about the lives of Kosovo Serbs. The Albanians often brought position papers, usually prepared by their American and European consultants. On one occasion, the Kosovar Albanians produced a seventy-page position paper on community rights, presumably written by their own expert; when the UNOSEK team read it, they could not believe how much the Albanians were willing to give up. Recalled Rohan, "We said to them, 'Are you sure you want to say this in your paper?'"

February 2006 initiated the fourteen-month process, with direct talks in Vienna between Belgrade and Pristina representatives on February 20–21, "under the auspices" of Martti Ahtisaari, as the UNOSEK press releases termed it.

The first round of negotiations focused on the issue of decentralization: the process of shifting governmental power from the central government in Pristina to municipal governments. Municipalities historically had been the political entities through which local government occurred. They functioned roughly like counties in many U.S. states, and townships in other states, with elected councils, mayors, and significant control over local police detachments and educational establishments. Their boundaries were contiguous and every part of Kosovo was in one municipality or another.

Thus, in Kosovo, two levels of government existed: the central government and the municipal governments. The Rambouillet Accords had recited that municipalities were the basic unit of self-government: "The basic territorial unit of local self-government in Kosovo shall be the commune. All responsibilities in Kosovo not expressly assigned elsewhere shall be the responsibility of the communes."[7] Kosovo's territory was divided into thirty municipalities.

---

[6] August 2007 interview with Albert Rohan, Vienna.

[7] Art I(8), Rambouillet Agreement, located at http://www.state.gov/www/regions/eur/ksvo_rambouillet_text.html.

Municipal boundaries had been defined by the government of Yugoslavia after World War II, and UNMIK had mainly ratified the boundaries with a few modifications. Elected municipal assemblies exercised legislative power and chose mayors to exercise executive authority over the territory of their municipalities. From a legal perspective, towns and villages had no separate governments; each was simply a cluster of houses and businesses with its own name, tucked within a greater municipality.

Decentralization was one of the best ways to ensure Serb involvement in the governance of Kosovo; it essentially gave the Kosovo Serbs a measure of self-government in the municipalities where they constituted a majority. The goal was a structure that would leave 80 to 90 percent of Kosovo's Serbs with majority control over the governments of municipalities where they lived. It was also true, however, that too much decentralization would make Kosovo ungovernable. There already were problems with lack of municipal responsiveness to central government legislation because of local political dynamics and because so many international programs were implemented at the municipal level.

Critics such as Chad Rogers, head of the National Democratic Institute (NDI) office in Pristina in 2006, for example, argued that the international community had gotten it backwards by emphasizing decentralization. NDI was an NGO funded by the U.S. Congress and tasked with providing aid to political parties and other institutions of democratization. It enjoyed a strong reputation for competence, effectiveness, and neutrality in local politics. Rogers argued that the international community should have insisted on effective centralization of authority first – only then, once an effective, democratic government was established in Pristina, it might be possible to devolve power to municipalities. Separately, some Kosovar Albanians, most prominently, Albin Kurti, leader of the Vetevendosje (Self-Determination) movement, argued that decentralization was a disguised pathway to partition. Creating Serb-majority municipalities and then giving them substantial political control and allowing them to form links with each other and with Belgrade would effectively create a Serb entity within Kosovo, like the Republika Srpska entity in Bosnia. Eventually, he argued, such an entity would insist on a union with Serbia, thereby splitting Kosovo, even if the rest enjoyed internationally supervised independence. However, decentralization was one of the major keys to a final status template that protected minority rights, and so it featured prominently in the negotiations, and had been a reality on the ground, even before a well-functioning government existed in Pristina. Decentralization also had to be at the core of practical negotiations, because it was part of the Contact Group's mandate for Ahtisaari, and it was a fait accompli under UNMIK administration of Kosovo.

One threshold issue in decentralization talks was particularly thorny: determining the number of municipalities to which power would be devolved. At the end of 2005, all but four of Kosovo's municipalities had Albanian majorities. The Serbian delegation wanted to redraw the boundaries so there would be more municipalities with Serbian majorities. The Serb position at the beginning – and end – of talks about decentralization was that Serbs had to have fourteen new municipalities.

Those municipalities and the protected church zones collectively would constitute a de facto Serb "entity," or a substate within Kosovo akin to Republika Srpksa in Bosnia, although the Serb delegation wanted to go beyond that model. Nominally a part of the unified independent state of Bosnia, Republika Srpska is practically a separate state that takes its political direction from Belgrade rather than Sarajevo.

Constructive dialogue was inhibited by the consistent Serbian focus on territorial acquisition – how much territory in Kosovo Serbs would "own." At one point Serb negotiators bragged that they had compromised by reducing their territorial demands from nine thousand to six thousand hectares. "Bully for you," Rohan responded, "but we are not counting acreage; we're focusing on legal protections for specific rights and privileges. We want to make sure that we create the kind of environment a monastery needs; we should not care how much real estate the monastery will own." The Serbs wanted to link protective zones for churches with restitution for church property taken by the Communist regime in 1945. "Restitution is an issue completely separate from what we are trying to accomplish here," Rohan insisted.

The Kosovo delegation was wary of the subject of decentralization because they adamantly opposed partition. Before final status negotiations had even begun, however, then–Prime Minister Haradinaj had taken the first difficult step and agreed to talk about the technical details of decentralization.

The Kosovar Albanians were, on the whole, constructive with their proposals; they took to heart the international community's advice that they had to begin with a serious proposal and not engage in temperamental bargaining that was too finely grained. However, UNOSEK and the Contact Group had to push them hard, especially to modify their initial opposition to asymmetric decentralization – an approach giving more rights to communities with Serb majorities than those with Albanian majorities. In the end it turned out they had taken this advice too literally, and held back little on which they could make further concessions. Conversely, once or twice, Kosovar Albanian negotiating team leader Lutfi Haziri was intransigent. He was adamant, for example, on the boundaries of a new Serb municipality in Gjilan, which was his home area, but he was persuaded to relent partially. In another case, however, involving the area around Obilic, a new municipality was rejected because it would have disrupted any reasonable plan to extract lignite and to generate electricity from it.

Despite the positive language of the initial UNOSEK press releases, however, there was still clearly a profound difference in overall point of view from each side. The day after the talks concluded, for example, a Kosovar newspaper quoted Lutfi Haziri as stating that the government of Kosovo would be ready to implement decentralization the day after achieving independence – despite the fact that Serbia remained just as adamantly against independence.

The second round of talks on decentralization took place in Vienna on March 17, 2006. This time the negotiators focused on local finance, intermunicipal cooperation and cross-boundary cooperation. If municipalities had taxing power and control over their own budgets, they would be more independent of Pristina. If Serb municipalities had ties to each other and to Belgrade, they would come closer collectively to constituting a separate Serb entity within Kosovo. As expected with advancement into slightly deeper issues, the discussions became more difficult. The Kosovar Albanians resisted a draft that provided for relatively informal contacts between municipalities, a municipal association, and contacts between the municipalities and other governments (which would mean Serbia in the case of independence). They suspected that such provisions represented a Trojan horse that would lead to the partition of Kosovo along ethnic lines. The UNOSEK team produced language from the charter of the Council of Europe providing exactly the same language[8] and said, "We're sure you don't want to do less in your decentralization plan than the Council of Europe provides."

This session resulted in two main points of agreement: first, financial subsidies from Belgrade to Serb municipalities in Kosovo were acceptable, on the condition that they be given in a transparent manner and be limited to activities within the authority of the municipalities. Second, both parties agreed that Kosovo municipalities had the power to make intermunicipal cooperation links, provided that this cooperation did not lead to an intervening layer of government between the municipalities and the central authorities.

The reality was that Kosovo already worked this way. The three municipalities north of the Ibar River that divided Mitrovica – Leposaviq, Zvecan, and Zubin Potok – had Serb majorities and were really governed from Belgrade. Civil servants in these municipalities (as in other Serb-predominant communities in Kosovo), which included local teachers, health care workers, and police officers, drew salaries and pensions from Belgrade; they disdained any connection with UNMIK or the central government in Pristina. Mitrovica itself was divided: UNMIK and the PISG ran the predominantly Albanian part south of the river; Belgrade ran the predominantly Serb part north of the river. The only other existing municipality with a Serb majority was Strpce, where the young Serb Major Ilic had been beaten for his cooperation with Jessen-Petersen.

---

[8] For example, Article 1 of the Council's "European Outline Convention on Transfrontier Co-operation between Territorial Communities or Authorities" of 1980 provides: "Each Contracting Party undertakes to facilitate and foster transfrontier co-operation between territorial communities or authorities within its jurisdiction and territorial communities or authorities within the jurisdiction of other Contracting Parties. It shall endeavour to promote the conclusion of any agreements and arrangements that may prove necessary for this purpose with due regard to the different constitutional provisions of each Party."

April 3 brought the third session on decentralization. Prior to the talks, Ahtisaari met with each delegation separately, to encourage them in the process. In particular, he urged Belgrade to reconsider its policy of encouraging Kosovo Serbs to abstain from local political processes, as well as its recent directive forcing any employees receiving salaries from both Belgrade and Pristina to choose one over the other. He noted the efforts of the Kosovo president and prime minister to reach out to minorities in Kosovo, emphasizing that, as they all worked toward a final status for Kosovo, improvement in the situation "on the ground" was vital.

The meeting itself focused on "Principles of Decentralization," a document UNOSEK had prepared based on the first two rounds of talks. An analysis of the document confirmed the areas of common ground previously agreed upon, but no further progress was made. The Kosovo delegation was constructive. It arrived with responses to the document, which was not the case on the Serbian side. The Kosovars were willing to decentralize power, but the Serbs desired decentralization of territories along ethnic lines, a contention that would rear its head repeatedly throughout the process.

Beginning on May 4, 2006, the fourth round concentrated on the creation of new municipalities and their boundaries. Of particular concern were municipalities with a Kosovo Serb majority. Both parties agreed on the necessity of "fair minimum size": a principle that all municipalities must be big enough to be functional, with the necessary infrastructure and economic viability. The Kosovo delegation proposed the creation of three new municipalities, and the extension of an already existing one. In contrast, the Serbian participants wanted the creation of fourteen new municipalities, and the modification of the boundaries of five others, to increase the percentage of Serbs within the new boundaries.

Upon their return to Pristina, the Kosovo delegation was quoted as saying that the differences between the two parties were obvious, had grown bigger, and were, from their point of view, unbridgeable. Lutfi Haziri said, "It will be very difficult to achieve some sort of rapprochement in the future." Ylber Hysa[9] commented on the impossibility of compromise due to the "extreme requests" of the Serbian delegation. The Serbian delegation, in contrast, characterized their requests as reasonable and refused to bargain further.

Closely intertwined with the subject of decentralization was the subject of "returns" by Kosovo Serbs who had been displaced by the threat of violence and who hoped to return to their homes. In June 1999, just before the UN's bombing campaign, Kosovo had about two hundred thousand Serb residents. A substantial percentage of these fled Kosovo after the conclusion of the bombing campaign, fearing the KLA and other instruments of Kosovar Albanian retaliation. Others refused to live under UN administration. Most went to

---

[9] Mr. Hysa was a member of the Kosovo Assembly and deputy chief of Veton Surroi's ORA party.

Serbia proper, although some sought refuge in Mitrovica and the other municipalities in the north. As early as 2002, UNMIK had issued a policy entitled "The Right to Sustainable Return," and UNMIK and a variety of NGOs had worked with the PISG to promote returns. The PISG established a Ministry of Communities and Returns in March 2005. Sharp differences existed between the Serbian and Kosovo delegations about the total number of refugees both outside Kosovo and of internally displaced persons – those still within Kosovo but not at their previous homes.

During one of its trips to Belgrade and Pristina, UNOSEKdiscovered that a draft "Protocol on Voluntary Return..." had been negotiated between the two sides many months before, without having been signed yet. The purpose was to establish clear procedures for an orderly return process. Apparently, drafts had been sent back and forth in slow motion, the change of leadership of the Serbian Kosovo Coordination Centre being given as one of the reasons for delay. The other obstacles were two controversial issues of substance: Belgrade wanted a return to "places of choice"; the Kosovars insisted on return to the original homes of returnees, claiming that this was UNHCR's normal practice (which seemed to be true) and pointing to the danger of "demographic engineering" by Belgrade. Rohan supported from the beginning the "places of choice" alternative (also advocated by Kai Eide in his 2005 report), pointing out to the Kosovars that in any normal country citizens can choose where they want to live and that it might even be an advantage if the small Serbian minority were concentrated in a few municipalities instead of being spread around the country in smaller settlements.

The other issue was whether permission for return should be given by UNMIK (Serbian position) or the relevant municipalities (Kosovar Albanian position). At the lunch break during one of the meetings in Vienna, Rohan took Kojen and the competent member of the Pristina delegation aside to settle the matter once and for all. They found compromise wording for both issues (the first based on return "to places of choice"). "I called UNMIK's Legal Adviser Borg-Olivier right from our luncheon table to check the language," Rohan says. "From the legal point of view, he gave his OK and in the press briefing following the meeting we could announce this (rare) achievement. Several weeks later, after a hiccup about who would sign the Protocol on the two sides, the ceremony took place in Pristina in the office of SRSG Jessen-Petersen."

Differences also existed about how much the refugees and displaced persons wanted to return to their former homes. Apart from rhetoric about the data on returns, the reality was that Belgrade and the Serbian delegation to the final status talks treated the unresolved returns issue as an important symbol of their claim that an independent, Albanian-dominated Kosovo would infringe on the human rights of Kosovo Serbs who had been displaced by Albanian human rights violations. If the numbers of potential returnees were large, and if few actually returned, Serbia could use this as evidence that the climate in

Kosovo was too hostile for them. On the other hand, the Serbian delegation knew that if more Serbs could be induced to return to Kosovo, or migrate there, an increasing Serbian presence could tip the balance of population and votes in existing or proposed municipalities.

On the Kosovar Albanian side, there were deep resentments – mainly concealed within politically correct conversation – against the Kosovo Serbs, most of whom were believed to have been complicit in the ravages of the Milošević regime's ethnic cleansing campaign. Most ordinary Kosovar Albanians were not eager to share political power with Kosovo Serbs, as they would have to do if Kosovo Serbs were more numerous. So the Albanian side wanted to minimize the official number of potential returnees as well as the special rights that would be granted to them if they did return.

It was crucial that both sides reach a workable agreement on a goal for the number of returns and their legal rights. All of the negotiators claimed to hope that most of the displaced Serbs would return, and committed themselves to creating a truly multiethnic community in Kosovo. It was nonsensical, however, to expend the time or the resources to create new municipalities for them only to end up with numerous "ghost towns" if they did not come back. At this point in the negotiating process, no compromise was reached on how to count potential returnees. Part of the problem were conflicting data. Belgrade's position was ambiguous. After first accepting UNMIK figures, which certainly were not always up-to-date, they came up with their own figures that never were substantiated.[10]

Later in May, Deputy Special Envoy Rohan visited Belgrade and Pristina to continue discussions on decentralization, returns, and other issues previously brought up in the talks. After his visit to Belgrade, UNOSEK spokesperson Hua Jiang claimed that the meetings went well, and that common stances had been found. In the Serbian press, however, negotiation team member Marko Jaksic made accusations that the mediators were treating the negotiations as an opportunity to fulfill only the wishes of the Albanian delegation, which resulted in the Belgrade team digging in their heels regarding their requests. In Pristina, Rohan asked the Kosovo team for more concessions regarding decentralization. The Kosovo delegation expressed surprise at this request; in their eyes, they already had offered more than their share of compromise.

May 23 saw the first round of talks on another vital subject: the protection of religious and cultural heritage in Kosovo. Much of Serbia's opposition to an independent Kosovo was premised on the argument that an independent, Albanian-dominated Kosovo would threaten Serbia's religious heritage, symbolized by many centuries-old churches and monasteries inside Kosovo's boundaries. At the center of Serbian national consciousness was the belief that the Serbian Orthodox Church had resisted Muslim domination through

---

[10] May 2008 e-mail exchange with Bernard Schlageck.

extension of the Ottoman Empire, beginning with the Ottoman victory on the Field of Blackbirds in 1389. The Church had long been one of the most virulently nationalist forces in Serbian politics, emphasizing the importance of its religious shrines located in Kosovo.

In surprising contrast to the impasse regarding municipalities, the May talks brought significant agreement between the two parties on protection of religious heritage. This occurred despite Belgrade's insistence that this issue was directly linked to that of decentralization – a view rejected by both Pristina and Ahtisaari's team. Both sides agreed that protective zones around religious sites were necessary, and established an expert group to discuss the criteria for establishing such zones, with zone boundaries to be decided on a case-by-case basis. All parties agreed that access to churches and monasteries – for pilgrims, authorities, and others – should be at the discretion of the respective institutions. Pristina conceded that the Serbian Orthodox Church should enjoy support in terms of welfare, social and pension benefits, or health insurance from any government that wished to provide it – including Belgrade. Differences remained regarding the size of the protected zones and the restitution of nationalized church property, but the session was still regarded as successful.

Rohan had advised the Kosovars not to resist Serb requests for protection of religious sites. "Whatever the Church wants, give it to them," he said. For the most part, the Kosovar Albanians followed this advice – but then the Serbs declined to agree in the end because neither the Kosovar Albanians nor UNOSEK were willing to treat new protected zones as property. A protected zone, in the view of UNOSEK and the Albanians, was analogous to a zoning restriction: certain activities would be prohibited in protected zones, regardless of who owned the property. The Serbian side insisted that protected zone meant outright property ownership by the Church, redressing acts of expropriation years before. The crux of the matter was Belgrade's conditioning any agreement to continued full authority of the Serbian government over all Serbian religious and cultural sites in Kosovo and restitution of the church property nationalized after World War II. Belgrade did not demand outright property ownership in every case, but insisted on restitution and, where restitution was not feasible, the power to purchase the respective areas. After not doing anything about Serbian Orthodox Church restitution claims for fifty years, the Serbian Assembly rushed a law through that provided for restitution of property taken half a century earlier by the communists. Meanwhile, Sanda Rascovic-Ivic, head of the Kosovo Coordination Centre in Belgrade and frequent member of the Serbian delegation, submitted an initial proposal that had enormous protected zones. Combined with existing and proposed Serb municipalities, the protective zones created a nearly continuous Serb area running through Kosovo – a result fully consistent with the continuing Serbian proposal for a Serb "entity" in Kosovo, as in Bosnia.

The negotiation over protecting religious sites was complicated by division within the Church itself. Artemije, Bishop of Raska and Prizren and informally styled "Bishop of Kosovo and Metohije," was the Kosovo Serbs' senior cleric. Although he had been an outspoken critic of Milošević throughout the 1990s, he was ferociously and destructively radical in his public statements about the negotiations, regularly referring to his Kosovar Albanian counterparts as the "terrorists."

On a 2006 trip to the United States, Artemije gave an incendiary public statement in support of Serbian negotiating points. American policy in Kosovo "will condemn my Christian people to extinction and create a new rogue state – this time in Europe," he warned. He described "the local Muslim Albanian administration" of Kosovo as being "controlled by members of a terrorist organization, the so-called Kosovo Liberation Army, which is closely tied to the Muslim Albanian mafia, [and] which runs drug and slave rackets across Europe." He did not hesitate to capitalize on Western outrage at recent atrocities in Iraq: "Among the characteristic jihad terror practices of the KLA is the beheading of victims, as seen in other countries with active jihad terror movements," he thundered. "On the Internet you can see photographs of uniformed KLA Islamic terrorists, whose identities are known but who have never been brought to justice, with heads of their Christian Serb victims."

Artemije was such a polarizing figure that before the first meeting to discuss religious sites, Rohan got an urgent message from two members of the Belgrade delegation requesting a meeting the night before. He met with them secretly in Vienna's Sacher Hotel Blue Bar. Their message was simple: "Keep Artemije from speaking at the meeting." "Well it's up to you who speaks for your side," Rohan said, and the visitors left.

The most constructive participant from the Church was Bishop Teodosije, vicar of the Diocese of Raska and Prizren, who was at one point appointed coordinator of church affairs for Kosovo Serbs, indicating that someone in Belgrade thought he would make a better representative of Kosovo Serb interests than Artemije. Teodosije's own public statements in the United States in 2006 illustrate the contrast between him and Artemije: "I am deeply aware that our future as citizens of Kosovo in fact lies in Kosovo, regardless of what its future status will be and what the colors of the flag will be," he said. "My primary concern is what kind of society it will be in terms of its quality, not only its appearance. The 'new reality' in Kosovo must not be rule by one people over another, but a society of free and equal citizens. That is why a hasty decision on the future status of Kosovo could very easily fossilize the rule of clans and 'war heroes' and profiteers, while the victims in this society will not be differentiated by ethnic affiliation but will be all those who want to live as free citizens in a democratic Europe. I say these words not only as a Serb but also as a concerned citizen of Kosovo and Metohija."

Rohan told the Serbian religious representatives not to ask for too much, on the grounds that ultimately their safety and security would be determined by the quality of their *modus vivendi* with the local population, not by the number of armed guards. When it came time actually to define the boundaries of the protective zones, UNOSEK brought the Belgrade and Pristina negotiations together with UNICEF and Council of Europe representatives at the Monastery of Decan. The session was intended to review models for protection of religious heritage in other contexts. The senior Serb representative was Dusan Batakovic, a well-known Serbian historian. The meeting went very well, but just as the group was ready to leave for a field trip to visit the sites and get to work on defining actual boundaries, Belgrade furiously called Batakovic home on the grounds that he had no authority from the Serbian delegation to be there.

Therefore, while there had been progress on establishing protective zones for Serbian religious sites in Kosovo, as well as their rough contours, the parties were at an impasse on whether protective zones should be treated as property of the Serbian Orthodox Church and linked with Serb-majority municipalities to form a separate Kosovo Serb political entity within Kosovo.

A week later, on May 31, the teams met again for talks on economic matters. The meeting was co-chaired by Rohan and Stefan Lehne, head of the UNOSEK working group on economy. Although little concrete progress was made, UNOSEK officials still found the talks beneficial as they allowed both sides to present their positions and understand each other's concerns. Many of the issues were directly tied to final status concerns as well, which prevented final decisions from being made. Pristina did agree to pay foreign debts incurred during the period of Yugoslav rule; Belgrade, however, refused to commit to provide statistical data necessary to allocate foreign debts between Belgrade and Pristina. Other issues brought up but left unresolved included debts from the Belgrade government to the Pristina government and vice versa; allocation of proceeds from the privatization of governmentally funded companies; documentation of the pension rights of Kosovo Serbs and Kosovar Albanian workers; rights to foreign currency accounts held for the benefit of Yugoslavia; and compensation to Kosovo for war damages caused by Serbia. Both parties agreed to exchange relevant information in preparation for future discussions.

The teams met again regarding religious and cultural heritage on July 18, 2006. Despite expectations of an agreement by the end of this set of negotiations, no progress was made. Both parties were given the opportunity to present their proposals on the issues; both parties' conclusions differed significantly from each other's and from those of the international community. Both the international proposal and Pristina contemplated protection of fifteen zones, for instance, while Belgrade requested first forty-two, then thirty-nine. Ylber Hysa of the Kosovo delegation blamed Belgrade for its unconstructiveness with its positions and demands, claiming that the issues were not between Belgrade and Pristina but rather between Belgrade and everyone else involved. Belgrade, for its part, accused Ahtisaari of bias, saying that his aim was independence for Kosovo but that he refused to say so openly. Belgrade said that the negotiations had reached their limit of potential, as the ostensibly "practical" issues were actually very much linked to final status determination, which inhibited compromise and progress.

On July 19, talks resumed on decentralization. In an attempt to stimulate further progress, Ahtisaari's team split the delegations into their own rooms and sent UNOSEK representatives back and forth to feel out each side's positions. While Pristina did offer two more municipalities and Belgrade reduced its demands slightly, the differences were still greater than the concessions. Pristina rejected the possibility of "asymmetric decentralization" – an approach in which greater competencies would be given to Kosovo-Serb majority municipalities than to Kosovar Albanian municipalities. Belgrade focused on the specifics of municipal government competencies, particularly the degree of authority over the local police and justice systems, and over Serbian language use and curricula in the educational system. The Serbian approach was to insulate Kosovo-Serb-dominated municipalities from decisions made by Kosovar Albanian governmental authorities in Pristina. Naturally, the Kosovo press blamed Serbian inflexibility for the lack of negotiation progress, while the Serbian press blamed the stubbornness of the Kosovo delegation. Nevertheless, the questions still remained: How much independent legal authority would be extended to the Serb municipalities, and would substantial authority truly induce displaced Kosovo Serbs and other minorities to return?

Despite criticism of the decentralization talks by Serbia's Tadić, who said they generated more worry than relief, the teams met again on August 7 to continue discussions. Pristina offered compromises regarding the appointment of municipal police, and agreed to allow Serb municipalities to cooperate with the Belgrade government, in line with the Council of Europe's convention. Lutfi Haziri insisted that the Kosovar delegation was willing to compromise on many issues, but it could not allow the division of Kosovo along ethnic lines. Belgrade's justification for this long-standing demand was that a division along ethnic lines would prevent Kosovo Serbs from being stripped of their basic rights, and that rights to education, health care, security, and freedom of movement were so basic as to allow no room for compromise. No progress was made. In an interview with the German press, Ahtisaari praised the Kosovar delegation for its constructive approach to decentralization, while criticizing Belgrade's unacceptable demands.

The next day, discussions centered on "community rights" – a euphemism for minority rights. The term *minority rights* was avoided because of the negative connotation it carried for many people; many Kosovo Serbs refused to be identified as a minority, because they counted themselves citizens of Serb-dominated Serbia rather than citizens of Albanian-dominated Kosovo. The Pristina delegation offered concrete proposals regarding issues such as representation in institutions, and a mechanism for protection of community rights including languages, media, and freedom of movement. Belgrade offered no proposal, reiterating its opinion that the issue belonged within the framework of status talks, referring to its position in the July 24 meeting on status.

These practical negotiations over decentralization, returns, community rights, and protection of religious sites were supposed to have been the easy part of final status negotiations. Although he knew that discussion of Kosovo's final status itself would be intractable, Ahtisaari had hoped that Belgrade and Pristina could narrow their differences over these practical issues. All of these issues were going to have to be addressed in any event, regardless of Kosovo's final status. Belgrade, however, was unwilling to participate seriously in a process that had the potential to strip away reasons to oppose Kosovar independence. In Belgrade's view, practical issues could not be separated from the fundamental question of whether Kosovo would remain a part of Serbia or become an independent state.

12 Negotiations over Status Itself

ON JULY 24, 2006, EVEN AS PRACTICAL NEGOTIATIONS WERE PROceeding, the first round of official talks to determine final status for Kosovo took place in Vienna. For these discussions, the delegations were led by the respective presidents: Boris Tadić of Serbia and Fatmir Sejdiu of Kosovo, who had replaced Ibrahim Rugova. The main purpose for this rendezvous was to allow each side to present and argue its respective position. Pristina stated that independence was its "alpha and omega" in these negotiations, while Belgrade reiterated that full independence remained unacceptable, and instead offered "autonomy" for Kosovar Albanians.

Despite this fundamental difference, both parties said they were pleased with the meeting. Kosovo President Sejdiu expressed his satisfaction afterwards, saying, "We presented our view to the international community by simply and directly arguing why Kosovo should be independent." The Belgrade delegation, for its part, was content with the fact that its arguments were based on European values, and that it had offered a full compromise in the form of the broadest autonomy within Serbia.

Ahtisaari largely left the management of intra-Kosovo political dynamics to others, but he and Rohan worked hard to nurture the capacity of the Kosovar Albanian delegation to participate effectively in final status negotiations, regularly confronting them with hard realities that necessitated compromise if they were to get anywhere close to their goal of independence. For the most part, the efforts by Ahtisaari and Rohan worked: the Kosovar Albanian side made many more compromises than the Serbian side, and the Kosovar Albanians were much more constructive in submitting detailed proposals than the Serbian side.

Sejdiu led the Kosovo delegation because of the death of Ibrahim Rugova in January 2006. Rugova's death resulted in a major reshuffling of Kosovo's political deck. The loss was widely lamented because he had been such an important symbol for so many years of Kosovar Albanian aspirations. Pragmatically, though, his demise provided an important opportunity to strengthen the PISG's capacity to function effectively. Haradinaj, still in Kosovo under close UNMIK control, enthusiastically participated with the United States and the UN in the formulation and execution of three major personnel decisions.

First, Kosumi was sacked as prime minister and replaced by General Agim
Çeku, head of the Kosovo Protection Corps (KPC, or TMK in Albanian).
At the time of his appointment, General Çeku was the most popular man in
Kosovo. He was regarded as a tough, effective manager with far better war
credentials than Kosumi, having served militarily in Croatia's conflict with Serbia, and as the KLA's Chief of Staff during the last few months of the NATO
bombing campaign. The KPC had been formed to absorb many of the former KLA fighters; although its formal role was limited to civilian emergency
management and its members were unarmed, most Kosovar Albanians viewed
KPC as an independent Kosovo's future army. Çeku, as its head, kept its former KLA fighters and commanders mostly under control for the internationals, while serving as a prominent symbol of Kosovar Albanian aspirations. He
also had amicable relations with both Haradinaj and Thaçi.

Rugova's death also shook up the Unity Team. With Rugova's terminal
illness, the powerful Speaker of the Kosovo Assembly Nexhat Daci viewed
himself as the natural leader of the Unity Team – he was, after all, the senior
official in the LDK after Rugova. However, he overreached, and Thaçi publicly rebuffed his claim to leadership. As Daci's frustration grew, he insulted
UNMIK and U.S. representatives in meetings, and they decided he had to go.
Daci was involuntarily removed from his position as Speaker, and replaced by
Kole Berisha. Berisha had a significantly smaller power base within the LDK
than Daci and thus was less of a threat to the internationals and to Thaçi.

Then, after internal jockeying, the LDK selected Fatmir Sejdiu as the new
party president, and the Assembly installed him as president of the PISG.
The leadership struggle within the LDK was intense. One report began, "Two
arrests, fist fights, and a display of guns were some of the highlights of the
congress of Kosovo's largest party, the Democratic League of Kosovo, LDK,
which met on December 9 to select a successor to Ibrahim Rugova."[1] Sejdiu
won 189 out of 349 valid votes, and his principal rival Daci subsequently withdrew and started his own party, the Democratic League of Dardania LDD.
Others who stayed with the LDK were uneasy with Sejdiu's selection. A longtime law professor at the University of Pristina and General Secretary of the
LDK, Sejdiu immediately proved to be an effective statesman. He was a far
more visible and conventionally dignified symbol of the Kosovo government
than Rugova had been in his declining years. Also, he generally did what the
internationals told him to do.

With Kosovo's government expected to be more effective – both domesti-
cally and in final status negotiations – optimism grew in Pristina, Vienna, and
Washington that Ahtisaari's mission could be wrapped up by the end of the

---

[1] Krenar Gashi, "LDK Leadership Fight Endangers Kosovo Government," *Balkan Insight*
(December 14, 2006), located at http://kosovo.birn.eu.com/en/1/70/2087/.

year. Ahtisaari's hope was to reach the level of agreement necessary to formulate a final status proposal by the end of 2006 – and his timeline was adopted and publicized by both U.S. government spokespersons and Kosovo's political leaders.

In the "elephant round" in July 2006, however, frayed relations were showing. The Austrian Foreign Minister hosted a lunch for the participants. Koštunica would not come to lunch and would not mix with the others in the corridors. Tadić, on the other hand, mixed, laughing, sometimes speaking English and sometimes Serbian. His Kosovar Albanian counterparts responded in kind.

Koštunica's personal discourtesy went to the heart of the dilemma: "How did the Serbs ever imagine that would reintegrate Kosovo into Serbia when they acted with such visible personal discourtesy to the very Kosovar Albanian leaders they would have to work with if Kosovo were to continue as a part of Serbia?" Wisner asks. "The only approach would be to force the Albanians by the scruff of the neck back into Serbian political life. Belgrade's leadership had made absolutely no effort to reach out to the Kosovar Albanians for eight years. There was never any real spirit behind endless Serbian proposals for autonomy – the letter of the law, yes, but not the spirit of reality."

The pressure on the direct sessions grew. On September 7–8, negotiating teams met again in Vienna, this time to discuss the matters of decentralization, cultural heritage, and community rights all at once. In most areas, there was no progress at all. Rohan was reporting the "sad news" that there could be no talk of a breakthrough. Surroi went even further, calling the discussion on minority rights "pitiful." The most significant advance regarded protective zones: Belgrade maintained the demand for thirty-nine, but was willing to reduce their aggregate size from 6,500 to 5,500 hectares (16,055 to 13,585 acres). Both sides agreed to the establishment of a committee to implement and supervise an eventual agreement on the protective zones – but this could not truly be considered progress, because they had already agreed to this concept back in May.

In the realm of culture, Dusan Batakovic (on behalf of the Belgrade negotiating team) offered his word that, if an acceptable agreement on protective zones could be reached, artifacts transferred from Kosovo to the Serbian Academy of Arts and Sciences would be returned in a gesture of goodwill, even though from a legal point of view they belonged to Serbia. Kosovo's Hysa dismissed the offer as a form of blackmail, on the grounds that Kosovo was entitled to the artifacts regardless of the course of the negotiations.

Consistent with the Contact Group's desire to have a proposal on Kosovo status by the end of the year, it was planned that by March of 2007, the UN Security Council would pass a new resolution that would introduce a new status for Kosovo. The intent was that this would replace Resolution 1244's reference to Serbia's sovereignty over Kosovo. The new proposal, however, would mention neither independence nor Serbia's sovereignty; rather, it would introduce an "interim state," a territory under continued international administration. Editorials in the Belgrade press, however, predicted that other countries would respond to the interim state by officially recognizing Kosovo's independence. Even in the face of this unwelcome development, and regardless of the results of the negotiations, the proposal, or the UN Security Council's new resolution, Serbian President Boris Tadić maintained that Serbia's aim was to keep good relations with the United States.

At the same time, Kosovo Prime Minister Çeku stated that the Kosovo Assembly might decide to declare its independence from Serbia unilaterally, although it would be better if the Security Council's new resolution clearly defined Kosovo's independence. He claimed that this was not intended as a threat, but merely a possible route to independence. Serbian officials, however, warned that such an action would be dangerous and could lead to bloody conflicts as other populations, such as the Bosnian Serbs and Albanians in Macedonia and Montenegro, followed Kosovo's lead, thus destabilizing the region.

On September 15, the teams met again regarding decentralization. Unsurprisingly, once again, no real progress was made. Rohan was quoted as saying that the moment was nearing when talks alone would no longer suffice, and a Kosovar newspaper offered a headline declaring that "UNOSEK has started losing its hopes." In fact, the parties regressed, as concessions previously made by the Serbian delegation in practical negotiations were now being made contingent upon acceptance of other requests.

UNOSEK had been working hard behind the scenes on the draft of the hoped-for resolution, which would be contained in the Comprehensive Proposal for Kosovo's Future Status. In September 2006, Ahtisaari met with Tadić to discuss the impact of Serbian parliamentary elections on the status process. In mid-November, Tadić announced that the elections would be held on January 21, 2007. Ahtisaari then called Wisner and said, "We have to postpone presentation of our plan until just after the elections." Wisner and everyone on the Contact Group agreed; they wanted to give as much space for constructive democratic movement in Serbian politics as possible. No one wanted presentation of an Ahtisaari plan to bias the Serbian election in favor of radical nationalists. A split between coalition partners Tadić and Koštunica was increasingly defined with reference to the final status process. So Ahtisaari issued a statement that he would present his proposal for the settlement of Kosovo status, not before the end of 2006, but posthaste after the elections.

Whenever Ahtisaari made his recommendations public, it still remained for the Security Council to adopt a new resolution, which was in some ways more dependent on the position of the Russians than on the content of Ahtisaari's proposal. Although the delay in holding elections was a stalling tactic from Serbia, it could be seen as providential, because it offered time for the Security Council to continue attempts to soften the Russian stance, for Europe to unify its position, and for Ahtisaari to refine the details of the plan. It was now possible that final status could be decided as soon as March 2007. "We lost six months," Ahtisaari said of the delay, "but we made good use of the six months."

13 The Ahtisaari Plan

AS PROMISED, AHTISAARI UNVEILED THE DRAFT OF HIS PLAN immediately after Serbian elections, on February 2, 2007 (his "recommendations" would come later). The document already had been reviewed by the Contact Group. In Belgrade, he handed the plan to President Boris Tadić; then, in Pristina, he presented it to President Fatmir Sejdiu and the Unity Team. He also met at the UNMIK Headquarters with representatives of the non-Albanian communities in Kosovo.

The reaction in Belgrade was hostile. The bloodshed of 1998 and 1999, the Djindjic assassination, and the March 2004 riots meant that the possibility of violence was never far from the minds of observers of the status process. For his part, Koštunica refused to receive Ahtisaari on the grounds that he (Koštunica) was without authority. He further claimed that no one could represent Serbia until a new government was formed – an especially ridiculous assertion because Koštunica himself regularly made major decisions on behalf of Serbia during this period. Undeterred, Ahtisaari arranged for a meeting with President Tadić.

UNOSEK leased a twelve-passenger Learjet® for Ahtisaari's small staff plus two security personnel for the short flight to Belgrade. When the group arrived at the Belgrade Airport, they were met with the pomp and circumstance usually attending a state visit and taken immediately into the VIP lounge at the airport. Not everything went smoothly. The multiple copies of the report were bulky; some were carried in ordinary large traveling bags and others in brown shopping bags emblazoned with the logo of an Austrian children's wear store. Then, as they were walking to the lounge, Ahtisaari discovered that his suit jacket was missing a button. Much consternation ensued until Kai Sauer discovered that he had extra buttons sewn to the inside of his own tailored suit. The Serbian welcoming committee scurried around, found a needle, thread, and scissors, and proceeded to cut a button out of Sauer's jacket and sew it on to Ahtisaari's.[1]

As the delegation motorcade headed into the center of the city to the presidential palace, security was tighter than many staff members had ever seen in Belgrade. Soldiers and MUP police manned almost every intersection. When

[1] June 2007 interview with Kai Sauer and Hua Jiang, New York.

the motorcade arrived at the presidential palace, it stopped under the kind of awning one might find at the automobile entrances to a hotel. No one opened the doors. Puzzled, the staff was about to say something – then, suddenly, heavy curtains dropped down on all four sides of the vehicle, after which Serbian personnel rushed to open the doors and escort Ahtisaari from the car. The Serbian government had learned from Djindjic's assassination, and was using the curtains to block a sniper's view of the car and its passengers. Although Ahtisaari's report was not welcome, the Serbian government did not want any harm to come to him on its watch.

Tadić was courtly and proper as always, but much more formal than on other meetings (he usually joked with Ahtisaari's press representative, but not on this occasion). Ahtisaari made brief comments to Tadić and the assembled Serbian officials. He described the proposal as a compromise that would lay foundations for a future Kosovo that would be viable and stable, where members of all communities could live a dignified, safe, and economically sustainable life and that would contribute to the security and stability of the region. Tadić made a brief, formally correct response, and the UNOSEK team headed back to the Belgrade Airport for their flight to Pristina.

In a news conference in Pristina after presenting his plan to the Kosovo delegation, Ahtisaari was pressed repeatedly for his position on independence. Finally, he winked and said, "Wait for my report to the Security Council."

Later in the month, Serbian and Kosovo delegations met with Ahtisaari in Vienna to discuss the proposal, which contained "General Principles" and twelve "Annexes." He promised to "consider constructive amendments and [be] willing to integrate compromise solutions that parties might reach." After the consultations, he would present the final version to the Secretary General.

General Kosovar Albanian reaction to the draft was that it was an independence package without using the word "independence," and they looked forward to a Security Council resolution that would give the Assembly of Kosovo the sovereignty necessary to declare their independence. Kosovo Serb reaction was decidedly less enthusiastic – the Serbian Archbishop Patriarch called it "unacceptable" because it foresaw division of Kosovo from Serbia.

Although statehood for Kosovo was implied by the proposal, Ahtisaari claimed to be less interested in borders than in aspects of the plan imperative to economic development in the Balkans, including Serbia, which would improve the lives of all the peoples in the region. The dire economic situation in Kosovo required the most urgent attention he said, and the proposal offered provisions to promote sustainable economic development, including Kosovo's power to apply for membership in international financial institutions. Additionally, the proposal included mechanisms for protecting the safety of non-Albanians and guaranteeing participation of minorities in governmental bodies; it also established a series of municipalities and self-rule in some areas, and identified protected zones for churches and historical heritage sites.

In these consultations, on February 21, March 2, and March 10, 2007, the Serbian and Kosovar delegations remained diametrically opposed on the question of the future status of Kosovo, which naturally spilled out to the rest of the issues. The Belgrade delegation picked over the proposal for every detail that implied statehood for Kosovo, while the Kosovo delegation tried to add further and more detailed explanations within the proposal. By this point in the process, all the negotiations felt like déjà vu, enough that former Serbian Foreign Minister Vuk Drašković spent part of one meeting attempting to build a mock bridge on the conference table out of notebooks, pencils, and coffee cups. The little structure was intended to illustrate the need for a bridge between the two sides – but his construction collapsed twice during the meeting. After the final meeting, with Pristina calling the document draft a "painful compromise" and Belgrade rejecting the proposal in its entirety, Ahtisaari declared the potential for negotiations exhausted. "I regret to say that, at the end of the day, there was no will from the parties to move away from their previously stated positions," Ahtisaari said. "I had hoped, and very much preferred, that this process would lead to a negotiated agreement. But it has left me with no doubt that the parties' respective positions on Kosovo's status do not contain any common ground to achieve such an agreement. No amount of additional negotiation will change that." He would finalize his proposal for submission to the UN Secretary General later in March.

In his report to the Secretary General on March 26, strongly supported by Secretary General Ban Ki-Moon, in Ki-Moon's transmittal to the Security Council, Ahtisaari broke any remaining suspense over the crux of his recommendation: the only viable option for Kosovo was independence, he said, with an initial period of international supervision.

The Secretary General forwarded two distinct Ahtisaari documents to the Security Council: a "Comprehensive Plan" and his "Recommendations." The Ahtisaari Plan was widely praised among human rights experts in Europe and the United States as the most detailed and sophisticated structure for protecting minority rights in a multiethnic society ever developed through international diplomacy.

Although the report lamented that agreement between Belgrade and Pristina was not possible on Kosovo's future status, and observed that no further negotiations would close the gap, it said that the international community must confront two realities. The first was that any attempt to reintegrate Kosovo into Serbia was doomed to fail. "For the past eight years, Kosovo and Serbia have been governed in complete separation," it read.

The establishment of the United Nations Mission in Kosovo (UNMIK) pursuant to Resolution 1244 (1999), and its assumption of all legislative, executive, and judicial authority throughout Kosovo, has created a situation in which Serbia has not exercised any governing authority over Kosovo. This is a reality one cannot deny; it is irreversible. A return of Serbian rule over Kosovo would not be acceptable to the overwhelming majority of the people of Kosovo. Belgrade could not regain its authority without provoking violent opposition. Autonomy of Kosovo within the borders of Serbia – however notional such autonomy may be – is simply not tenable.

Second, continued international administration was not sustainable. For one thing, Kosovar Albanian patience with being denied true self-government could not last:

> While UNMIK has made considerable achievements in Kosovo, international administration of Kosovo cannot continue. Under UNMIK authority, Kosovo institutions have been created and developed and have increasingly taken on the responsibility of managing Kosovo's affairs. This has set into motion a dynamic political process, which has reinforced the legitimate expectations of the Kosovo people for more ownership in, and responsibility for, their own affairs. These expectations cannot be realized within the framework of continued international administration.

Ahtisaari also asserted that continuing to hold Kosovo in limbo inhibited economic development:

> While UNMIK has facilitated local institutions of self-government, it has not been able to develop a viable economy. Kosovo's uncertain political status has left it unable to access international financial institutions, fully integrate into the regional economy, or attract the foreign capital it needs to invest in basic infrastructure and redress widespread poverty and unemployment. Unlike many of its western Balkans neighbors, Kosovo is also unable to participate effectively in any meaningful process towards the European Union – an otherwise powerful motor for reform and economic development in the region and the most effective way to continue the vital standards implementation process. Kosovo's weak economy is, in short, a source of social and political instability, and its recovery cannot be achieved under the status quo of international administration. Economic development in Kosovo requires the clarity and stability that only independence can provide.

While reiterating that independence was the only viable option, the report acknowledged Kosovo's limited capacity to ensure minority protection, to develop viable democratic institutions, to grow the economy, and to achieve interethnic reconciliation. Accordingly, Ahtisaari proposed that Kosovo's exercise of independence and its implementation of the concrete features of the Comprehensive Proposal be "supervised and supported" by international civilian and military authorities. He urged a "strong" but "focused" international authority over community rights, decentralization, and protection of the Serbian Orthodox Church and the rule of law. These international authorities would have the power to "correct actions," that is, to veto local governmental decisions that would "contravene the provisions of the Settlement proposal and the spirit in which they were crafted."

Under the plan, independent Kosovo would be supervised by three international authorities. An International Civilian Representative (ICR) would be appointed by an International Steering Group (ISG). This ICR would also serve as the EU Special Representative (EUSR). Although the ICR would be the final authority for interpreting the civilian aspects of the plan, he or she would not have executive or legislative powers, except for veto power over legislation adopted by the Kosovo Assembly and, likewise, the power to annul decisions by public authorities that contravened aspects of the plan. The ICR would be supported by an International Civilian Office (ICO) much smaller than UNMIK. The mandate of the ICR would extend for an initial period of two years and would be extended thereafter until the Steering Group determined that Kosovo had implemented the terms of the plan.

A second institution, the European Security and Defense Policy Mission (ESDP) (subsequently known as "EULEX"), directed by the EUSR, would assist Kosovo in developing its rule-of-law institutions. It would possess limited executive authority to investigate sensitive crimes, and retain the capacity to prosecute and judge the guilt or innocence of perpetrators. Meanwhile, KFOR would remain as the International Military Presence (IMP) until Kosovo was capable of providing for its own security.

Anticipating arguments from elements of the international community who feared that Kosovo would set a dangerous precedent for other independence-seeking minorities, the report concluded by emphasizing that Kosovo was a unique case: "In unanimously adopting Resolution 1244 (1999), the Security Council responded to Milošević's actions in Kosovo by denying Serbia a role in its governance, placing Kosovo under temporary United Nations administration and envisaging a political process designed to determine Kosovo's future. The combination of these factors makes Kosovo's circumstances extraordinary."

The "General Principles" section of Ahtisaari's plan committed Kosovo to a future as a multiethnic society that would govern itself democratically and with full respect for the rule of law. It also declared that Kosovo would have "an open market economy with free competition." It proposed the establishment of six new municipalities.

The rest of the relevant provisions for the establishment of an independent Kosovo were contained in twelve Annexes. Annex I mandated certain provisions for a new constitution for Kosovo, including that it incorporate the provisions of the Comprehensive Settlement committing Kosovo to a multiethnic society observant of human rights and fundamental freedoms. It further required the constitution to affirm that Kosovo has no official religion and that it be neutral on questions of religious beliefs. Minority representation in the Kosovar government, on the constitutional court and in other judicial institutions, was ensured. Specifically, it required the constitution to create a 120-member Assembly of Kosovo "elected by secret ballot, on the basis of open lists," and instructed the Assembly to reserve twenty seats for minority communities. It required a supermajority – including a majority of minority representatives in the Assembly – for laws changing municipal boundaries, laws relating to the rights of minority communities, laws on the use of language, and similar concerns of particular interests to minorities. The president of Kosovo was intended to represent the unity of the people, and Annex I authorized him to return once to the assembly for reconsideration any bill he considered detrimental to the legitimate interests of one or more communities.

Annex II specified the right of all members of all communities to express, maintain, and develop their own culture, receive public education in one of Kosovo's official languages of their choice, establish and maintain their own private education and training establishments, and receive public funding for such enterprises. Every citizen would be entitled to use his or her language and alphabet freely in private and in public, and to use the symbols of his or her community.

Annex III, drawing on the negotiations over decentralization, made municipalities the basic unit of local government in Kosovo and gave them "full and exclusive powers, insofar as they concern the local interest." It specifically allowed education in the Serbian language, using curricula or textbooks developed by the Ministry of Education of the Republic of Serbia. Municipalities were authorized to levy and collect local taxes, charges, and fees. The annex also allowed cooperation among municipalities, and cooperation with municipalities and government agencies in the Republic of Serbia. According to the document, "Such cooperation may take the form of the provision by Serbian institutions of financial and technical assistance, including expert personnel and equipment, in the implementation of the municipal competencies." It specified a number of new municipalities created specifically for Serb majorities. This part of the plan embodied the concept of asymmetric decentralization, with Serb-dominated municipalities enjoying rights and privileges denied Albanian-dominated municipalities.

Annex IV provided that judicial institutions, such as courts and public prosecutors' offices, must contain a specified number of minority representatives.

Annex V, drawing on the negotiations over protection of religious heritage, mandated protection and enjoyment of rights, privileges, and immunities by the Serbian Orthodox Church. It immunized assets of the Church from expropriation. It also established protective zones for specified monasteries, churches, and other religious sites.

Annex VI provided that Kosovo would assume its share of the external debt of the Republic of Serbia according to specified principles, also providing for international arbitration if Serbia and Kosovo could not agree on apportionment of the debt.

Annex VII provided that ownership rights in publicly owned enterprises would be transferred to the government of Kosovo, negating any claim that they were still held by the government of Serbia. It also provided that socially owned enterprises and their assets would continue to be managed by the

Kosovo Trust Agency, with oversight by a board of directors containing a majority of internationally appointed directors. It ratified judicial review of Trust Agency decisions by the Special Chamber of the Supreme Court of Kosovo. It also ratified continuation of the Kosovo Property Agency to resolve claims relating to private real property.

Annex VIII gave Kosovo authority over law enforcement, security, justice, public safety, intelligence, civil emergency response, and border control on its territory. This annex authorized a Kosovo Intelligence Service, and a new Kosovo Security Force (KSF) replacing the KPC, which would be disbanded. The KSF was limited to twenty-five hundred active members and eight hundred reserve members. Possession of heavy weapons such as tanks, heavy artillery, or offensive air capability was forbidden.

Annexes IX–XI addressed the structure and authority of the international supervision of Kosovo's independence. Annex IX detailed the mandate of the ICR. It authorized the ICR to annul laws or decisions adopted by Kosovo authorities and to remove from office any public official making serious or repeated failures to comply with the letter or spirit of the Comprehensive Proposal.

Annex X provided general authority for the European Security and Defense Policy Mission, specifying that its head would be appointed by the Council of the European Union.

Annex XI, detailed the responsibilities of IMP, providing that "the authorities of the IMP will be kept under review and, after consultation with the relevant parties and decision by the North Atlantic Council, adjust it accordingly." The North Atlantic Council is the governing body for NATO.

Annex XII set out a legislative agenda that the Assembly of Kosovo was obligated to adopt during the transition position to independence.

The substance of the plan was well within the mainstream of European thinking on the dissolution of Yugoslavia. The basic concept of supervised independence (sometimes called *conditional independence*) was the centerpiece of the approach Europe had taken to the recognition of the first states to secede from Yugoslavia in 1991.[2] Independence and recognition were preconditioned on a commitment to protect human rights and to afford special political protections to Kosovo Serbs. The details represented, not only the views expressed by the Belgrade and Pristina delegations, but they also reflected Ahtisaari's determination to avoid the heavy-handed monopolization of policy decision making that had made progress so difficult in Bosnia and in Kosovo under UNMIK. Decentralization reflected not only reality on the ground since 1999; it also was within the mainstream of European thinking on how to manage potential interethnic conflict without war, ethnic cleansing,

---

[2] See Caplan at 24 (characterizing European guidelines for recognition of states seceding from Yugoslavia as representing "a striking departure" from historic conventions on recognition).

or secession.[3] Only time would tell whether the Kosovo Serbs would cooperate and accept decentralized government as a viable way to be integrated into Kosovo's political structures or whether decentralization would lead to partition.

The UN-led process had been a major success to this point: it led to a very good plan tabled before the Security Council, reflecting the concerns of all parties. Two UN Secretaries General were especially supportive and really went out on a limb supporting the Ahtisaari process.

Despite all the daunting challenges that the UN faced, its institutional support for the Ahtisaari process and his recommendation represented a high-water mark in post–Cold War UN effectiveness. Both Secretary General Kofi Annan and his successor Ban Ki-Moon had unequivocally supported Ahtisaari – although there were some disagreements within the Secretariat between the Department of Political Affairs and the Department of Peacekeeping Operations. From the beginning of his tenure, Ban took a principled position in favor of the Ahtisaari recommendations and did not waver, despite considerable pressure from Moscow. In the Department of Peacekeeping Affairs, Jean-Marie Guehenno was particularly helpful as well. In the field, UNOSEK and UNMIK cooperated well in working out technical details for the period of transition to Kosovo's new status. This was no accident – well-respected former UNMIK officials were part of the UNOSEK staff.

The plan was comprehensive and the process producing it had been well managed. Ahtisaari had done what he was appointed to do, and expectations were high that the Security Council would approve his work promptly, permitting Kosovo to move into its next phase of supervised independence.

---

[3] See Caplan at 5–6 (analyzing European experience with cantonization and federalism as structures to provide a measure of autonomy to restless minority ethnicities, beginning with the South Tyrol region of Italy).

14 The Plan Runs into Trouble

EVEN AS THE FINAL TOUCHES WERE BEING APPLIED TO AHTISAARI'S plan and recommendations, the political tide was running in the wrong direction, although prompt support was expressed in some quarters. On the same date that Ahtisaari's Report and Plan reached the Security Council, the U.S. State Department issued a press statement supporting Ahtisaari's recommendations. Britain followed immediately.

Ahtisaari's reputation and status as a former president of an EU member state was expected to give his report and comprehensive plan special traction in Europe. Ahtisaari had good relationships with the senior U.S. diplomats closely involved with the final status negotiations. His reputation for constructive engagement in negotiating the 1999 Kosovo crisis preceded him. The United States was enthusiastic about the process Ahtisaari managed. Ahtisaari's reputation and the contents of his plan thus provided a bridge between the United States and Europe.

Rather than moving to formal consideration of the report, however, the Security Council began a period of "consultations," with Russia urging further bilateral negotiations between Belgrade and Pristina. The effort to derail Ahtisaari's work had begun.

Presentation of the plan had been delayed with the hope that moderates would gain power in Serbia's January 2007 elections. In New York, at the Security Council, it was difficult to oppose arguments that consideration of the Ahtisaari Plan should wait until things were sorted out in Serbia. Keeping Kosovo was Koštunica's battle cry, and it was hoped that putting the plan on the back burner might strengthen the position of the more pro-European forces aligned with Tadić.

The plan was delayed, but the moderates lost in Serbia. The strong nationalists of the SRS essentially won the elections. Of 250 parliamentary seats, the SRS won 81. President Tadić's Democratic Party came in second with sixty-four seats, and Prime Minister Koštunica's conservative alliance of DSS and the small New Serbia (NS) was third with forty-seven seats. G17+ allied its nineteen seats with Tadić. The new assembly elected Tomislav Nikolić as its Speaker; Nikolić was a former ally of Milošević who now led the ultranationalist Radical Party. He had called for a Greater Serbia and favored alliance with Russia rather than integration into the EU.

The election of Nikolić gave Koštunica the opening he needed to dictate the structure of the new Serbian coalition government. Koštunica and Nikolić conferred, and within hours Nikolić was no longer the Speaker, while Koštunica's party had captured the Ministry of the Interior. Some observers believed Koštunica had procured Nikolić's election as Speaker for just this purpose.

In May 2007, after intense bickering and maneuvering, Serbia's coalition government was assembled and Koštunica remained prime minister. Thirty-two-year-old Vuk Jeremić, Tadić's former adviser, served as Foreign Minister. Few Serbian voices with any significant following expressed anything but determination to hold on to Kosovo. G17+ was a lonely exception, and induced little resonance in Serbian public opinion. Former Foreign Minister Goran Svilanović had been explicitly in favor of letting Kosovo go – and as a consequence, he was denied Koštunica's support for a high-level international appointment. Another promising voice calling for a sensible policy on Kosovo was Čedomir Jovanović, a charismatic leader of the student movement against Milošević who had become the youngest member of the Serbian Assembly in history. Rumors of underworld ties combined with a campaign against his dovishness on Kosovo, however, marginalized him as well. The radicals in the SPS party adhered to a Milošević-like line on Kosovo, organizing protests in favor of war-crime fugitives Mladic and Karadzic, and occasionally vowing to organize armed intervention in Kosovo.

It became clear that Serbia was not going to mute its opposition to Kosovar independence. Russia, seeing opportunities to advance its own geopolitical agenda, began to distance itself from the other members of the Contact Group. As Russian opposition to the Ahtisaari Plan intensified, and the possibility of a Russian veto in the Security Council loomed larger, expected supporters began to jump ship – or at least to head for the lifeboats. European unity in support of his plan was premised on the idea of a UN Security Council mandate for its implementation. When that did not happen, centrifugal forces within Europe pushed Ahtisaari out of the diplomacy following submission of his report and plan.

At first, the desire for European unity worked in favor of a prompt resolution of status and adoption of the Ahtisaari Plan. Representatives of EU member states, even those who had voiced doubts about the Ahtisaari Plan formally or disagreed with the process, reassured their EU colleagues in private that they eventually would fall in line with the rest of Europe. The EU leadership spoke with one voice in designing the EU-led international civilian presence in Kosovo recommended in the Ahtisaari Plan, and consistently backed a UN Security Council resolution approving the entirety of the Ahtisaari Plan. As Rohan said in late May 2007, there would always be states that wished the Kosovo problem would go away, sparing them the necessity of making tough decisions. Delay would always be the most attractive answer for these states, no matter how powerful the rational arguments against delay.

Still, Europe should not be denied credit for doing a very difficult thing in the spring of 2007. Despite the inherent challenges of reaching any kind of decision through the sovereign foreign policies of its twenty-seven members, the EU promised that it would deliver support for the Ahtisaari Plan in New York, and it did. There were five to ten members who were skeptical or out-right opposed to the Ahtisaari process, but they agreed to remain silent and stay out of the way of the two permanent European members of the Security Council. They did just that, to the EU's credit. The desired result of a Security Council resolution was derailed by Russian opposition, not by any European backing away from its commitment to support a Security Council resolution.

Nevertheless, after the Security Council proved a dead end in mid-2007, the desire for European unity began to work against pro-independence EU members, frustrating their attempts to craft an alternative path to the Ahti-saari Plan. Russian intransigence had blurred Europe's collective will.

All along, knowledgeable European diplomats believed that European unity would be shattered if the Security Council did not adopt a new reso-lution. If other steps toward independence were taken – such as a unilateral declaration of independence by the Kosovo Assembly followed by U.S. recog-nition – it was unlikely that more than a handful of EU members would imme-diately follow suit.

The inability of the Security Council to adopt the plan required everyone to go back to the diplomatic drawing board, and at first it was not clear that the political will existed to do creative work there. Without a Security Council resolution it was hard to see how the transition to independence could occur in an orderly manner. In the end, Europe and the United States bonded behind implementation of the Ahtisaari Plan through UDIR with a stronger intra-European commitment and stronger transatlantic ties, but the route to that outcome was only dimly visible in the spring of 2007.

Some anonymous voices within the EU diplomatic community were telling the press that they doubted that Europe could do much more; to them the demise of the Security Council process meant a frozen conflict and diplomatic drift.[1] Others, however, were hopeful that Europe, aided by an understanding but firm United States, could prove its unity at a higher level and grapple suc-cessfully with the much harder problem of acting without a Security Council resolution. There was no clear plan for doing that in mid-2007, but one could be developed with a little more time.

Unable to produce a solid vote in favor of Kosovo's independence at a March 2007 ministerial meeting, reluctant members of the EU now began to say that the Ahtisaari process had not been transparent enough. Some of the

---

[1] See *Kosovo: Divisions After Independence* (September 3, 2007), located at http://www.b92. net/eng/news/politics-article.php?yyyy=2007&mm=09&dd=03&nav_category=93&nav_id= 43488 (discussing article in German newspaper *Frankfurter Allgemeine Zeitung* stating that the EU will spend years managing a frozen conflict on the southeastern perimeter, but a frozen conflict is better than a "hot" conflict).

smaller countries in Europe had not experienced Russian or Serbian intransigence face-to-face, and therefore held an unwarranted hope in further bilateral negotiations. By making its participation in the Ahtisaari Plan contingent on a Security Council resolution, the EU had basically outmaneuvered itself and had given Russia the keys to the process. Suddenly it was looking alarmingly like 1991 all over again, when the EU was unable to act collectively to respond to the impending danger of Yugoslavia's disintegration.

Russia was hardly oblivious to these fissures within Europe. Genuine transatlantic unity at the beginning of 2007 might have dissuaded Russia from spending its political capital on Kosovo, but Russia now saw opportunities to drive wedges between EU members, and between the EU and the United States.

The EU had bet that, with sufficient U.S. and European unity, Russia eventually would abstain from voting on a Security Council resolution, thereby enabling it to pass. This belief was not born simply from hope; it was a conclusion based on consistent Russian behavior in the Contact Group and elsewhere. In January 2006, in conjunction with the EU foreign ministers' meeting in London, the Contact Group added the proviso that any final status decision must be "acceptable to the people of Kosovo." Because the Albanians were the overwhelming majority in Kosovo, this meant independence. Russia, as a member of the Contact Group, signed on to this proviso. "Russia will not stand in the way of the inevitable," said Russian Foreign Minister Lavrov in an interview with the *Financial Times*.[2] "I don't believe there were signals from Russia that it would block the Plan in the Security Council," Jessen-Petersen says. "My Russian friends always said 'we want to be helpful.' We always had to accommodate some concerns of Russia, but when we did, Russia always allowed us to move to the next step."[3] Western negotiators thought that Russia would believe its interests best served by stability in the Balkans.

On the merits, there was nothing that Russia could possibly object to in the fifth draft of the Security Council resolution. The draft gave Russia everything it said it wanted – no explicit reference to the Ahtisaari Plan, no automatic implementation of the plan, special emphasis on returns, further emphasis on security for minorities, and a simple exchange of an EU mission for UNMIK. However, Kosovo's final status had become part of a larger game for Russia.

It is unlikely that the Quint simply misread Russian interests and intentions. The Russians consistently had agreed that independence would be the ultimate solution, while insisting that it not be imposed on Belgrade. Perhaps the West underestimated the strength of the second part of the Russian position, but that is not likely. At the onset of his mission, Martti Ahtisaari pointed

---

[2] Guy Dinmore and Daniel Dombey, "Russia and China Give Assurance They Will Not Stand in Way of Kosovo Independence," *Financial Times* (March 15, 2006), located at http://www.ft.com/cms/s/0/4114ba88-b3c8–11da-89c7–0000779e2340.html?nclick_check=1.

[3] July 10, 2008, interview with Soren Jessen-Petersen.

out to the Contact Group that Russia had only said what Kosovo could not be, and that the Contact Group had to move Russia toward saying what Kosovo would be. More particularly, at the beginning of the January 2006 meeting, British Foreign Secretary Jack Straw looked Lavrov in the face and said, "We have to be clear that independence is the ultimate answer." Everyone was present; it is hard to imagine a higher-level meeting. The EU Foreign Policy Chief Solana was there, as were the EU president and the Secretary General of NATO. Everyone was watching. Lavrov seemed to get the message and to be in an agreeable mood.[4] "There was nothing from Russia contesting Ahtisaari's statement in his first meeting with the Contact Group, when he said that independence was the likely result of his process," says Jessen-Petersen. "At that point, Russia could have said, 'Whoa! Stop. We don't agree with that,' but it did not." Ahtisaari said that someone must deliver to Belgrade the message that the Contact Group was headed toward independence. Russia agreed that the Quint countries could deliver the message to Belgrade privately. Russia said, "We won't deliver the message, but we won't say anything that undercuts it." Ahtisaari used the remainder of January working out a draft of eight principles to be communicated to Belgrade and Pristina. Russia tinkered with the language of the principle declaring that Kosovo could not go back to its 1989 status and eventually agreed to the text.

In the spring, Security Council approval still seemed possible. On April 3, 2007, Wisner made the following estimate of votes in the Security Council: for – United States, United Kingdom, France, Italy, Slovakia; abstain – Russia, China; undecided – Indonesia (leaning against), Qatar (likely for), Ghana, Congo, Peru (possible yes), Panama (possible yes). By April 22, his estimate was: for – United States, United Kingdom, France, Italy, Belgium, Slovakia, Qatar, Congo, Panama; undecided – Peru, Ghana, Indonesia, South Africa.

If Russia had acquiesced in the Security Council, the rest of the Security Council – those not from Europe and without close ties with the United States or Russia – would have voted for a Security Council resolution. These nations mostly took the position that Kosovo's status was not a global problem; it was a European/NATO/U.S. problem. Some wanted the Contact Group to solve the issue outside the Security Council, either via bilateral agreement or by allowing Kosovo to declare its own independence. A unilateral declaration of independence, followed by recognition, was fine by them; such is the way states are created. In Rohan's talks in New York, the non–European Council members did not advocate a solution outside the Security Council. What they said instead was that Kosovo was a European problem and that if the Europeans together had proposed a solution they would have agreed. Because the Europeans obviously did not have a unified position, they had to make a judgment according to their own criteria and interests. These states saw no advantage to giving a Security Council blessing to extracting 15 percent of one state's

---

[4] May 2007 interview in New York (British).

territory to create a new state. They feared the precedent this could set for many parts of the world where boundaries are far less well defined than in the Balkans. Once Russia created an impasse to a Security Council resolution, their reservations came to the fore.

Of course, the positions of the individual Security Council members were more varied and nuanced than this generalization suggests. Some, like Panama, had no real position. South Africa and Indonesia hated the subject because of their own problems with separatist elements, and Indonesia manifestly did not believe that Kosovo was just a European–United States matter. South Africa worried about fragmentation in Africa more generally. The Chinese, on the other hand, were inclined to let Europe and the United States sort out what the Chinese saw as a mess of their own making.

As it became clear that the Ahtisaari Plan would not be embraced quickly by the Security Council, solidarity among the Kosovar Albanians also threatened to unravel. Tension was rising between Hashim Thaçi, who wanted to be prime minister, and Agim Çeku, who was the prime minister with Ramush Haradinaj's support. The tension would cause the Unity Team to collapse if it was not managed adroitly, and the Kosovars trusted only the United States to manage it.

Until Haradinaj returned to custody at the commencement of his trial in March 2007, he was by most lights the most powerful man in Kosovo. He was widely perceived as giving orders to Çeku and Sejdiu, and internationals and Kosovo political leaders alike checked almost everything with Haradinaj before they made a final decision. In addition, he surely could be controlled: his continued freedom on provisional release depended on continued assertions by the SRSG that he was helpful in assuring peace and security in Kosovo as final status negotiations proceeded.

When Haradinaj returned to The Hague, his preoccupation with his trial opened a new vacuum in Kosovar politics, especially because it was uncertain what his future would be. One distinct possibility was that he would be acquitted (as he ultimately was) and would return to Kosovo as a hero, prepared to become the dominant political leader, unencumbered by formal public involvement in the final status process. If Kosovars were disappointed with final status, then Haradinaj might well lead them in a direction contrary to that preferred by the West. If he were acquitted by the ICTY, he would be relieved of the tight international control that had followed his indictment, and he would be free of any taint of association with the Unity Team. If he were convicted, he would be removed from the official political scene for several years – but his conviction might make him a martyr in the eyes of the Kosovar Albanian public, and could trigger a violent reaction. An obstructionist role for Haradinaj was not, however, a concrete fear of the architects of Western policy toward Kosovo. Everyone believed he had been transformed from a militant into a statesman. "It was not a factor in our thinking," says Wisner. Unity Team unity was.

A spring 2007 meeting, sponsored by the Rockefeller Brothers Fund, was helpful in reinforcing Kosovar Albanian unity. Held at the Fund's Pocantico Conference Center from April 12 to April 15, 2007, the conference on "Developing a Strategy for Kosovo's First 120 Days" involved the Unity Team and other political and civil-society leaders from Kosovo in charting an independent Kosovo's course under the Ahtisaari Plan. Co-chaired by Frank Wisner, Wolfgang Petrich, and Steven Heintz, the conference included all the members of the Unity Team and participation by former President Bill Clinton, former Secretary of State Madeline Albright, former UN Ambassador Richard Holbrooke, Under-Secretary of State Nicholas Burns, and Assistant Secretary Rosemary DiCarlo.

At the conference, Wisner and Burns privately confirmed with the Unity Team the existence of a Plan B contemplating a unilateral declaration of independence followed by recognition (UDIR). They emphasized, however, that the United States much preferred a Security Council resolution (Plan A) and would not go public with the existence of a Plan B lest that kill Plan A. "We will stand by our commitment to Plan B, if necessary," they said, however. On April 13 at the conference, President Clinton spoke movingly of the need for reconciliation. Later, after his speech, he called the president of Indonesia to urge him to back independence. The "Pocantico Declaration," signed at the end of the conference committed the Unity Team to stick together and identified concrete priorities for the immediate post-independence period.

Back in New York, the Security Council decided on April 19, 2007, to undertake a mission to Kosovo on the basis of the proposal by the Russian Federation so that its members could investigate conditions for themselves. The mission formally reported to the Security Council on May 4, 2007, essentially reiterating what was already well known about economic conditions, ethnic tensions, and the intractability of Belgrade's and Pristina's positions on final status.

On May 16, the Belgian Foreign Minister argued to Wisner that Russia would not veto a Security Council resolution, but the Russian position on Kosovo had hardened considerably. Putin's public-opinion ratings in Russia went up whenever he asserted Russian power. Rice and Merkel were taken aback by some of Putin's rhetoric but were determined to press forward.

At first, hopes for Russian acquiescence and concern to preserve a fragile European unity suppressed prudence: a commitment to prompt implementation of a contingency plan. Much of the EU simply was not prepared to make such a commitment yet. As a result, there was a certain amount of floundering in May and June of 2007, when acceptance of Ahtisaari's work by the Security Council proved more difficult than the Contact Group had anticipated. The EU went through a period of denial: surely Russia could be persuaded to join in some sort of final status plan. As Soren Jessen-Petersen said at the time, "The new trap may be that the West has prepared five different draft Security Council resolutions, each one sacrificing some part of the Ahtisaari recommendation. Russia may be waiting for draft eight or nine before it begins to negotiate. At that point, any semblance of a serious resolution to final status would have been surrendered by the West negotiating against itself."[5]

On May 22, 2007, National Security Adviser Hadley chaired an NSC principals meeting. Secretary of Defense Gates, Steve Kappas from the CIA, and the Chairman of the Joint Chiefs of Staff (JCS) attended, as well as Wisner. Secretary Rice briefed the attendees on Kosovo developments. The attendees cleared modifications to a French-circulated draft Security Council resolution. By the end of May, it became clear that a logjam at the Security Council would make it unlikely that the Kosovo issue could be resolved during the U.S. presidency of the Council.

Nevertheless, hopes persisted for some kind of breakthrough. President Bush prepared for a personal meeting with Russian President Putin at his parents' retreat in Kennebunkport, Maine, in early July 2007, after the window of opportunity for an early Security Council vote on the Ahtisaari proposal had already closed. The very scheduling of the meeting offered a new excuse for delay. Putin was to visit the Bush vacation home in Kennebunkport on the first and second of July, two days into the Russian presidency of the Security Council. If President Bush was trying to mend personal relations with President Putin, it hardly would be appropriate to poke the Russian in the eye days before Putin's visit by insisting on a Security Council vote that would dramatize Russian isolation on the Kosovo issue or, worse, by recognizing a Kosovar declaration of independence. Moreover, Russia, holding the presidency of the Security Council, was not going to schedule such a vote anyway.

Nevertheless, hope springs eternal, especially among those seeking to delay risky decisions. Some optimists mused that Putin and Bush might be able to agree that the Russians would endorse or at least not veto a Security Council resolution adopting the Ahtisaari Plan, perhaps with a few face-saving tweaks in the text of the plan – and that Russia would like for this to occur during its presidency of the Security Council so that Russia could demonstrate its commitment to international statesmanship after all.

There were no signs from the Russians, however, that Putin's position in private discussions with Bush would be any less obdurate than Russia's public position in the preceding weeks. So if any positions changed in Kennebunkport, it would likely be a weakening of the theretofore-firm American determination to adopt the Ahtisaari Plan immediately and eventually to recognize an independent Kosovo. The more hopeful scenario put entirely too much weight on the role of personal relations in international diplomacy, and on the persuasiveness of President Bush to turn around an interlocutor who was tough and sophisticated; it was far more likely that waiting for the outcome of Kennebunkport represented just another fruitless delay.

[5] July 2007 interview with Jessen-Petersen.

During June and July, work proceeded in the Security Council on the Ahtisaari Plan, ICO empowerment, NATO continuity, and an end to Resolution 1244. Russia balked at automatic resolution of Kosovo's status. Its public statements were bellicose, with palpable contempt for the U.S. and European position. At one point Deputy Foreign Minister Titov said to other diplomats, "We don't give a damn how many votes the U.S. has; we have what we need – one vote."[6]

In June 2007, the mood among European, U.S., and UN diplomats was decidedly grim. Expectations of swift Security Council approval had been replaced by fear that the whole process was unraveling. The field of maneuver was tightening. Russian opposition put the Europeans in a tight corner. There was no prospect of broad European consensus absent a Security Council resolution. French Foreign Minister Kouchner said to Richard Holbrooke, "The Russians have us over a barrel. European unity is more important than Kosovar Albanian aspirations." Europeans told the United States that a Security Council vote and a Russian veto would kill chances for European unity.

Some British observers, on the other hand, thought that an action-forcing event was necessary, and they were frustrated that the United States did not push harder, sooner. "The last six months have been a long string of magic dates and events which were supposed to produce a solution or at least movement, and they all have come and gone," said one senior British diplomat in July 2007. "Absent some change of facts on the ground, the matter will continue to drift. People are all over the place in the Security Council. Even the U.S. position is something of a mystery. Khalizid said, earlier in July, that the matter would be resolved one way or another within ten days, but at almost the same time, U.S. Assistant Secretary of State Fried was making a speech in Zagreb taking a far softer line, suggesting that the U.S. would not take any forcing action for many months. So everyone is trying to figure out how to square that circle." Inevitably, it would come in the form of a unilateral declaration of independence. "The best thing would be for the U.S. to tell the Kosovars they can go ahead and do that – now," the British diplomat insisted in the spring of 2007. "Once a UDI occurs, then the pressure will be on for some states, at least, to recognize Kosovo, and some will. Once that happens, there will be no possibility for further dithering by other EU members; they will either have to recognize Kosovo or be prominent in their refusal to do so. That is not an orderly process, but it would produce movement. The present process will just produce further dithering."

As another UN diplomat put it, "If this were Asia, there would have been demonstrations, a little bit of violence, a unilateral declaration of independence, and the matter would be settled and people could figure out how to

---

[6] Confidential interview, May 2008.

move on. But this is Europe, where people are less bold and quite fearful of disorder in decision-making processes."[7]

Indeed, some UN personnel and European diplomats seemed, in conversations during the summer of 2007, far more frustrated and impatient and disgusted with EU dithering than did the U.S. representatives. Part of that may have reflected a sense of obligation on the part of U.S. diplomats to maintain the face of U.S. diplomacy, but it also reflected a more realistic hard-nosed view of how negotiations work: they work well only when there is pressure from some kind of action-forcing event. U.S. protagonists focused more on the U.S. political capital accounts; U.S. policy makers were concerned about the long-term effects of another confrontation with Europe. The fear of U.S. unilateralism actually was greater within the U.S. government than within the international community. Conversely, having bashed the United States for acting unilaterally with respect to Iraq, and to a lesser extent with respect to Kosovo in 1999, many European diplomats wished for nothing more than U.S. unilateralism with respect to Kosovo's final status, as a stimulus for the EU to get its act together.

The United States' sidelining of the UN Security Council before the Iraq invasion, and the Bush administration's belligerent international posturing, put a scare into Europeans who cared about the continued viability of the UN and who saw the EU as a counterbalance to U.S. power. From this perspective, either forcing the Security Council vote on the Ahtisaari Plan and triggering a Russian veto, or inaction by the Security Council followed by a unilateral declaration of independence and U.S. recognition, would create a serious, concrete, and imminent threat to the UN's future capacity. In many European capitals, a vague threat of violence that might take years to develop was weighed against the immediate reality of further undermining the UN Security Council's credibility. In framing this comparison, one can see the logic of embracing a delay to allow further diplomacy.

The reality was that European diplomats were grasping at straws. U.S. policy makers continued to claim that the United States had not changed its position or backed away. There still was a hint of European sentiment that perhaps the United States should force a vote in the Security Council – although the United States rarely had done so in the past when a veto was expected. Still, the United States might be able to force a Security Council vote on Friday, June 8, or during the following weeks of June. Belgium was in the chair, and wanted a vote, even if Russia cast a veto, but France did not want to force a Russian veto. There really was nothing else that could be given to the Serbs. In fact, as Assistant Secretary of State Rosemary DiCarlo observed at the time, Serbia had been more reasonable three months earlier. In addition, Russia not only had not leaned on Serbia in favor of the Ahtisaari Plan, it had emboldened Serbia to be even more difficult.

---

[7] Confidential interview, June 2007, New York.

In desperation, the West essentially began negotiating against itself as Russia refused to say what it would accept. Between the date that Ahtisaari's recommendations were transmitted to the Security Council and July 20, at least five draft Security Council resolutions were prepared and discussed. The first simply adopted Ahtisaari's recommendations and rescinded Security Council Resolution 1244. The second and third softened the language adopting Ahtisaari's plan.

The rationale for the redrafting process was to present Russia with a looser, more ambiguous Security Council resolution to make it clear to the Russians that they could go along if they wanted, and to isolate the Russians from Europe if they did not go along. "There was Plan B, Plan C, and so on," says Wisner, "but these never crystallized because work on them was preempted by the Troika process."[8]

On June 7, 2007, freshly inaugurated French President Nicolas Sarkozy and his newly appointed Foreign Minister Bernard Kouchner threw what initially seemed to be a major monkey wrench into the faltering effort to isolate Russia. At the G8 Summit then underway in Heiligendamm, Sarkozy, with no warning (Kouchner claimed to be the instigator), proposed six-month further negotiations followed by freedom for Kosovo to declare independence. Alternatively, at the end of the six months, independence – or at least implementation of the Ahtisaari Plan – might be automatic if no negotiated agreement had been reached.

Before this bombshell, Sarkozy had been portrayed widely in the French and U.S. press as tilting toward the United States in geopolitical matters. His proposal in the face of U.S. determination that the Ahtisaari Plan be adopted by the Security Council was a major anomaly in any such tilt. Sarkozy's statement appeared to pull the rug out from under the EU and U.S. position at the time. His statement loosened the vice that had been intermittently tightening on Russia.

At least one UNOSEK senior staff member, however, thought at the time that the Sarkozy proposal presented new opportunities. A resolution could be written that would provide a six-month space for further negotiations, and it would declare supervised independence automatically at the end of the period. To be sure, this would be a far more draconian approach than the Security Council was used to adopting.

Of course one delay might be followed by further delay; it is easy to buy into one delay at a time. It was also possible, however, for the United States and backers of decisive action by the EU to extract promises from the doubters that the six-month period would be it – no more delay after that. That is exactly how things worked out.

Crucial to the dynamics was U.S. President Bush's statement, on June 10, 2007, in a joint press conference during his visit to Tirana, Albania: "I'm a

---

[8] May 2008 interview with Frank Wisner.

strong supporter of the Ahtisaari Plan," he said. "When does the process end? [T]he time is now.... I made it clear that, one, that we need to get moving; and two, that the end result is independence."[9] This unequivocal statement quashed any lingering expectations that Pristina would agree to anything less than independence on a short timetable. It also led Belgrade to charge that the United States had sabotaged the talks, leaving Russia free to obstruct and to support Serbian intransigence.

On June 12, the Quint political directors met in Paris. Wisner and Nick Burns "argued bravely" for preparatory negotiations on Plan C: recognition and support of Kosovo's independence outside the Security Council. Schaeffer would go no further than a Plan B; a Security Council resolution moot on the Ahtisaari Plan while empowering formation of the ICO, continued NATO presence, and 120 days of further talks. That plan was crystallized in a draft resolution during the second week of June. An alternative draft resolution authorized 120 days further negotiation, to be followed by automatic adoption of the Ahtisaari recommendations if no agreement emerged from the negotiations. This draft was circulated to members of the Security Council on June 20, and members of the Security Council discussed the new draft in a private session. Russia shot it down,[10] and no formal action was taken. Tensions in Kosovo increased again as Independence Day receded further into the future. Wisner called Çeku to reassure him.

At a meeting in Brussels on June 21, 2008, the EU ministers agreed to postpone a decision on Kosovo's final status, and urged Pristina and Belgrade to "have a new dialogue." The communiqué issuing from the meeting was silent on whether a new mediator should be appointed, which initially was interpreted as supporting a continued mandate for Ahtisaari and UNOSEK. UNOSEK's budget extended through the end of 2007, and a core, whittled-down staff had already agreed to remain through the end of the year. The timing was relatively fortunate: otherwise, the risk was enormous that if UNOSEK were disbanded, other individuals or institutions would fill the vacuum and begin some alternative process, essentially erasing any of UNOSEK's hard-won progress. During the Security Council deliberations in mid-2007, Ahtisaari visited the capitals of Spain, Indonesia, and South Africa twice to help sell the plan.

There was a Security Council meeting, with accompanying background discussions, on July 9. Russia had not changed its position one iota, and Indonesia had come down solidly behind Russia. The United States had not changed its position either, and there was no point to putting to a vote the fourth draft resolution for a period of further negotiations, a mandate for an EU mission, and more or less automatic implementation of the Ahtisaari proposal at the end in the absence of bilateral agreement. A fifth draft resolution was prepared

---

[9] Transcript of press conference, located at http://www.whitehouse.gov/news/releases/2007/06/20070610–1.html.

[10] May 2008 interview with Frank Wisner.

that would provide for 120 days of further bilateral negotiations and authorize an EU civilian presence in Kosovo but not make any provision for final status, such as the automatic implementation of the Ahtisaari Plan. Russia rejected it.

The pressure on Europe had increased but it was too late to do anything. Nothing would happen in the Security Council in six months. The matter would be taken up again in the late fall or early 2008 without the same momentum that had existed in mid-2007. Solana had made a major turnaround. Until late June and early July, he had favored delay to provide more time to rally European consensus. Now he was worried that if something were not done immediately, Europe would have to get involved later when Kosovo would be a much bigger mess.

On July 12, Nick Burns signaled to the Quint in Paris that the United States would accept no more than 120 days further negotiations. Burns and Wisner told Kouchner that Wisner would go to Pristina to counsel the Kosovar Albanians to be patient a while longer. Wisner did so, and found the Kosovar Albanians horrified by the prospect of four more months of negotiation. He reassured them of U.S. steadfastness, referring to President Bush's statement in Tirana. Wisner was convinced that the Unity Team would continue to unravel through the rest of July, and that it would implode altogether if there were no clarity about the U.S. and EU positions. The EU would not provide clarity; only the United States could. So, Wisner suggested to Secretary Rice that she invite the Unity Team to Washington to meet with her in late July. She liked the idea. Wisner called Çeku on July 17 because he and Surroi were still feeling pressures in Kosovo and urged him not to make any unilateral moves, but instead listen to the Secretary and move ahead in partnership. "Çeku agreed despite the harshness of my tone, and the stridency of my advocacy," Wisner said.

By mid-July, the United States had crystallized the following plan:

1. Run out the clock on getting a Security Council resolution embodying Plan A, with a specific authorization of the Ahtisaari Plan.
2. If unsuccessful with Plan A, move to a minimalist Plan B: a Security Council resolution authorizing international presences.
3. If unsuccessful with Plan B, persuade the Europeans to accept Plan C – coordinated recognition of a Kosovar declaration of independence.
4. If unable to secure Plan C, recognize Kosovo and persuade as many European states to recognize as possible.
5. Dan Fried would travel to Pristina and Belgrade and invite the Unity Team to come to the United States.
6. The Albanians would arrive on July 23 and Jeremić, representing Serbia, on July 27.
7. Ask the Secretary General to superintend a replacement negotiation strategy and eventual UNMIK confirmation of a UDI.[11]

---

[11] Confidential 2008 interview.

Nick Burns and Rosemary DiCarlo worked hard with their counterparts to inch the Europeans from Plan A to Plan B to Plan C. In London, on July 17, Burns was able to secure UK and French commitments – despite Kouchner's doubts – to Plan C.

On July 19, Nick Burns met with the Quint political directors and obtained agreement to a July 20 public statement saying that all chances for a Security Council resolution had been exhausted, blaming Russia for the impasse. The statement would allow 120 days for further negotiations. Germany and Italy would not agree to a further statement declaring that the members of the Quint would recognize Kosovo's independence at the end of the 120-day period if negotiations were unsuccessful, but Burns said the United States would not join a common front without such a commitment and that instead would recognize Kosovo on its own. Britain and France supported the U.S. position in an effort to leave Germany the choice of joining a consensus or being isolated. Fried and Rice would talk to the Germans to try to overcome Steinmeier's objections. Zal Khalizad would talk to the Secretary General to try to obtain his ownership of the 120-day negotiation process through the Contact Group, or, if the Russians would not agree, by the Quint, either with a common EU position or by EU Quint members with the United States and Russia.

On July 20, the West officially gave up on the Security Council. The fifth draft resolution, which omitted automatic adoption of the Ahtisaari Plan at the end of the 120-day period, was discussed. Russia was still opposed, and the draft was not put to a vote. This marked the official abandonment of the Security Council as an instrument for determining final status. The Security Council was at a complete impasse, and nothing would break the impasse absent something that changed the facts on the ground significantly.

European diplomacy was so focused on how to manage the mess then developing at UN Headquarters in New York that there was little energy left to consider what was going on in Kosovo itself, although the dynamics of politics in Kosovo were changing dramatically and threatened an explosion unless a new scenario for final status emerged.

The United States, however, continued to be concerned. An implosion of the Unity Team would make implementation of any plan extremely difficult. The Unity Team had been established as a substitute for a grand coalition government; Thaçi and Surroi were needed on the constructive side of final status talks while Kosovo's other most effective leader – Haradinaj – remained in jail. The Unity Team was fearful of doing anything that would deviate too far from what the U.S. and European leadership wanted them to do. They recognized that Kosovo was likely to get independence only if the United States pushed hard for it and was prepared to use its power unilaterally to recognize Kosovo. Thaçi and Sejdiu were most firmly in this position, although Thaçi was struggling to understand his options and to choose among them. He was increasingly preoccupied with his demand for national elections in Kosovo to be held without further delay. Çeku and Surroi were more restless – Surroi because he perceived that the United States needed some pressure of action or threatened action by the Unity Team in order to take the plunge, and Çeku because he was acutely embarrassed by having announced specific dates for independence and then having been proved wrong. It was not clear to any of them what kind of Unity Team position might accelerate U.S. unilateral action without alienating the United States. Any significant misstep could cause the United States to turn its attention elsewhere or to withdraw support from specific individuals on the Unity Team – any loss of American support could be fatal to their future political ambitions. Throughout the process, Blerim Shala, editor of Pristina's number two newspaper *Zeri*, was helpful in explaining the dynamics of Kosovar Albanian politics to the internationals.

Patience throughout Kosovo was surely running thin. When I went to Kosovo in July 2007, the view on the street in Pristina was one of disgust with the Unity Team and a growing lack of confidence in the entire Kosovo political elite. There was much frustration at the European Union, and trepidation about when the United States would deliver on its promise to help Kosovo achieve independence. Unvaryingly, ordinary people believed that the Unity Team had become essentially irrelevant, and that it was basically incapable of making any decisions or taking any initiatives. Even if that were not so, said Kosovars, the Unity Team's decisions would not make any difference; any relevant decisions would be made in Washington and Brussels. Public confidence in the Unity Team had eroded to virtually nothing.

The credibility of the international community was also low. There was a pervasive sense that the only thing the Kosovars could count on to produce independence was the United States, and the upcoming meeting with Secretary Rice was crucial.

On July 23, 2007, the members of the Unity Team met with Secretary Rice as planned. Going into the meeting, Thaçi was pushing for elections before year-end. Surroi and Çeku were arguing that the time had come for Albanians to take matters into their own hands and declare independence. Wisner called Çeku and pointed out that Washington would not react well to "blackmail." Çeku agreed but a Unity Team document purporting to be from Çeku to the other members urging that the Kosovars "seize the reins" appeared in the *Boston Globe* in a story written by David L. Phillips[12] who then had a "stressful" telephone conversation with Wisner.

In the meeting itself, the Pristina delegation was unified and calm. Sejdiu held the floor and committed to continued partnership with the United States.

---

[12] David L. Phillips, "Kosovo's Long Path to Autonomy," *Boston Globe*, July 20, 2007, located at http://www.boston.com/news/globe/editorial_opinion/oped/articles/2007/07/20/kosovos_long_path_to_autonomy/. Phillips served as Senior Fellow at the Council on Foreign Relations, a visiting scholar at Harvard, and as director of several NGOs, including the International Rescue Committee.

Burns made it clear that after every stone had been turned during the 120 days of negotiations, the United States would recognize Kosovo's independence if necessary. Rice sharply refused to set a specific date, however.

Secretary Rice "gave her word" that the United States would follow through, and National Security Adviser Hadley reiterated the message in a subsequent meeting with the Unity Team in the Roosevelt Room at the White House. Sejdiu agreed to continued partnership and avoidance of uncoordinated action by the Kosovars, and the other members of the Unity Team nodded.[13]

The meeting on July 27 between Rice and Serbian Foreign Minister Jeremić proceeded professionally and respectfully, benefiting from Jeremić's tenure and experience as a minister. Jeremić said that partition of an independent Kosovo along the line at Mitrovica was not Serbian policy. Secretary Rice emphasized that the United States was committed to an ongoing partnership with Serbia, and it would not allow Serbia to become a "football" in a geopolitical contest between the United States and Russia. Pointing to Thomas Jefferson's portrait on the wall, she reminded Jeremić that Jefferson had been a slave owner and that her ancestors were slaves. He would be astonished to be sitting in her chair today, she said, but he would have recognized that reality governs public affairs. The U.S. position on Kosovo was not anti-Serbia but acceptance of reality.[14]

Repeated delay in forcing a Security Council vote and eventual abandonment of a formal vote altogether signaled to Serbia and Russia that an appealing alternative to the Ahtisaari Plan was indeed available: indefinite delay. The prospect of further negotiations, without any plausible, merit-based alternative to the Ahtisaari Plan for protecting minority rights in Kosovo, eliminated the focus and structure that the Contact Group principles and Ahtisaari's conduct of the practical negotiations had provided. Now it was anyone's guess what would happen, unless international attention once again was focused on the Ahtisaari Plan.

Issues arising from determining final status outside the Security Council were much more difficult to resolve than anything arising in connection with Security Council implementation of the Ahtisaari Plan. Indeed, they proved so difficult that a critical mass of the European leadership initially shrank from considering the necessity for an alternative pathway. The absence of any alternative meant that Russia and Serbia saw no real downside to blocking Security Council adoption of the Ahtisaari Plan. Nothing would happen except delay, and both wanted delay.

If Europe had either presented a more solid front in support of the Ahtisaari Plan in the Security Council in early 2007 or quickly closed ranks behind an alternative way to implement it outside the UN in mid-2007, Russia would

---

[13] Confidential 2008 interview.
[14] Confidential 2008 interview.

have been confronted with the prospect of a major breach between it and Europe, and an undermining of its desire to be considered an equal partner with the EU and the United States in international relations. It was obvious, however, to anyone paying close attention throughout the first half of 2007 that the Europeans were having difficulty sculpting a face of European unity. The Russians were paying close attention.

The greatest challenges in forging Quint unity were Italy and Germany. Italy had been waffling all over the place, but was likely to be less of a problem than Germany. Germany was a significant source of concern throughout 2007. Foreign Minister Steinmeier "was very worrisome," President Merkel less so, according to one diplomat close to the Troika process. Steinmeier was reluctant to do anything bold that would cause public disaffection with his party. Steinmeier was greatly concerned about the new left-wing party in the Bundestag, which hoped to chip away at support for his Social Democratic Party by playing on popular German antagonism toward U.S. unilateralism. He was unwilling to take risks that helped his domestic opponents. Moreover, Steinmeier had been the personal adviser to Chancellor Schroeder and had given him advice to oppose unilateral military U.S. action in Iraq. This history would predispose him to resist U.S. pressure with respect to Kosovo. It also is reasonable to believe that his close relationship with former Chancellor Schroeder allowed Schroeder to urge Steinmeier to consider the effect on German–Russian relations of too hard a line on Kosovo. Schroeder, now active in the private sector, formally represented Russia on major energy business activities.

There was disagreement even within the UNOSEK staff about how vigorously Germany executed its leadership responsibilities: Germans headed both UNMIK and KFOR and Germany held the presidency of the EU in the critical months from January to June of 2007. Given all those factors, one might have expected Germany to take the lead in vigorous advocacy for the Ahtisaari proposal, to be energetic in whipping European states into line behind it, and to be firm with Russia. On the whole, that did not happen. The British, the Americans, and some parts of UNOSEK were frequently frustrated by the flabbiness of German leadership. Internal UNOSEK communications are rife with calls for German Chancellor Merkel to be reminded that Germany had to be more assertive. Some European observers, however, felt that Germany had done a good job when it held the presidency of the EU, but the dynamics of the EU were beyond Germany's control.

Other challenges to European unity existed as well. Not only the usual suspects – Greece, Slovakia, and perhaps Spain – were skeptical about independence, but smaller states and individual actors also demonstrated an unhelpful naiveté about the Kosovo problem, believing they could come up with some idiosyncratic solution that should be pursued instead of the Ahtisaari recommendation. For example, the Prodi government of Italy surprised UNOSEK and the leaders of the EU early in 2007 with statements raising doubts about the desirability of independence. "Italy, the least helpful member of the Quint, was always flipping and flopping and wringing its hands, trying to please everyone," said one senior diplomat privately.[15] Historically, Italy had been especially concerned with the Albanians, but in recent years it has been much more concerned about its business relations with Serbia and Russia. Its wavering policy undermined its international standing and made it a junior – and sometimes unwelcome – partner in the Contact Group. No one in a position of leadership within the EU had the capacity or the will, as of mid-summer 2007, to suppress these rationalizations for inaction.

Matters were made worse by a cacophony of diplomatic voices outside Kosovo that hinted they had plans for final status superior to the Ahtisaari Plan. Once the Ahtisaari process appeared likely to be followed by other diplomatic processes, envoy envy[16] sprang to the front of the stage. Carl Bildt consistently manifested this condition. In a blog entry posted on January 27, 2007, just as the Ahtisaari Plan was about to land at the Security Council, he declared his intention to go to Kosovo to speak to its leaders about the effect of final status on economic development. The highly publicized visit, undertaken on Bildt's own initiative, implied that Europe should reconsider its backing of the Ahtisaari Plan.

There were two huge missed opportunities for Europe. The first was the EU Council meeting in March/April 2007. The second was the G8 meeting in April/May. Nothing decisive on Kosovo happened at either of these meetings, and serious work had been deferred previously on the promise that the next meeting would prove decisive.

Then, when Nicolas Sarkozy became president of France and Bernard Kouchner became French Foreign Minister after the May 6, 2007, French elections, things took a turn for the better. Kouchner was co-founder of Doctors Without Borders, which had won the Nobel Peace Prize in 1999. Sarkozy's instincts were to close the gap between French and U.S. foreign policy, which was a harbinger of stronger support for the Ahtisaari process and recommendations. French persuasion was the key to bringing Germany on board.

Kouchner created some confusion before he settled in to a more constructive role. Kouchner enjoyed real, experience-based expertise on the Kosovo conflict. Kouchner had been the second SRSG in Kosovo, had his own views on Kosovo's future, and sought the limelight. It was not clear how closely he had followed developments since he left his post as SRSG in January 2001. Likely, he was confident that he knew better than anyone else – including Ahtisaari – how Kosovo's final status should be determined. Indeed, before the dust had fully settled on Sarkozy's startling proposal for a six-month delay, which became the centerpiece of the post-Ahtisaari diplomatic process,

---

[15] Confidential interview, July 2007.

[16] See generally James Traub, *The Best Intentions: Kofi Annan and the UN in the Era of American World Power* (2006).

and which Kouchner claimed credit for formulating, Kouchner traveled to Belgrade and indirectly broached the idea of partitioning Kosovo as one possible solution to consider during the 120-day negotiation period. This was an even more startling proposal than Sarkozy's, given that one of the three "no's" adopted by the Contact Group rejected partition as an outcome. In the end, however, Kouchner's prominence and his support for the Troika process helped build credibility for eventual European support for supervised independence. Although his reputation for grand pronouncements and gestures worried the final status negotiators, he and Sarkozy delivered in the end.

France would come down on the side of independence and help bring Germany on board, but it took a while to get the new personalities sorted out. Eventually Kouchner concluded that further negotiations between Belgrade and Pristina would be fruitless. Kouchner argued that an additional period for negotiations would undercut any belief that Belgrade and Pristina could agree and would persuade Germany and Italy that inaction was inimical to transatlantic relations and to Europe's credibility as an international actor.

Organizing an EU civil administration mission without a UN resolution also was difficult for pragmatic reasons. The EU and its member states had expressed their willingness to organize a civil administration mission for Kosovo in a permissive environment created by a new Security Council resolution. There was every indication, however, that not all member states would be willing to do so in a nonpermissive environment – one in which Russia and Serbia had not agreed to the new mission or one in which the Kosovar Albanians were defiant. In fact, ample authority existed under Resolution 1244 itself to deploy an EU mission, but no one in the West was eager to embrace the idea because it played into Russian hands. Russia had already said that 1244 offered all the authority necessary for another two to three years of the status quo with the EU replacing UNMIK, and the West wanted to maintain the integrity of its position that a new Security Council resolution was necessary or at least highly desirable. It was easier to hide behind legal questions than to solve the pragmatic problem.

Because no alternative pathway had solidified, members of the EU started with a clean slate on the question of acting without a Security Council resolution in late spring 2007. This was a far more difficult prospect than the "keep your doubts to yourselves while the Security Council deliberates" proposition, because the five to ten states that didn't like the Ahtisaari process or plan were now being asked to contribute significant resources to an EU mission without the cover of a UN mandate. It was not clear that they would be willing to do that. The problems could be worked out, but it would take some time and lots of political will.

15 The Troika Takes Over

IN JULY AND AUGUST OF 2007, THE UNITED STATES AND THE EU worked to organize the additional rounds of negotiation. After the Security Council impasse, U.S. Ambassador to the UN Zalmay Khalilzad was quoted as saying, "The Contact Group will lead a new process to move forward as proposed in the resolution. There will be 120-day negotiation, but outside the Security Council because the process there was blocked. Russia is in the Contact Group, but it doesn't have a veto there. Therefore, we have a new process that is not related to the Security Council."[1]

Ahtisaari asked to be excused from managing the 120-day process; his plan, he thought, was the best that could be achieved to serve the legitimate interests of Belgrade and Pristina, and it would be counterproductive to expose it to tinkering. "The last thing we needed was for the Plan to be reopened," he says. "I didn't want any further role for UNOSEK. My folks and I did not want to put the Plan into play for cherry picking by Serbia and Russia."[2] Better would be a process that would show all of Europe that every avenue for resolving Kosovo's status had been explored, leaving the Ahtisaari Plan as the only feasible option. "It was time now for the member states of the EU to step up and do their part. The Quint had to be in the driver's seat," Ahtisaari said later.

The Contact Group met in Vienna on July 25, 2007, to discuss further steps. The Ahtisaari Plan would remain as a concrete pathway forward, but its details would not be the subject of negotiations. Process options included shuttle diplomacy between Belgrade and Pristina, "proximity talks," in which the Contact Group would work separately with delegations from Belgrade and Pristina in the same physical location, while minimizing face-to-face talks between the two delegations, and a possible international conference in the fall. At first, it was contemplated that the entire Contact Group or – more likely – the Quint would actively supervise further negotiations. Kouchner, especially, held this view. Then the decision makers realized that a smaller group, with a German representative speaking for Europe, would be more

---

[1] See Warren Hoge, "Kosovo Independence Measure Withdrawn From UN Council," *New York Times*, July 21, 2007.
[2] February 2008 interview with Martii Ahtisaari.

effective. Kouchner was initially disappointed but came to support the idea and the work of the Troika.[3]

In that July 25, 2007, meeting, the Contact Group agreed that: (1) a U.S./EU/Russia troika would lead further negotiations, (2) the Contact Group would seek some kind of "blessing" for its efforts from the Secretary General of the UN, and (3) Martti Ahtisaari and his UNOSEK team would play only an advisory role rather than serving as official mediators.

The goals, beyond the substantive one of crafting a future status for Kosovo, were to keep Russia involved and to expand European unity on the Kosovo issue. The most desirable path for Russian involvement was its cooperation and support in the Security Council, if not for adoption of the Ahtisaari Plan, then at least for a Security Council mandate for an EU mission in Kosovo. If neither Security Council option proved feasible, it still was desirable to keep Russia involved to limit the intensity of its opposition to the direction for Kosovo that the United States and Europe agreed on.

Privately, some of the diplomats contemplating the further negotiation effort characterized the Troika process as a "charade." "We must give the appearance of taking these negotiations with seriousness without running the risk of actually taking them seriously; they can produce nothing," one senior diplomat said. "Their only value is to show doubters in the European Union that a negotiated solution is impossible. Afterwards, we can say, 'Look, we tried again; this time you can't blame failure on Martti Ahtisaari, whom you said was biased.'"[4]

The Troika process certainly was a charade in the sense that it had almost no prospect of producing agreement between Belgrade and Pristina on independence or any other fundamental change in Kosovo's legal status. It was not a charade in another sense, however: while falling short of producing complete unity, it played an essential role in forging a workable European position.

The Ahtisaari process had been premised on a Security Council resolution adopting his plan and recommendation. In the absence of a Security Council resolution, a critical mass of states had to be persuaded that final status should be resolved outside the Security Council. The most obvious course, going forward from July 2007 when the Security Council proved impotent, was to get Quint agreement on making Kosovo independent. If the Quint supported independence, then the United States and the EU could give a signal, the Kosovars could declare independence, and the United States and other members of the Quint could recognize Kosovo as a state. If – but only if – the Quint was solid, another fifteen or so members of the European Union could be expected to follow.

Germany was the key to Quint solidarity. France was solid, as was Britain. The Gordon Brown government maintained Britain's aggressive advocacy

---

[3] Confidential 2008 interview with senior European diplomat.
[4] Confidential interview, July 2007.

of independence. Mark Malloch-Brown, Minister of State for Africa, Asia, and the UN, had been Deputy Secretary General of the UN. Foreign Secretary David Miliband had worked closely with Tony Blair on Kosovo in 1999. Although there continued to be elements within the British Foreign Service that tilted toward Serbia and feared the implications of Britain's advocating independence for Kosovo,[5] senior British diplomats discounted the likelihood that Serbophile influence would become dominant again in the foreign ministry. Italy would go along with the other four.

The United States had conflicting interests in the negotiations over Kosovo's future. It was, on the one hand, committed to see the Kosovo project through to a conclusion. Despite early instinctive disdain for "Clinton administration projects," of which Kosovo clearly was one,[6] the president and his advisers recognized that a credible U.S. foreign policy depends on one administration keeping the commitments of its predecessors, a point that Wisner and Burns often stressed in NSC meetings. Resolving Kosovo's status also would reduce the need for U.S. military forces to manage a further crisis in the Balkans when they were needed in Iraq, Afghanistan, and elsewhere. On the other hand, no responsible presidential adviser would have counseled, "Forget your relationships with Russia and with Putin; and never mind opportunities for rebuilding U.S. relations with the EU. We must force independence for Kosovo, one way or another."

U.S. reluctance to act unilaterally on Kosovo was shaped by a realization that an important Russian objective was to split the EU and the United States further. The United States did not want to play into Russia's hands by pursuing the unilateral option without every conceivable effort to forge transatlantic unity. The European Union put enormous pressure on the United States in the spring of 2007 neither to put the matter to a vote and get an actual Russian veto nor to follow the UDI path precipitously. As a result, the United States maintained its patience, although President Bush's July 10 speech in Tirana promising independence "one way or another," made it clear that U.S. resolve continued. Wisner, Burns, and Rice reinforced this clarity in every diplomatic encounter throughout the summer and fall of 2007.[7]

The Troika comprised U.S. Special Envoy Frank Wisner, Wolfgang Ischinger, German ambassador to Great Britain and a former ambassador to the United States who had participated in the Dayton Accords, and Russia's top Balkans diplomat Aleksandr Botsan-Kharchenko (generally known as "Sasha"). Ischinger was widely admired in Germany, the United States,

---

[5] See Pettifer at 18.

[6] Condoleezza Rice, "Promoting the National Interest," 79 *Foreign Affairs* No. 1 at 45, 46 (January/February 2000) (arguing that Clinton administration foreign policy failed to separate the "important from the trivial"; acknowledging that strategic interests relating to NATO were involved in Kosovo conflict, but concluding that Clinton administration conducted Kosovo war "incompetently").

[7] May 2008 interview with Frank Wisner.

and throughout Europe. His career had been centered in Europe, the United States, and Bonn/Berlin, where he rose to the summit of German diplomacy. His years in Washington schooled him in U.S. politics and built U.S. confidence in him. "His command of English is flawless," says Wisner. "He makes it his business to know his partners, building up personal ties to supplement his official ones. Angela Merkel on the right; Steinmeier on the left, admire him as clearly the best German diplomat of his generation. Solana was right to select Ischinger for the Troika and give the Troika, its results, and the inevitable inability to bridge Serbian and Kosovar positions a distinctly European color."

"Wolfgang saw the necessity of European unity over Kosovo and believed by opening and closing every door, he could bring Europe to a conclusion which was both hard-headed and united," Wisner said. Everyone involved gave Ischinger high marks for honestly leaving no stone unturned in his efforts to find common ground between Pristina and Belgrade.[8]

Ischinger was tireless in his efforts to brief everyone and to keep them fully engaged in the progress of the negotiations. "Ischinger's unique insight," says Wisner, "was to get the two sides together at the head of state and head of government levels. Never let them say they had no face-to-face negotiations. He wanted to prove to Europe that every stone had been turned over to try to find compromise – and to jerk the rug out from under the Serb sniping at the Ahtisaari process on the grounds that 'we never got a chance to make proposals.'" Ischinger recognized the limitations of Britain, France, Germany, and Italy – the European members of the Quint – saying "We speak for Europe." He was determined to include everyone else as well, to increase the number of European states inside the tent on Kosovo. Ischinger travelled constantly from one European capital to another during the Troika's work. "I had 27 clients; Wisner and Sasha had only one each," he said afterward.[9] Ischinger travelled more than one hundred thousand kilometers (about sixty thousand miles) between the end of July and Christmas 2007. He met with the Rumanian president, the Greek foreign minister, and Carl Bildt in Sweden, visiting the United States three times and Russia twice.

Ischinger himself "had no illusions" at the start of the Troika process. "Early on, I had hopes that the Russians would work with us. If we did not keep meeting with them, we would get nowhere."[10] Ischinger not only worked closely with Sasha, he traveled to Moscow and met with Foreign Minister Lavrov, trying out different ideas for Kosovo's future status. Once or twice, he found glimmers of hope that Russia would support something like the 1972 treaty between the two German states.[11] In the end, however, Russia rejected

---

[8] May 2008 interview with Frank Wisner.

[9] October 2008 interview with Wolfgang Ischinger.

[10] October 2008 interview with Wolfgang Ischinger.

[11] Treaty on the Basis of Relations Between the Federal Republic of Germany and the German Democratic Republic and Supplementary Documents, Signed at Berlin, December 21, 1972, located at http://www.ena.lu/basic_treaty_21_december_1972–020302440.html.

every concrete alternative. Ischinger was not sure whether the intransigence came from the Russian Foreign Ministry or from Putin himself.

Wisner described Sasha as a "mild-spoken, beautifully mannered, and slight man. He knows Serbia and is a true Balkan expert. He speaks Serbian; he knows the leaders and he has superb insights into their positions. These he shares in the name of collegiality – a principle he clings to. Sasha said from the beginning of the Troika process that Russian Foreign Minister Lavrov gave him explicit instructions to make the Troika work, in the name of overall Russian–European–American harmony. Sasha advanced ideas; he shaped our ideas (Wisner's and Ischinger's) to take Serbian views into account and arguably to seek a way ahead. He kept his word and was discreet; by and large he stuck by Troika press discipline."[12] Sasha had Russian-accented but idiomatic and subtle command of English.

"He had slightly less influence in Moscow than Wisner had in Washington and I had in Germany," Ischinger recalls. "He was very helpful and generous with goodwill. But he had to operate according to detailed instructions developed through an extremely cumbersome Russian process." Wisner and Ischinger, on the other hand, were authorized to operate more freely, relying on their judgment. They were not told "do not do this." Instead, the message was, "We understand the challenges you face. You are doing a good job. Keep it up."

Relations among the three members of the Troika were warm and constructive. "My relations with Wisner were quite good," said Ischinger. "Both he and I were experienced."[13]

On July 31, Wisner called Ischinger and committed the United States to good-faith participation in the 120-day negotiation process. It would use the Ahtisaari Plan as the roadmap and would resist partition. He expressed serious doubts that any negotiated outcome could be achieved, acknowledging that Ischinger faced a tough challenge in bringing the Europeans along in accepting reality. No European leaders believed that Belgrade and Pristina could compromise on an issue that both saw as existential. He stressed that the Troika must speak with one voice. Ischinger agreed, but said he had been charged by Solana with trying to see if a compromise was possible.

The Secretary General provided his blessing on August 1, 2007, and welcomed the Troika initiative. He expressed hope that their talks would result in agreement on final status, and he required a report of Contact Group efforts to the Secretary General on December 10, 2007.

Wisner and Ischinger met in London on August 9 and Ischinger then hosted a dinner for the members of the Troika and all the Balkan political directors of the Contact Group. Botsan-Karchenko noted that the Troika offered an opportunity to demonstrate that Russia, the United States, and

---

[12] May 2008 interview with Frank Wisner.
[13] October 2008 interview with Wolfgang Ischinger.

Europe can do joint diplomacy even against long odds and a background of sharp disagreement.

Despite these areas of agreement, several serious disagreements remained. Russia continued to push for no time limits and implementation of final status only when agreed to by Belgrade, Pristina, and all members of the Contact Group. Moreover, Russia rejected the Ahtisaari plan as the basis for negotiations – except perhaps for those parts Serbia liked. Wisner and Ischinger were mindful of the risks of opening up the details of the Ahtisaari Plan to cherry picking; it was useful to leave the plan as the default – the only fully thought-through concrete proposal. Russia wanted to determine negotiation procedures first, before any substantive negotiations took place. The other parties agreed that a 120-day time limit should be set. The U.S. team's position was that the 120-day clock started ticking immediately, so it was fine if Russia wanted to talk about procedures, even if it chewed up two months. The United States settled on December 10, 2007, as a firm deadline for the Troika process.

Wisner left the dinner convinced that compromise was worse for Serbia politically than defeat. Nevertheless, a handful of Europeans argued that direct negotiations between Belgrade and Pristina might produce agreement on a status for Kosovo that differed significantly from the Ahtisaari Plan. Autonomy, partition, and confederation were their only concrete concepts. In the back rooms of what one European diplomat called "the flea circus," partition was a favorite idea, despite having been firmly removed from the negotiating table under the Contact Group's "three no's" and rejected by the Serbian government. French Foreign Minister Kouchner kick started a discussion of partition on a mid-July trip to Belgrade, although he later denied proposing it. Influential senior members of the international community strongly resisted the partition idea and were prepared to walk away if it looked like partition was taking life in bilateral negotiations. The north might be de facto independent of any governance from Pristina, they argued, but both Serbia and an independent Kosovo were on their way into the EU. After five to ten years, the EU political and legal infrastructure would make borders, whether formal or informal, less meaningful. The consistent advice from senior internationals on the ground in 2006–2007 was, "Don't rock the boat in the north; wait for European integration of Serbia and Kosovo to take care of the problem."

The first meeting between the Troika and the Belgrade authorities occurred on August 10. Tadić was polite, and Jeremić radiated cheerfulness. Koštunica, however, made a presentation characterized by one participant as "tough and sour," taunting Wisner with the idea that his trip to Belgrade represented a triumph for Serbia. In subsequent discussions that evening, Samardzic rebuffed a Confederation of Independent States (CIS)[14] analogy offered by Ischinger, saying that it implied separate sovereignty and that the example of

---

[14] The Confederation of Independent States was formed after the breakup of the Soviet Union from its constituent states.

Montenegro showed that confederations among sovereign states end badly. He also rejected partition of Kosovo because it would acknowledge Kosovo's separation from Serbia and would open a Pandora's box with respect to Vojvodina, the Preshevo Valley, and Macedonia.[15]

In actuality, there were two separate Serbian delegations: Jeremić represented Tadić and Samardzic represented Koštunica. "They came from two different universes."[16] Meetings with leaders of the Kosovo Serbian community left no doubt that they had received their instructions from Belgrade – mostly from the Koštunica faction – and were following them.

The Troika went to Pristina the following day and met with the Unity Team, which made it clear that it would participate in the Troika negotiations but had no intention of modifying its commitment to independence. Wisner planted the idea that Pristina could take advantage of an opportunity to be constructive if it proposed a "treaty of friendship and cooperation" that would commit Serbia and an independent Kosovo to protect free trade, free movement of people, and cooperation in the justice, cultural, and health spheres – an idea that resonated with the other members of the Troika and with the Unity Team. It resulted in a formal proposal along those lines at the London meeting on September 17–19.

In contrast to the split in the Serbian delegation, the Team of Unity presented a solid front. "Surroi was really smart and he understood the world," and Thaçi handled himself well in the negotiations with Serbia, frequently resisting the provocations no doubt tempting him to be as abrasive as Samarazic."[17] The Serbs, however, had a legal department and came from a background of serious professionalism, while the Kosovar Albanians only "had a bunch of people not as well equipped as the Serbs."[18] The two visits left intact the conclusion that there was no negotiating range on the subject of status. Nevertheless, in both of these initial meetings, the Troika urged both sides to bring forward new ideas.

Round II of the Troika process occurred in Vienna on August 30. The Albanians "put on a disappointing show," with no proposal on a good-neighbor policy, and presented a confused outline of principles. The Belgrade delegation was more polished in its presentation, giving a slide show on its proposal to give Kosovo full autonomy on internal matters while reserving to Belgrade authority on defense, foreign policy, borders, monetary policy, and foreign affairs. Kosovo, however, would have no administrative or parliamentary presence in Belgrade. Because the Albanians had so little trust in

---

[15] See ICG, *Bridging Kosovo's Mitrovica Divide*, Europe Report No. 165 at 8 (September 13, 2005) (reviewing disadvantages of partition and criticism flabbiness of international opposition to it).

[16] October 2008 interview with Ischinger.

[17] October 2008 interview with Ischinger.

[18] Confidential 2008 interview with a participant in the negotiations.

the Serbs, the proposal envisioned international enforcement of the deal and adjudication of disputes.

Wisner questioned the Serb representatives about the details of their proposed autonomy for Kosovo. "What does it envision with respect to Albanian representation in Belgrade and participation in the Serbian government?" he asked. "They never had good answers. It was like proposing that Arkansas would get no funding from the U.S. government and would have to fly the American flag but have no representation in Congress," Wisner said. "They threw sand in our eyes with ridiculous proposals, wasting our time." Other international participants in the Troika meeting sarcastically asked the Serbs if they would allow the 20 percent of the total population of Serbia comprising Albanians to be reflected by giving 20 percent of the Serb embassies to Albanian ambassadors, and to give 20 percent of the cabinet seats to Albanians. Informally, the watchword was "How about Hashim Thaçi as Serbian Minister of Defense?" The Serbs reviled Thaçi because he had been the political leader of the KLA.

"The Serbian autonomy proposal was bullshit," said another participant.[19] It was written by one of their Swiss German advisers, reflecting a narrow and artificial view of international law. Wisner did a masterful job of cross-examining Samarazic on the proposal, asking him at one point how Kosovar Albanian views would be reflected if Serbia were to negotiate a treaty with Russia. "Their answers were horrible – 'the Albanians don't want to be represented.' I would have had a hard time selling it in Europe. Even the Russians said that it was a horrible paper."

"We were off to a slow start," Wisner observed privately.

On September 8, U.S. State Department spokesman Kurt Volker was quoted by *Agence-France Presse* as saying, "If Kosovo unilaterally declares independence, the United States will recognize that independence, as, we believe, will others, since that is the only solution for the Balkans."[20] His statement made the United States seem to have marginalized the Troika negotiations. The United States could not afford anything that would undermine the Troika's effort to forge transatlantic unity. The U.S. State Department scurried to respond to adverse Russian and Serbian reaction. The statement was simply a product of Volker not being fully briefed on the U.S. position, said the State Department. Meanwhile, the most senior figure in the Serbian Kosovo-Metohija Ministry specifically threatened violence should Kosovo unilaterally declare independence. "Tempests in teapots," Wisner remarked.

Nevertheless, the United States had to walk a tightrope; it had to continue to push for independence and to leave no doubt that independence was its preferred outcome regarding final status. It had to continue to keep up the

---

[19] Confidential 2008 interview.
[20] Confidential discussion regarding State Department reaction to Volker interview, Washington, DC, September 2007.

pressure lest diplomatic drift take over once again. It also had to support – genuinely to support – the Troika process. Otherwise, the intended effect of building European solidarity would not be realized, and the wedge that Russia was driving between the United States and Europe would be successful.

By mid-August, some European diplomats at the fringes of the Troika-led discussions were dismissive about talk of the inevitability of independence and said that Europe instead should focus on managing Kosovo indefinitely as a "frozen conflict," such as that in Cyprus, the West Bank and Gaza, and Taiwan.[21] Several EU states continued to oppose independence for Kosovo. "The Greeks were thinking only of Cyprus; they did not know how to distinguish Kosovo from Cyprus if Kosovo became independent. The Rumanians and Slovaks had concerns over their large ethnic minorities. Spain, at first, thought it could manage its internal problems. In late November and early December of 2007, the Spanish Foreign Minister Miguel Ángel Moratinos had told the Troika, "I think we can handle this," but Spanish opposition to independence hardened after Christmas when the European baton was passed from the Troika to the Quint, from which Spain was excluded.[22]

Then, other, more assertive views began to take center stage. In an EU ministerial meeting in Viana Do Castelo, Portugal, September 8, 2007, EU attention shifted subtly away from hopes that the Troika-led negotiations would produce any kind of bilateral agreement toward contingency plans for European response to a UDI. At the same time, European foreign ministers and heads of state began making statements insisting that, whatever transpired, Europe must remain unified. European unity, of course, was a two-edged sword: It could mean, as it had in the early development of a European position on the Ahtisaari plan, that Europe must unite behind independence. On the other hand, it could mean that those states opposed to independence should be able to prevent any other European state from recognizing Kosovo after UDI.

At this point, U.S. analysis agreed with European analysis: the key to the Troika negotiations lay with Germany. If the other members of the Quint showed solidarity, that would bring Italy along, and then others outside the Quint. If Germany chose further delay, matters would become extremely difficult for the French, who would not want to be stuck out on a limb by themselves. In addition, it surely would mean the loss of Italy.

Part of the German skepticism was the product of some Social Democrat leaders feeling close to Tadić, who was an active member of the association of European social democratic parties. Ischinger's involvement in the Troika was crucial to solidifying Germany's support for the outcome. German President

---

[21] See generally "Balkan Bagatelle," *The Economist*, December 13, 2007, located at http://www.economist.com/world/europe/displaystory.cfm?story_id=10286536 (independence of Kosovo may result in frozen conflict).

[22] Confidential 2008 interview with senior European diplomat close to the Troika.

Merkel was an astute manager of German politics. She knew that if, say, Portugal or France represented the European position within the Troika, it would be much easier and more persuasive for Bundestag members to oppose any outcome. On the other hand, if a German – particularly someone as widely respected as Ischinger – represented Europe and could say at the end of the process, "We left no stone unturned; agreement between Belgrade and Pristina is not possible; European support for conditional independence under the Ahtisaari Plan is the only feasible way forward," it would be hard for significant opposition within the Bundestag to take root.

Ischinger also was close personally to Foreign Minister Steinmeier. He understood Steinmeier's political problems and helped him resolve them. Ischinger worked hard to keep doubtful members of the Social Democrats informed of what the Troika was doing and what the realistic possibilities were.

At first, the Troika decided that it would not make proposals itself, lest that discourage Belgrade and Pristina from developing their own proposals to accommodate the interests of the other side. By early September 2007, however, Ischinger said, "We have to change; we must make our own proposals."[23] He sought authority to do that from an EU ministerial meeting held in New York in late September and got a clear mandate to be proactive. Thereafter he decided to put before the parties as a model the 1972 treaty between West and East Germany.[24] Among other things, the document had the virtue of simplicity: it was only two pages long and comprised ten paragraphs.

As adapted to the context of Kosovo, the key principles were:

> Kosovo and Serbia will live side by side in peace. They will work to establish good neighborly relations.
> Kosovo and Serbia will act in full accordance with the UN Charter and the relevant OSCE documents.
> Kosovo and Serbia will refrain from any use of, or threat with, force. They will settle their differences by peaceful means.
> Each government will be solely responsible for the administration of its respective territory.
> Serbia will not seek to establish a physical presence in Kosovo.

A "nonpaper" describing the proposal was prepared in Berlin and reviewed with the U.S. State Department and the Russian Foreign Ministry. The core of the concept was that the agreement be either silent or ambiguous on status, so that both Kosovo and Serbia could maintain their respective positions on Kosovo's status, allowing other states to do likewise. The agreement would create a "community," which would allow Serbia to claim that

---

[23] October 2008 interview with Wolfgang Ischinger.
[24] See Floy Jeffares, "The Gentle Revolution: German Unification in Retrospect," 20 *Denver J. Int'l L. and Pol.* 537, 539 (1992) (analyzing 1972 treaty between two Germanys).

there was still a common sovereign superstructure over Kosovo, while simultaneously allowing Kosovo to characterize it as an international arrangement. Kosovo and Serbia would agree to disagree on interpretation of this agreement, without such disagreement nullifying the operative clauses of the agreement. In other words, the agreement to disagree should be only about status, not about other parts of the agreement. The agreement would be asymmetrical, in the sense than some obligations would be imposed only on Kosovo and not Serbia, for example international presences, and their scope of obligation to consult the other.

The United States thought that the ambiguous language must allow Kosovo to achieve clear international legal personality. It also wanted to discuss what would happen if the document were agreed to. Would it go to the Security Council for approval? How would the Ahtisaari proposal for an International Civilian office and EULEX be implemented? What would be the scenario for recognition of Kosovo's new status?

After the members of the Troika had resolved these issues among themselves, they gave it to the Belgrade and Pristina delegations. In the end, Moscow declined to support it and the parties put it aside, although some of the same ideas were reflected in Pristina's proposed Treaty of Friendship and Cooperation.

Round III took place on September 17–19 in London. The Belgrade delegation was unresponsive to further Troika questions on its autonomy proposal. "What was in it for the Albanians," Wisner asked, "who would be stuck with a foreign policy as to which they had no power to help formulate, and Belgrade has no power to enforce compliance with it inside Kosovo?" The Troika was left with the impression that Serbia wanted sovereignty over Kosovo with no responsibility for governance.

The Pristina delegation was well prepared this time, giving a presentation on the Treaty of Friendship and Cooperation, deftly orchestrated by Sejdiu, with well-executed speaking roles for each of the other members of the Unity Team. Their proposal envisioned independence, with concrete institutional frameworks for cooperation between Kosovo and Serbia on displaced and missing persons, entry by Kosovo into Euro-Atlantic institutions, cooperation with NATO and OSCE, and joint bodies to guide economic, judicial, and educational cooperation, including a council of ministers. The idea was that an independent Kosovo and an independent Serbia could have an institutionalized dialogue over common issues, organized through regular meetings of some kind of council. The idea was similar to that embodied in Ischinger's two-Germanies model.

Russia considered the idea, but then backed away as soon as Koštunica attacked it. The plan crafted by the Kosovar Albanian team was an effort to be constructive, but the Serbian side was disdainful. "Who came up with this?" one of the senior Serbian officials asked privately. "The Albanians," responded one of the Western participants. "Impossible," said the Serbian official, "Albanians are incapable of conceptual thought. I've known them all my life."[25]

Round III was a clear win for the Albanians, without, however, any indication of common ground on the question of independence.

Part of the Belgrade delegation – the part led by Tadić – was, however, willing to compromise on language defining NATO's role, in a communiqué worked out by the Contact Group on October 22. The Russians were opposed to explicit language inviting NATO expansion into the Balkans. The new Serb proposal was to provide that Serbia would "cooperate with" NATO through the Partnership for Peace. Koštunica opposed even that modification.

The United States kept the pressure on. In her presentation to the Contact Group Ministerial meeting on September 27, 2007, Secretary Rice said, "These negotiations are not open-ended. They will conclude by December 10th....If there is no agreement by December 10th, then...the Ahtisaari recommendations...provide the best way forward....We should also be clear about the options realistically available: Independence for Kosovo is inevitable, supervised independence to be sure, but independence nevertheless."

In the Troika session with the negotiating teams on October 13–16, 2007, in Brussels, the Kosovar Albanians rejected the Serbian autonomy proposal and the Serbs gave even shorter shrift to the Albanian Friendship and Cooperation Proposal. The Troika, becoming more proactive, presented both sides with a draft statement of fourteen conclusions for them to review and revise. In preparation for the meeting with the parties, Javier Solana, the foreign policy spokesman of the European Union and former Secretary General of NATO, had met the members of the Troika and "cheered them on."[26]

Solana had consistently demonstrated his lack of enthusiasm for further fragmentation of what little remained of Yugoslavia, seeking to defer the independence of Montenegro for as long as possible, and declining to jump on the bandwagon of supporters of independence for Kosovo. As a Spaniard, he was not unmindful of Spain's struggle to quell separatist elements in the Basque community in Spain. Solana had worked closely with U.S. General Wesley Clark to keep the NATO alliance from falling apart during the 1999 bombing campaign, but he also had hung on to the idea of some kind of residual Yugoslav confederation. Solana had insisted, for example, that aspirations for Montenegrin independence be deferred by cobbling together a "union of Serbia and Montenegro," forestalling a referendum on independence for Montenegro, and then insisting on a supermajority as the referendum threshold.

After the Security Council impasse in mid-2007, however, he quickly embraced the urgent need to avoid a diplomatic – or shooting – war over

---

[25] Confidential interview with the person who heard the remark.
[26] May 2008 interview with Wisner.

Kosovo. Consolidation of the European position was, in his view, essential.[27] Solana was at the center of the advocates for a post-Ahtisaari 120-day period of negotiations. Solana had barely taken charge of the post-Ahtisaari negotiation period when leaks from Brussels began to suggest that a desirable outcome of the 120-day negotiation period would be a confederation of Serbia, Kosovo, and Montenegro – an idea that had never enjoyed much currency except when Solana was driving the discussion. Solana's refusal to jump on the bandwagon of independence in early 2007, however, increased his credibility as a patient architect of European unity.

When he called Ischinger to ask him to join the Troika, he initially expressed concern that Ischinger might be too independent. Ischinger promised to consult with Solana closely, even daily if necessary. It would not be productive, in Ischinger's view, to outrun what Solana could sell to the doubters in Europe.

After the dinner and Solana's pep talk, the Troika members met to discuss the end game, considering three options: a CIS formula, with two sovereigns loosely linked with common institutions; a "special relationship," under which neither side would concede sovereignty but would cooperate through joint institutions on practical issues such as community rights and protection of religious sites; and autonomy for several years with an eventual plebiscite on independence. They concluded that Belgrade would reject the CIS option and were unable to agree on the third option because of Russian refusal to set a date for the plebiscite. They decided to focus on the second option and reflect it in the revised conclusions document.

On October 21–23 in Vienna, both sides expressed unhappiness with the Troika's draft conclusions. The Belgrade delegation had redrafted them in a way that foreclosed any possibility of Kosovar agreement.

On October 23, the Troika sponsored a face-to-face negotiation in New York. All three Troika members urged both Belgrade and Pristina to speak to each other. The tendency so far had been for each side to make and defend proposals to the Troika, with little consideration to likely reactions from the other side. Again, Tadić was polite and Koštunica was insulting, spicing his remarks with references to "Albanian terrorists." The parties did talk to each other for the first time since Ahtisaari's "elephant round," but they found no common ground.

On November 4–6 in Vienna, the Troika members worked with each other and with the two negotiating teams on the fourteen conclusions, with much of the argument focusing on the role of Resolution 1244, about which everyone agreed they had conflicting interpretations. It was clear that status-neutral confederation was unacceptable to the parties.

---

[27] October 2008 interview with Wolfgang Ischinger.

Under pressure from Thaçi, UNMIK allowed Kosovo elections, postponed from the fall of 2006, to be held in November 2007. Turnout was less than 50 percent, reflecting the alienation of the Kosovar Albanians and Belgrade's insistence that the Kosovo Serbs boycott them. Thaçi's PDK got the largest number of votes, 34.3 percent, and the LDK vote shrank to 22.6 percent. Haradinaj's party, the AAK, received 9.6 percent. The new parties of Pacolli New Kosovo Alliance (AKR) and Daci (LDD) received 12.3 percent and 10 percent, respectively.[28]

The Troika reassembled with the parties on November 21 in Brussels. The Belgrade delegation rejected the Troika proposal for a "status-silent" statement of conclusions. The Pristina delegation rejected the Serbian-proffered models of Hong Kong and Aland Islands because they did not involve independence. Wisner posed the following questions to the Belgrade delegation:

1. Is there scope for a partnership between Serbia and Kosovo?
2. Can we focus on ideas that affect the lives, property, and security of ordinary people?
3. Can we identify priorities important to Serbia, Kosovo Serbs, and the Church?
4. Specifically, can we find cooperation in the fields of economy, social development, health, justice, missing persons, and refugees?
5. Is it possible to set up bodies to provide for cooperation and coordination?
6. Is it possible to sidestep the issue of status?

Koštunica rejected the questions as inadmissible because they violated international law by contemplating partnership among equals.

The final Troika round occurred in Baden and Vienna on November 25–28. Despite Ischinger's hopes that a three-day meeting in Baden might, like the Dayton negotiations over Bosnia, produce a compromise, it did not. The parties simply reiterated their positions. Afterwards, the members of the Troika worked over the language of a draft report of their efforts to the Secretary General. The final joint meeting occurred on November 26 and 27, followed by dinners, both of which Koštunica skipped. Tadić promised privately that Serbia would not resort to violence or stir up trouble in Bosnia. Koštunica vowed revenge, without similar commitments to avoid violence or other destabilizing efforts.

When this part of the process concluded, the Troika felt obligated to report to the UN, especially because the Contact Group was operating under a Secretary General request. Some observers believed that the earliest the UN reporting and discussion process could be completed was March 2008. They also believed that there were many opportunities for delaying it past that time.

[28] ICG, *Kosovo Countdown: A Blueprint for Transition*, Europe Report No. 188 at 6 (reporting election results).

Ischinger and Wisner were firm in their determination that the Troika would report to the Secretary General by December 10. "The Troika's mandate was for 120 days," Wisner says. "It ended on December 10. On that date, we would give our report to the Secretary General, saying 'We exhausted every possibility for a negotiated solution to Kosovo's status.' Of course we expected a short period for rumination inside the Security Council. Then there would be the Christmas holiday, and then we would wait for the Serbian elections."

Significant sentiment remained in Europe that the Kosovo status issue did not need to be rushed. There was a sense in some quarters that the United States, although working hard to achieve a common transatlantic position through the Troika, had handicapped the process and foreclosed useful possibilities for agreement by taking such a public position that independence was the answer, particularly in President Bush's speech in Tirana. That put the United States unambiguously on the Kosovar Albanian side and eliminated the possibility of Pristina agreeing to anything short of independence. Moreover, the United States made it clear that there would be no more delay after December 2007.[29] "Belgrade argued that we had ensured failure of the Troika negotiations by Bush's speech in Tirana," Wisner observes. "But what were we supposed to say to the Albanians instead? 'Would you kneel on the floor?' How would we have enforced that? Who would impose such humiliation on the Albanians? And Russia torpedoed the chances for a negotiated solution by its promise to Serbia that it would never allow that which Serbia opposed. That closed down the possibility of Serbian compromise."

None of the alternatives to the Ahtisaari plan surfaced by experts on the Balkans had resonated with either Belgrade or Pristina. These new and not always welcome ideas did have a payoff, however: their expression made it difficult or impossible for any European diplomat to claim that more time would permit forging agreement between Belgrade and Pristina. No one believed that the specifics of the Ahtisaari Plan could be modified to become more acceptable to Serbia. The reality was that the Ahtisaari recommendation gave so much to the Kosovo Serbs as to make Kosovo nearly ungovernable, with overlapping international and elected authority and weakened central government. In the end, then, what looked like an unraveling process made it possible to forge an agreement where it counted: within Europe.

There had been some talk that the Troika's work should be followed by an international peace conference. In the end, the United States and Europe recognized that a peace conference would be little more than cover for drift. Such a conference was never seriously considered by the Troika. Kosovo's final status question was very different from the prospects for ending the war in Bosnia, and no one could identify concrete results that could be obtained from a peace conference after the 120-day period. An international conference could be useful only if the parties narrowed their differences sufficiently that

[29] Confidential 2008 interview.

a conference could produce agreement. That never happened, so there was no point in organizing a conference. A decision must be made now.

The two actual objectives of the Troika process – to provide a more transparent but fruitless period of negotiations while engaging in a far more important, but less visible, effort to forge Quint unity – were within reach.

Russia made a fundamental mistake, not only by placing itself squarely on Belgrade's side but also by telling Koštunica that the United States and the EU would never dare to move forward with independence in the face of Russian and Serbian objections.[30] Lavrov had said to Ischinger early in the Troika process, "We are not more Serbian than Serbia." Ischinger responded, "You should be Russian rather than Serbian at all."[31] However, Russian perceptions of Russian interests were not hospitable for agreement on Kosovo's status. "Why in hell should we give a gift to the U.S.? We'd be seen as a loser. We'll keep Kosovo in reserve to trade off against other issues," one high-level European diplomat characterized Russian policy makers as thinking.

Russia's opposition to Kosovo's independence was the product of its goal of reframing the U.S./Russian strategic relationship. Europeans usually tried to find a solution that was good for everyone; Russia saw it as a zero-sum game. It certainly was not based on any consistent position on international law, as events in Georgia in 2008 showed.[32] In any event, there was no significant price to be paid by Russia if it refused to agree on a path toward independence for Kosovo.

Ischinger thinks that violence would have been a real risk if the Troika had delayed a decision. He believes, however, that the range of possibilities in 2007 would have been broader if the United States and the Europeans had worked more creatively with the Kosovar Albanians in 2005 and 2006.[33] Also, the Ahtisaari process might have embraced a strategy that envisioned a longer process. Ischinger says, "We should have started years earlier – even before the 1999 conflict – on a separate effort to figure out Kosovo's future. But in 1995 the levels of consciousness on Kosovo were not sufficiently developed in Paris and London to make that possible."[34] In addition, an ex-U.S. ambassador thought the United States could have offered Russia some incentives to agree on Kosovo. "The Clinton administration would have offered to suspend the missile deal with Poland," he said.[35]

The NSC principals met at the White House during the week preceding November 19–21 with Secretary Rice and National Security Adviser Hadley present. Some NSC staff had pushed for delay, but the group concluded that the United States and the Troika must stick to the December 10 deadline

[30] Confidential 2008 interview.
[31] October 2008 interview with Wolfgang Ischinger.
[32] October 2008 interview with Wolfgang Ischinger.
[33] October 2008 interview with Wolfgang Ischinger.
[34] October 2008 interview with Wolfgang Ischinger.
[35] Confidential 2008 interview.

with UDIR anticipated in mid-January. A brief delay to accommodate the Serbian elections might be in order, but everyone was mindful of the Serbian habit of using elections or coalition-formation as an excuse for extended delay over Kosovo. Most participants recognized that, if the United States let the announced deadline of December 10 slip, it would pay a heavy cost in the credibility of its diplomacy around the world.

In a final meeting on December 2, the members of the Troika finalized its report to the Secretary General, incorporating some last-minute Russian changes and rejecting others aimed at another round of negotiations without time limit. Thereafter, the Troika traveled to Belgrade and Pristina to brief the parties on the report.

During November and December, Wisner sat down in D.C. with representatives of State, the JCS, the NSC staff, and the CIA to review what could go wrong. One possibility was Kosovar-Albanian-sponsored interethnic violence. Another possibility was Serbian-sponsored interethnic violence. More likely, they thought, was a Serbian wink and nod to allow infiltration of armed Serbian thugs into Kosovo to stir things up. A fourth possibility was that Belgrade and Moscow would destabilize Bosnia, encouraging separatist action by the Bosnian Serbs. A fifth possibility was that Russia would take provocative action in Transnistria, Abkhazia, or South Ossetia.

On December 7, Wisner briefed Secretary Rice and Nick Burns, and Secretary Rice met in Brussels with the foreign ministers of the UK, Germany, France, and Italy. They followed up with a letter to their European colleagues urging unified European action and support of an EU mission to Kosovo.

As the Troika report was being finalized on December 4, 2007, Wisner and U.S. Office Pristina Charge d'Affairs Tina Kasdanow met with the Unity Team at the USAID mission in Pristina. Wisner told them that the United States was determined to see Kosovo through to independence, but that there must be a coordinated declaration of independence, not a unilateral one. To accomplish that, the Europeans had to be on board and they "had a series of bridges to cross: a foreign ministers meeting on December 10, a heads of government meeting on December 14, and a Security Council meeting on December 19."[36] Also, there would be detailed discussions with Secretary General Ban Ki-Moon and his staff to ensure that they take the necessary steps to enable independence under Resolution 1244. The United States would point out that Resolution 1244, even if it were not replaced by another resolution, did not bar independence. The language in Resolution 1244 recognizing Serbian sovereignty is in the preamble, and therefore does not constitute a "decision" by the Security Council. UN members are obligated only to recognize and apply "decisions" by the Security Council.[37] The reference to the

---

[36] May 2008 interview with Wisner.
[37] Art. 25 UN Charter (referring to "decisions" of the Security Council).

Helsinki Act brings with it the Helsinki principle that all of its principles must be interpreted in *pari materia* with the others, including human rights and security in Europe. The reference to Annex II makes it clear than any implied prohibition against independence applies only during the interim stage and not to final status itself.[38]

The Kosovo political leadership must keep absolute silence and engage in no uncoordinated or unilateral acts, Wisner told them. On December 10 itself, when the Troika would issue its report to the Secretary General, they should commit themselves to international cooperation and adherence to the Ahtisaari Plan. They must lobby in Europe and worldwide and they must prepare legislation called for in the Ahtisaari Plan, holding in abeyance any laws that require sovereignty, such as those relating to a defense ministry and an intelligence service. They should put off plans for a new Kosovo security force until after independence. Kosovo should be ready with a declaration of independence by mid-January, although the date of its adoption might need to be postponed to accommodate Serbian elections. The Declaration should commit Kosovo to the Ahtisaari Plan and invite military and other international presences. He acknowledged risk, and emphasized that the Kosovar Albanians must take responsibility for complete security, even in the face of Serb retaliation or provocation. "Not a house can burn," he said. All the members of the Unity Team solemnly agreed, with considerable emotion.

Separately, Wisner urged Sejdiu and Thaçi to move promptly to form a new government, based on the results of the November elections. Shortly thereafter, the PDK and LDK announced a coalition government with Thaçi as prime minister and LDK leader Sejdiu continuing as president. Thaçi resisted pressure to include Haradinaj's AAK in the coalition. Thaçi was sworn in as prime minister on January 9, 2008. Haradinaj himself was not acquitted until April 3, 2008, after the coalition was formed and independence had been declared.

One last obstacle needed to be avoided and then the plan could be implemented through UDIR. The obstacle was the Serbian presidential elections scheduled for early February, which resulted in the reelection of Boris Tadić as president of Serbia. Once those elections were over, the stage was set for UDIR.

Ahtisaari himself was little involved in the Troika-led negotiations. To maintain good relations – or perhaps only good appearances – a UNOSEK member was invited to participate in all the Troika meetings. One significantly involved U.S. diplomat remarked, however, "UNOSEK still maintains an office in Vienna and is paying people's salaries, but I don't think they have anything to do."

---

[38] State Department briefing paper.

Adroitly subordinating ego to pragmatism, Ahtisaari understood that by receding into the background while the Troika worked to forge a critical mass of European support for his plan, he would remove himself as an excuse for continued Serbian and Russian criticism of the process. Keeping UNOSEK on the sidelines would leave his plan intact as the framework for an independent Kosovo.

16 Independence Day

SUCCESS FOR THE EU, THE UNITED STATES, AND KOSOVO OCCURRED
on February 17, 2008, when the Kosovo Assembly declared independence under the Ahtisaari Plan. Widely feared risks of general unrest did not materialize.

Although President Sejdiu and Prime Minister Thaçi, joined by U.S. and European diplomats, had refused to confirm the specific date on which the Kosovo Assembly would declare independence, a flood of press and media stories claimed that it would be either Sunday, February 17 or Monday, February 18. On Saturday, February 16, a flight from London to Pristina was packed with Albanians.

One Albanian passenger was taking his nine-year-old son back to Kosovo for Independence Day. He lived in London, but was originally from Pristina, and his son was born there. "We are going to be free like any other country," he said to Chad Mair, one of my former students who was sitting next to him on the flight. "We will have freedom. I don't know how to say it. Now is the end." He expected Kosovo to be recognized by most countries. "I do not expect problems – who will [cause] problems now?" he asked. "Everything is controlled by Albanians, KFOR. There are not the same issues as the United States has in Iraq and Afghanistan."

He disclaimed any hatred for the Kosovo Serbs. "I don't believe the Serbians in Pristina can't leave their homes [for fear of being beaten or intimidated]. I am from Pristina and have lived there for twenty-plus years," he said. "I know who is Serb and who is Albanian, but it doesn't matter to me."

Mair's flight arrived at the airport in Pristina a little before 4 P.M. A large throng of people waited to meet the plane. There were lots of hugs and every indication that families were being reunited after a long separation. His taxi driver spoke little English, but got very excited when Mair said he was from America. "Go America!" he said repeatedly. "Thank you America!" There was a small police presence along the roads, but nothing extraordinary – three or four police cars glimpsed in the twenty-minute drive from the airport to Pristina. Mair saw two empty KFOR trucks, but nothing else.

Mother Teresa Street was full of people walking and in cars. Albanian flags were flying from car windows, taped to the hoods of cars, or held aloft by cheering passengers in the cars. There were also many American flags. The people on the streets, some wearing flags as capes, were mostly young, in their teens and twenties. Most of the cars were packed full, laying on their horns and blaring traditional Albanian music. The pedestrians seemed to be going nowhere in particular, but were simply basking in the moment. People had congregated in two major gatherings at several spots along the main road, where the police had blocked it. A hundred people were dancing. Music was coming from loudspeakers. The weather was bitterly cold and snowing, but no one seemed to be paying any attention to the weather. Photos were being taken near historic statues; everybody seemed to be enjoying themselves and the scene.

The Grand Hotel bar was full of journalists and locals, where the Pristina Media Center was still active at midnight. Some two thousand journalists were reported to be in Kosovo, and no hotel rooms were available for more. Chants of "UCK, UCK" could be heard in the hotel and on the street.

The local television news began with a rundown of Prime Minister Thaçi's activities that day, especially his press conference with former KLA spokesman and revered Albanian nationalist Adem Demaci. News then moved on to global reactions to the imminent declaration of independence. It specifically referred to celebrations by the Albanian population in New York, and showed the Croatian prime minister expressing his support.

By midnight, pedestrian traffic had diminished significantly, but there were still many cars on the streets and much noise from the mostly young celebrators.

Meanwhile, out of the public view, trouble was brewing in the assembly. LDK members of the assembly, still resentful over what they perceived as Thaçi's marginalizing the LDK when he put his cabinet together, erupted when they heard that Jakup Krasniqi, PDK speaker of the assembly, had removed Rugova's portrait from the assembly chamber. They threatened not to attend on Sunday. Hurried phones calls occurred from the U.S. Office to Thaçi, and from Thaçi to Krasniqi, and the portrait was back in place when the assembly chamber opened.[1]

Sunday morning, music blared from the loudspeakers of businesses and apartments, car stereos, and large, concert-style speakers mounted on vehicles. Shortly before noon, the news reported that Thaçi had sent a letter to Jakup Krasniqi, as head of the parliament, asking for an emergency meeting of parliament at 3 P.M. Krasniqi gave a radio interview acknowledging receipt of Thaçi's letter and another from President Sejdiu. He declared that the parliament would meet in three hours, with two items to discuss: independence and its attendant symbols.

At noon, Radio Kosova reported on Albanians celebrating in Sweden, Macedonia, and the United States, and cut to President Bush expressing

---

[1] Confidential interview, August 2008, Pristina.

continuing U.S. support for independence. "We have been waiting for this for centuries," said one overwhelmed Kosovar. "I cannot put into words the feelings I have right now."

Police had blocked the roads leading into Pristina to prevent cars from coming in, but there were still cars moving around inside Pristina. The Pristina Chamber of Commerce made an agreement with businesses in the city center to give away free food and drinks. Despite the extreme cold, Sunday's crowds of pedestrians appeared to include more families with children than the previous night.

Mair waded into the crowds to get a sense of Kosovar emotion. "There is no bigger day for us," said one man in his sixties or seventies. "Today was not only done by Albanian people, it was done by other nations. I do not feel the cold, because I have been waiting for this day for a long time." His pleasure was palpable. "Today is not only for Kosova people, but for all Albanian people," he declared. "If not for America, today would not happen. We wouldn't be free." He had come with his family to Pristina from where they lived in the Llapi zone to "walk around, celebrate, sing. Then," he said, "we will go home to be with our family and celebrate some more."

Another man in his seventies was there with his own family. They were from Pristina. He looked forward to celebrating with loved ones and "no Kalashnikovs," he laughed. "When I turned fifty-one," he said, "there were demonstrations in 1991 and I had the feeling that I would be able to experience this day. I felt that it either happens while I am alive or it doesn't happen at all." He was mindful, he said of the "generations who have waited for this day, but could not be here for it." For himself, he said, "I was never happier in my life. There are not words to describe this day. My hope," he said, "is that institutions develop and that all citizens do not suffer, but experience sustained welfare. We also must return the favor to all those who made contributions to the liberation of Kosova."

Mair walked through the center again shortly after noon. The main street was shoulder to shoulder with people of all ages. He described it as "very peaceful and calm. It seems like most were just taking in the scene, and just wanted to be there and be a part of it. Most were smiling and happy. A lot of flags were evident – mostly Albanian, but many others, such as U.S., UK, EU, Italy, Germany, France, Turkey. It was absolutely freezing – to the point that my pen was frozen and wouldn't work – but that didn't seem to stop anyone." Later, the news estimated crowds of three hundred to four hundred thousand people roaming the streets of Pristina.

When the parliament convened, the proceedings seemed relatively subdued, all things considered. Thaçi and Sejdiu looked extremely nervous, perhaps because of the squabbles with the LDK of the evening before, but also surely because they were on history's stage. "We are changing the whole map of Europe," said a somber Krasniqi, stumbling verbally as he announced the order of the proceedings. "Peace and justified freedom can only exist in societies where there are equal rights. Kosova has never had friends like it has today." Thaçi took the podium and greeted everyone. "The time for freedom is here," he declared in Albanian, and he emphasized that Kosova would be a country of equal opportunity and equal rights. He then made the same declaration and pledge to Kosovar Serbs, speaking in Serbian.

Then, at 3:34 P.M. on Sunday, February 17, 2008, Jakup Krasniqi read the Declaration of Independence, which began thus:

1. We, the democratically elected leaders of our people, hereby declare Kosovo to be an independent and sovereign state. This declaration reflects the will of our people and it is in full accordance with the recommendations of UN Special Envoy Martti Ahtisaari and his Comprehensive Proposal for the Kosovo Status Settlement.
2. We declare Kosovo to be a democratic, secular, and multiethnic republic, guided by the principles of nondiscrimination and equal protection under the law. We shall protect and promote the rights of all communities in Kosovo and create the conditions necessary for their effective participation in political and decision-making processes.
3. We accept fully the obligations for Kosovo contained in the Ahtisaari plan, and welcome the framework it proposes to guide Kosovo in the years ahead. We shall implement in full those obligations, including through priority adoption of the legislation included in its Annex XII, particularly those that protect and promote the rights of communities and their members.
4. We shall adopt as soon as possible a Constitution that enshrines our commitment to respect the human rights and fundamental freedoms of all our citizens, particularly as defined by the European Convention on Human Rights. The Constitution shall incorporate all relevant principles of the Ahtisaari Plan and be adopted through a democratic and deliberative process.

As he read the declaration, emotion quickly escalated in the room. People outside were hushed. Some cameras from local stations stayed focused on parliament to show images of each member signing the Declaration; others showed the scenes on the streets of Pristina and Prizren.

After the Declaration, people were shouting, dancing, and celebrating in the streets. Smoke from the fireworks formed a cloud just above their heads. The weather remained blisteringly cold, but no one seemed to be paying any attention. Occasional gunshots rang out in the distance, without the menace of violence. "I have never seen so many happy people," Mair said later. "You continuously hear people saying words like 'miracle,' 'unbelievable,' or 'never been happier.' People who were married and with children were describing today as the most momentous and important day of their lives."

A stage was erected near the parliament. The crowd in front and for a good two hundred yards back was packed from edge of sidewalk to edge of sidewalk. The crowd bubbled over with good cheer; spontaneous conga lines formed, and people pushed and danced their way through the crowd. Groups of youths formed circles to dance and sing. The trees along streets were full of people: ten people in a tree that looked like it could barely hold two. Red and white balloons circled the new light poles lining the streets.

The first act to go onstage was a group of traditional Albanian dancers. The concert, like the day's celebration, seemed to be as much about history as about the freedom and statehood just obtained. Although sporadic chanting could be heard through the day in reference to fallen KLA soldiers, there were otherwise very few patches or other KLA/UCK symbols. Many people wore t-shirts with a picture of Adem Jashari and the words "Bac, u kry," which translates roughly as "Respected one (hero), the end [is here]," signifying the continued symbolic importance of Jashari's death to the Kosovar Albanian struggle for independence. There was also a fifteen-foot flag in the center with the same slogan and another flag near the sports center. "Many people I talked to asked if I knew the history of Kosova, not since the war, but for the past six hundred years," Mair reported. "This wasn't merely breaking free from Serbia, but a throwing off of the chains of oppression six centuries old."

The government shot fireworks from behind the Grand Hotel. The crowd had not thinned at all. People were not celebrating or demonstrating emotion just for the video cameras or journalists, but appeared oblivious to their presence. There was very limited police presence, and no show of international forces. Mair saw no instances where the police had to intervene, or even warn people, nor did he see any situations that even required police presence. "It was extremely peaceful and calm celebration," he affirmed, "just like Thaçi asked for."

"We have been waiting for this day for a long time," said an eighteen-year-old young man who took the bus from his village to Pristina each day to be where the celebrations were. "We fought for it and we deserve it. Hours have passed and now we are just waiting for other countries to recognize that we are our own state." He described the mood: "The government asked us to celebrate peacefully and not to provoke anyone," he said. "We followed their request."

On Monday, Pristina was essentially back to business as usual. The streets were completely open to auto traffic except around the Grand Hotel; although the occasional car horn was heard, and the occasional Albanian flag seen, the city of Pristina in no way resembled the jubilant chaos of the day before. Still, hints of the previous day's events lingered: the streets were littered with debris and the remnants of expired fireworks, and stickers and other placards proclaiming independence were affixed to anything and everything. KFOR patrols were more obvious than they were the day before, but acted relaxed, like they were not expecting anything to happen. Overall, the police presence was limited.

The mood of some passersby was less buoyant on Monday as well. "I was at home yesterday watching it on TV," said one eighteen-year-old from an industrial zone just outside Pristina. "I wasn't expecting much, and what happened was what I expected, nothing more, nothing less." He expressed disappointment because "we aren't fully independent. Resolution 1244 is still there, the SRSG is still here. I think we will be another Bosnia-Herzegovina. Maybe we will get full independence with integration [into the EU], but that will probably be ten years away. Everything will just take time." Another pair of high-school-age kids from Pristina were tentative about the future. "We celebrated massively," they admitted. "We are more free now. It means much more. Of course we expect something more, more jobs for youngsters. Also, we expect improvements in the education sector. We are quite optimistic. We remember everything from the war. Somehow, we thought that yesterday would happen, even during the war. We knew it would happen sooner or later. It had to happen."

A few other young people were critical later as they drank coffee. "We were shocked when Thaçi used the Serbian language," one said. Another thought the ceremony in the assembly chamber was too political. "How could Thaçi have referred to Jashari and not said a word about the Haradinaj family, who also sacrificed?"

For the most part, however, the significance of the declaration of independence could hardly be overstated. "For me personally, it is the biggest, biggest, biggest thing that has happened. It is great to have this freedom of breath," said the husband of an older couple. "Since the first student demonstrations, this street has been the center of violence and of peaceful protests. I was an organizer of the first student demonstration. Since that day, hundreds of protests have been held, with yesterday being the culmination and realization of those demonstrations and dreams."

One twenty-five-year-old from Pristina said that Sunday had been "one of the best days. We have been waiting for it for two thousand years. Not one, but *the* most important day." He remained cautious, however: "Now we have to see how the people will work, how they will handle the freedom," he said. "I am 50/50 on whether it will work. It will always be hard. We are three years under supervision and they can always take away independence."

One man saw independence in optimistic, if starkly pragmatic, terms: "Yesterday, I worked seventeen hours and got paid six Euros total. That will change, it has to change," he said. "The police have to get paid more. Teachers as well. Even doctors, nurses need more. I strongly believe that there will be direct foreign investments to stimulate the economy and salaries. Tax collection also has to be improved. Also, we must have an official list of everyone who is working. Too many people are 'unofficially' working and not paying taxes." He also saw a future for Kosovars returning from diaspora: "Almost every family here has someone working abroad," he said. "These people will start coming back when the economy is improved."

Gani Rafuna, a longtime schoolteacher, welcomed the declaration. "This dream of Albanians has existed for six hundred years," he said. "Since then, all Albanians have wanted to experience this day. Generations of Albanians have passed away without experiencing it. This nation has experienced the most horrible things a nation could experience. Thank God and the United States that justice was decided at the right time." He was philosophical on the question of timing. "In all cases, justice is late, but eventually it gets to the right point." In his school, he said, "The mood was incomparable, meaning that the faces of all students and teachers were endlessly happy. It is now the students saying 'Let's go, let's work,' knowing that the dreams have been obtained but that there is still a lot of work to do."

Meanwhile, in Serbia, both President Tadić and Prime Minister Koštunica were in a less celebratory mood: they gave televised addresses saying that Serbia would "annul" all documents relating to the creation of a "false state" on the sovereign territory of Serbia. They denounced the United States for bullying the European Union into recognizing Kosovo's "illegal declaration." They said that Serbia would never recognize Kosovo and Metohija's independence.

In Belgrade, rioters attacked the U.S. and other Western embassies, television crews, and a McDonald's restaurant. Police at first were able to prevent significant damage, but then they were withdrawn and Belgrade rioters destroyed cars, traffic signs, and containers. Further riots broke out in Belgrade the next day. The McDonald's was destroyed, but the police protected the embassies.

On Monday, February 18, the United States, followed by Britain and France, recognized Kosovo as an independent state. The EU foreign ministers, meeting in Brussels, released a compromise text saying that member states "will decide, in accordance with national practice and legal norms, on their relations with Kosovo." The statement also said that the independence of Kosovo "does not set any precedent." Albania and Turkey recognized Kosovo, and the Hungarian foreign minister announced that she would recommend recognition to the Hungarian parliament. The three Baltic states – Estonia, Latvia, and Lithuania – announced that they would grant recognition. Rumania's parliament and Georgia declared that they would not grant recognition. Abkhazia and South Ossetia, separatist provinces of Georgia, had declared that they would follow Kosovo's lead. Serbia recalled its ambassador from Washington. Spain and Cyprus issued statements refusing to recognize Kosovo. China and Russia characterized the declaration as illegal and an assault on Serbian sovereignty.

In a UN Security Council meeting on February 18, Serbian President Tadić expressed Serbia's formal opposition to the Declaration of Independence:

> The Provisional Institutions of Self-Government of the southern Serbian province of Kosovo and Metohija, under interim United Nations administration, unilaterally and illegally declared their independence on Sunday, February 17. This illegal declaration of independence by the Kosovo Albanians constitutes a flagrant violation of Security Council Resolution 1244 (1999), which reaffirms the sovereignty and territorial integrity of the Republic of Serbia, including Kosovo and Metohija. Serbia, let me recall, is a founding State Member of the United Nations.

If a small, peace-loving, and democratic country in Europe that is a United Nations Member State can be deprived of its territory illegally and against its will, a historic injustice will have occurred, because a legitimate democracy has never before been punished in that way.

"The Serbian State was born in Kosovo, and it represents the central part of our identity. I shall be frank with the Council: this is a situation in which a peace-loving country where a proud and European people lives is having a part of its identity, tradition, and history snatched away. This act annuls international law, tramples upon justice, and enthrones injustice.

If the members of the Security Council allow this illegal act to stand, they will demonstrate that right and justice can be disrespected in the world. They will demonstrate that, unfortunately, this body of the world organization is losing its authority.

After this act, the world will no longer be the same. Serbia, a European State, will continue to fight for law and justice in a dignified, peaceful, and civilized way in such a world as well. We shall never give up our legitimate interests and shall continue our peaceful and diplomatic struggle in pursuit of our legitimate European perspective.[2]

On Tuesday, February 19, a mob of several thousand Serbs blew up KPS/UNMIK border posts at Banja near Zubin Potok, at Jarinje in the far north of Kosovo, and threatened the nearby town of Leposavic. KFOR troops evacuated the UN and KPS personnel and used bulldozers to move earth onto the access roads. The Serb attackers responded with their own bulldozers to remove the roadblocks and a standoff resulted. It appeared that KFOR had secured the two border posts by Wednesday, closing the border at those two places but leaving it open elsewhere.

On Wednesday, February 19, Germany and Norway granted recognition. China announced that it was renewing its small contingent of UN police even as it denied recognition. Taiwan granted recognition the day before. Denmark and Italy followed on Thursday, February 21. Kyrgyzstan, Poland, and Latvia followed with recognition on Thursday.

A "Kosovo is Serbia" rally drawing hundreds of thousands was planned for 5 P.M. on Thursday in Belgrade. The 150,000 demonstrators got out of control and set fire to the U.S. and British embassies in Belgrade, ransacked the McDonald's again, and looted stores. Earlier on Thursday, several hundred retired Serbian army reservists attacked Kosovo riot police and their Czech KFOR backup near the border crossing of Merdare, much further east than the initial attacks. Merdare is close to the Kosovar Albanian-dominated city of Podujeve. The attack lasted about twenty minutes and then the veterans withdrew. Serbian Minister for Kosovo Slobodan Sarardzic said that the destruction and other attacks on the border posts "might not be pleasant, but it is legitimate."

---

[2] Statement by Boris Tadić, President of Serbia, to UN Security Council, S/PV.5839 (transcript of Security Council meeting, February 18, 2008) at 4.

In Banja Luka, the capital of the Republika Srpska entity of Bosnia, about a thousand Serbs engaged in a mostly peaceful protest. Its leaders blamed the less-than-expected turnout on lack of support from Bosnian Serb politicians.

On Friday, UN police fired tear gas to keep nearly five thousand Serb protestors from crossing the bridge from North Mitrovica to the Albanian-dominated South Mitrovica. On Friday, Russia's ambassador to NATO, Dmitry Rogozin, threatened force in response to any action by NATO overstepping its authority under Resolution 1244. Later, however, he said, "There won't be any war between Russia and NATO over Kosovo...although this issue will ruin our dialogue." By Sunday, the Belgrade prosecutor's office announced initial arrests and further investigations over the attack on the U.S. and British embassies, and the Serbian government backed away from any implication that it endorsed the embassy attacks.

While Serbia and Russia expressed their outrage over UDIR, their ability to confront it directly was limited. Even if Russia had the military resources to support aggressive Serbian military action in Kosovo, it had no way to get its troops to Serbia. Ukraine and Romania would not likely grant overflight rights, and Poland and Hungary certainly would not, defeating the possibility of moving troops by air. Russia lacked the sealift capability to introduce troops through Macedonia or Albania, and neither was likely to give transit rights. In any event, no one anticipated a military response by Russia. The most likely Russian response was to stir up trouble in the Caucasus, likely sponsoring formal secession by already largely separate regions of Georgia, and to cozy up to Iran.

Serbia, for its part, was unlikely to introduce troops into Kosovo. It remembered well the cost of the NATO bombing of Serbia proper less than ten years before, and the Serbian defense establishment did not support military intervention in Kosovo. The most Serbia could do was to incite violence in the Serb-dominated areas north of Mitrovica, and encourage the Bosnian Serbs to revolt against the Bosnian government and its international backers. If KFOR stood firm in the north of Kosovo, as it appeared to be doing through the end of the week following independence, Belgrade-sponsored violence in that part of Kosovo could not get very far. And the response in Republika Srpska to militant calls for violence was underwhelming.

It appeared that the maximum Serbian and Russian response would be limited to sharp words and recall of ambassadors. In the longer term, of course, independence might have the effect of drawing Serbia more firmly into Russia's sphere of influence and away from the EU. There were some reports, however, of Serbia, perhaps with Russian assistance, arming Kosovo Serbs in the enclaves.[3]

---

[3] See generally ICG, *Fragile Transition* at 4–5 (reporting on means used by Belgrade to control Serb-majority territory in Kosovo).

There remained the question of how the Ahtisaari Plan could be implemented in the face of Russian opposition backed up by its veto in the UN Security Council. Russia could prevent the UN from terminating UNMIK and turning over its authorities to the Kosovo government and to the new Ahtisaari institutions: ICO and EULEX.

17 Kosovo's Future

THE PEOPLES OF KOSOVO ARE BETTER OFF WITH AN INDEPENDENT state than without one. Failure to adopt the Ahtisaari Plan would have meant an eventual guerrilla war or unsupervised independence with its potential for poor governance and lack of respect for minority communities. If a guerrilla war had developed, a changed geopolitical climate would not have permitted the same quick results obtained by the KLA in 1998 and 1999. Violence, had it broken out, would have been protracted, tempting Islamic militants to offer their services in support of the resisters. Kosovo, whatever its challenges, is clearly on a peaceful path to its future.

Independence provides reasonable prospects for achieving the basic goals of both the 1999 international intervention and the goals of the UN when it put the Ahtisaari process in motion:

- Democratic government
- Ethnic tolerance in political and legal systems
- Economic progress in a market economy
- Security against renewed armed conflict in the region

Democracy

Independent Kosovo clearly enjoys democratic governance with an elected assembly, a government selected through traditional parliamentary processes and vigorous competition between the government and an opposition. These features are not new with independence; they have been manifest at least since the fall 2004 elections and developed during the two rounds of elections before that. How Kosovo's democracy evolves depends on the international community staying out of the way and the commitment of government and opposition leaders to important domestic priorities.[1]

---

[1] The analysis in this chapter draws on scores of conversations I have had over a ten-year period about Kosovo's politics with political activists, NGO leaders, and ordinary Kosovar Albanians and Kosovo Serbs, focused by my experience as a former member of the White House staff, a senior subcabinet officer, and a candidate for the U.S. House of Representatives. These

The quality of Kosovo's democracy depends more on its elected leadership than on the international community. Those exercising political power in Kosovo after independence do not have a history of passivity and that holds promise for success. President Fatmir Sejdiu was Secretary General of the LDK and a longtime professor of international law at the University of Pristina. Prime Minister Hashim Thaçi was the president of the PDK, former prime minister of the interim government after the war, and former political director of the KLA. Assembly Speaker Jakup Krasniqi had been a regional LDK leader before the war, the public spokesman for the KLA during the war briefly, and was Secretary General of the PDK.

Although Kosovo's independence was the result of Great-Power politics, it also was the result of self-help. The road began with the NATO bombing campaign in 1999, followed by UN Resolution 1244's political trusteeship for Kosovo. These steps by the Great Powers resulted not from calculated, proactive policies hatched in Brussels, Washington, and New York; they were the result of a handful of fed-up Kosovar Albanians starting a guerrilla war in Kosovo. The launching of the long-delayed final status process in 2005 was also not the result of a strategic international timetable adopted beforehand; it was a reaction to the March 2004 riots. The course of the negotiations that produced the Ahtisaari Plan was shaped by the consistent involvement of the Unity Team, and by the perception that instability and violence in Kosovo would result if the process did not produce independence. Every step of the way, the Kosovar Albanians had forced Europe and the United States to make tough decisions. Then, after the 2007 general elections in Kosovo, Sejdiu and Thaçi, the key leaders of the Unity Team, became the government of Kosovo and thus had the opportunity to implement what they had asked for.

"Thaçi needs to go to school," Veton Surroi had said disdainfully in late 1999, dismissing Thaçi's capacity for effective political leadership. Now, Thaçi had gone to school. He built a political party that confounded ongoing reports that it was about to fragment or to dump him as its leader and then emerged as the most successful party at the ballot box just before independence was declared. After a few stumbles, he organized a vigorous parliamentary opposition to the 2004–2007 LDK–AAK coalition government. He worked cooperatively within the Unity Team. During the 2007 election campaign, he presented a confident face to the electorate for his party and for himself as a possible prime minister. He built on efforts, begun in the 2004 election campaign, to present his party through American-style campaign techniques: featuring his still-young and handsome face on billboards, visiting schools, nursing homes, and small businesses with camera crews in tow, and making good use of campaign consultants from the United States, Israel, and Austria. Thaçi revamped

included regular conversations with Hashim Thaçi, Ramush Haradinaj, Fatmir Sejdiu, Jakup Krasniqi, Bajram Rexhepi, Rrustem Mustafa, senior UNMIK, EU, and U.S. State Department officers.

the PDK, acquiring several smaller parties, and adding to its slate some new younger faces, including one of the most popular Kosovo rap singers, twenty-seven-year-old Memli Krasniqi. While he was a staple of postwar Kosovo politics, Thaçi's role in opposition had distanced him from the unpopular LDK–AAK coalition government, and he managed to present himself as a new face, even as he served as the most prominent member of the Unity Team.

After the 2007 elections, he was forceful in putting together a PDK–LDK coalition, resisting international pressure to include everyone in a grand coalition, and he bargained hard with his coalition partners over the details, ensuring that he had genuine control over his government.[2]

Now, as prime minister, he had graduated to the premier leadership position for postindependence Kosovo. His legacy would depend on his success in dealing with a number of challenges in guiding Kosovo onto a successful post-independence path, and sparing Kosovo from becoming a failed state. He had succeeded in working with Europe and the United States to produce independence. Now he must show that he could govern better than the predecessor coalition. He was off to a good start, imposing discipline on a government that had no history of discipline.[3] Still, his challenges were daunting: he must inspire the Kosovar Albanians to do much by themselves, but he also must do so within a context in which many preconditions for success remain in the hands of international actors.

International Politics

Major forces shaping Kosovo's future were beyond the control of Thaçi's government, although its reaction to them matters. Most broadly, the wider international community must accept Kosovo as a member. Serbia and Russia would continue to interfere with the integration of Kosovo Serbs into Kosovo's political fabric and to destabilize Kosovo, but Thaçi's government must nevertheless find a way to implement the Ahtisaari Plan, which is premised on Kosovo Serb participation. Formally, the authority of any government of Kosovo is circumscribed because Kosovo's sovereignty is limited. Article 147 of the new Kosovo constitution states: "The international civilian presence shall be the final authority regarding the interpretation of the Comprehensive

---

[2] Accord, ICG, *Fragile Transition* at 18 ("During the first 120 days, the PDK/LDK coalition government under Hashim Thaçi was disciplined and improved Kosovo's image abroad").

[3] "Prime Minister Thaçi and his small inner circle are determined to exercise top-down control, unlike previous coalition governments in which a figurehead prime minister presided impotently over ministers who set their own agendas. Overall, the administration has exuded a greater sense of purpose than its predecessor and remains popular, but centralization of decision making in a very narrow circle around the prime minister is causing delays and poor intragovernmental communication." ICG, *Fragile Transition* at 19.

Proposal for Kosovo Status Settlement, dated March 26, 2007 [the Ahtisaari Plan]. . . ."[4]

Russia ensured continued confusion over the locus of decision making in Kosovo by blocking repeal or modification of Security Council Resolution 1244, and intimidating UN Secretary General Bai Ki Moon from transferring authority under Resolution 1244 cleanly from UNMIK to the ICO and EULEX.[5] The only legitimate authorities in Kosovo, the Russians argued, were the government of Serbia and UNMIK under Resolution 1244. Independence was a legal nullity, and the Ahtisaari Plan – including its ICO and EULEX – a dead letter. By the end of 2008, EULEX still had not fully deployed, and a downsized UNMIK was thrashing about, trying to build bridges with Belgrade and facing opposition from the Kosovo government as it did so. Serbia's success in obtaining a UN General Assembly vote to seek an advisory opinion from the International Court of Justice on the legality of Kosovo's independence[6] promised to cloud Kosovo's status for an indefinite period.

The impasse in the Security Council confronted independent Kosovo with a four-way split in governance. The elected local government must deal with not three – as the Ahtisaari Plan envisioned – but four separate international presences: ICO/ICR, EULEX, UNMIK, and KFOR. The Ahtisaari Plan envisioned a 120-day transition period at the end of which UNMIK, having transferred its competences either to the elected government or to ICO, would close up shop. Legislative and executive power would lie entirely in the hands of the local government, with ICO exercising a limited veto power with respect to implementation of the Ahtisaari Plan and EULEX supplementing local resources in the justice and law enforcement spheres.

The refusal by Russia and its allies on the Security Council to allow the Secretary General to order UNMIK to transfer its powers to EULEX, however, meant that UNMIK could retain, or purport to retain, executive and legislative powers for an indefinite period of time. EULEX accordingly was hesitant about deploying. This set up the certainty of a collision between Kosovo government institutions and UNMIK.

EULEX finally began to deploy seriously in early 2009 under a "six-point" plan that characterized the deployment as "status neutral." The government

---

[4] United Nations, *Comprehensive Proposal for the Kosovo Status Settlement*, S/2007/168/Add.I at §12.3 (March 26, 2007) [hereinafter "Ahtisaari Plan"]. It makes ICP's decisions binding on all public authorities. Ahtisaari Plan, Annex I, art. 11.

[5] See International Crisis Group, "Kosovo's Fragile Transition," Europe Report No. 196 (September 25, 2008 ("Ahtisaari Plan has been undermined by the international organizations meant to help implement it"; EULEX has deployed slowly; ICO is a "shell").

[6] UN General Assembly, Request for an advisory opinion of the International Court of Justice on whether the unilateral declaration of independence of Kosovo is in accordance with international law, Resolution 63/3 (adopted October 8, 2008).

of Kosovo formally rejected the six-point document[7] but did nothing to block it. Under the six-point plan, UNMIK would formally oversee EULEX operations with respect to police, customs, justice, transportation and infrastructure, boundaries, and Serbian patrimony (mainly sites of the Serbian Orthodox Church).[8] The Secretary General of the UN admitted the impotence of UNMIK: "While my Special Representative is still formally vested with executive authority under Resolution 1244 (1999), he is unable to enforce this authority."[9]

The six-point plan was fundamentally inconsistent with Kosovo's constitution and its status as an independent state. It was worse than Security Council Resolution 1244 in seeming to be "status neutral"; unlike Resolution 1244, it did not even recite formally that the governing authority in Kosovo exercises authority over the entire territory of Kosovo.

The six-point plan strengthened the de facto partition of Kosovo and legitimated the exercise of effective sovereignty over part of it by Belgrade. It validated Serbia's continued imposition of its historically racist policy on Kosovo without participation in decision making by Kosovar leadership. It reinforced Europe's backing away from the Ahtisaari Plan.

In October 2008, the same month that the Secretary General announced the six-point plan, on a petition by the government of Serbia, the UN General Assembly requested an advisory opinion from the ICJ on the legality of Kosovo's Declaration of Independence.[10]

The ICJ was established by Article 92 of the UN Charter, which authorizes it to function in accordance with its "statute." A case can reach the ICJ through two distinct avenues. The first avenue involves "contentious cases" – disputes arising between two state entities, under Article 34 of the Statute of the ICJ. The second involves a request by the General Assembly or other organs of the UN for an advisory opinion.[11] Only states are eligible to be parties in contentious-case litigation, and the states involved must consent

---

[7] S/2008/692, Annex I, para. 2.

[8] Report of the Secretary General on the United Nations Interim Administration Mission in Kosovo (November 24, 2008), S/2008/692, located at http://daccessdds.un.org/doc/UNDOC/GEN/N08/518/31/PDF/N0851831.pdf?OpenElement (describing six-point plan for coordination between UNMIK and EULEX).

[9] S/2008/692 at 7.

[10] "On October 8, 2008, the General Assembly of the United Nations adopted resolution A/RES/63/3 in which, referring to Article 65 of the Statute of the Court, it requested the International Court of Justice to 'render an advisory opinion on the following question: Is the unilateral declaration of independence by the Provisional Institutions of Self-Government of Kosovo in accordance with international law?' The Request for an Advisory Opinion was transmitted to the Court by the Secretary General of the United Nations in a letter dated October 9, 2008, which was filed with the Registry on October 10, 2008." ICJ Press Release, No. 2008/34 (October 10, 2008).

[11] UN Charter art. 96.

to the jurisdiction of the ICJ. Serbia avoided the "contentious case" proce-dure, because ICJ recognition of jurisdiction over Kosovo would automatically validate Kosovo's sovereignty.

There are three possible outcomes of this latest Serbian gambit to frus-trate Kosovo's independence: (1) the ICJ could decline to exercise jurisdiction; (2) the ICJ could find that Kosovo's independence is legal; or (3) the ICJ could find that Kosovo's independence violates international law. Kosovo's case in favor of the legality of its independence is strong. Customary international law recognizes a sovereign state as (1) an entity that has a defined territory and a permanent population, (2) under the control of its own government, and (3) that engages in, or has the capacity to engage in, formal relations with other such entities. Kosovo easily satisfies the first and third requirements. There is little dispute that Kosovo has a well-defined territory with a permanent pop-ulation. Kosovo also satisfies the third requirement because it has engaged in formal relations with other state actors, including the fifty that have so far rec-ognized it as an independent state. An issue may exist with respect to the sec-ond requirement, whether Kosovo is completely under the control of its own government, given the terms of international supervision of its sovereignty under the Ahtisaari Plan and Security Council Resolution 1244. It also is open to dispute whether the government of Kosovo exercises effective authority over the Serb-predominant areas north of the Ibar River and in the enclaves in the south.

In mid-October, the Court decided to invite the "authors" of the "uni-lateral declaration of independence by the Provisional Institutions of Self-Government of Kosovo" to make "written contributions to the Court." It set April 17, 2009, as the deadline for written statements to be submitted, and July 17, 2009, as the deadline for party comments on the statements.[12]

The ICJ likely will decide to exercise its jurisdiction and arguably already has done so by issuing its scheduling order. Then the arguments on the merits will begin.

However, the point is not the merits of the case; the point is that an ICJ decision on Kosovo's independence will take years. A case involving the geno-cide convention between Serbia and Croatia was filed in 1999 and has not been decided yet.[13] The protracted nature of the ICJ process will give Serbia and Russia exactly what they want: more uncertainty.

Investors and Kosovars will use uncertainty as an excuse for sluggish investment in Kosovo. It will be like before February 17, when Kosovo's

---

[12] Accordance with International Law of the Unilateral Declaration of Independence by the Provisional Institutions of Self-Government of Kosovo (Request for an Advisory Opinion), 2008 General List No. 141 (Order, October 17, 2008).

[13] In its judgment of November 18, 2008, the Court rejected preliminary objections by Serbia to its jurisdiction, but did leave the merits for further proceedings. Case Concerning Application of the Convention on the Prevention and Punishment of the Crime of Genocide (*Croatia v. Serbia*) (Judgment on Preliminary Objections, November 18, 2008).

friends said, "Foreign investment is discouraged by uncertainty about Kosovo's status." Now, they will say, "Foreign investment is discouraged by uncertainty over the outcome of the ICJ case."

Kosovo's political leaders cannot do much about the ICJ case. They can, however, do something about the other factors that do more to discourage investors than uncertainty over Kosovo's status or the legality of its independence. If they succeed in these endeavors, Kosovo's success as an independent state will be undeniable by the time the ICJ rules and no one will care what the ICJ says. If they fail, victory for Kosovo in the ICJ will make little difference in the lives of its peoples or to international attitudes toward Kosovo.

Disagreements between Kosovo officials and international overseers were inevitable, just as they were between UNMIK and Kosovo's elected leaders before independence. Constructive evolution of supervised independence requires that both sides concentrate on resolving their differences rather than creating impasses.

A crucial difference exists, however, between the UNMIK political trusteeship and the postindependence period. Kosovo now is a sovereign state. International authorities could be present only with the permission of the government of Kosovo. Its Declaration of Independence and Constitution provide for the role of ICO and EULEX, but not for continued UNMIK presence after a limited transition period. The government of Kosovo now enjoyed the legal power to say simply, "We appreciate accomplishments of the UN civil administration from 1999 to 2008, but we no longer consent to have UNMIK here." At some point, the government of Kosovo must have the courage to say that, even if some international elements were twitchy about the certain controversy that would follow such action. The problem with this course of action is that the six-point plan and UNMIK's involvement in implementing it is the only remaining mechanism for diluting otherwise complete control by Belgrade over the Serb areas of Kosovo. The government of Kosovo lacks the police and military capacity to enforce its authority over the Serb areas unilaterally. For that matter, it lacks the capacity to expel UNMIK by force. Therefore, it is pretty much stuck with whatever the UN and the EU decide.

Apart from questions about extension of authority over the Serb areas is the question of the relationship between the government of Kosovo and the international Ahtisaari authorities: ICO and EULEX. Although the initiative rests with Kosovo's elected political leaders, the international community (particularly the EU and the United States) must manage the geopolitical context within which they can lead. As Ahtisaari said in mid-2008, "It's independence that is important, not the details of international supervision of Kosovo."[14] The Peace Institute's Daniel Serwer offered a sound framework

---

[14] August 2008 interview with Martii Ahtisaari.

in his March 2008 congressional testimony.[15] His first precept is international restraint:

> Kosovo needs massive assistance, but it also needs wise restraint to develop as a state. While providing international judges and prosecutors as well as police monitors, we need to be careful not to create dependency: politicians who feel no obligation to take on tough issues because they know the internationals will act. States need to make their own mistakes. We should intervene only to prevent the potentially fatal ones.

The international community needs to avoid the confusion of the UNMIK period, when a weak UNMIK administration in Pristina blocked elected Kosovo officials from exercising authority. It was not that the SRSG was weak; Jessen-Petersen clearly was not. "The problem," said Ischinger, "was a very large UN organization, with personnel of uneven quality. They did not give the Kosovo institutions enough to do. Even the license plates were printed locally by German diplomats. That meant that the Kosovar Albanian leadership had little to focus on except final status."[16]

After independence, Kosovo's political leadership had to decide whether to look outward for its legitimacy or inward. Neither could be pursued singlemindedly. Before Independence Day, the most important thing a Kosovar Albanian politician could do for his or her career was to keep the international community happy – especially the United States. This was the real constituency; not the local population. After Independence Day, that changed, although the internationals remain an important constituency. They decide how much money comes into the country through donors' conferences, the first of which occurred on July 11–12, 2008. The internationals control relations with Belgrade and with the Kosovo Serbs through KFOR and UNMIK. They have the power to veto legislation and to remove political officials, at least when such intervention could be linked to interpretation or application of the Ahtisaari Plan, a justification not too difficult for any decent lawyer to construct. Therefore, it may be, as Albin Kurti's claimed, that formal independence would make little difference: Kosovo's political leaders would be selected in Washington and Brussels and all the important decisions would be made there. However, such a robust role for the international community was hobbled by the overlapping mandates of UNMIK, ICO, and EULEX and by tepid European support. Therefore, the international authorities could block certain action by the government of Kosovo by refusing to fund it or by refusing to provide the security forces to overcome resistance. However, they were not likely to be decisive.

---

[15] Testimony of Daniel Serwer, Vice President for Peace and Stability Operations, United States Institute for Peace, before the Senate Foreign Relations Committee (March 4, 2008), located at http://foreign.senate.gov/testimony/2008/SerwerTestimony080304a.pdf.

[16] October 2008 interview with Wolfgang Ischinger.

A central problem in the international realm is the lack of robust public support in other states for Kosovo as a new state. There is no widespread
hostility to Kosovo's independence, outside Russia, Serbia, and the EU members who have refused to recognize Kosovo. Neither is there enthusiasm, however. Most people are indifferent now that Kosovo has been replaced on the
evening news by Georgia, developments in Pakistan and India, and the Soma-
lian pirates. The government of Kosovo needs to do much more than it has
to building popular support in other countries. No effective, proactive, public
relations campaign is evident, and Kosovo badly needs one.

In April 2004, as the dust was settling from the March riots, Michael
Kunczik was making some good suggestions at a Symposium on Final Status
for Kosovo held at Chicago-Kent College of Law. Kunczik is a professor of
journalism at the University of Mainz, Germany, and the author of the 1997
book *Images of Nations and International Public Relations*.

His paper, prepared for the Symposium, asserted, "Public opinion in the
West has been decisive in all phases of the Kosovo conflict and is of central importance today.... New countries or new governments have to introduce themselves to world public opinion." They have to do so, he explained,
through a carefully constructed public relations campaign comprising several
distinct phases.

In Phase I, embassies and consulates abroad, and ministries at home, must
become skilled at producing materials for the press, including images, and
surely including good material on the Web – the cheapest and easiest way to
present a face to the world. In this phase, Kunczik suggests emphasizing information that casts a country and its people in a favorable light: information on
painters, sculptors, architects, musicians, writers, works of art, cultural events,
and athletics. In Phase II, he suggests using "the aura of famous persons to
cultivate a country's image" by exhibitions and visits abroad by artists and
athletes. Upon such a foundation of foreign appreciation of the talents of the
people of Kosovo, the campaign then can move to Phase III, where the message shifts more explicitly to the activities of statehood, such as initiatives to
combat corruption and install good government, success in building a sustainable economy, and respect for democratic values and human rights. All three
phases, he says, must begin with foreign journalists, but also should include
other opinion leaders such as upcoming young politicians, young managers in
the business community, and intellectuals.

This is sound advice, but so far, the government of Kosovo is not following
it. Effective public relations in 1997 and 1998 were decisive in building international support for Kosovo's struggle against Serbian oppression. It could be
decisive now in building support for Kosovo's statehood. However, the effort
must begin. It has not begun yet.

Until early 2009, the Kosovo government's Web site had no page for its
Ministry of Foreign Affairs. Its Ministry of Culture still had an essentially
blank page as its only offering in English. Its Ministry of Trade and Industry had

no functional Web page, in either Albanian or English until late 2008 – only a technical message from the Web server administrator. These omissions do not concern frills. The first thing a foreign reporter does when he or she is writing a story is to check for Web resources. When he or she finds empty pages on the Kosovo government Web site, that journalist is not likely to write favorably about Kosovo's progress. These pages, instead of being empty, should be full of photographs and biographical data about Kosovo's people, featuring its musicians, visual artists, actors, playwrights, and athletes. They should feature some of the works and accomplishments of these creative people.

Lack of resources is not a credible explanation; lack of will is the problem. Hundreds of young Kosovars have the requisite knowledge to construct Web pages, and they are underemployed. Indeed, I encouraged a group of young AUK students to build a mock Web site for the Ministry of Culture and offered it to the Minister of Culture. He was unresponsive. An effort in 2009 to get Kosovo to develop a sports-oriented film for entry into the U.S. Sports Film Festival elicited interest only from private filmmakers and theaters, not from the government or from the government-funded National Theatre.

Domestic Politics

Ironically, the impasse between ICO/EULEX and UNMIK provides more political space for the elected leadership than might have been the case if the transition had gone according to plan. Much now is within Thaçi's control. He must maintain coherent leadership despite continuing resentment within the LDK and challenges from Ramush Haradinaj, who has emerged as an energetic leader of the opposition. He must reduce political alienation within Kosovo, particularly among the young. He shepherded a new constitution through the Kosovo Assembly and now must obtain results meeting the essential requirements of Ahtisaari's plan. He must get corruption under control. He must find a pathway to economic prosperity.

Mass popular constituencies inside Kosovo matter more now than international authorities. The ultimate test for the Thaçi government – and for its successors – will come when the euphoria over independence runs its course. Kosovars would look around them and examine their prospects for economic success. They would ask themselves if electricity interruptions were fewer in number and shorter in duration. They would consider whether educational opportunities for their children had improved. At this point, if it looks like the Thaçi government is not delivering, it will be turned out of office, no matter how good its relations with Washington or Brussels. That possibility is a hallmark of democratic accountability.

Public opinion in Kosovo has shifted dramatically since the UNMIK days on who is responsible for Kosovo's political situation. In June 2003, 60 percent considered UNMIK responsible, and fewer than 20 percent held the government of Kosovo and its political parties responsible. By the end of 2008,

47 percent held the government of Kosovo and its political parties responsible, while only 27 percent held UNMIK responsible. A similar trend was apparent regarding responsibility for Kosovo's economic situation. In June 2003, 60 percent held UNMIK responsible and 20 percent held the government and the parties responsible. In December 2008, 60 percent held the government and parties responsible and only 20 percent held UNMIK responsible.[17]

Thaçi cannot achieve results in the economic, law, and political realms unless he maintains coherent leadership in a political culture that is still immature. It had been focused for a hundred years or longer (much longer, depending on who is counting) on criticizing outside "occupiers." Now Thaçi must forge effective political coalitions focused on delivering results. To overcome the legacy of policy paralysis,[18] he must deal with three problems. The first was the fact that the LDK was divided and sullen about its participation in a coalition led by Thaçi.[19] Despite its second-place vote returns in the 2007 elections, the LDK was still the best-organized party in Kosovo. It had a ten-year advantage over the other parties in that respect, with well-developed components at the municipal level throughout Kosovo, a generation of political activists experienced in using all the levers of political power, and two generations of voters accustomed to voting for the LDK. Its role as a junior partner in the coalition was an uncomfortable one, as much the product of internal divisions as of broad support for the PDK. President Sejdiu's control over LDK factions was tenuous,[20] and Thaçi must work closely with him and other LDK supporters to broaden genuine support for his coalition government within all parts of the LDK. Moreover, there had been strains within Thaçi's own PDK ever since it was formed – especially between those members and leaders who were part of the KLA and those who were not. Thaçi must manage LDK and PDK party processes so that agreement and initiative comes out of party institutions instead of stalemate and indecision.

The second threat to coherent leadership for Kosovo was Ramush Haradinaj,[21] although he also showed the potential for leading an effective opposition and any successor government to Thaçi's. As Kosovo celebrated

---

[17] December 2008 Early Warning Report Fast Facts at 2.

[18] See generally European Commission, Kosovo Under UNSCR 1244 2007 Progress Report 8 (November 6, 2007) (SEC [2007] 1433), located at http://ec.europa.eu/enlargement/pdf/ key_documents/2007/nov/kosovo_progress_reports_en.pdf [hereinafter "2007 EU Report"]; id. at 8 (the assembly made some progress in the legislative field, but its administrative and policy-making capacities remain limited); id. at 7–9 (PM office has improved but lack of capacity, particularly at the local level, remains problematic); id. at 10 (overall, Kosovo's public administration remains weak and inefficient. Some progress has been made in reforming the public administration, but reforms are at an early stage).

[19] See generally International Crisis Group, *Kosovo After Haradinaj*, Europe Report No. 163 at 12–24 (May 26, 2005) (analyzing Kosovo's political parties).

[20] See generally ICG, *Countdown: A Blueprint for Transition*, European Report No. 188 at 18 (December 2007) (describing split within LDK over possible coalition with PDK).

[21] See ICG, *Fragile Transition* at 22 (discussing Thaçi–Haradinaj rivalry).

independence on February 17, 2008, posters featuring Haradinaj's image sprouted up throughout Pristina. His popularity remained strong despite his war-crimes trial and controversy over his defense fund.[22] His acquittal of all charges on April 3, 2008,[23] caused enthusiastic celebrations in Kosovo. During his prime ministership and during the long period of his behind-the-scenes dominance of the LDK–AAK coalition that continued after his resignation, Haradinaj built ties with internationals and with power centers in the LDK. He was especially close to Deputy SRSG Steven Schook, who was quoted as saying that he liked to "get drunk with Haradinaj once a week," and who was the target of unsubstantiated rumors that he disclosed the name and whereabouts of one of the protected witnesses against Haradinaj in his ICTY trial.[24]

Haradinaj has enormous innate political talents, more spontaneous than Thaçi's, who is stronger on strategy and is more conventionally polished. He was a natural magnet for lingering public disaffection with Thaçi and his coalition partners, and a credible leader of a vigorous political opposition. Relations between him and Thaçi were poisonous. Thaçi was adamant, even in the face of considerable international pressure including from the United States, that Haradinaj and his AAK party be excluded from the new coalition government, and had not met with him since he returned from The Hague. So Haradinaj was outside the tent, throwing stones at those inside, motivated to get even for the stones that Thaçi's opposition threw at his coalition when they were in office. In addition, because Haradinaj played no formal role in the Unity Team, he was free to focus criticism on the terms agreed to by the Team in order to obtain independence. Haradinaj initially concentrated his criticism on the Thaçi government's incompetence in encouraging more states to recognize Kosovo.[25]

Haradinaj, however, faced challenges, too. Even his most enthusiastic supporters said that he must get his own party under control,[26] getting rid of or

---

[22] Astrit Haraqija, Minister of Culture in the Haradinaj-dominated government, and Bajrush Morina, an official at the ministry, were indicted by the ICTY, accused of pressuring a protected witness not to testify against Haradinaj. *Prosecutor v. Haraqija*, Case No. IT-04–84-R77.4 (Indictment January 8, 2008). They were convicted and sentenced in late 2008. Jahja Lluka, former adviser to Haradinaj, Milazim Abazi, director of Kasabank, and Hashim Sejdiu, manager of Kasabank, went on trial in late October 2008 for money laundering and failure to report financial transactions, in connection with their administration of the Haradinaj defense fund. All three pleaded not guilty.

[23] Haradinaj was represented by an unusually able team of lawyers, while the prosecution appeared to be bumbling and generally incompetent.

[24] See Walter Mayr, "The Slow Birth of a Nation," *Spiegel Online International* (April 24, 2008), located at http://www.spiegel.de/international/world/0,1518,549441,00.html.

[25] See *Kosovo's Fragile Transition* at 23 (describing Haradinaj's criticism of the Thaçi government, particularly regarding foreign-state recognition and integration of Serbs in the north).

[26] See 2007 EU Report at 12 (the use of Ministry of Justice premises for actions in support of an indicted party leader [presumably referring to Haradinaj] is a cause of concern); id. at 23 (one key witness in the Haradinaj trial died and other witnesses have been intimidated; protection of witnesses needs to be enhanced).

putting behind the scenes former Energy Minister Ekrim Çeku and former Trade-and-Industry Minister Bujar Dugolli, whose rumored corruption was accepted as a fact by political activists, regardless of party or personal attachment. He also must rein in his younger brother Daut, who used his prominence as an AAK officer during Ramush's trial to behave in a thuggish and generally embarrassing manner.

Simultaneously, he must cement relations with one or more of several power centers in Kosovo politics naturally inclined to oppose Thaçi and Sejdiu. The first was the disaffected group of former LDK ministers, angered by not being part of the new cabinet. Lutfi Haziri was the most prominent of these – former deputy prime minister and minister for local government, and leader of many of the Unity Team negotiations with Ahtisaari and Belgrade. Sejdiu had little power to deliver what they wanted and they well could conclude that they were more likely to realize their goals with Haradinaj than with staying in the LDK and the Thaçi coalition. Kadri Krejziu, former LDK speaker of the assembly, was another potential Haradinaj recruit. His situation was similar to that of Haziri and the former ministers, but he and Haziri had different geographic bases and were rivals within the LDK.

Nexhat Daci and his LDD, and Behgjet Pacolli and his AKR, were also obvious targets, although each had baggage. Daci, many said, was a spent force and continued to be loaded down by reports of corruption when he was president of the assembly. He also continued to smart from Haradinaj's "betrayal" when Haradinaj joined in the cabal with the U.S. office in deposing Daci from his assembly post in the spring of 2006. Pacolli did not earn a reputation for political prowess in the 2007 campaign, but his new party did get about 12 percent of the vote. Whether he could subordinate his own ego in an alliance with Haradinaj would test the power of his pragmatism. Probably more damaging for Daci and Pacolli was the widespread belief that the United States opposed a more significant role for either of them in politics.

More ambitiously, Haradinaj might be able to split the PDK, for example, peeling away Fatmir Limaj, Minister of Telecommunications and Transportation in the 2008 coalition. Ever since he was acquitted by the ICTY, Limaj had been rumored to be unhappy with Thaçi and ready to jump ship if he could not depose Thaçi as leader of the PDK. However, Thaçi was holding Limaj closely, and rewarded him with a cabinet post after Limaj's unsuccessful bid to become mayor of Pristina in the 2007 elections.

Regardless of Haradinaj's strategy, the lure of office would increase Thaçi's gravitational pull for those already in the coalition government or affiliated with one of the two coalition partners. Those already holding office would be reluctant to trade the reality of power for the speculative possibility that they might return to power in a different government. For those in one of the two coalition parties but not holding office, a shift to Haradinaj would not immediately improve their economic situation: Haradinaj controlled no spoils, and joining him would alienate those who already had the power to reward them in the future. Few would be so bold in staking their futures on a comeback by Ramush Haradinaj. At the end of 2008, Thaçi had the lead over Haradinaj in popularity. Polls conducted by UNDP showed that 23 percent of respondents trusted President Sejdiu and Prime Minister Thaçi, while 14.2 percent trusted Ramush Haradinaj. Pacolli and Daci were at 5 percent.[27]

The entire calculus would change, of course, if the public soured on the Thaçi's government's ability to deliver what they want, and if opinion surveys showed that those associated with the Thaçi government or one of its parties were likely to lose an imminent election. Then the gravitational pull of the leader of the opposition would increase relative to Thaçi's, and a political reconfiguration would be more likely. Until early 2009, Thaçi and Haradinaj were engaged in a tug of war over when elections would be held. A literal interpretation of the Ahtisaari Plan requires new national elections nine months from June 10, 2008 – the date on which the Ahtisaari Plan "entered into effect." That would result in elections in March 2009. Haradinaj's public statements favored early elections, if not in March 2009, then later in the year. However, Sejdiu and Thaçi, with support from Peter Feith (reportedly on instructions from Javier Solana), decided to defer elections until 2011.[28] Haradinaj objected, but there was not much he could do to reverse the decision. Deferring elections actually might be to Haradinaj's advantage because it would give more time for disappointment with the Thaçi government to build up. As the first anniversary of independence approached, Feith was generous in his praise of Thaçi: "As an International Community Representative, I want to . . . congratulate Prime Minister Hashim Thaçi, my dear friend Hashim, for the achievements during the last year, for consolidation of institutions, for the efforts of Kosovo, its international position, work with communities in the internal aspect, reforms, all these are extremely positive."[29]

A third obstacle – and the most important long-term threat – to coherent leadership by Thaçi was pervasive political alienation, particularly among the young. The turnout in the November 17, 2007, elections was only about 45 percent, in the face of deep and pervasive cynicism among both Kosovo Serbs and Kosovar Albanians about the capacity of the political elites in Pristina to make a difference in their lives. In the December 2008 poll, approximately 25 percent did not trust any of the political leaders or did not know whom to trust.[30] Public opinion polls showed that political pessimism in mid-2008 stood at 39 percent, only two points lower than in December 2007, but far lower than the 57 percent recorded in July 2002.[31]

To a significant extent, political alienation is a problem in all countries in transition. Throughout Eastern Europe, populations had thrown off the yoke

---

[27] UNDP Kosovo, Fast Facts – Early Warning Report #23 at p. 5 (December 2008).
[28] UNMIK Media Monitoring Headlines, January 19, 2009 (quoting translation of story in Zeri).
[29] UNMIK Media Monitoring Headlines, February 14, 2009.
[30] UNDP Kosovo, Fast Facts – Early Warning Report #23 at p. 5 (December 2008).
[31] 2008 Early Warning Report at 18.

of communism, motivated by dreams of how their lives would improve after they achieved independence. The credibility of communist regimes was low as they earned reputations for enriching themselves from public resources and repressing dissent. Ordinary people had learned not to trust public institutions.[32] Then, after transition away from socialism proved far from easy, the public mistrust of government easily attached to newer, more democratic regimes and political elites. The same phenomenon operated in Kosovo. The removal of the Serbian yoke by the international community left many political and economic aspirations unfulfilled. The Kosovar Albanians mistrusted their leadership. The Kosovo Serbs, under pressure from Belgrade, did not vote in the elections and thus had little interest in Kosovo's elected political leadership, whom they saw as illegitimate.

The sense of alienation and passivity increased because the early stages of final status were too easy and the middle stages uncertain. Throughout 2005 and 2006, it looked like it would be a straight shot from Ahtisaari's appointment to Security Council approval of an independence resolution. So everyone "grilled the fish while it was still in the sea," as Dastid Pallaska, an outspoken young Kosovar Albanian lawyer, said.[33] Their early celebrations came back to haunt them, especially in the Unity Team's case. "Now they look like fools, and they are powerless to do anything about it," Pallaska said in the summer of 2007 when things were going badly at the UN.

For the moment, the major Kosovar Albanian figures who delivered independence were enjoying something of a political honeymoon. Mid-2008 approval ratings for the president of Kosovo were up fourteen percentage points from December 2007 to a level of 75 percent. The approval ratings of the prime minister stood at 71 percent.[34] As the bloom of Independence Day fades, however, and the realities of policy making and implementation retake public consciousness, this underlying lack of confidence in Kosovo's political leadership would have to be dealt with, and it would not be easy. Satisfaction with the institutions of the president and the prime minister stood at 71 percent and 63 percent, respectively, at the end of 2008, down three and six points from the spring in which independence was declared.[35] The decline was inevitable but hardly precipitous.

The cynicism tars Kosovo's entire political elite, and any genuine mobilization of the alienated majority probably must await some completely new face in Kosovo politics, someone with charisma, a compelling message, and only

---

[32] See Daniel N. Nelson, "The Worker and Political Alienation in Communist Europe," 15 *Polity* 182, 183 n. 1 (No. 2, Winter 1982) (finding that blue-collar workers in Eastern Europe, including Yugoslavia, were alienated from communist elites; characterizing literature as concluding that modernization expands political participation beyond capacity of institutions, creating a "revolution of rising frustrations").

[33] August 2007 interview with Dastid Pallaska in Pristina.

[34] 2008 Early Warning Report at 17.

[35] December 2008 Fast Facts at 2.

muted ties to the past – to the KLA or to the UNMIK period. No one could even identify such new faces in early 2009, and if they existed, they surely would not come to the fore for another five years or so.

If Thaçi cannot deliver on the economic front, and if a coherent opposition could not get people excited at the prospect that it could do better, a dangerous pattern already established by the time Thaçi took office would become the norm: people in Kosovo would go about their daily lives paying less and less attention to politics, stitching together enough resources to live from low-paying jobs, the grey market, remittances, and other family support. The soil would continue to be fertile for organized crime linked to international criminal networks, and young people might heed the ever-present call by extremist elements within Islam.

Here is how one young Kosovar architect, Driton ("Toni") Kulakaj, described his life in July 2007:

> There are limitations everywhere I go. If I want to go somewhere and seek some architectural business, I can't do it. It's not my fault that I can't go abroad to seek business. I have the money, but I can't go because I have to go a month ahead of time to get a visa and then nothing will happen. I want to start a business, but it's very difficult because nobody will come in here to do business – with the conditions here – or to invest. It's not my fault that I have to sit here with my life and wait, wishing for somebody else to straighten things out.
>
> We are frustrated. That's the problem. More and more people take it out by cheating other people, lying – like the international community does to us. It's like being in prison. They make all the people prisoners.
>
> Our history has created a situation. Our present has robbed the people of a fighting heart. They have put our hearts in jail.

Some of Kulakaj's frustration was driven by the protracted final status process and was expressed before independence was declared. However, much of the frustration was born from obstacles to his professional success, obstacles that independence does not necessarily remove. In a discussion with Kulakaj in August 2008, six months after independence, his attitude had not brightened.[36]

Other young people were even more scathing in their expression of disdain for the new political elite. As one young person put it before independence was declared, "Sejdiu and Thaçi don't care about whether Kosovo becomes independent; they only want to make sure the elections occur soon so that they can squeeze out the others and the two of them run Kosovo's government. Why should someone want to run a province where all the decisions are made by somebody else? But that's what they want and, when you think about it, you can't blame them. They ride around in leather seats in chauffeur-driven automobiles, and that's a lot better than sneaking through the woods not sure when you are going to get shot at."[37]

---

[36] August 2008 interview with Driton Kulakaj.
[37] Confidential interview, July 2007, Pristina.

In governing, the Thaçi government, like past Kosovo governments, faces a particular capacity gap, fueled by the political alienation of the young. It has experienced political leaders, who by now understand the collective and personal interests that define politics in Kosovo. They also understand how to work with – and against – the international community. They understand how to craft a message that resonates with the general population. It also has a cadre of civil servants who know how to carry out government programs, although political-faction loyalty, indifferent work ethnic, lack of results orientation, and uneven technical skills continue to plague their ranks. The greatest gap is in the middle – individuals who can bridge the space between policy and politics.

Kosovo is flooded by think tank reports on virtually every aspect of public policy. Some are generated by foreign government and intergovernmental agencies such as USAID, the European Agency for Reconstruction ("EAR"), or their contractors. Some are generated by international NGOs such as the International Crisis Group or the European Security Initiative. An increasing number are generated by local consulting groups such as MDA, KIPRED, ReInvest, and the Institute for Advanced Studies.

Kosovo, however, needs a stronger capacity to take the intellectual capital generated by these think tanks and translate it into coherent and viable political programs in the energy, economic, or justice sectors. In the past, the political leaders did not fully trust the intellectuals, and the intellectuals disdained partisan politics. Thaçi, Sejdiu, Krasniqi, and Haradinaj need someone at their sides who can say, "If you embrace this part of the USAID report on privatization of the electricity company, it will gain support from this part of your constituency and anger this other part." Kosovo needs to shed a political culture in which policy proposals are publicized briefly, given lip service, and then forgotten about, while the political parties put all their energies into jockeying for favor with the internationals, more foreign donor support, and competition over the spoils. Substantive programs must emerge to which those with political heft are genuinely committed. Kosovo needs more pragmatic politicians and businessmen and women, not more think tank consultants and NGOs.

Ethnic Tolerance

The conceptual core of the Ahtisaari Plan is the creation of a political and legal environment in which Kosovo Serbs feel safe and perceive opportunities for themselves in a state governed primarily by Kosovar Albanians. In the weeks immediately following independence, Belgrade was making reconciliation of Serbian and Albanian Kosovars as difficult as possible by encouraging attacks against UN, EU, and Kosovo symbols of authority in the north, and intimidating Kosovo Serbs employed in the Kosovo courts and by the Kosovo Police Service, demanding that they resign en masse. This institutionalized resistance to Kosovo's independence was problematic. "The Ahtisaari

Plan... firmly embeds separate Serb institutions into the legal structure of the Republic of Kosovo and privileges them with enhanced authority and the benefits of external support. The plan effectively fragments Kosovo's sovereignty into two sets of institutions, one of them with fully authorized influence and financial support of a neighboring state.[38] In their effort to provide Kosovo's Serbs with adequate security guarantees and meet Belgrade's objections, international negotiators have enshrined in the heart of independent Kosovo institutions similar to those used by nationalist Serbs in the early 1990s to launch their projects of separation and ethnic cleansing in Croatia and Bosnia-Herzegovina."[39]

Still, Kosovo was not an armed camp, with a handful of Kosovo Serbs hunkered down behind barricades and KFOR machine guns.[40] In Mitrovica, the famously divided city, the bridge was open, with a few KPS police cars parked at either end. An occasional pedestrian passed over in one direction or the other carrying plastic bags of bread. To be sure, flags of Serbia flew prominently on the north side of the bridge, while the red and black Albanian flag proliferated on the south side of the bridge. Nevertheless, the atmosphere on a March 2008 Sunday morning was anything but tense. A French KFOR observation post on the top of one of the buildings overlooking the bridge from the south was manned by a few bored-looking soldiers. No tanks, no groups glaring at each other across the bridge, and no riot police.

Further south, cars whizzed through the Serb enclave of Qakalavica astride the Prishtina-Skopje road, taking no notice unless a passenger pointed out where the Serbs live. Two other Americans and I were welcomed warmly in a Serb-run restaurant there in March 2008. Likewise, the route from Pristina to Gjilane, a little further east, passes through the Serb enclave of Gračanica, where Kosovo Serbs were washing cars, chatting in cafes, and walking along the road unmolested and apparently unconcerned, noticeable to passersby only because a colleague points out that they are Serbs.

Near the Kosovo-Serbian border in the vicinity of the Preshevo Valley, the municipality of Kamenica hosts Albanian and Kosovo Serb families living and working cheek to jowl: a Serb house, an Albanian house next to it, and then another Serb house. Young Serbs tend cattle on one part of a field, while young Albanians look after their small flocks on another part of the same field.

---

[38] Donia, *Elusive Finality*.
[39] Donia, *Elusive Finality*.
[40] See BBC, "Kosovo Lives: A Mixed Village," August 4, 2008, located at http://news.bbc .co.uk/2/hi/europe/7526184.stm (reporting interview by Nick Thorpe of Kosovo Serb, who says she has good relations with her Albanian neighbors, feels no physical threats, and is free to travel throughout Kosovo and to Serbia). The interviewee lives in Vidanje, near Klina, deep in KLA-dominated territory. But see Robert J. Donia, *Creeping Crisis: The Serbian Government's Plan for Kosovo* (July 7, 2008) (describing "the grave threat to stability that Serbia is incrementally implementing in Kosovo" and suggesting it is inconsistent with Serbia's aspiration to joining the EU).

Kosovar Albanian residents here were proud of their Serb neighbors, bragging that one Serb family has the greatest skills in the community in farming techniques. "We are not much interested in politics here," the proprietor of an auto shop said. "We have always worked and lived together without problems." He pointed out that here, unlike in the north of Kosovo, a substantial Serb population concentration exists on the Kosovo side of the border, but on the Serb side of the border the population is predominantly Albanian. It is more difficult for radicals from Serbia proper to stoke fears and hostility by Kosovo Serbs, who, for their part, realize that their future, like their past, is inside Kosovo.[41]

Efforts to isolate Serb communities and to break the thin ties they have with the Pristina government were likely to continue. Whether they succeed depends to a significant degree on the attractiveness of participation in the regular political life of Kosovo.[42] To the extent the Thaçi government makes a reality of its rhetoric to open its arms and doors to participation by minorities in government and civil affairs, the Serbian sabotage initiative would be weakened. Thaçi consistently said the right things. "Talk to your son and tell him to return.... You can tell your son he can return today, you have my pledge and the pledge of Kosovo's institutions that we will help him in this respect," Thaçi told a local Serb in the village of Videjë, near Klina. "All those that want to return to Kosovo can do so, because Kosovo is the country of all those that want to live here."[43]

Possibilities for a *modus vivendi* are exemplified by the statement of one prominent Kosovo Serb:

'I cannot bring myself to acknowledge Kosovo's independence, but I am prepared to abide by the law of the land,' Dr. Trajkovic told me. The law of the land, of course, is the Ahtisaari Plan, as the new Constitution specifies. 'I've concluded that you westerners are great at planning for wars, but horrible at

---

[41] See Helsinki Committee for Human Rights in Serbia, *Forgotten World: Kosovo Enclaves –* Part II, (June 2008), located at http://www.helsinki.org.yu/doc/2nd%20and%203rd% 20missions%20to%20Serb%20enclaves%20in%20Kosovo,%20report.doc (reporting on project "Serb-Serb Dialogue in Serb Enclaves in Kosovo"); id. (reporting that some villagers in enclaves were "critical of the representatives from Kosovska Mitrovica, who, as they put it, constantly obstruct their integration into the Kosovo society"); id. (reporting on successful effort by Kosovo Serbs in Staro-Gracko to obtain funding from Kosovo government and NGOs for projects; villagers "display interest in cooperation and readiness to partake in Kosovo institutions").

[42] Donia, *Elusive Finality* (North Mitrovica and adjacent Serbian-majority municipalities are, de facto, governed from Belgrade; it is a fiction that the territory is part of Kosovo). Donia, *Elusive Finality* (Kosovo Serbs get their health care, licenses, passports, pension payments, and municipal services from institutions financed by Belgrade at a sum roughly equal to one-third of Kosovo's total budget, spent on 6 percent of Kosovo's population). Donia, *Elusive Finality* (Serbian institutions in the enclaves generally ignore both UNMIK and the Kosovo government).

[43] UNMIK Division of Public Information, *Media Monitoring Headlines* (July 16, 2008) (quoting Koha Ditore).

planning the peace,' she opined. 'But this Ahtisaari Plan is technically okay.' Having reluctantly acknowledged the realities of today's Kosovo, she opted to focus on the work of her clinic and advancing the interests of Kosovo's Serbs rather than engaging in political machinations orchestrated from Belgrade. She even dared to hope that the long-term demographic attrition of Serbs in Kosovo's enclaves might be reversed, and Serbian refugees might return to better prospects and greater security in Kosovo.[44]

A significant ethnic divide exists, however, on the prospect for interethnic relations.[45] At the end of 2008, only 8.6 percent of Kosovar Albanians thought that further aggravation of interethnic relations threatened the stability of Kosovo, while 55 percent of Kosovo Serbs thought so.[46] An unsurprising divide also existed on popular opinion about how independence was declared. Among Kosovar Albanians, 89 percent were satisfied or very satisfied, while 92 percent of Kosovo Serbs were dissatisfied or very dissatisfied.[47] Seventy-eight percent of Kosovar Albanians and non-Serb minorities believe interethnic relations are improving. Only 3 percent of Kosovo Serbs believe so, a huge decrease from June 2007, when more than 90 percent of Kosovo Serbs thought relations were improving.[48] Most Kosovar Albanians believe the problem is the influence of Belgrade, following by the lack of readiness of Kosovo Serbs to be integrated into Kosovo society. Kosovo Serbs believe the problem is the attitude of Kosovar Albanian leaders, followed by insufficient efforts to promote integration.[49]

About 50 percent of Kosovar Albanians are willing to work and live with Kosovo Serbs, while only 20–40 percent of Kosovo Serbs are willing to work or live with Kosovar Albanians, a significant decline since late 2006. A poll conducted in November 2008, however, showed a significant increase in the number of Kosovo Serbs willing to work with Kosovar Albanians: 43 percent, compared with 35 percent in July 2008. The corresponding percentage of Kosovar Albanians willing to work with Kosovo Serbs stood at 55 percent in the same poll, up seven percentage points since July 2008.[50] Almost no members of either group were willing to condone interethnic marriages,

---

[44] Robert J. Donia, *Elusive Finality: Dispatch from Newly Independent Kosovo* (June 3, 2008), located at http://www.ifimes.org/default.cfm?Jezik=en&Kat=10&ID=377 [hereinafter "Donia, *Elusive Finality*"] Dr. Rada Trajkovic is the director of the Clinic of Gracanica, who directs the staff of six hundred and fifty health professionals.

[45] See generally 2007 EU Report at 21 (Kosovo Serb community still sees their freedom of movement being restricted for security concerns; returnees' houses are still the targets of violent attacks).

[46] Fast Facts, December 2008 Early Warning Report at 5.

[47] 2008 Early Warning Report at 21.

[48] 2008 Early Warning Report at 33.

[49] Id.

[50] UNDP Kosovo, Fast Facts – Early Warning Report #23 at p. 6 (December 2008), located at http://europeandcis.undp.org/home/show/D963850E-F203–1EE9-BDE5BC00EB70C6E3.

however.[51] About half (48 percent) of Kosovar Albanians thought interethnic relations would normalize over the long term, while only 28 percent of the Kosovo Serbs thought so.[52]

Surprisingly, the percentage of Kosovo Serbs who reported a positive change in their economic circumstances by getting a job (12 percent) or starting a family business (6 percent) exceeded the corresponding percentage of Kosovar Albanians (7.5 percent and 2.5 percent, respectively).[53]

Russia, Serbia, and others opposed to independence for Kosovo will continue to claim that Kosovo Serbs are being mistreated. Yet if independent Kosovo's new government continues to bend over backward to demonstrate concern for the welfare of Kosovo Serbs, it is not unreasonable to expect that Kosovo Serbs gradually will embrace the reality that their futures lie with Pristina and not with the failed policies of Belgrade past.

Economy

The Kosovar Albanian public was mostly concerned about the economy,[54] and their concerns fuel their political alienation. The assessment and priorities document prepared by Kosovo's Ministry of Economy and Finance for the July 2008 donors' conference candidly summarized Kosovo's economic position:

> Due to the many difficulties over the last two decades and in particular through the postconflict period, Kosovo faces many economic developmental challenges. It has the highest unemployment numbers in the region, highest poverty numbers, and the weakest economic growth performance. International support across a broad number of fronts has delivered economic and political stability.
>
> Kosovo's initial position contains a number of strengths. It has a young population and significant natural resources. The social structure is characterized by the existence of networks both formal and informal that provide safety nets for the poor and the unemployed. The foundations for a liberal market economy and modern system of accountability are in place and international partners are supporting many dimensions of the developmental process.
>
> But the challenges ahead are enormous.[55]

[51] 2008 Early Warning Report at 34.
[52] 2008 Early Warning Report at 45.
[53] December 2008 Fast Facts at 3.
[54] UNDP and USAID, Earning Warning Report Kosovo 19 (January 2008); December 2008 Fast Facts at 4 (75 percent of Kosovar Albanians identify economic situation as reason for feeling worried and anxious).
[55] Medium Term Expenditure Framework 2009–11 at 6 (July 12, 2008), located at http://www .seerecon.org/kdc/MTEF%20%202008–2011%20June%2012.pdf. See also 2007 EU Report at 24 (Some progress has been made toward creating an enabling environment for a successful transition to a functioning market economy, but uncertainty about status clouds every area of economic policy); id. at 28. Overall, the weak technology base (combined with a lack of price competitiveness) and the low endowment with qualified human capital remain major impediments to Kosovo's capacity to cope with competitive pressure and market forces).

According to statistics compiled by UNDP and USAID, favorable trends existed on GDP growth, workers' remittances, commercial bank loans, and the trade balance. Negative trends existed on the amount of foreign assistance, bank deposits, inflation, the number of job seekers, and returns. GDP per capita and basic pensions were neutral.[56]

Kosovo is a small state, with no past economic successes to its credit. Tito invested heavily in Kosovo to jump-start industrialization, but most of the resulting industry was tied into Yugoslavia-wide trade networks, and those are now gone. UNMIK had only modest success in promoting private-sector growth and job creation outside the trade sector. Small- and medium-sized enterprise development was not a priority. Foreign investment promotion was sporadic and hobbled by restrictions on representatives of the Kosovo government going on official missions unless they spoke through the UN. Privatization is a success, measured by numbers of enterprises now in private hands, but the participation of foreign investors has been modest.

Kosovo's economy depends on expenditures by internationals associated with the UN civil administration and with the many NGOs now present in Kosovo for a significant percentage of its GDP, on foreign assistance for about 15 percent of its GDP, and on "remittances" sent into Kosovo from Kosovars working abroad for another 15–20 percent.[57] For decades, it has been the custom for at least one younger member of extended Kosovar Albanian families to go abroad to find work and to send money home. While much of this money is consumed meeting the daily needs of family members still in Kosovo, it adds to the overall capital stock. A viable economic program must include plausible steps to prevent a sharp depression as these expenditures are reduced – as they surely will be now that independence is a reality. Even after privatization is completed, it is far from clear which sectors of the economy offer comparative advantage to Kosovar producers of goods and services.[58] Considerable insight and experimentation will be necessary to find Kosovo's place in the regional and world economy. Its balance-of-trade deficit is equivalent to about 58 percent of GDP.[59]

---

[56] UNDP and USAID, Early Warning Report Kosovo, Report #20/21 Special Edition, January–June 2008 (June 2008) [hereinafter "2008 Early Warning Report"] at 6 (table: Selected Economic Indicators).

[57] UNDP, Early Warning Report No. 19, at 6 (January 2008) (table: Selected Economic Indicators).

[58] See generally 2007 EU Report at 28–9 (Almost half [47.8 percent] of all businesses were in retail and wholesale, followed by food processing [9.3 percent], construction and other social personal services [both 5.3 percent]; informal economy remains sizeable, affecting competitiveness of economy; agriculture continues to suffer from unresolved property rights issues and poor levels of capital investment; as a consequence, Kosovo was unable to harness its potential for import substitution in the case of unprocessed and processed foodstuffs, thereby failing to use a powerful mechanism for reducing its external deficit).

[59] UNDP, Early Warning Report No. 19, at 6 (January 2008) (table: Selected Economic Indicators).

The European Commission organized a donors' conference for Kosovo on July 11, 2008, in Brussels. Representatives from thirty-seven countries and sixteen international organizations attended meetings chaired by Director of the Western Balkans for the Commission. Ahmet Shala, Minister of Economy and Finance for Kosovo, presented Kosovo's economic strategy and investment priorities. Attendees pledged more than €1,2 billion (nearly $2 billion) to address socioeconomic development and international debt servicing needs set forth in the "Medium Term Expenditure Framework (2008–2011)" document prepared by Shala's ministry.[60]

Some aspects of Kosovo's economic infrastructure are strong now, but critical gaps exist. Kosovo's Internet connectivity is among the best in the world. It has a nationwide broadband wireless backbone, which allows businesses and individuals to obtain high-speed Internet connections at prices at or below those available in Western Europe and the United States. The telephone infrastructure, especially that for cell phones, is robust. The airport in Pristina is modern, and served by several major airlines with daily flights to hubs throughout Europe and Turkey. Major road construction projects sponsored by the European Union have left Kosovo with a good internal highway backbone of mostly two-lane paved roads. Rural roads are less satisfactory, many of them unpaved and poorly maintained. A well-organized and inexpensive system of intercity buses allows the population without automobiles to move about freely all over Kosovo.

Kosovo's electricity supply, however, is erratic and its transportation links to the outside world are inadequate. No one will invest in anything except the lightest retail, service, and trade establishments unless investors can be assured of reliable electricity supplies. This is not possible now. When UNMIK took over in 1999, it was well understood that, while Kosovo had substantial reserves of lignite, its two major electricity generating plants (Kosovo A and Kosovo B) were of obsolete design, insufficient capacity and poorly maintained. Kosovo has the largest lignite (soft coal) reserves in southern Europe, so it could be an exporter of electricity – lignite accounts for approximately 50 percent of total coal consumption in Europe, usually exported in the form of electricity rather than being shipped for long distances. Instead of investing in the construction of a new plant (Kosovo C) along with enhancements in lignite mining capacity, the European Union, in charge of the economic aspects of UNMIK's political trusteeship, elected to attempt rehabilitation of Kosovo A and Kosovo B. The rehabilitation was not a success and work still had not started on Kosovo C at the end of 2008. At best, the project would not be completed fully until 2020. As independence was declared, award of the initial contracts was still being delayed by wrangling over alleged corruption in the ministry and the publicly owned enterprise responsible: the Energy Corporation of Kosovo (KEK).

---

[60] See http://www.seerecon.org/kdc/.

A second infrastructure gap involves transportation access to international markets. Kosovo's only practicable access to seaports is through Macedonia and Greece to the south, through the port of Thessalonica, or through Albania to the west, through the port of Durres.[61] Kosovo's rail system is decrepit and lacks links through Albania and through Macedonia and Greece. It is entirely unsuited to handle large volumes of freight, even if shipper density were adequate to support it. Highways are inadequate for large volumes of trucks. Segments within Kosovo are modern and well maintained, but their two lanes are clogged with traffic. Routes through Albania are close to impassable even for four-wheel-drive passenger vehicles. The best of the existing highway links to Durres, Pan European Corridor 8, runs through Macedonia, where Kosovo's access to ports depends on continued cooperation by a government nervous about Kosovo's independence. A consensus existed as early as 2003 that high priority should be given to construction of new, four-lane highways from Pristina to the port of Durres on Albania's coast, and construction was underway by 2007. Progress on the project, however, which requires expensive construction through Albania's rugged mountains, has been fitful, ensnared in political squabbling in Albania, international indifference – or outright opposition – to stronger links between Kosovo and Albania, and the ever-present allegations of corruption. The projected completion date of 2009 was in jeopardy.

The human infrastructure for economic development is encouraging, although significant gaps exist.[62] Kosovo has an ample supply of labor in its rapidly growing youth population. A significant fraction of Kosovars under age thirty-five have spent time in Europe or the United States working, getting university degrees, and learning English and German. No "brain drain" is evident: most young Kosovars who have worked or been educated abroad are eager – for now – to come home to participate in building a prosperous and democratic independent Kosovo.[63] Kosovo's young people are, on the

---

[61] In early 2009, discussions were underway between the prime ministers of Kosovo and Albania on possible use by Kosovo of the Albanian port of Shengjin, over another highway that would be constructed from Shengjin to Gjakova. See "Kosovo Asks to Use Albanian Port of Shengjin," *New Kosova Report*, February 19, 2009 (also referring to construction of highway to Durres), located at http://www.newkosovareport.com/200902191627/Business-and-Economy/Kosovo-asks-to-use-Albanian-Port-of-Shengjin.html.

[62] See generally 2007 EU Report at 25 (unemployment stood at 44.9 percent of the active labor force in 2006, but a large number of registered unemployed may be active in the informal economy; partly due to the estimated size of the grey economy, registered unemployment does not yet systematically reflect the dynamics of the economy).

[63] The author's discussions with many young Kosovar Albanians and a handful of Kosovo Serbs reveal a strong desire to return to or to remain in Kosovo to build a new society. This contrasts markedly with a number of conversations with Bosnians and Croats, who usually express a desire to leave. See generally Gregory Weeks et al., "Four Accounts on Brain Drain in the Balkans," 4 *South-East Eur. Rev. for Lab. and Soc. Affairs* 13 (2003), located at http://www.google.com/search?sourceid=navclient&ie=UTF-8&rlz=1T4SNYI_

whole, resourceful and enthusiastic. Those who have experience with international organizations have a good work ethic. They respond well to good management that emphasizes the importance of meeting deadlines, achieving results, and being on time for appointments. Wage levels are higher than one might expect, given the oversupply of labor, because international employers bid up wage levels. As the international presence declines, wage levels will likely soften.

One of the hallmarks of Kosovar society is the strong orientation toward entrepreneurship. Largely excluded from the formal economic system during ten years of repression by the Milošević regime, Kosovars learned to survive by setting up business ventures with little capital and access to infrastructure. Informal business networks exist throughout the region, into northern Europe and North America. Almost every family is in some kind of business, concentrating more on service and retail trade rather than manufacturing and processing. This pool of entrepreneurs offers significant opportunity to those who have the capacity to tie entrepreneurship to sources of adequate capital and modern business methods.

After the Serbs withdrew in 1999, underlying pride and entrepreneurial spirit began to build a market economy, and have continued ever since then to strengthen it. Shops, filling stations, and Internet cafés sprouted up through Kosovo. There is a long way to go, but it is clear that much is possible when ordinary people are freed to build a country with cheerfulness and pride, rather than being prisoners of sour, backward-looking, defensive isolation that blames others for economic disappointment.

Accounting and auditing services are available and professional. A public agency sets accounting standards and licenses accounting professionals. A reliable credit rating and reporting system is not available, however.

Kosovo has made good progress in establishing a rule of law, in the economic sphere as well as in the political and human-rights spheres – at least regarding the substantive content of law.[64] Its court system is seriously deficient, however, burdened by enormous backlogs, riddled with corruption – intensified by low judicial and support-staff salaries and saddled with a lawyers' culture that focuses on personal relationships instead of legal analysis.[65] Public approval ratings for Kosovo's courts stood at 21 percent, the

---

enUS309US309&q=brain+drain+balkans (reporting on actual brain drain in Bosnia and elsewhere in western Balkans; describing possibility of same phenomenon in Kosovo, despite eagerness of young Kosovars to return and remain).

[64] See 2007 EU Report at 27 (Kosovo has developed an appropriate legislative and institutional framework for a functioning market economy).

[65] 2007 EU report at 27 (use of courts to resolve property issues remains underdeveloped; corruption and uncertainty over property rights remain a major impediment to economic activity, due partly to Kosovo's final political status being unresolved and partly to disputed land registries or missing business cadastres; deficient rule of law is hampering business development).

lowest ranking of all Kosovo's institutions.[66] Any pronouncement by the law is meaningless unless it is applied by the courts. A well-designed reform of bar associations and lawyer licensing implemented after the war potentially allows the addition of better educated and more professional lawyers to the practicing bar. There still, however, is an acute shortage of well-qualified business lawyers knowledgeable about the new legal framework and oriented toward market transactions. The current Kosovo attorney licensing rules do not permit the admission of attorneys licensed in other jurisdictions, even for a particular case. The combination of these restrictions and the limited competence of the local bar presents a further barrier to foreign investment.

Kosovo must produce a labor force that can compete successfully in international labor markets. Not only must its computer programmers, graphic designers, and architects be able to hold their own against competitors in India, Britain, the United States, or Finland, Kosovo's nurses must meet the standards necessary so they can take advantage of aggressive efforts to fill nursing shortages in Canada and elsewhere with immigrant labor. The educational system inherited from the past does not produce such human capital, and education has gotten worse, with primary and secondary schools operating in three shifts, an ill-advised and clumsily implemented effort to revamp the curriculum completely, and a demoralized and grossly underpaid teaching staff. It does a poor job of inculcating basic skills, and it tends to overemphasize and reinforce Albanian nationalism. Universities struggle to fill the gap. The public university is very weak, and has so far resisted efforts at dramatic reform;[67] the gap is being filled by a large collection of independent institutions, the best of which is the American University in Kosovo,[68] where all instruction is in English, and about a hundred new students enroll annually in degree programs in business administration and information technology. Other good private universities exist, such as the University of Business and Technology, but many are no more than diploma mills. The Thaçi government took a desirable step on July 16, 2008, when it issued an order closing most of the profit-making universities.

Kosovo's financial-services sector is basically sound. Kosovo has a good banking system. Internal savings rates are high, and Kosovars proved more willing than many expected to deposit their savings in the array of well-run banks established after the war. The major banking enterprises are tied to

---

[66] 2008 Early Warning Report at 17.

[67] Enver Hasani took office as rector of the University of Pristina shortly after independence and spawned hope of significant reform. He is a widely respected and outspoken international law expert with high academic standards and a willingness to challenge entrenched interests at the university and in the political parties.

[68] I have worked over a ten-year period with the Law Faculty at the University of Pristina and with the leadership of the American University in Kosovo since its commencement on a variety of projects to improve legal education.

banking concerns in Western Europe, and use best practices in terms of internal auditing and conservative loan policies.

Many wealthy individuals with family, social, or past business ties to the Balkans have made significant investments in medium-sized enterprises and building and highway construction. Multinational corporations and individuals lacking any previous connection with Kosovo have expressed interest, but have been more reticent, mostly because of uncertainty about the legal status of Kosovo. Independence removes this excuse, and the Kosovo government must intensify its investment-promotion activities.

Privatization of "socially owned" and "publicly owned" enterprises has been controversial, but largely successful. The privatization agency, Kosovo Trust Agency, recovered well from a yearlong hiatus in 2003–2004 due to maladministration by a senior German official who was sent to supervise privatization. A special court dominated by international judges, set up to adjudicate claims arising from privatization, however, functioned slowly and with insufficient transparency. For example, it was extremely difficult for counsel for potential inventors to get access to the decisional law of the privatization court. The amount of genuinely foreign investment brought into Kosovo by the process has been modest; most workers and others depending on the Socially Owned Enterprises (SOEs) were left in the lurch; the funds paid by investors that could have been invested in Kosovo are held in banks outside the country. A November 2007 opinion by the privatization court[69] raised questions about the legality, under European human rights law, of major features of the conceptual structure of Kosovo's privatization system (similar to many other privatization approaches in Europe).

Physical capital, human capital, and the institutional matrix for entrepreneurship need to concentrate on those areas of economic development where Kosovo enjoys competitive advantage. This does not imply institution of a managed economy, but it does imply greater awareness in both public and private sectors of where Kosovo's best opportunities lie. Kosovo's economic prospects are brighter if it continues on its path of integrating its economy with others in the region, emphasizing products and services where it has something special to offer. Already, substantial financial and trade ties with Slovenia and Croatia augment capital and open up markets for products and services from Kosovo. The large ethnic Albanian populations in the Republic of Albania,

---

[69] In the matter of *Alexander Hadzijevic and Vera Frtunic v. KTA and SOE Trepca Hotels restaurant Parajsa* (Hotelier Company Ibar), SCC-06–0010 (Spec. Chamber, November 20, 2007); see generally OSCE, *Privatization in Kosovo: Judicial Review of Kosovo Trust Agency Matters by the Special Chamber of the Supreme Court of Kosovo* 31 (May 2008) (discussing Special Chamber case law and faulting Special Chamber for not publishing its decisions either in the Official Gazette or on the Internet), located at http://www.osce.org/documents/mik/2008/05/31255_en.pdf.

Macedonia, Serbia, and Montenegro make available informal channels for investment and trade; these will strengthen naturally.

Current macroeconomic and tax policies designed by the international community during UNMIK's reign are among the most business-friendly in Europe, focused on minimizing the legal barriers to starting businesses, simplifying and minimizing tax burdens, and facilitating free trade. Going forward, the government of Kosovo must resist pressures to erect trade barriers and to impede business formation through nontransparent municipal licensing requirements, mechanisms always desired by inefficient local businesses that fear competition. Present and past governments developed ties with European policy makers in charge of EU enlargement, and it is important that momentum continue in this direction.

Kosovo is still a predominantly agricultural economy, with most agricultural production taking place on small family-owned or village-run subsistence farms. Substantial reform in the methods of farming would be necessary for Kosovo to become a significant exporter – or even to be self-sufficient – in raw agricultural products. Agricultural processing, on the other hand, is a significant investment opportunity. Already wine production, soft drink and beer processing and bottling, and dairy-product processing have attracted significant foreign investment.

Thus far, tourism is a largely untapped opportunity for Kosovo. Its geography is beautiful, varied, and largely unspoiled. A popular ski resort operates in southern Kosovo. Hotels and restaurants in the cities are of high quality. Those features, combined with Kosovo's history and prominence in the news, present the possibility for attracting a significant number of foreign tourists. Investment in tourism is attractive because of large job-creation potential, relatively low capital costs, and the opportunity to earn significant foreign exchange.

Kosovo's good Internet infrastructure, the large number of young professionals with good information-technology skills, and the now widely recognized potential of e-commerce to allow small enterprises access to world markets represents another largely untapped opportunity. Most Kosovar businesses and nonprofits of any size have Web pages, but little has been done so far to establish e-commerce and other forms of Internet intermediation and software services in Kosovo.

The best course for Kosovo's economic future is for the government to ensure a macroeconomic climate in which business can make a profit; and take a machete to the many nit-picking opportunities for local government to stymie a business start-up while fueling petty – and not so petty – corruption at the same time. Entrepreneurs will figure out whether investment should occur in electricity production, tourism, chicken cultivation, software, or something else. The priority for the Thaçi government should not be competitiveness assessment; it should be ensuring that government employees at all levels of government do their jobs, honestly, efficiently, and cheerfully.

Corruption

Corruption in the public and private sectors is poison to both democracy and economic development.[70] Kosovo's culture provides too much space for corruption. Its long history of resisting "oppression" by "occupying forces" – the Ottomans, then the Serbs, and then UNMIK – encourages a spirit of defiance, secrecy, and noncompliance with formal norms, including formal norms of honest government. In this context, reliance on informal family and friendship connections in order to survive and prosper also increases the reluctance to turn anybody in. Ratting out somebody in Kosovar society means betraying the bonds that have permitted everyone to survive. In addition, there is a general mistrust of government, based on a belief that it is ineffective, not motivated by improving the lives of the ordinary people, and thoroughly corrupt. This leads to a preference for "informal" private enterprise, and the valid belief that some forms of corruption are necessary to provide space for informal entrepreneurship.

By objective measures, corruption in Kosovo and the rest of the Balkans is no worse, and may be less of a problem, than in Western Europe. A report issued by the UN's Office on Drugs and Crime in May 2008 concluded that "The vicious circle of political instability leading to crime, and vice versa, that plagued the Balkans in the 1990s has been broken." Still, "the region remains vulnerable to instability caused by enduring links between business, politics, and organized crime."[71] The conclusion is controversial especially among prosecutors, who argue there is considerable underreporting. The European Commission has identified corruption and organized crime as major problems for Kosovo.[72] There also may be, however, overreporting. The public understands corruption poorly. Although ordinary citizens in Kosovo complain about corruption, their definitions of corruption are diffuse. Too many citizens believe that merely seeking a profit is a form of corruption. Many

---

[70] See generally *Operation Kosovo, Combating Corruption in Kosovo* (rev. October 29, 2006) (eighty-five-page report on adapting public-corruption investigative and prosecutorial techniques in the United States to special circumstances in Kosovo), available at www.operationkosovo.kentlaw.edu.

[71] UN Press release, "Greater Stability in the Balkans is Lowering Crime, reports UNODC" (May 29, 2008), located at http://www.unis.unvienna.org/unis/pressrels/2008/uniscp566.html.

[72] See 2007 EU Report at 13 (due to a lack of clear political will to fight corruption, and to insufficient legislative and implementing measures, corruption is still widespread and remains a major problem); id. at 13–14 (overall, some progress was made in the fight against corruption, but corruption is still widespread and constitutes a very serious problem; one of the problems is that asset disclosures by public officials are not public); id. at 46–8 (legislative framework to tackle organized crime is still incomplete, particularly in the area of witness protection, undercover agents, the anti-mafia law, and the law on organized crime; money laundering and narcotics and human trafficking remain significant problems); id. at 48 (little progress can be reported in the area of organized crime and the combating of trafficking in human beings. The fight against organized crime, including human trafficking, remains one of the major challenges).

citizens of Kosovo believe (correctly) that they depend on petty corruption in order to advance legitimate individual and family interests. Burdensome and irrational permit requirements and fees fuel this belief. Public attention needs to be refocused on behavior that undermines a market economy rather than on behavior that energizes it. A market economy depends, of course, on profit seeking – so an effective anticorruption effort must constantly distinguish between ordinary entrepreneurship and public corruption.

Opinion surveys in 2008 showed that 30 percent of the population believes that corruption exists on a large scale.[73] As long as public corruption is widely perceived to be a significant reality, foreign investors will be reluctant to invest in Kosovo, local businesspeople will have an incentive to evade responsibilities imposed by the law, and ordinary members of the public will become further alienated from the democratic political process.

Thaçi has been vigorous in committing his government to root out public corruption, imposing new rules that limit use of public resources by ministers. He must build on this good beginning by organizing successful investigation and prosecution, not sparing those associated with the coalition parties.

An effective anticorruption campaign in Kosovo must be careful to pick the right targets. Targeting ordinary profit-seeking and low-level smuggling and evasion of tax and permit requirements, for instance, is not the place to start. The most damaging types of corruption like embezzlement, kickbacks, and bribery occur at the highest levels of government: that is where anticorruption campaigns should focus. To spend limited anticorruption resources on anything else is distracting and wasteful. Likewise, when human trafficking or drug dealing is the target, raiding a house of prostitution and jailing the prostitutes and their customers, or prosecuting the lowest-level drug dealer, gains short-term publicity but does little about the real problem. Lower-level law violators must be targets only for the purpose of turning them into cooperating witnesses against those who run the networks.

Security

Security, the dominant concern motivating international intervention in 1999, is clouded by continued wrangling over the legitimacy of Kosovo's independence, an undeniable factual and legal reality that both Serbia and Russia refused to accept. Both states threatened other states that recognized Kosovo's independence, seeking to hold the total number as low as possible – although most of Serbia's neighbors (Slovenia, Croatia, Bulgaria, Montenegro, and Macedonia) resisted the pressure and recognized independence by the end of 2008.

---

[73] 2008 Early Warning Report at 47.

As significant, Russia and Serbia were embarked on an effort to make it impossible to implement the Ahtisaari Plan, an integral part of the supervised independence formula. "The Serb nationalists in Belgrade dug deep into the Milošević playbook and appear to have adopted and followed strategies from the 1990s that successfully mobilized Serbs to challenge their respective republic's governments."[74] Belgrade has, so far, ensured that Kosovo Serbs do not cooperate in decentralization. Moscow is making sure the transition from UNMIK to the ICO and EULEX does not go smoothly. Both are trying to isolate Kosovo by lobbying other states not to recognize Kosovo – beyond the fifty-five that already had. The Thaçi government was off to a weak start in countering the lobbying. Skender Hyseni, the new Kosovo Foreign Minister, was widely regarded as weak. He had spent his career as an LDK staff guy, mainly functioning as a gatekeeper to Rugova's presence. The organization of Kosovo's foreign missions, appointment of ambassadors, and special envoys was sluggish.

If these forces cause a paralysis in governmental decision making with respect to domestic priorities and discourage foreign investment in Kosovo, the long-term reaction could be violent. However, the recipe is not the same as that which produced violence in the 1990s. Targets for guerrilla action are unclear; there is no modern-day equivalent of Serbian "occupiers" of the Milošević era. There is no clear leadership for violent reaction corresponding to the Planners in Exile and the Defenders at Home who produced the KLA. There is no arms route through a failed state, as Albania provided in the late 1990s.

Interethnic violence is possible, however. It could start with Kosovo Serbs, encouraged by Serbia, or it could start with Kosovar Albanians. Like the 2004 riots, its outbreak could leave it unclear who started it. Initially, at least, it would be less intense than the KLA initiatives. It would be diffuse, mostly spontaneous, and poorly organized, and therefore even harder to quell than the KLA resistance.

The likelihood of Serbian or Russian military action to reverse Kosovo's independence was never significant. Nevertheless, Serbia's program to make Kosovo ungovernable by poisoning relations between the new Kosovo government and Kosovo Serbs further keeps the threat of low-level violence alive for the foreseeable future, as with the February attacks on border posts on the northern border between Kosovo and Serbia, the attack on the courthouse in Mitrovica in July 2008, and the threatened attacks on a water supply project north of Mitrovica in September.[75] Indications are that the Tadić government

---

[74] Donia, *Elusive Finality*.

[75] See ICG, *Fragile Transition* at 4 (reporting on border postconflict, courthouse attack, skirmishes over water pipes west of Mitrovica, and confrontations in Strpce).

has been less active in encouraging such violence than was the Koštunica government.[76]

Another threat is violent Albanian reaction to what the Albanians see as Serb provocations: low-level violent resistance by Kosovo Serbs to symbols of Pristina authority or to EULEX, refusals to recognize the authority of the Kosovo government in the north and in Serb enclaves elsewhere in Kosovo, and prominent display by Kosovo Serbs of symbols of continued loyalty to the government in Belgrade.

If the Serb-dominated north intensifies its refusal to accept Kosovo and EU authority, it would be natural for opinion leaders in the Kosovar Albanian community to portray this as the north seceding from Kosovo. The response might be Albanian attacks on Serb enclaves in the south. The Serb enclaves were well armed, and Serbian intelligence services have been regular presences wherever Kosovo Serbs predominate. Violence between Albanians and Serbs could then intensify in or near Serb population centers in Kosovo. Serbia could use this as a pretext for intervening militarily, either with regular Serbian forces or – more likely – with material support for Serb irregular forces, to protect Kosovo Serbs.[77] The West then would have to decide how NATO should respond.

The specter of violence was receding in late 2008, however, not advancing. Hopes were high that the new coalition government in Belgrade, which excluded Koštunica, would gradually put the Kosovo issue on a back burner as it focuses Serbian energies on the economy and accession to the EU.

The long-term threat to security in Kosovo is that ordinary citizens may give up on democracy and rule of law, caring little whether corruption and organized crime networks deepen their penetration into Kosovar society. Honest entrepreneurs would go elsewhere to seek their fortunes. Street crime would rise from its present low levels. In such a downward spiral, the ground would be fertile for terrorist networks to gain a foothold.

In such a social context, some Kosovar Albanians fear that the siren call of religious extremists could become potent for the first time in Kosovo. Although a majority of Kosovar Albanians are Muslim, they are strongly secular. During the 1998–1999 conflict, KLA leaders, unlike Bosnian government leaders during the war in Bosnia, consistently rebuffed offers of assistance from Islamic fundamentalists.[78] With frustration over progress as an independent state, however, this might change. Enver Hasani, Rector of the University of Pristina, told me in July 2007 that he detected rapidly growing interest among his university's students in radical brands of Islam. Others, in other university settings, disagreed. One young faculty member at AUK, Robert

---

[76] ICG, *Fragile Transition* at 26 (opining that Tadić government may put less energy into blocking Kosovo's independent political development).

[77] Confidential August 2007 interviews with senior UNMIK officials, who had intelligence about possible sources of violence.

[78] Perritt, KLA at 29, 119 (describing refusal by KLA to accept help from Islamic militants).

Muharremi, said, "I don't see any sign of a turn to Islam among my students. I don't think it's at all likely, considering Sanjak[79] and Tetovo[80] where there are many more religious nuts who are much more active. There's been no mass veering toward Islam in either of those places. Kosovo has always been much more secular and mistrustful of religion. I just don't believe it would happen here. I have lived in Germany and I know the signs. I didn't see any of them here, even when frustration was high about delays in final status." It was heartening that Kosovo's Independence Day celebration was devoid of prominent displays of Islamic militancy.

Security was satisfactory during the first year after independence. Overall, feelings of insecurity were down, compared with earlier periods.[81] Security remained fragile, however. Among Kosovo Serbs, the dominant reason for feeling worried or anxious were security concerns at the 70 percent level, while fewer than 10 percent of Kosovar Albanians identify security as their dominant concern.[82]

Conclusion

The diplomatic, political, and economic challenges are daunting, but the people of Kosovo have unusual energy and commitment to building a bright future for themselves and their families. Now they have the political and legal space to do that, and they have coherent elected leadership. The rest is up to them. They have long wanted it this way.

[79] The Sanjak region of western Serbia has a predominantly Muslim population.
[80] Tetovo is the largest Albanian city in Macedonia.
[81] 2008 Early Warning Report at 7 (table: Public Opinion Survey Results).
[82] 2008 Early Warning Report at 31.

18 Implications for the International Order

ANALYSIS OF THE DIPLOMATIC PROCESS LEADING TO KOSOVO'S independence leads to the following conclusions: First, Russia could not have been brought around to any solution acceptable to the Kosovar Albanians or to Europe and the United States. Russia wanted something inimical to Europe, the United States, and the people of Kosovo – continued uncertainty and instability in the Balkans.

Second, Serbia was a prisoner of a historical myth implanted through the years, and a racist sense of ethnic superiority that made it impossible for it to credit the aspirations of the Kosovar Albanians and thus to craft a solution acceptable to both sides. Regardless of its leadership's calculation of Serbia's national interests, public opinion represented too many obstacles for statesmanship.

Third, Martii Ahtisaari and the Western members of the Troika demonstrated how to forge transatlantic unity by forging personal relationships of trust and by paying careful attention to the local politics of important constituencies.

Fourth, international law's role in the process was poorly understood, but the independence of Kosovo marks a significant step into an international law that balances sovereignty against the responsibility to protect.

Fifth, the output of intelligence agencies was irrelevant to the negotiations and the determination of negotiating positions mainly because of the poor quality of the intelligence.

Sixth, decision making occurred, as it usually has in the Balkans, only under the threat of violence, although effective diplomacy forestalled the actual outbreak of violence.

Seventh, the process showed that the United Nations is useful for many things, including for structured negotiations over contentious issues such as Kosovo's future status, but the UN Security Council does not provide a reliable decision-making forum because of the inevitable possibility of disagreement among the permanent members. An institution that allows for paralysis in international decision making is not a suitable centerpiece of the international system.

As the world has moved toward democracy, international diplomacy has become more complicated. Even when political elites and officeholders agree on what their respective state interests require, their power to strike a deal is constrained by popular opinion at home. That popular opinion is shaped by local culture, past humiliations on the international stage, historical myths defining their nations, and a variety of opinion leaders from civil society, many seeking to benefit from whipping up antagonisms against other states and cultures.

Russia

Public opinion in Russia and Serbia, combined with a rational assessment of Russia's national interests, made it impossible for either to agree on a viable future status for Kosovo. Nothing could have been done by Martti Ahtisaari, Europe, or the United States that would have brought Russia on board with any solution acceptable to the Kosovar Albanians, Europe, and the United States. Russia wanted something inimical to Europe, the United States, and the people of Kosovo – continued uncertainty and instability in the Balkans.

Russian opposition to the Ahtisaari Plan was an indirect product of Russian democracy and realism in Russian diplomacy. The evolution of Russian foreign policy on Kosovo since Yeltsin's capitulation to the NATO bombing campaign in 1999 illustrates the power of popular opinion in Russia, even as robust Western engagement in 1999 illustrated the power of popular opinion in the United States and Europe. Paradoxically, Putin has responded to mass opinion in Russia even as he embarked on antidemocratic initiatives. His international belligerence is enormously popular among ordinary Russians – as are his antidemocratic reforms in Russia's political system.[1] It was a rational political act for Putin to use the Ahtisaari Plan as an opportunity to poke the United States in the eye and to further build his popular support at home.[2] There is no evidence that Russian popular sentiment will encourage Russian policy makers to be any less belligerent in the future. Confrontation with the West, particularly with the United States, pays big political dividends in a more democratic Russia.

Apart from mass Russian opinion, cold-eyed assessment of Russian interests from a Russian perspective suggests that moderation on Kosovo is

---

[1] See Charles King, "The Five-Day War: Managing Moscow After the Georgia Crisis," 87 *For. Aff.* No. 6, at 1, 9 (November/December 2008) (reporting that Russia's 2008 intervention in Georgia was "wildly popular in Russia," citing public opinion polls showing 80 percent support); Stephen Sestanovich, "What Has Moscow Done? Rebuilding U.S.–Russian Relations," 87 *For. Aff.* No. 6, at 12, 22 (November/December 2008) (Putin built his popularity on the idea that foreigners have no right to judge Russia); id. at 23 (confrontation with the West has paid enormous political dividends in terms of Russian popular opinion); Edward Lucas, *The New Cold War: Putin's Russia and the Threat to the West* 7 (2008) (Putin's "ratings rocketed, turning Putin from backstage zero to national hero in four months, as he fueled public panic about terrorism in Russia, and restarted the war in Chechnya").

[2] See Lucas at 199 (Russia's main aim with respect to Kosovo may simply have been to "look tough").

unlikely to mark Russian policy in the future. Ahtisaari's senior political adviser Kai Sauer said in June 2008: "Russia's opposition to the Ahtisaari Plan was not of a principled nature, and it wasn't about the process. It was about geopolitics. The Russians say differently, but all you have to do is to look at a map of Gazprom assets and connections to see how dependent Europe is becoming on Russian energy supplies," Sauer says. "As to Abkhazia and Transnistria, Russia is going to do whatever its strategic interests and tactical calculations dictate. Russian initiatives on these issues will not be driven by Kosovo's independence."

Russia's invasion of Georgia later in 2008 and its recognition of the independence of South Ossetia and Abkhazia showed that it did not conduct its foreign policy consistent with the view of international law it had espoused in connection with Kosovo's status. Instead, it seemed to embrace the legal position the United States had taken with respect to Kosovo.[3]

Ahtisaari, Ischinger, and Wisner did not misread Russian intentions or mishandle Russia during the negotiations over Kosovo's final status; they were simply confronted by the crystallization of Russia's realization that intransigence on Kosovo represented an opportunity to advance Russian strategic interests. That crystallization occurred even as Ahtisaari and the Quint were working off early signals that Russian might cooperate on the Kosovo issue.

One hypothesis can be rejected: that Putin did not know what Lavrov and the other Russian negotiators were doing in the run-up to and in the early stages of the Ahtisaari process, and once he found out he brought them up short. Knowledgeable Contact-Group-level participants rule out the possibility that there was any kind of disconnect between Lavrov and Putin. They credit Lavrov and the Russian ambassador to the UN, Vitaly Churkin, as being very well informed about Kosovo and highly sophisticated about diplomacy and internal Russian politics. It is more likely that Putin's own view shifted.

Increasing press and media attention to the Ahtisaari process and to the likelihood that the result would be independence for Kosovo resonated negatively with popular opinion in Russia. Putin, determined to secure his succession after his term as president expired in 2008, decided to take a harder line on Kosovo simply because it was popular in Russia. A March 2006 *Financial Times* story headlined "Russia and China pledge not to block new Kosovo" reported a commitment by Lavrov to Secretary of State Rice to abstain in a

---

[3] See "Medvedev's Statement on South Ossetial and Abkhazia," *New York Times*, August 26, 2008 (announcing recognition), located at http://www.nytimes.com/2008/08/27/world/europe/27medvedev.html?ref=europe; Clifford J. Levy, "Russia Backs Independence of Georgian Enclaves," *New York Times*, August 26, 2008, located at http://www.nytimes.com/2008/08/27/world/europe/27russia.html?pagewanted=1&_r=1 ("Mr. Medvedev used an interview on Tuesday with Russia Today, the Kremlin-financed English-language channel, to turn the West's rationale on Kosovo against it").

proposed UN resolution granting independence to Kosovo.[4] "I was furious," says Ahtisaari. "This forced Lavrov to begin backing away publicly from his cooperation with the process. Whoever leaked the story procured a very short-sighted victory."[5]

Not only Kosovo but also missile defense and other issues of East–West relations provoked a series of confrontations against the United States and the West. Putin gave a clear signal of a general hardening of position in his February 10, 2007, speech at the 43rd Munich Conference on Security Policy. Opening with a pledge to "avoid excessive politeness," Putin proceeded bitterly to criticize U.S. unilateralism, military assertiveness, and disdain for international law.

A confrontation with the United States on this range of issues, including Kosovo, was advantageous to Putin for two reasons. First, toughness might cause the United States to blink on at least some of the issues of concern to Russia, preoccupied as it was with the mess in Iraq and growing criticism in the United States of the Bush administration's unilateralism. Kosovo could be used as a prominent source of leverage for Putin's strategies in the Caucasus region. It was worth a try. Even if the United States did not back away from positions already declared publicly, it might be reluctant to start new fights in the Caucasus. Second, confronting the United States aggressively was not only popular with the man or woman on the street in Russia; it also would satisfy desires at the personal level among senior Russian policy makers to get even for the humiliation inflicted in the 1999 conclusion of the NATO bombing campaign, when Russia was seen by some – including major segments of the Russian national security elite – as abandoning its ally Milošević in favor of the U.S. position. Putin wanted to show that Russia would not lie down once again in front of the United States as it had done in 1999.

As domestic politics invited reexamination of the possibility of Russian acquiescence in what easily could be perceived as a predominantly U.S. desire for Kosovo's future, it is not hard to see how a Russian analyst would conclude that Russian interests actually are advanced by prolonged turmoil in the Balkans. There would be no downside for Russia – or at least Russia perceived no downside – if the final status talks failed. Russia might even enjoy a collapse of Kosovo into violence, which it could blame on the United States for creating the mess in 1999.

If the U.S. initiative to make Kosovo independent succeeded, Russia could use the scenario to its advantage in Georgia and Ukraine. The U.S. and EU leadership would have expended so much energy and political capital on Kosovo that they would have less to spend on a meaningful response to

---

[4] Guy Dinmore and Daniel Dombay, "Russia and China Pledge Not to Block New Kosovo," *Financial Times*, March 14, 2006, located at http://www.ft.com/cms/s/0/24b5d91e-b399–11da-89c7–0000779e2340.html?nclick_check=1.

[5] February 2008 interview with Martii Ahtisaari.

Russian intervention in Georgia and continued pressure on Ukraine. Moreover, controversy over the norms of international law and their application to Kosovo would blunt claims that Russia violated international law in Georgia or Ukraine. All Russia needed to do was to make achievement of transatlantic unity as difficult as possible and to protest the moves toward Kosovo's independence as inconsistent with international law.

Russia also had strategic interests in fostering closer relations with Belgrade in the energy supply and distribution context. The Putin government recognized the power of capitalism as a tool of imperial power. No one feared that the Russian Army would invade Kosovo to secure it for Serbia – but Russia need not send Red Army troops into the Balkans to reestablish dominance there; it need only send investment from its state-controlled corporations. The greater the uncertainty and insecurity in Kosovo, the less Western investors would be likely to make commitments there, leaving more room for Russian investors, and hence Russian control – perhaps greater than it had enjoyed when Tito was alive and Yugoslavia intact.

It was not that Russian strategic interests aligned with Serbia's interests, in the sense of a traditional alliance. No one involved believes that Russia really cared about Serbia or the Kosovo Serbs. However, pro-Russian and anti-European sentiment in Serbian popular opinion could be helpful to Russian interests. The fault line between Russia and the EU and NATO could be drawn at the Albanian border if Serbia inclined more toward Moscow than Brussels and if Kosovo was kept in limbo. In this limited respect, the hardening of the Russian position resulted in part from Serbia's inflexibility. If Serbia had been less intransigent, or if the factions in Serbia had been more equally split, Russia could have pulled back from spending its international political capital on behalf of Serbia. That is not what happened in Serbia. Not only was Serbia unified in opposition to independence and the Ahtisaari Plan, significant signals emanated from Belgrade that Russian/Serbian opposition, followed by UDIR, might produce a result very desirable for Russia: Serbia's backing away from eventual European integration and a reinvigoration of a Serbian/Russian alliance in international affairs.

Meanwhile, a prolonged mess in Kosovo would tie down and preoccupy the United States and Europe. If Russia managed its part of the final status process right, it might get a result in which Kosovo was left in limbo, Europe was split, and relations between the United States and Europe worse. As those possibilities became more credible, intransigence became more attractive to Russian leaders. European and U.S. policy makers wrongly assumed that Russia monolithically saw its future in the twenty-first century as tied to a robust and expanding European community.

Russia surely perceived cracks in Europe's ostensibly united front and set about skillfully to exploit them. If Europe had been more monolithic and more vigorous in its support for Ahtisaari, Russian behavior might have been different. Rational negotiators determine and adjust their positions in negotiations based on their assessment of what will happen if a negotiated agreement is not reached.[6] Perceiving that disagreement over implementation of the Ahtisaari Plan would result in Euro-American unity collapsing and a continuation of the status quo in Kosovo, it was rational for Russia to block the Ahtisaari Plan. On the other hand, if Russia thought that an impasse between it and the Euro-American alliance would be followed by UDIR and robust implementation of something less favorable to their interests than the Ahtisaari Plan, rational pursuit of self-interest might have induced it to agree. Russian and Serbian recalcitrance, therefore, was the result of Europe and the United States not making UDIR sufficiently credible.

The best outcome for Russia was a divided Europe, a worsened split between the United States and Europe, a Serbia drawn closer into the Russian orbit, and prolonged uncertainty and turmoil in Kosovo. After all was said and done, however, the Russian policy of divide and conquer failed. The United States did not blink. Europe was not split – at least not as badly as Russia had hoped. Despite Ahtisaari's warning, Russian foreign policy ended up being made in Belgrade, and – worse yet, by Koštunica and the radicals, whose approach ultimately was not embraced by the Serbian public. The center of gravity in Serbian politics preferred European integration. "It is amazing how Russian clumsiness in handling the final status process rendered Russia irrelevant on the international stage," Wisner commented. "They proved that they could not deliver on anything. They cut their maneuvering room off. And now they have no real Serbian allies except Nikolic and Koštunica, who have marginalized themselves in Serbian politics."

Moreover, Russia created yet another example of how the UN Security Council could not be relied on as the primary institutional framework for resolving difficult questions of international peace and security, thus weakening a body where Russia, by virtue of its veto power, actually can control the course of international diplomacy.

Getting the worst, even as it worked for the best, resulted from tactical Russian missteps in the early stages of the negotiation over Kosovo's status. In retrospect, the opacity of Russia's position in the early stages actually accelerated UDIR. If Russia had taken a harder line against independence early in the Ahtisaari process, U.S./EU solidarity might have been forestalled – or the United States might have backed away. Alternatively, if Russia had shown more willingness to consider alternative Security Council resolutions providing for implementation of the Ahtisaari Plan while deferring a decision on independence, it well might have bought an agreement to delay final status from the United States and the EU.

Independence represents a defeat for Russian foreign policy, which might lead to Russian withdrawal from cooperation with Europe and the United States on other issues. It also might lead, however, to more constructive

---

[6] See discussion of BATNA concepts in chapter 10 n.17 and accompanying text.

engagement in the future. Russian diplomats consistently emphasized, throughout the Ahtisaari and Troika processes, the Russian commitment to a dialogue with the West, even as differences between the two sides widened over Kosovo. Europe and the United States can apply a lesson learned from Kosovo about the Russians: firmness produces better results than ambiguity about intentions. Russia can apply its own lesson: real engagement on the merits produces better results than drawing a line in the sand defined by a client state and sticking to it.

Serbia

Serbia is a prisoner of a historical myth implanted through the years, and a racist sense of ethnic superiority that made it impossible for it to credit the aspirations of the Kosovar Albanians and thus to craft a solution acceptable to both sides. Regardless of Serbian leaders' calculation of Serbia's national interests, public opinion represented too many obstacles for statesmanship. The best way to have resolved the question of Kosovo's final status would have been through an agreement with Serbia. That Serbia did not cooperate in making this possible illustrates the power of popular opinion and of past humiliation in shaping that opinion. Hope sprang eternal in Western capitals that Serbia, now that Milošević was gone from the scene, would repudiate its past adherence to a virulent nationalism and substitute a commitment to European values and integration into the EU. This always was an unduly optimistic formulation. It ignored the fact that Milošević had risen to power on a tidal wave of popular support in Serbia, organized around racist nationalism and a myth that Serbs had always been victims of international forces aligned against Serbia. Milošević was not out of step with Serbian popular opinion; he gave voice to it. Now Milošević was gone, but the psychic wounds of the NATO bombing campaign were unhealed. Koštunica and the radicals saw their futures tied to continued exploitation of Serbian resentments.

EU – and to a lesser extent, U.S. – policy makers were not oblivious to this reality, but they also recognized a parallel reality: Serbia was geographically a part of Europe and its integration into Europe was very much in the long-term interest of other European states and of the United States. Whatever Kosovo's future, the transatlantic community also had to address Serbia's long-term future vis-à-vis the rest of Europe. Any solution to Kosovo's status had to be accompanied by initiatives that would be attractive to the Serbian leadership and public. The most prominent possibility was a commitment to accelerate Serbia's accession to the EU, with fewer preconditions. Throughout the Ahtisaari and Troika periods of diplomacy, EU officials were concurrently announcing one after another inducements for Serbia to join the EU. They accelerated EU accession process for Serbia and decoupled it from the Kosovo negotiations. They let up on pressure for Serbia to arrest war-crimes indictees Mladic, Karadzic, and other suspects. They (along with the United States) signed agreements for Serbian membership in the Partnership for Peace, the precursor of NATO membership, and made agreements for Western investments in Serbia's energy and other sectors. During this period, the prevailing approach was to present Serbia with a series of carrots, few explicitly linked with Serbia's position on Kosovo. While the context may have implied that the price for these prizes was moderation of Serbia's position on Kosovo, it also was possible to infer that there was no price: that Serbia could do whatever it wanted on Kosovo and still get the prizes.

The Peace Institute's Daniel Serwer offered sound advice in his March 2008 congressional testimony.[7] The international community also must stop giving Serbia "freebies:"

> Brussels and Washington sought to buy Serbian acquiescence in Kosovo's independence by offering gratuities to Serbia, including improved trade relations, more than one billion Euros in financial assistance, a moderation of insistence that Serbia turn over prominent war-crimes fugitives, and an accelerated pathway to EU membership. Serbia has pocketed these incentives and provided little in return since 2003.

He concludes that Kosovo is not the problem; Serbia is, with the Koštunica government's consistent efforts to "turn back the clock." He urges Washington and Brussels to "get smarter." "Washington and Brussels should also signal that they are determined not to give Serbia any more freebies.... Offering more freebies without conditions will have the opposite effect [compared with guiding Serbia to a constructive place in the international community], encouraging reactionary forces in Serbia and strengthening its alliance with Russia."

This tendency to offer Serbia only carrots, with no preconditions – Daniel Serwer's "freebies" – will come back to haunt Europe in the long run. Serbia may be brought along toward EU membership, but if the EU does not insist that Serbia confront its past and repudiate it, Serbia will be a malign influence as a member of the EU. If Serbia does not eventually reconcile itself to Kosovo's independence before joining the EU, Kosovo will remain as a source of instability, now inside the EU.

Manifestly, however, it would not be effective U.S. or EU policy to insist that the Serbian government immediately and explicitly embrace an independent Kosovo. Serbian public opinion is not ready for that. Tadić's coalition is shaky, and Koštunica and the radicals, some within the SDS, Tadić's coalition partner, will continue to remind him of that fact – and make sure that Serbian popular opinion continues to be worked up about Kosovo, reiterating arguments that U.S. and EU policy is anti-Serbia.

Efforts must continue to nurture other voices. Čedomir Jovanović for example, is one of the few voices in Serbian politics with a pro-Kosovo view. He led student protests that led to Milošević's downfall and later joined

---

[7] Testimony of Daniel Serwer, Vice President for Peace and Stability Operations, United States Institute for Peace, before the Senate Foreign Relations Committee (March 4, 2008), located at http://foreign.senate.gov/testimony/2008/SerwerTestimony080304a.pdf.

Tadić's party, the DS, and was elected to parliament in 2000 at age twenty-nine. He was expelled from the DS for meeting with underworld figures and then founded the Liberal Democratic Party (LDP). In 2005, Jovanović was featured in *Newsweek*, which quoted him as saying that Kosovo Serbs should no longer call Belgrade their capital as Kosovo is already de facto independent.[8] He went on to state that in order to move forward, Serbia must acknowledge its war crimes and reform the Orthodox Church as one of main organs that was complicit in Milošević's regime.[9] He remained neutral in the runoff between Boris Tadić and Tomislav Nikolić, because Tadić was as inflexible on Kosovo as Nikolić. Jovanović, in a statement on October 20, 2008, stated that his party, the LDP, would support President Tadić's government only on the matter of entrance into the EU. Jovanović criticized Tadić for not looking to the future and criticized the government for its negative reaction to Montenegro and Macedonia's acknowledgment of Kosovo independence, stressing the future of Serbia lies in working with all neighboring countries.[10]

The most that can be hoped for is that the Tadić coalition will remain in power for an extended period and that it will gradually let Kosovo slide to a back burner on its array of priorities. Already there are some modest signs that this may be happening. Foreign Minister Jeremić had signaled that he may be willing to allow ambassadors of those states recognizing Kosovo to return to Belgrade,[11] and Tadić had said that he will acquiesce in whatever position Jeremić takes on this issue. Tadić also was reported as saying on July 17, 2008, that Serbia should not be "rigid" on matters relating to Kosovo.[12] In February 2009, Tadić said that Serbia would not oppose Kosovo's membership in international financial institutions such as the International Monetary Fund and the World Bank.[13] Longer term, young politicians like Jovanović may gain

---

[8] Zoran Cirjakovic and Rod Norland, "Now What? Dayton 10 Years Later," *Newsweek*, December 5, 2005 (describing Jovanović's maverick politics and noting that admiring female supporters wore buttons saying "CEDO, MARRY ME").

[9] Jovanović ran for president in the January 2008 elections accounting for 5.6 percent of the vote. Preliminary Results: Nikolić, Tadić, Headed for Run-Off (January 20, 2008), located at http://www.b92.net/eng/news/politics-article.php?yyyy=2008&mm=01&dd=20&nav_id=47072 (announcement of percentages of vote for top five candidates in presidential election).

[10] LDP to Support Govt. "Only in EU Matters." (October 20, 2008), located at http://www.b92.net/eng/news/politics-article.php?yyyy=2008&mm=10&dd=20&nav_id=54362.

[11] See "Government to Return Ambassadors," Radio B-92 (July 24, 2008), located at http://www.b92.net/eng/news/in_focus.php?id=91&start=30&nav_id=52168.

[12] "Tadić to Continue State Policy on Kosovo," Radio B-92 July 16, 2008, located at http://www.b92.net/eng/news/in_focus.php?id=91&start=75&nav_id=51968 (quoting President Tadić as saying that Serbia will continue to oppose Kosovo's independence but its policy must not be "rigid").

[13] See, "Serbia Happy for Kosovo to Join Global Financial Bodies" (February 12 2009), located at http://www.nasdaq.com/aspxcontent/NewsStory.aspx?cpath=20090212\ACQDJON200902121144DOWJONESDJONLINE000505.htm&&mypage=newsheadlines&title=Serbia%20Happy%20For%20Kosovo%20To%20Join%20Global%20Financial%20Bodies%20-%20President.

more support. In late October 2008, Tomislav Nikolić became the head of a new moderate party, the Serbian Party for Progress. Aleksandar Vučić, former secretary general of the radical party SRS, became Nikolić's deputy. The move signified a shift toward the center for the two former leaders of the radical party, the strongest single force in the Serbian Assembly after the 2008 elections. Both Nikolić and Vučić left the SRS because they favored European integration for Serbia.

Top EU diplomats must be sophisticated in shaping this evolution of Serbian policy. Every opportunity for Serbia to be constructive in sorting out the participation of Kosovo Serbs in the transformation of Kosovo should be seized. Belgrade should not be confronted with unnecessary demands for an explicit modification of its policy toward Kosovo in the short run, but no doubt should be left that accepting Kosovo's independence is the price of ultimate entry into the EU.

Transatlantic Diplomacy

Martii Ahtisaari and the Western members of the Troika demonstrated how to forge transatlantic unity by cultivating personal relationships of trust and by paying careful attention to the local politics of important constituencies. The success of the Ahtisaari and Troika processes, the first occurring within UN machinery, the second occurring mostly outside it, represents an achievement in transatlantic diplomacy. The United States proved that it could once again work effectively in a multilateral context, providing leadership while accommodating the concerns of its European negotiating partners. Eventual transatlantic support for Kosovo's independence was the result of U.S. patience, good European leadership, Russian overreaching, and Serbian militancy.

U.S. firmness played an essential role in forcing Europe to coalesce, accompanied as it was by a clear commitment to work through European concerns. The United States used exactly the right combination of patience with intra-European diplomacy and tough-minded willingness to go it alone if absolutely necessary – a willingness communicated to the Europeans unambiguously. Nevertheless, despite the ultimate success, missteps along the way made the achievement more difficult. Although popular opinion and past humiliations worked independently to determine Russian and Serbian positions on Kosovo, cracks in European unity and an underappreciation of the hallmarks of effective negotiation strategy made it easier for Russia and Serbia to try to block transatlantic policy goals for Kosovo. The missteps illustrate the challenges ahead for a meaningful European role in international diplomacy and for U.S. multilateralism.

The Kosovo experience supports four inferences about the dynamics of intra-European politics: First, carefully calibrated U.S. firmness made it clear that European indecision risked a breach in the transatlantic harmony sought by nearly every European leader. Second, failure to agree on Kosovo would further undermine EU credibility, which already was in tatters after rejection of the draft EU constitution in 2005 plebiscites in France and the Netherlands. Third, Russia and Serbia overplayed their hands, causing Europeans to want to push back. Fourth, on the merits, UDIR presented fewer risks to European interests than diplomatic drift and the existence of a failed state in Kosovo.

Its effective interaction with Europe, producing sufficient European unity to achieve Kosovo's independence, illustrates some lessons about the opportunities and limitations of U.S. multilateralism for the future. It also illustrates the interaction of multilateralism and unilateralism. The U.S. invasion of Iraq in the face of strong European opposition gave rise to fears that Europe and the United States would not be able to act in concert on security threats in the future. A failure to find common ground on Kosovo would deepen this fear. Russia's hardening position caught the United States in a dilemma. It needed to leave no doubt about its policy, lest momentum in Europe collapse, but it risked stimulating a confrontational Russian attitude by being too explicit that independence was the only practicable outcome, and by threatening that the United States was prepared to act unilaterally outside the UN Security Council to procure it.

Initially, it was hard to predict what would happen after failure in the UN Security Council: would the United States let up on the pressure? Would it act precipitously, thus widening transatlantic and intra-European rifts? Alternatively, would it work behind the scenes with key European figures to figure out a way to forge a unified approach that would get the Ahtisaari Plan adopted outside the Security Council? The basic idea of UDIR had already crystallized more completely in the minds of U.S. policy makers than in some crucial European ones. Should the United States proceed directly to UDIR, or should it accept the risk of further diplomatic work within the EU?

At the same time, the EU needed to prove its capacity for political decision making, both as an effective counterbalance to U.S. power and to buttress its credibility with other states. An impasse on Kosovo would represent a major failure for European unity. The EU was determined to regulate international relations effectively within Europe, and to prove that it could be a reliable player in diplomacy. Kosovo was a major test of EU effectiveness. Fifteen years earlier, Europe had failed its test in Croatia and Bosnia. European leadership was determined not to fail the test of Kosovo.

The leadership succeeded in crafting enough unity to move forward, but its success was muted by the refusal of the five EU member states to join in the majority consensus and to recognize Kosovo. This fissure in European unity has significant consequences. Apart from the fact that it weakens the EU role in this European matter on the international level, it encourages those who actively impede the work of EULEX, putting the success of the largest civilian mission of the EU in its history in serious danger. Moreover, the five make it more difficult for moderate forces in Serbia to come to terms with the new reality. One senior Serbian official said, "How can we possibly be less Serbian than the five EU countries?"[14] If the recognition of Kosovo had been part of the EU's body of European law that had to be accepted on the road to EU membership, a gradual change of attitude in Belgrade would have been much easier – despite political rhetoric to the contrary in Serbia. Regrettably, neither Solana nor any of the rotating European presidencies applied much pressure on the five to change their attitudes.

Nevertheless, the magnitude of the U.S./European achievement on Kosovo should not be underestimated. It can be appreciated by considering the attractiveness of doing nothing – and its likely costs. In mid-2007, before the Troika process started, Security Council adoption of the Ahtisaari Plan was dead, although hope lingered in some quarters that Russia, for some obscure reason of its own, might change course. The second path, 120 days more negotiation under Contact Group auspices, was about to be launched. Everyone involved, however, knew that the path ended at a fork: the fork staunchly opposed by Russia but preferred by the United States and Britain, and probably France, was UDI followed by recognition by a critical mass of states. The other fork was stalemate and diplomatic drift, treating Kosovo as a "frozen conflict."

Stalemate and drift would be much easier for anyone who did not live in Kosovo, although it was not on the table for the Troika itself. In the short term, drift would not require anyone to make a tough decision. In the very short term, serious unrest in Kosovo was unlikely, as long as the international community could promise some other potential pathway to independence, like an international peace conference, just over the horizon in 2008. While UNMIK and the Kosovar political leadership would not have any credibility left, ordinary Kosovar Albanians and Kosovo Serbs would just turn inward and do whatever they could to protect their physical and economic security, without regard to official institutions or law.

Russia would be comfortable with this scenario. In addition, Europeans and Americans would not have to figure out the answers to hard questions such as: Who would organize the process of recognizing an independent Kosovo? Who would organize the EU mission and the military security mission? Who would authorize it if the Security Council did not? How would NATO avoid paralysis, given that NATO works through a consensus with an implicit veto for each of its members? In addition, some of its members included those who were opposed to independence in the first place. How could the value of European unity be maintained if some members were adamant in their refusal to recognize?

Ultimately, the leadership of Europe recognized that drift would deepen political alienation in Kosovo, and profound political alienation is hardly a step toward effective nation building. If the Albanian population of Kosovo moved once again – as it had during Ottoman Empire times and during Milošević's apartheid regime in the 1990s – to depend upon quasi-legal or frankly illegal

---

[14] Confidential communication to the author, February 2009.

networks for economic sustenance and political organization, the result would be a worsening of corruption and organized crime penetration of Kosovar Albanian society. That would make any future effort to build democratic institutions and a rule of law in Kosovo much more difficult. It also would make Kosovo attractive as a beachhead for organized crime targeting other parts of the world. In addition, even darker possibilities existed. Failed states are good breeding grounds for terrorist networks. In 1997 and 1998, the Milošević regime in Serbia claimed that Kosovo was a breeding ground for crime and Islamic terrorism. It was not then, but it could become such a place if the final status process drifted off into the indefinite future. In the absence of a plan for UDIR, the international community's efforts in Kosovo would have crafted the perfect recipe for a failed state, one that would produce swarms of refugees, develop terrorism, and fuel international crime.

Serbian and Russian intransigence helped Europe to unify. Those who believed Ahtisaari had not tried hard enough or had jumped too quickly to the conclusion that independence was the only credible way forward were forced to concede that Serbia would agree to nothing realistic. The details of the Ahtisaari Plan represented a sound approach to protecting the rights of Kosovo Serbs. Belgrade's lack of interest in the plan fueled the widening perception that Belgrade did not care about the human rights of its own nationals in Kosovo. Its reiteration of its plan for autonomy for Kosovo lacked credibility because it refused to engage seriously in a discussion of details and, more important, because the plan was revealed to give Kosovo even less than it had in 1989. In 1989, autonomy within Serbia meant full Albanian participation in all the political institutions of Serbia. The new "autonomy" would deny such participation. Kosovo would be allowed only to continue what it had under UNMIK administration, threatened by the reintroduction of Serbian police and military units, and the prospect that a future Serbian regime might decide to rescind autonomy – just as Milošević did in 1989 – after international forces withdrew. "They could have made our lives miserable [referring to the path to conditional independence]," said one participant in the Troika negotiations.[15] "They made our jobs easier by not coming up with something decent."

Belgrade was rigid. It would not look at any alternative to its autonomy proposal for fear it would weaken its position on independence – not the CIS formula, not the two-Germanies model, not territorial division. "It rejected the idea that it must sell autonomy to the Albanians before it could be a serious proposal. It made no attempt to sell it, and would not recraft it to make it more palatable to the Albanian side," Wisner says.

Serbian refusal to consider alternatives to independence such as partition or confederation undermined arguments that there were concrete alternatives to supervised independence under the Ahtisaari Plan. Serbia could have caused further delay in resolving the Kosovo status question had it engaged in

---

[15] Confidential 2008 interview.

serious exploration of one of these alternatives. It did not. Milošević had regularly, with respect to Bosnia and Kosovo itself, caused the West to back away from confrontation by pretending to consider accommodation. The new leadership of Serbia not only disdained European concerns, it lacked Milošević's subtle trickery in diplomacy.

In the end, Europeans who argued that further negotiations would produce a solution were left high and dry. Russia and Serbia snatched defeat from the jaws of victory by overplaying their hands. As Russian rhetoric over Kosovo became more belligerent, and as Serbia refused to give serious consideration to any plausible alternative to the Ahtisaari Plan, European commitment to decisiveness and to unity strengthened. More and more, European diplomats were asking each other whether European policy was going to be set in Moscow or in Brussels. Growing Russian control over European basic industry and energy resources also were sources of concern, as Russia had twice threatened to cut off natural gas flows to Europe, ostensibly over disputes with Belarus and then Ukraine.[16] A renewed threat to Europe from the East was becoming undeniable, and Europe had to show its unity in resisting Russian demands. The Kosovo issue was an opportunity to do this. Now, there was nothing much that Russia could do about UDIR. If independence were delayed for a year or two, however, Russia's capacity to make trouble would be greater. The only way for Europe to save face and build credibility as an effective diplomatic actor was to figure out a way to implement the Ahtisaari Plan without a Security Council resolution and without Russian agreement.

Substantial European solidarity in support of Kosovo's independence also was the result of the way Solana structured the Troika process. Ischinger, as an individual, could coherently represent European concerns to the other two members of the Troika, and he could communicate a consistent message to the European capitals. He observes, "If you want an EU position, you need a credible person, not a committee."[17] During negotiations over final status for Kosovo, the Quint's leadership periodically made the Spanish and the Dutch furious because they were left out. When all of the members of the EU were confronted with an issue, they rarely were able to reach a clear decision. Similar problems had bedeviled the negotiations over the Dayton Accords.[18] Ischinger, as the European member of the Troika, also was skilled and credible enough to help Germany work through its internal political problems – the key to Quint and then EU unity.

Ahtisaari, of course, was an individual, and while he officially operated under a mandate from the UN Secretary General, his status as a distinguished

---

[16] See C. J. Chivers, "As Ukraine Balks at Gas-Price Rise, Russian Company Renews Cutoff Threat," *New York Times* (December 31, 2005).

[17] October 2008 interview with Wolfgang Ischinger.

[18] See Holbrooke at 242 (describing how two of the European co-chairmen of the European delegation to the Dayton negotiations said that Carl Bildt could not speak for their governments; quoting Henry Kissinger's question, "What is Europe's phone number?").

European former president was expected to enable him to forge a European consensus behind his plan. In retrospect, said one senior European diplomat, "Martii should have spent more time visiting European capitals. But protocol made it difficult for him to do that. As a former president of a member state, he faced greater formal obstacles in having private, candid discussions than would have someone with somewhat lower level experience."[19]

Whether or not diplomacy over Kosovo could have been more nearly perfect, it was successful. Everyone dodged a bullet. The EU and the United States had closed ranks. The Kosovar Albanians got what they wanted. Violence was averted. The capacity of the opponents of independence to do anything terribly disruptive was minimized. The stage was set for moving beyond Kosovo to further integration of the Balkans into European economic and security frameworks.

The problems in crafting an orderly plan for UDIR were daunting. UDI could result in a completely unsupervised independence, or it could be supervised if the Ahtisaari Plan could be adopted by some other international entity (unlikely) or (more likely) accepted by the Kosovar Albanian political leadership as the price of support for UDIR. UDI without international supervision was not an option considered by the Troika.

All of the questions about moving forward outside the Security Council had answers, and the 120-day Troika process gave time to develop the answers. The EU worked out a common policy – essentially, "Do what you want regarding recognition" – then assembled a coalition of interested states willing to put together an EU mission to replace UNMIK. No serious rifts developed questioning a continued NATO presence. "The result is as good an example of transatlantic unity as I can remember," Ahtisaari said afterwards. "It is never easy, but everyone worked together effectively to produce a very good result."

"They did a good job," said Ahtisaari. "Paris, London, and Washington were very clear-eyed and firm. Berlin and Rome stuck to the EU line despite internal political difficulties. Italian Foreign Minister Massimo D'Alema was quite good in all of his public statements. Even Spain, while refusing to recognize independent Kosovo, did nothing to block EULEX, KFOR, or anything else of substance. I have always focused on results. Whatever means produce results are desirable. I never had a hang-up about the Troika process. It worked."[20]

International Law

International law's role in the process was poorly understood, but the independence of Kosovo marks a significant step into an international legal regime that balances sovereignty against the responsibility to protect. Arguments about how to resolve international disagreements usually are couched, at least in

---

[19] A 2008 confidential interview with senior European diplomat.
[20] July 2008 interview with Martii Ahtisaari.

part, by references to international law. Either side to a dispute can clothe its position with greater moral force by arguing that the other side has a legal duty to modify its behavior.[21] In addition, once a dispute is resolved through diplomacy, the resolution usually is memorialized in a treaty that everyone must treat as a source of legal obligation under the famous maxim, *Pacta Sunt Servanda*.[22]

The problem is that most general norms of international law are indeterminate; there is room for both sides to frame legal arguments supporting their positions with more or less equally persuasive force. While treaties, like any legal text, can be written with precision, to narrow the range of future interpretative disagreements, agreement usually is possible only by deferring the most difficult questions through ambiguous language. Kosovo's final status was no exception. The breakup of Yugoslavia spawned spirited arguments among international lawyers over how the "right" of self-determination, recognized implicitly in the UN Charter and the UN Declaration of Human Rights,[23] should be reconciled with the obligations to respect sovereignty and

---

[21] "Appeals to norms, precedents, 'salience,' etc., naturally can be – and usually are – part of the conventional bargaining process. What gives 'bargaining' its peculiar characteristic, however, is the latent presence of coercion." Law and other norms provide "standard solutions which the parties can utilize if they want. It also offers an organized way of reasoning and arguing." *Friedrich v. Kratochwil, Rules, Norms, and Decisions* 181 (1989).

[22] *Fujitsu Ltd. v. Federal Express Corp.*, 247 F.3d 423, 433 (2d Cir. 2001) (explaining concept). The Latin phrase translates as, "pacts must be followed." The motto signifies that states have an international legal obligation to fulfil the duties they undertake when they enter into treaties. Certain duties are said to be so fundamental that they are "universal" – binding on states even if they do not obligate themselves through treaties. There is, however, no real enforcement mechanism if they violate these duties. It is thus appropriate to consider international law more as a set of norms than a set of rules, although most lawyers and scholars refer to international law as comprising rules.

[23] See Enver Hasani, *Self-Determination, Territorial Integrity, and International Stability: The Case of Yugoslavia* 19–20 (2003) (explaining that *uti possidetis* principle in international law – respect for existing borders – emerged with respect to Latin American colonial borders in early nineteenth century); id. at 51 (explaining how *uti possidetis* was used after collapse of Soviet Union to limit instability otherwise likely to emerge from ethnic nationalism); id. at 85–7 (characterizing Åland Islands case and leaving open question of when self-determination would justify postrevolution secession; quoting Commission of Jurists as saying that self-determination was not absolute right but must be applied on case-by-case basis; citing James Barros, *The Åaland Islands Question: Its Settlement by the League of Nations* [New Haven: Yale University Press, 1968]); id. at 88 (quoting League of Nations Commission of Rapporteurs on Åland Islands case as saying that self-determination can result in secession only as an "exceptional solution, a last resort when the State lacks whether the will or the power to enact and apply just and effective guarantees," citing League of Nations, Document B7.21/68/106/VII at 22–3). The Council of the League of Nations ultimately held that Finland should enjoy continued sovereignty over the Åland Islands. Decision of the Council of the League of Nations on the Åland Islands, Minutes of the Fourteenth Meeting of the Council (June 24), League of Nations Official Journal 697 (September 1921), located at http://www.kultur.aland.fi/kulturstiftelsen/traktater/eng_fr/1921a_en.htm.

existing borders, at the heart of the Oslo Declaration.[24] Part of this argument also involved disagreements over the 1974 Constitution of Yugoslavia: the differing privileges and powers of republics like Croatia and Slovenia contrasted with autonomous provinces like Kosovo.

Once Yugoslavia had broken up, and the KLA had forced the UN and NATO to intervene to displace the practical exercise of Serbian sovereignty over Kosovo, UN Resolution 1244 provided a treaty[25] framework for determining Kosovo's future. Because the parties could not agree in 1999 on what Kosovo's future should be – independence or a return to Serbian control – they finessed this issue in the text of the resolution, allowing Belgrade and Pristina and their supporters later to claim that each was in the right, legally.

Some of the opposition to adopting the Ahtisaari Plan was couched in two contradictory legal arguments. The first claimed lack of precedent for the Security Council to carve a new state out of an existing one; the second, paradoxically, rested on the illegality of moving forward toward independence without a new Security Council resolution. Adherents to the second argument also said that a Security Council resolution was required to deploy a new EU mission to Kosovo, replacing UNMIK. For the most part, those whose arguments rested on legalities, Koštunica being the archetype, were politically predisposed against independence. However, those who claimed to be inhibited by the legal arguments against independence, including Koštunica, showed no interest in hearing legal arguments in favor of independence or engaging in serious legal analysis. Law was a cover for a political position, not its determinant.

Even when those advancing legal arguments were not disingenuous, they were unsophisticated in their understanding of law. Using models of law and legal compliance drawn from domestic contexts for the international context is questionable: international law works through a different set of regimes and institutions than the hierarchy of legislatures and courts available within states.[26] Moreover, even in the domestic setting, legal obligations are contestable, and political reality often frustrates compliance with the letter of

---

[24] See Hasani at 119–22 (explaining politics of formulating the Helsinki Determination statement on inviolability of state boundaries, which also "legally unbinding," had considerable impact on European attitudes toward self-determination).

[25] In this context, a Security Council resolution can be characterized as a treaty, because its text is negotiated among the members of the Security Council before they are willing to accept it in a formal Security Council meeting.

[26] See Richard Caplan, *Europe and the Recognition of New States in Yugoslavia* 77 (2005) ("[I]t is more constructive to view international law not as a pale imitation of municipal [domestic] law but as an institution characterized by its own distinctive features."). See generally Harold Jongju Ko, "Review Essay: Why Do Nations Obey International Law?," 106 *Yale Law J.* 2599 (1997) (book review essay, analyzing scholarship on compliance with international law); Anne-Marie Slaughter et al., "International Law and International Relations Theory: A New Generation of Interdisciplinary Scholarship," 92 *American J. Int'l Law* 367 (1998) (reviewing literature).

the law. President Lincoln defied a federal court order in *Merryman*[27] that he release a suspected secessionist after he suspended the writ of habeas corpus.[28] President Eisenhower was initially disinclined to enforce the judicial order that compelled integration of the Little Rock schools.[29] More recently Tom Dart, the sheriff of Cook County, Illinois, announced that he would not enforce mortgage foreclosures[30] although the law seemed to require it.

International law was not the driving force for determining Kosovo's future, nor could it have been. To say that it did not drive the decision, however, is not to say that it played no role. All the contending sides were careful to develop arguments that their preferred outcomes comported with international law. Certain options that would have been available in a purely lawless world, such as directly military intervention, were never discussed. Some options, such as partition, were discussed but eventually abandoned, in part because of legal obstacles to partition's legitimacy. Some aspects of international law work extremely well, such as that pertaining to the allocation and use of radio frequencies, even if the parts contemplating that the Security Council resolve major threats to international peace and security do not. In addition, even in the Security Council, international law provides a useful framework for political discourse.

Intelligence

The output of intelligence agencies was irrelevant to the negotiations and the determination of negotiating positions mainly because of the poor quality of the intelligence. Casual observers of international diplomacy assume

---

[27] Ex parte *Merryman*, 17 F. Cas. 144 (D. Md. 1861).

[28] See William Baude, "The Judgment Power," 96 *Geo. L. J.* 1807 (2008) (discussing *Merryman* case), Jennifer Mason McAward, "Congress's Power to Block Enforcement of Federal Court Orders," 93 *Iowa L. Rev.* 1319, 1361 (May 2008) (analyzing Lincoln's refusal to enforce judicial decision requiring release of suspected secessionist held under presidential suspension of habeas corpus).

[29] See Jennifer Mason McAward, "Congress's Power to Block Enforcement of Federal Court Orders," 93 *Iowa L. Rev.* 1319, 1361 (May 2008) (analyzing Eisenhower decision); Judith A. Hagley, "Massive Resistance – The Rhetoric and the Reality," 27 *New Mexico L. Rev.* 167, 187 (1997) (discussing Eisenhower's reluctance to enforce court orders requiring desegregation of schools); compare Mary L. Dudziak, "The Little Rock Crisis and Foreign Affairs: Race, Resistance, and the Image of American Democracy," 70 *So. Cal. L. Rev.* 1641, 1687 (1997) (quoting Eisenhower statement to press that he could not imagine using troops to enforce court orders) with id. at 1650 (Eisenhower ultimately acted to uphold rule of law). Of course, Eisenhower's ultimate use of troops can be cited for the proposition that he ultimately felt bound by the law to use executive power to enforce a decision that he disagreed with politically and morally.

[30] Cook County Sheriff's Office, "Cook County Sheriff Suspends Foreclosure Evictions" (October 8, 2008 (press release), located at http://www.cookcountysheriff.org/press_page/press_evictionSuspension_10_08_08.html (announcing suspension of all mortgage florec losure proceedings).

that information provided by intelligence agencies plays a major role in determining the course of negotiations. This was not true in the development of independence for Kosovo. U.S. and British intelligence about the KLA was consistently bad.[31] Secretary of State Madeleine Albright was so starved for information about the KLA, she regularly pestered Ambassador Walker to tell her what he had learned about the characteristics and leadership of the KLA.[32] Both Ahtisaari and the members of the Troika report that they rarely gained anything useful from intelligence briefings. "My best sources were my own meetings in Pristina, with liberals in Belgrade, NATO, and NGOs," said Ischinger.[33]

Violence

Decision making occurred, as it usually has in the Balkans, only under the threat of violence, although effective diplomacy forestalled the actual outbreak of violence. While public dialogue about international diplomacy generally exaggerates the role of international law and intelligence agencies, it usually demeans the role of violence. Yet all of the robust international steps in the late twentieth century to manage the dissolution of Yugoslavia occurred only after violence was escalating, first in Croatia, then in Bosnia, and then in Kosovo. Only violence, it seemed, could ratchet up the costs of inaction sufficiently to cause political leaders to make tough decisions. There were a few exceptions, such as the United Nations Preventive Deployment Force (UNPREDEP), which was deployed to Macedonia under Security Council Resolution 983[34] in 1995, replacing elements of the Bosnian UN force, the United Nations Protective Force (UNPROFOR), which had been deployed to Macedonia earlier. Despite a brief outbreak of fighting in 2000–2001 between Macedonia's government and Albanian separatist forces, the UN military presence helped force interethnic controversies into peaceful political channels.[35]

Under this legacy, the threat of violence was essential to force a decision on Kosovo in the early twenty-first century, and so it had to be kept alive. It is an achievement of diplomacy that the independence of Kosovo was achieved without a further outbreak of serious violence in the Balkans, but the achievement occurred very much under the threat of renewed violence. EU and U.S. decision makers believed that Kosovar Albanian frustration over the slow pace of deciding Kosovo's future status was on the verge of spilling into the streets, with something worse than the riots of 2004 or the KLA insurgency of 1996–1999.

---

[31] See Perritt, KLA at 140.
[32] February 2008 conversation with William Walker.
[33] October 2008 interview with Ischinger.
[34] UN SCR 983 (1995).
[35] See http://www.un.org/Depts/DPKO/Missions/unpred_r.htm (summary of subsequent developments regarding UNPREDEP).

Threats, however, often take on a life of their own, and this was surely true in Kosovo, where the hold of the political leadership on public affection was so low. The Kosovar Albanian leadership had to show some kind of proactive initiative or it would completely lose control over events. The Kosovar Albanians held back from that risk. At the end of July 2007, the U.S. and European states were leaning hard on the Kosovars not to declare independence unilaterally, even as the pressure was building inside Kosovo for the Kosovar political leadership to do something. When I pressed them in late summer and fall of 2007 to explain what would happen in the absence of a Security Council resolution, a typical Unity Team response was, "We do not want to speculate." When I pressed them to explain what form violence might take in Kosovo once popular patience ran out, knowledgeable Kosovar Albanians could offer no concrete scenarios. Furthermore, Kosovars could not identify political figures around whom popular outrage might coalesce, and indeed insisted there were no such political figures offstage.

It was in the interest of proponents of Kosovo's independence to stress the potential for violence, but it was not in their interest to invite too close an examination of the actual potential, let alone to demonstrate that potential. Kosovo and its sympathizers needed to paint credible pictures of catastrophe in the absence of adopting Ahtisaari's plan, but they did not want to make it easier for those who wanted to delay tough decisions to conclude that nothing significant would change in Kosovo in the near to medium term. If the situation on the ground in Kosovo would be pretty much as it had been for the previous eight years – high unemployment, high and growing cynicism about democracy, and a grudging kind of cooperation with international civil administration – that surely would be a recipe for delay.

Although the threat of violence or its sporadic occurrence might arrest the internationals' tendency toward drift, it could just as easily undercut a constructive diplomatic process. If violence in Kosovo resumed, the Serbian and Russian position could be strengthened, because then both could claim a moral victory: violence would suggest Kosovo had indeed not been ready for self-government, and that UNMIK and KFOR could not manage their mission – to keep things under control.

The leadership of Kosovo began getting some private advice in June 2007 that it needed to be more obstreperous or threatening. The Kosovars – both the leadership and the general public – might have served their own interests better with more peaceful protests with large turnouts. This would have increased the pressure on the international community to find some kind of solution acceptable to the Kosovar Albanians. It also would have provided a kind of safety valve for growing public frustration. Tens or hundreds of thousands of Kosovar Albanians could have taken to the streets, in noisy but peaceful demonstrations under the banner of "No more delay!" The Unity Team then would have had a more urgent argument that "We can't hold our people back; we must declare independence." No one except Albin Kurti, however, was organizing such protests, and he experienced precipitous declines in participation. Kurti, a former political prisoner and spokesman for the KLA, led Vetevendosje, a Kosovar Albanian political movement opposed to the final status talks. His credibility was eroding, however, because of his rejection of any internationally supervised process and his leadership capacity was blunted by a prolonged – and probably illegal – period of detention by UNMIK authorities.[36]

Kosovo's political leadership was afraid to encourage demonstrations because they might get out of control. They worried about their own diminishing influence with the general public in Kosovo – especially the young. The EU and the United States certainly were not about to encourage the Kosovar Albanians to do anything that might get out of control.

In the end, arguments by Wisner and Burns in the United States and by their counterparts in the EU that violence would be the inevitable result of deferring a decision on Kosovo's status were credible without mass action, violent or otherwise, in Kosovo. The six-month delay and the cooperative strategy by Kosovo's political leadership proved to be a success in forging EU and transatlantic unity. The action-forcing event that everyone recognized as necessary to mobilize decision making was U.S. firmness rather than an outbreak of violence.

Determination of final status for Kosovo began with the riots of 2004, but concluded without further violence.

UN Security Council

The diplomacy resulting in Kosovo's independence showed that the United Nations is useful for many things, including for structured negotiations over contentious issues such as Kosovo's future status, but the UN Security Council does not provide a reliable decision-making forum because of the inevitable possibility of disagreement among the permanent members. An institution that allows for paralysis in international decision making is not a suitable centerpiece of the international system.

The Ahtisaari process and its Troika-led sequel intensified questions about the UN Security Council's effectiveness in dealing with threats to international peace and security while also demonstrating how UN-led negotiations can result in a sophisticated framework for managing interethnic conflict and international supervision of emerging states. Much of the debate about Kosovo's status involved the permissibility of deciding Kosovo's status without a UN Security Council resolution. This argument is couched in legal terms, but it implicates deeper political and institutional issues. The UN-sponsored process

---

[36] Amnesty International, *Albin Kurti – A Politically Motivated Prosecution?*, EUR 70/014/2007 (December 20, 2007), located at http://www.amnesty.org/en/library/asset/EUR70/014/2007/en/EUR700142007en.html.

leading to the Ahtisaari Plan was a success, but the effort to get the Security Council to adopt it was not. The plan was a highly sophisticated mechanism for managing Kosovo's inevitable transition to sovereign independence. It was unequaled in its comprehensive and detailed institutional framework for assuring minority rights and political autonomy, while providing sufficient authority for the elected central government of Kosovo to govern. Yet neither Russia nor Serbia seemed interested in the merits of the plan as the matter moved to the UN Security Council.

The structure of the Security Council under the UN Charter has always harbored the possibility that the UN will be unable to make a decision when the major powers that have a veto in the Security Council disagree. An actual veto, or the prospect of one, means that a threat to international peace and security may exist, but the UN may be unable to deal with it. The Troika process demonstrated that no internationally crafted proposal could have bridged the gap between Belgrade and Pristina. Given the Russian determination to support Belgrade's position and to avoid any policy that might weaken the Serbian position and a determination by other permanent members of the Security Council to support Pristina's position, no Security Council decision was possible.

Refusing to act without a UN decision would have allowed the Kosovo situation to fester, thereby undermining international peace and security – the very condition the UN was established to avoid. That a critical mass of international actors embraced UDIR was an achievement of multilateral international diplomacy. Paralysis in the Security Council simply reinforces the conclusion that the UN system can accomplish many things, but it is not always a reliable forum for deciding tough questions.

What happens when the Security Council is deadlocked? Is paralysis the answer? The Bush administration forthrightly took the position that the United States has a responsibility to act even when the UN will not.[37] This embrace of unilateralism defined Bush administration foreign policy, largely because of the invasion of Iraq. However, it did not originate with the Bush administration. The Clinton administration also acted outside the UN framework in Kosovo in 1999.[38] So did the Kennedy, Johnson, and Nixon

---

[37] See Winston P. Nagan and Craig Hammer, "The New Bush National Security Doctrine and the Rule of Law," 22 *Berkeley J. Int'l L.* 375, 405 (2004) (interpreting *President's Remarks at the United Nations General Assembly*, http://www.whitehouse.gov/news/releases/2002/09/20020912–1.html# (posted September 12, 2002, 11:04 A.M. EDT)] as declaring that the United States reserved the power to attack Iraq unilaterally).

[38] See Satish Nambiar, *India: An Uneasy Precedent, Kosovo, and the Challenge of Humanitarian Intervention: Selective Indignation, Collective Action, and International Citizenship* 260, 265 (Albrecht Schnabel and Ramesh Thakur, United Nations University Press, 2000) (describing the Kosovo intervention as against both NATO's charter and outside of the Chapter VII powers of the United Nations Charter); United Nations Secretary General (March 24, 1999) SG/SM 6938 "Secretary General Deeply Regrets Yugoslav Rejection of Political Settlement: Says Security Council Should be Involved in any Decision to Use Force." ("It is indeed tragic

administrations in Vietnam.[39] The fact that the UN endorsed Western intervention in Korea resulted from the tactical miscalculation of the Russians in boycotting the Security Council meeting at which intervention was authorized.[40] Despite widespread European criticism of the U.S. invasion of Iraq, most of Europe worked with the United States to resolve Kosovo's status outside the UN. It is reasonable to conclude that a pattern of state practice is emerging that permits such action.[41]

Security Council endorsement of international action is desirable, to be sure. The existence of a Security Council mandate makes it easier for states to cooperate in a coherent manner to carry it out. The absence of one makes it easier for some states to sabotage an effort agreed on by a majority. The absence of a new Security Council resolution permitted Russia and Serbia to interfere with the implementation of the Ahtisaari Plan after UDIR. Russia pressured the Secretary General not to proceed promptly and decisively to transition from UNMIK authority in Kosovo to ICO and EULEX authority. Serbia was determined to force the Kosovo Serbs to refuse cooperation with the Kosovo government, EULEX, and ICO, on the grounds that UNMIK remained the only legitimate international authority in Kosovo.

It may be that if the United States had been more muscular in forcing a Security Council vote in the summer of 2007, Russia might have been more accommodating rather than being isolated by using its veto. Then, there were eleven votes in favor of the Ahtisaari Plan, and three or four likely abstentions, with only one possible veto. A year later, there would not be anywhere close to eleven votes in favor of Kosovo's independence because of changes in the rotating membership, the obvious lack of European unity, and forceful Serbian and Russian lobbying. The result of failing to press for a vote in 2007 is that the UN Security Council is even less credible as an instrument for resolving major international disagreements.

that diplomacy has failed, but there are times when the use of force may be legitimate in the pursuit of peace ... but as Secretary General, I have many times pointed out, not just in relation to Kosovo, that under the Charter the Security Council has primary responsibility for maintaining international peace and security – and this is explicitly acknowledged in the North Atlantic Treaty. Therefore, the Council should be involved in any decision to resort to the use of force.").

[39] Richard A. Falk, "Legality of United States Participation in the Viet Nam Conflict: A Symposium," 75 *Yale L. J.* 1122, 1144 (1966) (stating that between 1954 and January 1966 the United States used military force despite the UNSC's failure to endorse).

[40] Anjali V. Patil, *The UN Veto in World Affairs 1946–1990: A Complete Record and Case Histories of the Security Council's Veto* 193 (UNIFO, 1992) (describing events in June 1950 decision of the UNSC to recommend that UN member states should assist South Korea in the absence of the Soviet Union, which was boycotting the UNSC for failure to seat the People's Republic of China).

[41] A norm of customary international law arises when a pattern of state practice couples with *opinion juris* – state belief that the conduct is legally mandated. It is uncertain whether these criteria for law formation apply to interpretation of treaties, including the UN Charter.

The pattern set with respect to Kosovo, both in 1999 and in 2007 and 2008, is likely to be the pattern of the future. States will put threats to international peace and security before the Security Council, but they will not be prisoners if the Security Council is unable to act. They will recognize that states have interests and also have obligations to act when the international machinery breaks down. That is what the United States and Europe did in 2008, and they were right to do so.

Conclusion

For once in the Balkans, political transformation occurred through international diplomacy without prolonged violence as a stimulus. The hope is that the Ahtisaari and Troika processes provide a model that will be followed in the future – and that diplomats and decisions will be worthy to stand in the shoes of Ahtisaari, Rohan, Jessen-Petersen, Wisner, Ischinger, Bostan-Schenko, Sejdiu, and Thaçi.

Glossary of Acronyms

AAK	Alliance for the Future of Kosovo, Albanian political party led by Ramush Haradinaj
ABA/CEELI	American Bar Association's Central and East European Law Initiative
AKR	New Kosovo Alliance
CIA	Central Intelligence Agency
CIS	Confederation of Independent States
DOS	Democratic Opposition of Serbia
DS	Democratic Party, political party in Serbia
DSS	Democratic Party of Serbia, political party in Serbia
EAR	European Agency for Reconstruction
ESDP	European Security and Defense Policy Mission, subsequently known as EULEX
EU	European Union
EUSR	EU Special Representative
FRY	Federal Republic of Yugoslavia
ICG	International Crisis Group
ICJ	International Court of Justice
ICO	International Civilian Office
ICR	International Civilian Representative
ICRC	International Committee of the Red Cross, a humanitarian group assigned responsibilities by The Hague and Geneva Conventions
ICTY	International Criminal Tribunal for the former Yugoslavia
IDP	Internally Displaced Person
IMF	International Monetary Fund
IMP	International Military Presence
IRA	Irish Republican Army
ISG	International Steering Group
JCS	Joint Chiefs of Staff
KDOM	Kosovo Diplomatic Observer Mission
KFOR	Kosovo Force (NATO force in Kosovo)
KLA	Kosovo Liberation Army
KPC	Kosovo Protection Corps

KVM	Kosovo Verification Mission, monitors of Holbrook/ Milosevic Agreement
KSF	Kosovo Security Force
LDD	Democratic League of Dardania
LDK	Democratic League of Kosovo, Albanian political party led by Ibrahim Rugova
LDP	Liberal Democratic Party
LPK	Popular League for Kosovo, successor to LPRK
LPRK	Popular League for the Republic of Kosovo, predecessor of LPK, militant Albanian exile group, forerunner of KLA
MUP	Serbian Interior Ministry
NATO	North Atlantic Treaty Organization
NDI	National Democratic Institute
NS	New Serbia
NSC	National Security Council
NDI	National Democracy Institute, an NGO funded by the U.S. Congress that promotes democracy in countries in transition
NMLA	National Movement for the Liberation of Kosovo
ORA	Reformist Party ORA, founded by Veton Surroi
OSCE	Organization for Security and Cooperation in Europe
PDK	Democratic Party of Kosovo, Albanian political party led by Hashim Thaçi
PISG	Provisional Institutions of Self-Government
SFRY	Socialist Federal Republic of Yugoslavia
SOE	Socially Owned Enterprise
SPS	Socialist Party of Serbia
SRS	Serbian Radical Party
SRSG	Special Representative of the Secretary General
UCK	Albanian initials for KLA
UDI	Unilateral declaration of independence
UDIR	Unilateral declaration of independence, followed by foreign-state recognition
UN	United Nations
UNDP	United Nations Development Program
UNESCO	United Nations Educational, Scientific and Cultural Organization
UNHCR	United Nations High Commissioner for Refugees
UNMIK	United Nations Interim Administration Mission in Kosovo
UNOSEK	United Nations Office of the Special Envoy for Kosovo
UNPRODEP	United Nations Preventive Deployment Force
UNPROFOR	United Nations Protective Force
USAID	United States Agency for International Development

USIP	United States Institute of Peace
USIS	United States Information Service, part of the United States Information Agency (USIA) the public diplomacy arm of the U.S. government, subsequently folded into organizational units reporting to the Under-Secretary of State for Public Affairs and Public Diplomacy

Bibliography

Albright, Madeleine, *Madam Secretary*. New York: Miramax Books, 2003.

Bali, Asli U., "Justice Under Occupation: Rule of Law and the Ethics of Nation-Building in Iraq." *Yale J. Int'l L.* 30 (2005): 431, 469, n. 119.

Bannon, Alicia L., "The Responsbility to Protect: The UN World Summit and the Question of Unilateralism," *Yale L. J.* 115 (2006): 1157, 1158.

Baude, William, "The Judgment Power," *Geo. L. J.* 96 (2008): 1807.

Brooks, Rosa Ehrenreich, "Failed States, or the State as Failure?" *U. Chi. L. Rev.* 72 (2005): 1159.

Campbell, Greg, *The Road to Kosovo: A Balkan Diary* 239–49. Boulder, CO: Westview Press, 2000.

Caplan, Richard, *Europe and the Recognition of New States in Yugoslavia*. New York: Cambridge University Press, 2005.

Carnegie Endowment for Peace, *The Other Balkan Wars: A 1913 Carnegie Endowment Inquiry*. Carnegie reprint, 1993.

Clark, General Wesley K., *Waging Modern War*. New York: Public Affairs, 2001.

Clark, Howard, *Civil Resistance in Kosovo*. London, UK: Pluto Press, 2000.

Cubrilovic, Vaso, *The Expulsion of the Albanians* (1937), http://www.aacl.com/expulsion2.html.

Daalder, Ivo H. and O'Hanlon, Michael E., *Winning Ugly: NATO's War to Save Kosovo*. Washington, DC: Brookings Institution, 2000.

Davies, Norman, *Europe: A History*. Oxford: Oxford University Press, 1996.

Donia, Robert J., *Elusive Finality: Dispatch From Newly Independent Kosovo*, International Institute for Middle East and Balkan Studies, http://www.ifimes.org/default.cfm?Jezik=En&Kat=10&ID=377.

Dudziak, Mary L., "The Little Rock Crisis and Foreign Affairs: Race, Resistance, and the Image of American Democracy," *So. Cal. L. Rev.* 70 (1997): 1641, 1687.

European Commission, *Kosovo Under UNSCR 1244 2007 Progress Report 8* (November 6, 2007) (SEC [2007] 1433), http://ec.europa.eu/enlargement/pdf/key_documents/2007/nov/kosovo_progress_reports_en.pdf.

European Stability Initiative, *Towards a Kosovo Development Plan. The State of the Kosovo Economy and Possible Ways Forward* (August 24, 2004), http://www.esiweb.org/index.php?lang=en&ID=156&document_ID=58.

———, *Travails of the European Raj* (2003) (report available on ESI website, http://www.esiweb.org/index.php?lang=cn&ID=156&document_ID=59.

Evans, Gareth, "From Humanitarian Intervention to the Responsibility to Protect," *Wis. Int'l L. J.* 24 (2006): 703, 704.

Fakukulteti Juridik I Universitetit te Prishtines, *E drejta – Law* (nr. 1–2) (2003).

Falk, Richard A., "Legality of United States Participation in the Viet Nam Conflict: A Symposium," *Yale L. J.* 75 (1966): 1122, 1144.

Fischer, Bernd J., "Enver Hoxha and the Stalinist Dictatorship in Albania," in Bernd J. Fischer, *Balkan Strongmen* 239, 246 (2007).

Fisher, Roger, Bruce M. Patton, and William L. Ury, *Getting to Yes*. New York: Penguin Books, 2nd ed. 1992.

Ford, Christian Eric and Oppenheim, Ben A., "Neotrusteeship or Mistrusteeship? The 'Authority Creep' Dilemma in United Nations Transitional Administration." *Vand. J. Transnat'l L.* 41 (2008): 55.

Glenny, Misha, *The Fall of Yugoslavia*. New York: Penguin Books, 1992.

Gordy, Eric D., *The Culture of Power in Serbia*. Pennsylvania: Pennsylvania State University Press, 1999.

Hagley, Judith A., "Massive Resistance – The Rhetoric and the Reality," *New Mexico L. Rev.* 27 (1997): 167, 187.

Halberstam, David, *War in a Time of Peace: Bush, Clinton, and the Generals*. New York: Scribner, 2001.

Hamilton, Rebecca J., "The Responsibility to Protect: From Document to Doctrine – But What of Implementation?" *Harv. Hum. Rts J.* 19 (2006): 289, 293.

Hammes, Thomas X., *The Sling and The Stone: On War in the 21st Century* 2. St. Paul, MN: Zenith Press, 2004.

Harris, Grant T., "The Era of Multilateral Occupation" *Berkeley J. Int'l L.* 24 (2006): 1.

Hasani, Enver, *Self-Determination, Territorial Integrity, and International Stability: The Case of Yugoslavia* 19–20. Vienna: National Defence Academy Institute for Peace Support and Conflict Management, 2003.

Holbrooke, Richard, *To End a War*. New York: Random House, 1998.

Hosmer, Stephen T., *Why Milosevic Decided to Settle When He Did*. Santa Monica, CA: RAND, 2001.

Human Rights Watch, *Under Orders; War Crimes in Kosovo*. New York: Human Rights Watch, 1999.

———, *Kosovo: Failure of NATO, U.N. to Protect Minorities: Reform of Security Structures Needed as New Administrator Takes Office* (July 26, 2004), http://www.hrw.org/english/docs/2004/07/27/serbia9136.htm.

———, *Failure to Protect: Anti-Minority Violence in Kosovo*, March 2004 at 28 (July 2004) (vol. 16, No. 6(D))

International Commission on Intervention and State Sovereignty, *The Responsibility to Protect: Report of the International Commission on Intervention and State Sovereignty* (December 2001).

Independent International Commission on Kosovo, *Kosovo Report*. Oxford: Oxford University Press, 2000.

International Crisis Group, *A Kosovo Roadmap (I): Addressing Final Status, Europe Report No. 124* (March 1, 2002).

———, *Kosovo's Fragile Transition, Europe Report No. 196* (September 25, 2008).

———, *Bridging Kosovo's Mitrovica Divide, Europe Report No. 165* at 8 (September 13, 2005).

———, *Collapse in Kosovo* (April 22, 2004), http://www.crisisgroup.org/library/documents/europe/balkans/155_collapse_in_kosovo_revised.pdf.

_____, *Kosovo: Toward Final Status, Europe Report No. 161* (January 24, 2005).

_____, *Kosovo After Haradinaj*, Europe Report No. 163 at 12–24 (May 26, 2005).

_____, *Countdown: A Blueprint for Transition*, European Report No. 188 at 18 (December 2007).

James, Lawrence, *Raj: The Making and Unmaking of British India.* New York: St. Martin's Press, 1997.

Joyner, Christopher C., "'The Responsibility to Protect': Humanitarian Concern and the Lawfulness of Armed Intervention," *Va. J. Int'l L.* 47 (2007): 693, 703–10.

Judah, Tim, *Kosovo: War and Revenge.* New Haven, CT: Yale University Press, 2000.

Kaplan, Robert D., *Balkan Ghosts.* New York: Vintage Books, 1994.

King, Charles, "The Five-Day War," *Foreign Affairs* (November/December 2008): 2–11.

King, Iain, and Mason, Whit, *Peace at Any Price: How the World Failed Kosovo.* Ithaca, NY: Cornell University Press, 2006.

Kissinger, Henry, *Diplomacy.* New York: Touchstone, 1994.

Knoll, Bernhard, "From Benchmarking to Final Status? Kosovo and the Problem of an International Administration's Open-Ended Mandate," *Eur. J. Int'l L.* 16 (2005): 637.

Ko, Harold Jongju, "Review Essay: Why Do Nations Obey International Law?" *Yale Law J.* 106 (1997): 2599.

Kola, Paulin, *The Search for Greater Albania.* London: Hurst & Co., 2003.

Kratochwil, Friedrich V., *Rules, Norms, and Decisions.* Cambridge: Cambridge University Press, 1989.

Kunczik, Michael, *Images of Nations and International Public Relations.* Philadelphia, PA: Lea's Communication, 1997.

Libal, Michael, *Limits of Persuasion: Germany and the Yugoslav Crisis, 1991–1992.* Westport, CT, Praeger, 1997.

Lucas, Edward, *The New Cold War.* New York: Palgrave, 2008.

Malcolm, Noel, *Kosovo: A Short History.* New York: New York University Press, 1998.

Mandelbaum, Michael, "Foreign Policy as Social Work," *Foreign Aff.* (January/February 1996).

Massa, Salvatore, "Secession by Mutual Assent: A Comparative Analysis of the Dissolution of Czechoslovakia and the Separatist Movement in Canada," *Wis. Int'l L. J.* 14 (1995): 183, 212–13.

McAward, Jennifer Mason, "Congress's Power to Block Enforcement of Federal Court Orders," *Iowa L. Rev.* 93 (May 2008): 1319, 1361.

McCarthy, Justin, *The Ottoman Peoples and the End of Empire.* London: Arnold, 2001.

Mertus, Julie A., *Kosovo: How Myths and Truths Started a War* 286. Berkeley, University of California Press, 1999.

Murphy, John F., *The United States and the Rule of Law in International Affairs.* Cambridge: Cambridge University Press, 2004.

Nagan, Winston P., and Craig Hammer, "The New Bush National Security Doctrine and the Rule of Law," *Berkeley J. Int'l L.* 22 (2004): 375, 405.

Nambiar, Satish, *India: An Uneasy Precedent, Kosovo, and the Challenge of Humanitarian Intervention: Selective Indignation, Collective Action, and International Citizenship* 260, 265 (Albrecht Schnabel and Ramesh Thakur, United Nations University Press, 2000).

Nelson, Daniel N., "The Worker and Political Alienation in Communist Europe," *Polity* 15 (No. 2, Winter 1982): 182, 183 n.1.

Norris, John, *Collision Course: NATO, Russia, and Kosovo*. Westport, CT: Praeger, 2005.

Owen, David, *Balkan Odyssey*. New York: Harcourt Brace, 1995.

Operation Kosovo, *Combating Corruption in Kosovo* (rev. October 29, 2006), www.operationkosovo.kentlaw.edu.

Patil, Anjali V., *The UN Veto in World Affairs 1946–1990: A Complete Record and Case Histories of the Security Council's Veto* 193. UNIFO, 1992.

Pellet, Alain, "The Opinions of the Badinter Arbitration Committee: A Second Breath for the Self-Determination of Peoples," *E. J. I. L.* 3 (1992): 178, http://www.ejil.org/journal/Vol3/No1/art12–13.pdf.

Perritt, Henry H., Jr., *Kosovo Liberation Army: The Inside Story of an Insurgency*. Chicago: University of Illinois Press, 2008.

———, "Structures and Standards for Political Trusteeship," *U.C.L.A. J. Int'l and Foreign Aff.* 8 (2003): 385.

———, "Economic Sustainability and Final Status for Kosovo," *U. Pa. J. Int'l Econ. L.* 25 (2004): 259.

———, "Providing Judicial Review for Decisions by Political Trustees," *Duke J. Comp. and Int'l L.* 15 (2004): 1.

———, "Note on the 'Political Trustee' Concept," Symposium – Final Status for Kosovo (Chicago: Chicago-Kent College of Law, April 16, 2004), http://operationkosovo.kentlaw.edu/symposium/note-on-political-trusteeship.htm).

Pettifer, James, *Kosova Express!* Madison: University of Wisconsin Press, 2005.

Popovski, Vesselin, "Sovereignty as Duty to Protect Human Rights," *UN Chronicle Online Edition*, December 1, 2004, http://www.un.org/Pubs/chronicle/2004/issue4/0404p16.html.

Rice, Condoleezza, "Promoting the National Interest," *Foreign Affairs* 79 No. 1 (January/February 2000): 45, 46.

Schwabach, Aaron, "Yugoslavia v. NATO, Security Council Resolution and the Law of Humanitarian Intervention," *Syracuse J. Int'l L & Com.* 27 (2000): 77, 83.

Sell, Louis, *Slobodan Milosevic and the Destruction of Yugoslavia*. Durham, NC: Duke University Press, 2002.

Serbian Academy of Arts and Sciences, Memorandum from the Serbian Academy of Arts and Sciences (1986), available at http://www.haverford.edu/relg/sells/reports/memorandumSANU.htm.

Sestanovich, Stephen, "What Has Moscow Done." *Foreign Affairs* (November/December 2008): 12–23.

Schott, Jared, "Chapter VII as an Exception: Security Council Action and the Regulatory Ideal of Emergency." *Northwestern U. J. Int'l Hum. Rts* 6 (2007): 24.

Slaughter, Anne-Marie Slaughter, et al., "International Law and International Relations Theory: A New Generation of Interdisciplinary Scholarship." *American J. Int'l Law* 92 (1998): 367.

Stahn, Carsten, "Responsibility to Protect: Political Rhetoric or Emerging Legal Norm?," *Am. J. Int'l L.* 101 (2007): 99, 102.

Sullivan, Stacy, *Be Not Afraid, For You Have Sons in America*. New York: St. Martin's Press, 2004.

Traub, James, *The Best Intentions: Kofi Annan and the UN in the Era of American World Power*. New York: Farrar, Straus and Giroux, 2006.

Troebst, Stefan, *Conflict in Kosovo: Failure or Prevention*. Flensburg, Germany: European Center for Minority Issues, 1998.

U.S. Institute for Peace, *Special Report No. 100: Kosovo Decision Time: How and When?* (February 2003).

UNDP and USAID, *Early Warning Report Kosovo, Report #20/21 Special Edition, January–June 2008* (June 2008).

United Nations, *Report of the Secretary-General on the United Nations Interim Administration Mission in Kosovo*, S/1999/779 (July 12, 1999).

United Nations, *United Nations Peace Operations Year in Review 2004: UNMIK – Holding Kosovo to High Standards* (December 2004), http://www.un.org/Depts/dpko/dpko/pub/year_review04/yir2004.pdf.

Vickers, Miranda, *The Albanians*. London: I. B. Taurus, 1995.

Wachtel, Andrew Baruch, *Making a Nation, Breaking a Nation: Literature and Cultural Politics in Yugoslavia*. Palo Alto, CA: Stanford University Press, 1998.

Wangsgard, Stephan A., "Secession, Humanitarian Intervention, and Clear Objectives: When to Commit United States Military Forces," *Tulsa J. Comp. and Int'l Law* 3 (1996): 313.

Weeks, Gregory, et al., "Four Accounts on Brain Drain in the Balkans," *South-East Eur. Rev. for Lab. and Soc. Affairs* 4 (2003): 13, http://www.google.com/search?sourceid=navclient&ie=UTF-8&rlz=1T4SNYI_enUS309US309&q=brain+drain+Balkans.

West, Rebecca, *Black Lamb and Grey Falcon*. New York: Penguin Books, 1968.

West, Richard, *Tito and the Rise and Fall of Yugoslavia*. New York: Carol and Graf Publishers, 1994.

Woodward, Susan L., *Balkan Tragedy*. Washington, DC: The Brookings Institution, 1995.

Yordan, Carlos L., "Why Did the UN Security Council Support the Anglo-American Project to Transform Postwar Iraq? The Evolution of International Law in the Shadow of the American Hegemon." *Journal of Int'l L. and Int'l Relations* 3 (2007): 61.

Index

... ...IES AT MEDWAY ...RS AT MEDWAY ... ...WAY,